Renegotiating the Welfare State

Why have some countries been more successful in welfare state reform than others? Is corporatist concertation experiencing a revival in Europe? Do policy makers in different countries learn from each other and is there a prospect for concertation at the European level?

This book examines the experiences of various countries in reforming their welfare states through renegotiations between the state and peak associations of employers and employees. Not too long ago, this corporatist concertation was blamed for bringing about all the ills of the welfare state but since then corporate institutions have learned from their bad performances, modified their structures and style of operation, and assumed responsibility for welfare state reform.

Now, consensual bargaining is back on the agenda of both policy makers and of social science twenty-five years after the start of the corporatist debate. This topical volume with its internationally respected panel of contributors will appeal to all those interested in the welfare state and labour relations. It includes chapters focusing on the Netherlands, Austria, Sweden, Denmark, Germany, Switzerland and Ireland as well as a section looking at the role of corporatist concertation in the European Union.

Frans van Waarden is Professor of Public Policy and Organization at Utrecht University. He has been a Visiting Scholar/Fellow at Stanford University, the Netherlands Institute for Advanced Studies and the European University Institute in Florence. **Gerhard Lehmbruch** is Emeritus Professor of Political Science at the University of Konstanz, Germany, and has been President of the German Political Science Association and Vice-president of the International Political Science Association.

Routledge/EUI Studies in the Political Economy of Welfare
Series editors: Martin Rhodes and Maurizio Ferrera
The European University Institute, Florence, Italy

This series presents leading-edge research on the recasting of European welfare states. The series is interdisciplinary, featuring contributions from experts in economics, political science and social policy. The books provide a comparative analysis of topical issues, including:

- reforms of the major social programmes – pensions, health, social security
- the changing political cleavages in welfare politics
- policy convergence and social policy innovation
- the impact of globalization

1 Immigration and Welfare
Challenging the borders of the welfare state
Edited by Michael Bommes and Andrew Geddes

2 Renegotiating the Welfare State
Flexible adjustment through corporatist concertation
Edited by Frans van Waarden and Gerhard Lehmbruch

3 Comparing Welfare Capitalism
Social policy and political economy in Europe, Japan and the USA
Edited by Bernhard Ebbinghaus and Philip Manow

4 Controlling a New Migration World
Edited by Virginie Giraudon and Christian Joppke

Renegotiating the Welfare State

Flexible adjustment through corporatist concertation

Edited by Frans van Waarden and Gerhard Lehmbruch

Routledge
Taylor & Francis Group

LONDON AND NEW YORK

First published 2003 by Routledge
11 New Fetter Lane, London EC4P 4EE

Simultaneously published in the USA and Canada
by Routledge
29 West 35th Street, New York, NY 10001

Routledge is an imprint of the Taylor & Francis Group

© 2003 Frans van Waarden and Gerhard Lehmbruch for selection
and editorial material; individual contributors for their contributions

Typeset in Baskerville by Exe Valley Dataset Ltd, Exeter
Printed and bound in Great Britain by Antony Rowe Ltd, Chippenham, Wiltshire

British Library Cataloguing in Publication Data
A catalogue record for this book is available from the British Library

Library of Congress Cataloging in Publication Data
Renegotiating the welfare state: flexible adjustment through corporatist
    concertation/edited by Frans van Waarden and Gerhard Lehmbruch.
        p. cm.
    Includes bibliographical references and index.
    1. Welfare state. 2. Comparative government. I. Waarden, Frans van,
    1950– II. Lehmbruch, Gerhard.

JC479.R46 2003
330.12´6—dc21   2002152036

ISBN 0–415–22345–8

Contents

Illustrations

Contributors

Klaus Armingeon is Professor in Political Science and Department Chair at the University of Berne, Switzerland. He studied political science and history at the University of Tübingen, got his PhD at the University of Konstanz and his Habilitation in Heidelberg. He also worked at the University of Mannheim. He has published extensively on corporatist incomes policy, trade unions, labour relations, media and democracy, globalization and the nation state, and German, Swiss and Austrian politics and political institutions.

Gerda Falkner is Professor at the University of Cologne and connected to the Max Planck Institute for the Study of Societies in the same city. Formerly she worked at the University of Vienna. She wrote a Habilitation on European social policy and has published on corporatism, social policy, the welfare state and European integration.

Jürgen Grote is researcher at the University of Konstanz in Germany. He studied in Marburg, London (LSE), and the European University Institute in Florence, and held earlier positions in Brussels (European Commission) the EUI in Florence and Mannheim. He has published on organized interests, Italian politics, regional policy, European integration and policy networks.

Anton Hemerijck is Vice-director of the Scientific Advisory Council to the Dutch Government (WRR). He studied economics and political science in Tilburg and wrote his PhD on the history of Dutch corporatism at the University of Oxford. He studied at the Massachusetts Institute of Technology, and held appointments at the Universities of Tilburg, Amsterdam, Rotterdam, and Leyden. He has published on political theory, political economy, corporatism, the welfare state, interest associations, social policy and is co-author (with Jelle Visser) of a successful monograph on corporatist reform of the Dutch welfare state (*The Dutch Miracle*, Amsterdam University Press 1997).

Sven Jochem works at the Centre for Social Policy Research of the University of Bremen and has published on social democracy, social policy and Scandinavian politics and political institutions.

Gerhard Lehmbruch is Emeritus Professor of Political Science at the University of Konstanz, Germany, and has been President of the German Political

Science Association (DPVW) and Vice-president of the International Political Science Association (IPSA). He was in recent years visiting professor in New York (New School for Social Research) and the University of Tokyo. He has published extensively on corporatist concertation, institutionalism, sectoral governance and German unification.

Philippe Schmitter is Professor of Political Science at the European University Institute in Florence. He studied in Geneva (Graduate Institute for International Studies) and Berkeley, and held earlier appointments in Chicago and Stanford. He was visiting professor at the Universities of Paris-I, Geneva, Mannheim and Zürich, and was Fellow of the Humboldt Foundation, Guggenheim Foundation and the Palo Alto Centre for Advanced Studies in the Behavioral Sciences. He has published books and articles on comparative politics, on regional integration in Western Europe and Latin America, on the transition from authoritarian rule in Southern Europe and Latin America, and on the intermediation of class, sectoral and professional interests.

George Taylor is Director of the Centre for Public Policy and a Lecturer in political science at the National University of Ireland in Galway. He has published on state theory, environmental politics and Irish politics. He has completed an edited book *Irish Public Policy*, with Irish Academic Press and is currently writing a book on Negotiated Governance and the Irish Polity.

Coen Teulings is Professor of Economics at the University of Amsterdam and director of the Tinbergen Research School, in which several Dutch universities combine their graduate programs in economics. He wrote a PhD on the economics of centralized bargaining and has published on labour economics, wage policy, economic institutions and corporatism.

Brigitte Unger studied economics at the University of Vienna and wrote her PhD on problems of financing public debt at the Vienna University of Economics and Business Administration. She undertook post-graduate studies at the Institute for Advanced Studies in Vienna. She wrote her Habilitation on room for manœuvre for national economic policy. She was Schumpeter professor at Harvard and visiting fellow at Stanford University and was nominated 'global leader for tomorrow' by the World Economic Forum in Davos in 1993. She has published on public finance, sectoral economic governance and corporatism.

Frans van Waarden is Professor of Public Policy and Organization at Utrecht University. He studied sociology, history and political science at the Universities of Toronto and Leyden, held earlier appointments at Leyden and Konstanz, and has been visiting scholar at Stanford University, the Netherlands Institute for Advanced Studies NIAS and the European University Institute in Florence. He has published on labour relations, co-determination, history of technology, textile industry, industrial policy, collective action, business associations, corporatism and state–industry relations.

Acknowledgements

The editors and publishers would like to thank the European Trade Union Confederation for their kind permission to reprint Chapter 11, 'The renaissance of national corporatism: unintended side-effect of European economic and monetary union, or calculated response to the absence of European social policy?', by Jürgen Grote and Philippe Schmitter. This article was originally published in *Transfer* 1–2/1999.

Part I
Introduction

1 Renegotiating the welfare state through corporatist concertation

An introduction

Frans van Waarden

Content and organizational form of welfare states

The term 'welfare state' is often used in a rather indiscriminate manner. The emphasis is on 'welfare' rather than on 'state'. What is meant is usually not so much a 'state' as a regime for the provision of welfare programmes. The state could play a role in such provision, whether directly or indirectly, but this does not necessarily have to be so. A more precise term would be 'welfare society', with the state being a variable in it.

However, the use of the word 'state' is more than a mere slip of the tongue. Even if entirely absent, the state would still play a role in it, albeit in a negative way: by its absence, or by tolerating private arrangements of organizations in civil society. That tells us something about the role of the state in that particular society as well. Indeed, 'welfare states' are also 'states', and that aspect has remained underdeveloped in the 'welfare state' literature. They are expressions of state traditions, and of traditions in the relation between state and civil society. As witnessed by the familiar typology which Esping-Andersen (Esping-Andersen 1990) developed, following the earlier work of Titmuss: liberal, social democratic and corporatist welfare regimes.

These different national welfare regimes refer both to organizational form and to the substance of the welfare provisions. Actually, the terms refer in the very first place to the organizational form: who provides and/or regulates the programmes, what conception of state–economy relations lies behind them. Nevertheless, most of the welfare state literature deals with the substance of the programmes, the degree and type of protection provided, their consequences for economy and society, and the changes therein over time. The use of the names of the organizational regimes for the substance of the programmes implies however that form has apparently consequences for substance. This is implied by the terms of Titmuss and Esping-Andersen. The terms refer to a dominant political ideology in the relations between state and society/economy, which has consequences for the substance of welfare state programmes, as indicated in Table 1.1, which summarizes the most important characteristics of the different welfare states.

Table 1.1 Varieties of welfare states

Variable	Liberal welfare state		Corporatist-conservative	Social-democratic
Dominant value *Substance*	Universalistic but residual	Particularistic	Particularistic	Universalistic
Type of social security	Means and needs tested social assistance	State-subsidized voluntary insurance	State Compulsory social insurance (Workmen's compensation)	Flat-rate state pension (People's insurance)
Name associated symbolically			Bismarck	Beveridge
Predominant in country:	USA, AUS, CDN	USA, AUS, CDN	D, I, A, NL	S, N, DK, UK
Coverage, size of welfare clientele	small	small	medium large	large
Criterion for eligibility Welfare for	the poor	the affluent middle class	employees	all citizens which satisfy objective criteria like age or having children
Generosity:				
– level of benefits	low	variable	high	medium low
– Max. duration of benefits	indefinite	variable	limited	indefinite
– Principle of calculation of benefits	flat-rate, based on need and means	contributions paid	former wages	flat-rate, based on general needs

– Principle of funding	taxes	premiums	premiums	taxes
– waiting periods	no	variable	some programs	usually
– strictness of control	high	low	low	low
– redistributive character	vertically, from rich to poor	horizontally, among contributors	horizontally, within category	horizontally and vertically
– stigmatization	yes	no	no	no
Organizational Form				
Institution protected or central in allocation	the market	the market	family, church, private associations	state agencies
State involvement in:				
– funding	high	low	medium	high
– regulation	high	low	low	high
– administration and implementation	high	none	none	high
Typical administrators	local/municipal government	Private insurance companies/ company pension funds	corporatist bi- or tripartite bodies	state agencies
Role of interest associations in formulation and implementation	low	none	high	medium

Inspiration/source: Alber 1982: 40–48; Esping-Andersen 1990: 25–54.
Note: USA=United States of America; AUS=Australia; CDN=Canada; D=Germany; I=Italy; A=Austria; NL=The Netherlands.

Under a liberal ideology the state yields to the market. Citizens are primarily responsible themselves for their insurance against the risks of sickness, disability, unemployment, and old age. They can buy such security on the market from private insurance companies. The state merely provides a minimal collectively financed safety for the very needy, a system of poor relief, and assistance in kind in housing, social and health care. By contrast, social democratic ideology holds the state primarily responsible for insuring citizens against the risks of working life. The programmes are universalistic. They provide a decent benefit to all, at a level equal for all citizens. Contributions however, usually collected through taxes, are income-related. The system is hence quite redistributive in character. Corporatist regimes give an important position to private interest associations on the labour market in the formulation and implementation of programmes; this implies that programmes are often specific to (categories of) workers, so called workmen's compensation plans. Contributions and benefits are related to wages earned. Within specific programmes there is some redistribution. Overall, the programmes tend to be rather generous.

Welfare state programmes in the different types of regimes are hence rooted in different relations between the state and the society/economy, in different styles of state intervention in civil society and in the economy; these have also found expression in a number of other political, legal and administration institutions, and in general and political cultural values, such as universalism/particularism, egalitarianism, or pragmatism/legalism. Together, these institutions and values form more or less integrated systems, which have been the product of long-term processes of state formation. Both the systemic character and their long history tend to make them pretty persistent over time.

Problems, criticism, crisis

The close link between form and substance implied that when problems arose with the substance of the programmes, when criticism mounted, the organizational forms got their share of the blame.

Industrial restructuring, recession, rising unemployment, individualization and aging of the population were factors that increased the use and costs of welfare state programmes, with the result that policy-makers were confronted with social security expenditures that seemed to have taken off into uncontrolled and sustained growth. This happened at the very same time that economic internationalization – a factor also behind industrial restructuring – made those policy-makers believe that their countries were forced to moderate or even reduce wage costs, including the costs for welfare state programmes, and to increase the efficiency in public expenditures in order to stay competitive. The self-imposed constraints of the EMU provided a additional impetus for public austerity among European countries. Large-scale long-term unemployment was considered to be an indication of welfare state dependency among an increasing size of the population – an issue popularized by Charles Murray among others in the USA – and such 'perversions' of the welfare state supposedly required an intensive overhaul of the system. All these developments posed challenges and threats to welfare state programmes.

In corporatist welfare states, the organizational form got its part of the blame. Corporatist concertation came to be held responsible for bringing about all the ills of the welfare state: uncontrollable growth of social security expenditures, high wage costs, loss of competitiveness in world markets, rising unemployment, budget deficits, welfare dependency; and an incapacity for reform: inflexibility and immobilism in policy-making, protection of vested interests, hostage holding of governments, sclerosis of economic governance institutions, etc. A famous and stereotypical case has been the Dutch disability compensation plan. The large-scale use of benefits under this plan (with at its peak about 20 per cent of the working population receiving a disability benefit) could be traced to earlier sectoral concertation externalizing the costs of industrial restructuring to the collective disability pension plan. Employers' associations and trade unions had jointly steered redundant older un- or semi-skilled workers in mining, shipbuilding or textiles, who had no chance of getting a job in new industries, to the disability compensation plan, which provided higher benefits (80 per cent of last wages until retirement) than a regular unemployment benefit. Thus, corporatism and welfare programmes came to be seen more and more as the problem, rather than the solution that it originally had been – to the problems posed by the uncertainties of capitalist life.

Reforms

Given the various problems, almost all governments of developed welfare states set out to reform their welfare state programmes in the past two decades. They have done so in different ways, with different policy goals, channels and instruments; and also in different times, periods and phases. Most reform policies – and the literature on them – have focused in the first instance on substance – as the goal was to control expenditures to make the system more financially stable. Given the close link between substance and form, sooner or later the organizational forms came also under attack. However, at the same time these organizational forms have also been channels for formulating and/or negotiating reform.

The first major attempts at reform were made in the late 1970s and early 1980s in the Anglo-Saxon world, with the conservative revolutions of Reagan in the USA and Thatcher in Britain. They tried to reduce the already minimal liberal welfare state programmes even further. Befitting the policy style typical for state–economy relations in these countries, and befitting the political convictions of the then leaders, the latter choose a radical, impositional and adversarial strategy. Paul Pierson (Pierson 1994) has shown in his study of these policies, 'The Retrenchment of the Welfare State', that these policies were not very successful. To some extent his study is a study in policy-immobilism.

A decade later other European countries followed, countries with more developed welfare state provisions. They pursued less ambitious and radical goals. Not a complete overhaul of the system was attempted, but a modification reducing the malign consequences of the welfare state: welfare state dependency, long-term unemployment, immobilism, uncontrollable public expenditures, loss of national competitiveness. They followed different reform styles and used different channels for formulating reform, in line with their different traditions of state intervention in the economy, and their different regulatory styles. The emphasis has been on concertation and negotiation instead of imposition; on consensualism instead of adversarialism; on stimulating bottom-up initiatives and self-regulation from civil society instead of top-down authoritarianism. This included using channels and institutions of corporatist concertation, which were well established in some countries, while others have attempted to create such. The organizational forms were used to renegotiate the substance of the programmes. Such attempts have been made in most continental European countries: the Netherlands, Denmark, Finland, Belgium, Ireland, Italy, Germany, Spain.

They all seemed to agree with Visser and Hemerijck when they write (Visser and Hemerijck 1997): 182):

> Societal consensus is crucial for effective reform of the welfare state. In all welfare states there are many veto points and actors with powers to obstruct. A politics of imposition is likely to provoke conflicts which may retard or even reverse the process. Modernization of the welfare state ... requires the construction of a political will and long-term commitments, built on norms of trust and networks of civil engagement, in order to overcome the inevitable opposition of groups who will lose.

Unlike the Anglo-Saxon retrenchment attempts, these governments still fitted the model that Ehrmann already described in 1961 as the 'modern form':

> Today extensive consultation between group leaders and civil servants is generally considered as a fundamental democratization of the administrative process. ... there exists by now in all countries widespread agreement on the propriety and convenience of continuous consultation both when the (state) bureaus are drafting legislation and when they administer enacted laws.
>
> (Ehrmann 1968, orig. 1961: 259)

It should be noted however that the new forms of corporatist concertation differed from older ones. States have rethought their policy regarding involving interest associations in policy formulation and implementation; and they have tried to find new modes of regulating the economy and the welfare state. The mix of state, market and associations has been reshuffled, with states reasserting some of their responsibilities and trying to make more room for market coordination in providing welfare state programmes. While associational governance was pushed towards the background for some time, it has now been revived. European governments have again turned to centralized corporatist concertation to 'oil' welfare state reform. These initiatives have met with different success. Some countries have been more successful than others in reforming their welfare states and adjusting them to changing circumstances.

Reinventing corporatism: reform through renegotiation

The revival of corporatist concertation has been a curious one. Originally institutions of corporatist concertation were blamed in part for the financial problems and a perceived sclerosis of continental conservative welfare states. 'Corporatist is dead. Long live corporatism!', wrote Schmitter over ten years ago (Schmitter 1989). He meant however two different kinds of corporatism. The dead one was macro-level centralized socio-economic concertation and negotiation. The alive one was concertation at the sectoral level, also called meso-corporatism.

However, since Schmitter wrote these words, macro-level concertation has also experienced a revival. In some countries corporatist institutions seem to have been able to learn from bad performance and experience, to modify their structures and styles of operation, and the social partners have again been willing to assume responsibility for socio-economic performance of the nation. Governments have encouraged social partners in doing so and/or have taken initiatives for centralized concertation. In quite a number of countries attempts have been made to revive or newly introduce centralized concertative bargaining during the 1980s and 1990s. The success of some countries with this has encouraged others to follow the lead. Country experiences differ of course, among others in the capacity of institutions to change. These differences are related among others to the historical presence or absence of a tradition of corporatist concertation, and to the (perceived) seriousness of the various policy problems, including the threats and opportunities of internationalization.

One of the first countries going this way again has been a country with a traditionally open economy, vulnerable to internationalization – and a country with a strong corporatist tradition: the Netherlands. The 1982 Wassenaar Accord between the peak associations of employers and workers set the stage for wage moderation and serious modifications of social security (in exchange for working-time reduction), and laid the foundations for the remarkable economic come-back fifteen years later. By now it has almost acquired mythical proportions. Subsequent central agreements concerned employability, vocational training, parental leave and child care, all measures to increase the popularity of part-time work and to raise the labour participation ratio. In April 1996 the Dutch peak associations of labour and capital concluded the 'Flex-agreement', which deregulated the labour market in exchange for more security for flex-workers on the labour market. This agreement, incidentally, also broke a government stalemate over this issue. It was codified in the 1999 Act on Flexibility and Security, which provided a legal framework for social partners to regulate further the position of flex-workers. Corporatism as the resolute decision-maker, instead of the long-despised decision-staller?

Sooner or later several countries followed this example. In Italy, social partners and the government concluded a tripartite national agreement in 1993, introducing two-level collective bargaining with different standards for wage setting. At the sectoral level the norm should be the expected inflation, at the company level the improvement of company productivity. A new central pact in 1998 linked sectoral bargaining to the projected average inflation level in the EU rather than the Italian figure. The Portuguese concluded a tripartite strategic concertation pact in 1996 for the period 1996–9 recommending to the bargaining partners at the sectoral and company level that wage increases should remain at half the productivity increase. Other countries where similar centralized social pacts were concluded were Norway (1993, for the period till 1997), Ireland (1997, Partnership 2000 for the period 1997–2000), Belgium (1998, for the period till 2000), Finland (1997), Austria (1996, '*Sparpaket II*').

There have been important differences between the various country experiences. Some were early with the revival of centralized corporatist concertation (the Netherlands), others late (Austria, Belgium), and yet others where it never really developed fully (Switzerland) or where a revival did not take place (Sweden). For some countries it was really a 'revival', that is, it took place in a country with a strong corporatist tradition (the Netherlands), for others it was relatively new (Ireland, Portugal, Italy). And in yet others central corporatist concertation has never really been away (Austria).

Curiously enough, early attempts at concluding central social pacts in countries with a corporatist tradition failed at first. The Dutch had tried several times before their successful Wassenaar Accord. The Belgian social partners failed still in 1996, and were only successful in December 1998. The Austrian government tried for the first time in postwar history to conclude a Budget Consolidation Package in 1995 without involving the social partners. The attempt failed and in the subsequent year the social partners came with the successful initiative for the *Sparpaket II*. Attempts by Chancellor Kohl to revive the *Konzertierte Aktion* with the *Bündnis für Arbeit* to counter the serious economic problems failed. New attempts by the present Schroeder government have been somewhat more successful.

Some countries with strong corporatist traditions have also tried to popularize the model of consensual bargaining within the European Union. The Dutch chair of the European Union organized in January 1997 an international high level conference on social policy and consensual bargaining as economic assets rather than liabilities. The Austrian chair of Europe did the same in September 1998.

Thus consensual bargaining or corporatist concertation seems to be back on the agendas both of policy-makers and of social science, a little more than twenty-five years after the start of the corporatist debate with the publication of Schmitter's well-known article 'Still the Century of Corporatism?' (Schmitter 1979 (orig. 1974)) and Lehmbruch's study on 'Konkordanzdemokratie' (Lehmbruch 1967).

Principal questions posed by the book

The contributions to this volume study and discuss these attempts at renegotiating the welfare state through channels of corporatist concertation. They try to find answers to some of the following questions.

1   Where and in what countries has centralized consensual bargaining experienced a revival?
2   What have been the issues and subjects of such renewed corporatist concertation? Have different policy issues been interlinked?
3   What is the difference between the earlier experiences of welfare state reform in the USA and the UK? Is corporatist concertation providing an alternative to the command and control and drastic policy measures of those who set out with the retrenchment of the welfare state, Thatcher and Reagan?
4   What can explain this renewed enthusiasm for social pacts?
5   How successful have these social pacts been? How stable? How real, in the sense that they actually influenced the behaviour of lower-level bargaining? Have they provided constraints to other parties, or windows of opportunity? Have some countries been more successful in this respect than others?
6   If so, which conditions for success can be identified? Which variables make for the difference between a flexible, adaptive and pragmatic corporatism, on the one hand, and sclerotic corporatism, on the other hand?
7   What future is there for institutions of corporatist concertation? Is internationalization not also a direct threat to corporatist concertation? Does it not make such institutions outdated and obsolete? Or is it on the contrary providing a stimulus for renewed vitality? Does concertation not require some national autonomy in socio-economic policy-making? In short, what is the future of corporatism in an age of increased internationalization and need for reform of the welfare state?
8   Are there any prospects for concertation at the European level?

In the remainder of this introduction we will provide a summary of some of the tentative answers to these questions, found in the individual contributions to the volume.

Issues, subjects

Most social pacts served several goals at the same time: they were meant to help reduce unemployment; and to aid states in consolidating their budget. Under a Keynesian policy regime these would have been considered contradictory goals; not so under a policy regime inspired by policy theories of supply-side economics, which has gained prominence since the 1980s. Both goals could be served by moderation of overall gross wage costs. It was believed that moderating wage costs would improve the cost competitive position of a country in comparison with its major trading partners and hence the prosperity if not survivability of various economic sectors important for employment; moderation of especially the minimum wages and other wages at the bottom of the pay scale would reduce the tendency of firms to automatize less skilled work and to maintain or even recreate lower-skilled jobs; moderation of wages in the private sector would also mean moderation of wages in the publicly financed sectors and of social security benefits, often linked to wage developments; and this would aid the state in reducing budget deficits; and of course a decrease of unemployment and an increase in the labour participation ratio would reduce costs of unemployment and other social programmes, and raise the income-based tax-income. Less costs and more income would also contribute to budget consolidation.

The first and foremost subject of these pacts were the *direct wage costs*, the average increase in wage levels. Almost all first social pacts concluded contained limitations of average wage raises. Unions were persuaded to accept this because they were made to believe that such would improve the unemployment situation. In addition, the government offered specific measures to help reduce unemployment, e.g. special programmes (subsidies, tax rebates) for the young, the elderly, the disabled, women or ethnic minorities.

Sooner or later, however, other factors influencing gross wage costs and labour participation got to be included, such as working hours, working conditions and flexible work. A reduction of the statutory working week has been considered in several countries, as a way to share scarce jobs. In many countries it was an issue introduced by the unions. Inclusion of weekly working hours in social pacts was a way to get support from them. Flexible work has been considered both an instrument for sharing scarce work (by the unions) and an instrument of greater flexibility of production organizations (by the employers). The Dutch central 'flexicurity' pacts facilitated the creation and maintenance of temporary and part-time work, and improved the legal status of temporary employment agencies; in exchange for measures which increased the security of such flexible work: pension rights; job protection after some period of having worked, special collective wage agreements for temporary labour intermediation bureaus.

Last but not least, welfare state programmes became the subject of centralized concertation. They do not only form a major part of gross wage costs, but were also considered to influence the work incentives and hence unemployment and the participation rate. Two different paths were followed, one regarding the generosity of programmes and one concerning their use, the so-called 'volume' policy. The first line of policy tried to reduce the generosity by a retrenchment of welfare state programmes, i.e. a lower benefit levels, longer waiting periods, etc. Such policies served to reduce costs directly, and to sharpen incentives for looking for work, hence reducing the volume of benefit receivers and thus indirectly also the costs of programmes. The so-called 'volume' policy was directly aimed at reducing the number of benefit recipients. The Dutch tried to reduce the numbers of recipients by several laws, all literally called 'Law for reducing the use of . . .' (sickness, disability pension plan, unemployment insurance). This included measures to make programme entry more difficult, measures to reevaluate benefit recipients, creating additional incentives to look for work including some moderate forms of work-fare; and programmes to aid the inactive part of the population in finding work. That is, social security reform led sooner or later, and also to a different degree in different countries, to more active labour market policies. Sometimes such policy intentions and measures were directly included in social pacts; in other cases such policy was carried out through one-sided state regulation, but supported by declarations in central social pacts, which were to provide a base of legitimacy.

Social pacts also contained reform of funding bases of welfare state programmes. An example was the Finnish pact on 'EU buffers', concluded in 1997. Social partners agreed to create two buffer funds for pensions and unemployment insurance, to be fed by somewhat higher social security contributions in periods of economic boom; and to be used during recessions. Thus the effects of cyclical shocks on social security, which Finland could counter less after its entry into the EMU, were to be cushioned somewhat.

These various policy fields are often interlinked. The links can be immediate: wage restraint was usually the new starting subject of social pacts and where social security benefits were linked to wage increases this also set a cap on the growth of welfare state expenditures. External effects could, however, also be negative. Early retirement as a way to reduce the pressure on the labour market, a popular measure in the late 1980s, increased the costs of pension plans. Policies could also be interlinked in the sense that reform in the one field required reform in another. Reduction of the volume of benefit receivers often required a more active labour market policy. Hemerijck, in his contribution to this volume, even perceives a logic of sequential interdependence between policy fields:

Shifts in macro-policy, wage formation, social security, and labour market policy were sequentially related. Over time, policy reforms across different policy areas created the conditions and the demand for one another, and neither of these domain-specific policy changes could have been successful on their own account.

The renewed relative success of central concertation in socio-economic policy increased its popularity and led to a (renewed) diffusion to yet other policy areas, where cooperation by those subject to the policy and greater legitimacy for such policies were sought. This was the case both in 'old' policy fields with well-established relevant (peak) associations, such as health policy; and relatively new policy areas where such associational positions were less well established, such as environmental policy. Concerted cooperation between state agencies and industrial associations in such fields may have had different names and legal forms, e.g. 'gentleman's agreements' or 'covenants' under civil law. However, they look suspiciously much like corporatist concertation.

Causes: internationalization cause rather than threat

There were two main categories of motivations for such pacts. An urgent first reason was European monetary integration. This required governments to keep inflation and budget deficits within the norms agreed upon. Wage restraint was considered necessary to keep inflation low, and for controlling public expenditure on civil servants' salaries, thus allowing budget consolidation. Hence, European integration and monetary union seem to have been an incentive for governments to conclude (again) social pacts. Many of the social pacts in the second half of the 1990s explicitly refer to the need for the country to satisfy the Maastricht criteria for EMU-participation. This holds for the Italian, Portuguese, Irish, Belgian and Austrian agreements.

A second motive for governments to try to get social partners to conclude central contracts was 'regime competition'. National competitiveness had to be increased by keeping wage increases below that of the major neighbouring trading partners. With this came a danger that it would result in a 'race-to-the-bottom' of countries undercutting each other's levels of wage increases.

Indeed, quite a few of the new centrally concluded social pacts were explicit forms of 'competitive corporatism': competition between sets of national corporatist institutions, competing in their outcome for more moderate wages; often by explicitly referring to wage and inflation levels of neighbouring countries. Thus, for example, the Belgian intersectoral agreement concluded in December 1998 for the period 1999–2000 set a norm for maximum wage increases for 1999–2000 of 5.9 per cent. This figure was calculated on the basis of assumed increases in the neighbouring trading partners France, Germany, and the Netherlands. The Norwegian social pact covering the period between 1993 and 1997 went even further: it fixed as the norm for wage increases the rates of Norway's main competitors minus 2 per cent.

Thus we may conclude that internationalization has been an important cause behind the revival of central corporatist concertation. This is a curious conclusion considering that not too long ago it was precisely internationalization and globalization that quite a number of both social scientists and politicians considered a major threat to corporatist institutions and practices.

Neo-liberal policy-makers have used the perceived threat of internationalization to try to undermine such economic governance arrangements, even, or rather, especially, in countries with corporatist traditions. Thus, leading Dutch politicians and top civil servants in the economics ministry embarked 1995 on a long-term comprehensive plan for deregulation of the traditionally Dutch species of 'organized capitalism', including the abolishment of some institutions for corporatist concertation. (This notwithstanding that simultaneously, elsewhere, centralized concertation was gaining in popularity.) In backing up their policy plans these policy-makers often referred to 'globalization', as leaving the government no other choice. Policy competition between countries would necessarily have to lead to the abolition of such institutions, as they were considered liabilities rather than assets to the competitive position of nation-states.

Not only proponents of neo-liberalism viewed internationalization as a threat. Those more favourably disposed to economic governance were also concerned about the effects of internationalization. Schmitter wrote in 1992:

> The Single European Act poses a special threat to a wide range of class, sectoral and professional arrangements – in particular to the operation of 'private interest governments' (PIGs) – within the twelve member states of the Community. . . . The countries of Europe could be deprived of some of their most venerable and distinctive socio-economic institutions, many of which have contributed significantly to sustaining their respective national versions of a generically European style of 'organized capitalism' and to underwriting their capability to compete effectively within the specialized niches of 'diversified quality production'. . . . The fact that Austria, Sweden, Finland and Switzerland have all announced their wish to become full members of the EU could eventually deprive us of some of the richest native accumulations of governance mechanisms in existence.
>
> (Schmitter 1992: 2, 7–9, note 36, 50)

And Streeck added: 'The "negative" mode of integration implied in "mutual recognition", a subtle form of de facto deregulation, undermines national corporatisms even where the national political resources of labour are still comparatively strong' (Streeck 1992: 111). Many others, from trade unionists to industrial relations researchers (e.g. Keller 1995), have expressed a related fear of 'social dumping'. They argued that unrestricted competition from countries with low wages and low social security protection would exert a downward pressure on wages, working conditions and social security in countries with higher levels of these. And with governments and employers less able and/or willing to make concessions, unions would be less inclined to agree to social pacts, thus uprooting corporatist institutions and practices.

And indeed, under the fury of neo-liberalism and the perceived threat of globalization, corporatist concertation seemed to have lost some of its legitimacy for a while and has had to singe some of its feathers. Several concerted economies with well-organized and regulated markets, such as Sweden, the Netherlands, Germany and Austria have instituted policies of deregulation, privatization and dissolution of organizations of corporatist concertation. The Dutch government considered for a while curtailing or even abolishing the statutory compulsory trade associations which exist in about one-quarter of the Dutch economy. Voluntary trade associations have had to reduce some of their self-regulatory activities, and governments have been hesitating about delegating the implementation of EU-directives for which they are held legally responsible to private interest associations. The statutory extension of sectoral wage agreements has been questioned by economic advisors because of their supposed rigidities and by lawyers because of the lower density ratios of the contract partners. Price regulation by the Austrian Paritätische Kommission was abolished when the country entered the European Union. The politically and culturally well-established Austrian compulsory Chambers seemed for a while to lose out in legitimacy, as one 'scandal' of overpaid Chamber functionaries with accumulated functions followed another in the press. A popular vote on the legitimacy of compulsory membership was feared but eventually reconfirmed the Chamber system. For a while a complete liberalization of the Austrian system of market entry and vocational training system in the small trade sector (*Gewerbeordnung*) was considered. And macro-corporatist concertation seemed to lose in importance as the disciplinary capacity of the peak associations as against their member-associations and unions has decreased.

However, as argued, the last few years have seen a return to central social pacts. At least macro-level concertation seems to be back from having been away. 'Corporatism is dead. Long live corporatism', wrote Philippe Schmitter a few years ago (Schmitter 1989). At that time he meant that macro-corporatism, to which most attention in the corporatism discussion originally went, has practically disappeared, but that corporatism at the sectoral level was still very much alive and kicking. Now it seems that one could turn around the meaning of the statement. Quite a few corporatist institutions and practices at the sectoral level have experienced a silent (or less silent) death; while macro-corporatism seems to have entered a second life. And in both cases internationalization and in particular European integration seems to have been a major factor behind death and life.

Conditions

What have been the conditions for a successful conclusion of central social pacts? Which factors have enhanced their conclusion, and/or have hindered if not blocked them? And under which conditions could they have become stable and successful? In the end this boils down to identifying the factors that *enabled* and *induced* the parties concerned to agree to a central social pact, to observe it and to defend it for the rank and file.

If we compare the different country experiences on which authors report in this volume we can identify a number of factors, which we can group under the headings 'actors', 'incentives', 'situation' and 'institutions'.

Actors: capacity and willingness

An important condition for successful corporatist concertation is the existence of parties which are able to and can afford to bind themselves in central social pacts, and which are able to deliver upon what they have agreed to, to ensure its observation by the 'rank and file'. The older corporatist literature from the 1970s and 1980s has called this the 'Achilles' heel' of corporatism. Parties that are not able to provide some minimum guarantees that the agreements will be observed are not attractive partners for others in negotiations. Does this condition still hold; and is it being satisfied once more?

On the side of the state, this requires an administration with enough authority, self-confidence and a reputation for autonomy and neutrality, to allow them to maintain close contacts with organized interests, to delegate policymaking to them and to maintain consensual relations, without immediately being suspected of bias and corruption. As Peters (1989: 156) wrote:

> Societies that have had among the most positive conceptions of the public bureaucracy – Germany, the Netherlands, and the Scandinavian countries – have been much more successful in accommodating the role of pressure groups into policy making than have political systems that have a less exalted conception of their civil servants. In fact, a relative positive evaluation of the civil service may be required to allow the civil servants latitude in dealing with the pressure groups and in making accommodations to their commands.

And Wilson (1985: 159) added: 'A teacher whose authority is assured may be able to adopt a more friendly and relaxed approach than a teacher whose authority seems highly uncertain.' The contrast is especially striking in comparison with the USA, where lower legitimacy of politicians and administrators means that close cooperation between state agencies and private interests is more readily seen as 'corruption' or 'capture' (Bernstein 1955; McConnell 1966; Mitnick 1980). One might add that where administrators have a more open attitude towards industry, the latter might see them less as natural adversaries. Hence it will be more likely to consult, cooperate with and get involved in corporatist arrangements. In general: a more positive public attitude towards the state, politicians and civil servants alike, reduces mutually the cultural if not structural separation between state and society and that allows for closer cooperation. In continental Europe France is the anomaly. Not that the state does not have the authority, self-confidence and neutral reputation. On the contrary. There a barrier to central social pacts is the paternalism of the French state and its traditional distrust of organized interests.

In most of the other continental European countries, experimenting again with central social pacts, this condition on the side of the state seems, however, to have been met. And it has also not really changed over the last decades, so in this respect there has been no difference in the conditions for the 'old' corporatism of the 1950s–1960s, and the revival in the 1990s.

The state should, however, not only be legitimized to involve private interests in public policy, but also to deliver upon whatever it has promised or included in central social pacts. Too many checks and balances in the political system may detract from the capacity of the state to do so. Federalism, dualism in the relation between government and parliament, a strong parliament, two competing and both powerful parliamentary chambers, judicial review and the possibility of referenda may all reduce the capacity of governments to govern, and may even threaten to lead to political paralysis as, for example, Lazare (1996) has argued. Such reductions of governability may also restrict the power of the government to bind itself in central social pacts.

Typically, several corporatist countries do not have many checks and balances in their system of political institutions. The Netherlands and Austria, for instance, do not have strong dualism between executive and legislative, the second chamber is relatively weak, and the Netherlands has no federalism, judicial review nor referenda, while Austria may have them, but all three in a rather weak form. By contrast, the limits imposed by strong federalism to central state authorities on committing themselves to organized interests are demonstrated in the Swiss case. Armingeon in this volume concludes in his chapter on Switzerland that

> Swiss corporatist institutions could never attain such a dominant position in economic and social policy making as in other countries [because] the results of the corporatist bargains have to be accommodated to the results of governmental and parliamentary decisions of

at least four large parties and the decisions of twenty-six autonomous cantons and their populations.

This has first limited the expansion of welfare state programmes, and subsequently reduced the need for cutbacks. In Germany, federalism was no hindrance to a *Bündnis für Arbeit*, but that was because economic and social policy were rather centralized. Furthermore, political fragmentation may be offset by political parties, who can act as 'integrator' (Friedrich 1968: 341; Lehmbruch 1998) and coordinate positions of political actors in different state institutions, and this even more so in a political culture emphasizing the importance of consensus- and compromise-finding, as is typical for most corporatist countries. Most corporatist countries have such 'integrator' parties and a consensual culture. Overall, these institutional conditions for governability are rather stable over time, and indeed have not really changed over the last decades.

While there has not really been a change in the *capacity* of the state to involve itself in central corporatist concertation, there definitely has been some fluctuation in the *willingness* of states to do so. As already indicated, in some countries like Sweden and the Netherlands, corporatism has been blamed for a while for the 'sclerosis' and inflexibility of the welfare state. The Dutch government has for some time given preference to advice by ad hoc expert committees, headed by former leading entrepreneurs such as Wagner of Shell, and put the social partners and their official advisory bodies such as the Social Economic Council (SER) at a distance. Parliament even accepted a proposal in 1994 to abolish the legal duty of the government to get the advice of the SER on any intended socio-economic measures. In the Netherlands the pendulum has swung back in the meantime, and the government has been again cooperating closely with the social partners in socio-economic policy, including welfare state reform. In Sweden this has been less the case, but that is also due to the unwillingness of the employers' associations to commit themselves to central social pacts. Currently, the willingness on the part of the state has become somewhat of a problem in Austria, where the present christian-democratic/conservative-liberal coalition seems less inclined to listen to the social partners, in particular labour in the form of the Arbeiterkammer.

On the side of interest associations a condition for successful central corporatist concertation is the presence of strong, nationally organized and encompassing interest associations, which can aggregate a great diversity of interests and which have enough internal disciplinary capacity to ensure the observation of agreements by their members. This poses two more or less contradictory imperatives to interest associations.

In order to perform the functions of preference aggregation and reformulation to more general interests well, interest associations and their functionaries need a certain autonomy, a certain discretionary space to interpret interests, to give and take in the negotiations between subgroups of members, and in external negotiations with other interests as well. So do members of parliament by the way, who are elected without duty of consultation, in order to allow them to move their positions in reaction to the exchange of information and arguments. This requires a certain distance to the membership, which is realized in many associational systems by a hierarchical structure of associations and peak associations and by the stepwise selection of functionaries. Peak associations are further removed from the membership than their affiliates. Union members elect union leaders, and these in turn appoint representatives in peak associations and other organizations at higher levels of aggregation in the system of interest associations.

Hierarchy and indirect elections of functionaries entail prospective dangers of limiting participation and increasing alienation of members from the association. Individual members may not recognize their individual interests any more in the much more generalized and often more 'technical' interests distilled in the aggregation process by economically trained functionaries, who may have developed in their frequent interaction with negotiation partners from the other side some understanding for their interests and constraints, a process which is not and cannot be followed by the rank and file.

Such alienation may threaten the other imperative which interest associations are under, namely the need to have some organizational capacity to mobilize, control and discipline the membership whenever necessary, and to ensure the observation of agreements by the membership. This could require instruments of coercion, such as compulsory membership and various sanctions. Furthermore, it may necessitate hierarchic centralization between peak associations and their affiliates. However, too blatant use of such instruments may again threaten to alienate members from their associations, and affiliates from peak associations, and thus be self-defeating.

An added problem of close and permanent cooperation between private associations and state agencies, whereby the first may even assume public tasks, is that associational functionaries may come to be seen more as 'servants' of the state or as an independent oligarchic clique, rather than as representatives of the interest group. Furthermore, increasing independence and discretionary authority also of course entail the danger of abuse of power, of corruption, by associational functionaries, thus threatening their legitimacy in the eyes of the members, and reducing their organizational capacities.

Alienation, loss of legitimacy, loss of discretionary space and loss of internal disciplinary capacity, this is what has happened to comprehensive systems of interest intermediation in the countries where corporatism once reigned. It started in the Netherlands and Sweden and eventually reached the stronghold of corporatism, Austria. This is manifested in lower density ratios, lower participation in associational elections, in public criticism of compulsory membership (in Austria), of associational self-regulation and of the practice of extending collective wage agreements negotiated by associations which represent only a minority of the working population; and it has been particularly evident in electoral gains of political parties critical of social partnership or of close involvement of associations in public policy, such as the liberal FPO in Austria or the VVD and 'Lÿst Pim Fortuyn' in the Netherlands. It has affected both trade unions and employers' associations. Various factors have contributed to this. First of all, the disintegration of the pillars or *Lager* to which these associations belonged and from which they derived their identity. Second, the loss of appeal of political ideologies in general. Third, the increased individualism of members, with the rise in education and social mobility of members, makes them less inclined to follow directions of the leadership of the groups and associations to which they belong. Fourth, corruption scandals have contributed to a loss in legitimacy.

A case in point is Austria. Public criticism on the organizational base of Austrian corporatism, the compulsory Chamber system, mounted in the first half of the 1990s. A popular revolt seemed to be near. Indications have been the very low participation rate in the Arbeiterkammer elections in 1994 (30 per cent instead of the usual 50 per cent); a loss of the established parties SPÖ and ÖVP and a gain of the FPÖ in the Chambers; and successive disastrous results of the first two parties in the general elections in 1994 and 1998, and huge gains of Haider's FPÖ, the opposition party which has made a point of attacking the *Proporzdemokratie*, the elite oligarchy of leaders of interest associations, Chambers and the government. The media blamed it on the typical abuses of an established oligarchy, not subject to many political controls: the 'self-service republic' of the associational functionaries, the accumulation of functions and salaries by the socio-economic elite (the president of the Arbeiterkammer collected triple salaries and earned, with US$16,000 dollars a month, 2–3 times more than a cabinet minister (*Der Standard* 7 October 1994)), the *Vetternwirtschaft* (nepotism), *Filz* (corruption) and *Privilegien* (privileges), the *Absicherung der Pfründe* (securing benefices). Already after the elections of 1994 the relatively progressive paper *Der Standard* wrote: 'Eine Reform-Regierung müßte das Kammer-System umkrempeln, müßte sich viel rigoroser von den Doppel- und Dreifach-Funktionären verabschieden, müßte die Verfilzungen zwischen Politik und Sozialversicherung beenden, müßte drastische Sachreformen einleiten. Vor allen: Die Parteien müßten sich selbst ändern – in Richtung Bescheidenheit und Effizienz. Ob das die vielen, an Pfründe und Privilegien gewöhnten Kammer- und Gewerk-schaftsfunktionäre hinnehmen werden?' (10 October 1994).[1]

In the meantime, however, the criticism in Austria has again subsided somewhat. Important in this respect was the outcome of a referendum on the compulsory membership of Chambers. The Austrians voted with a clear majority in favour of maintaining it. This has again legitimized the existence and political self-consciousness of the Chambers.

Notwithstanding the problems experienced by more or less encompassing peak associations in almost all continental European countries, these associational systems have not broken down everywhere. They have shown themselves to be quite resilient to the challenges listed. One reason could be that member mobilization may have become less important as a source of power. Their institutional power, their access to the arenas of political decision-making, seem to have acquired a life of their own, becoming rather stable and institutionalized. In addition, in some countries like the Netherlands associations have amassed quite significant financial reserves, so much that at least financially they could survive as organizations for decades, even if they lost all their members. Symbolic of the political influence of peak associations in the Netherlands is that they have become the most important recruitment area for leading politicians. The previous Prime Minister Kok was formerly the leader of the largest trade union confederation, and his predecessor Lubbers made a career in the metalworking employers' association. Hence in countries such as the Netherlands, Austria, Finland and Ireland the associational preconditions for central social pacts have remained firmly in place or have regained their earlier importance.

The most important exception is Sweden, as we can read in the chapter by Jochem. Here the peak employers' association SAF, originally in the 1930s the driving force behind the centralization of labour relations in Sweden, seems to have enduringly given up on centralized corporatist concertation. The legitimacy for it has been lacking among its members and the organization has been both unwilling and unable to lead the members back to the central bargaining table. However, Sweden was not quite alone. In Germany the employers' associations have also experienced an internal rank and file revolt – especially in the Eastern part of the country – against central commitments, and this has contributed to the difficulties of concluding central social pacts there. The fragmentation of the German system of business associations between a peak employers' association BDA and a peak trade association BDI has added to the problems. It allowed rivalry to develop between both. The BDI has challenged the prerogative of the BDA in the field of labour relations and has tried to give its members, sectoral trade associations, a task in wage negotiation. Both in Sweden and in Germany employers have given preference to a more decentralized, and presumably more flexible, system of wage negotiations. The economist Teulings in this volume provides good logical and empirical arguments that such a position should not really be in the employers' interest. Centralized bargaining makes for easier overall wage restraint.

While employers' associations have hindered the return of central corporatist concertation in Sweden and Germany, resistance in the ranks of the trade union movement has obstructed the conclusion of central social pacts in Belgium and France. In Belgium the unions backed out of some central agreements at the very last moment.

Incentives

Why should parties in central social pacts have been willing to conclude them? In large part because they provided incentives for each other, either negatively, or positively. They were threats to each other; or possible aides or alliances.

The existence of powerful comprehensive peak associations means that they can offer enough resistance to state plans for welfare reform if not involved and committed in the decision-making process. The failure of the first Austrian *Sparpaket* in 1995 is a case in point. At the same time, the existence of such integrated associational systems means also that states have potentially attractive partners in central consultations, partners that represent rather moderate positions given their comprehensive character, and partners that somehow also manage to enforce agreements internally.

Conversely, a strong and self-confident state, which clearly indicates that it will go at it alone with reform measures if the social partners refuse collaboration, provides an important incentive to get trade unions and employers' associations to return to the central bargaining table and to make concessions. Credible threats of state intervention can and do chastise social partners. Hemerijck in this volume has called this the 'shadow of hierarchy'. An example of this process was the determination of the Dutch Cabinet under Lubbers to introduce wage measures and to reform the invalidity pension plans in 1981–2. This determination brought the social partners to eventually conclude the by now famous Wassenaar Accord of 1982. Paradoxically enough, by first reaffirming the primacy of politics the government managed to reinforce corporatist concertation. A second example was the initiative of the Austrian social partners to introduce a budget consolidation package, after the government had made quite clear that it was intent upon doing so. The 'cold shoulder' that the new 1999 centre-right coalition has shown to the social partners may in time produce similar results to those seen earlier in the Netherlands. A third case was the Belgian inter-sectoral pact concluded finally in 1998. An earlier attempt by the social partners in 1996 to agree voluntarily failed. Subsequently the government took legal measures in order to ensure that Belgium could qualify for participation in the EMU. It introduced a 'competitiveness law', which fixed the legal wage norm for 1997–8, stipulating that average wage increases should not exceed those in the neighbouring countries France, Germany and the Netherlands. Under pressure of this state intervention the social partners were able to reach an agreement in 1998. They preferred their own contract over government regulation. This case demonstrates again the importance of European integration. Whereas in the past the national central banks provided the 'whip' for wage negotiations (Iverson *et al.* 2000), now this task was taken over by the European Monetary Union.

A final and major incentive for engaging in central social pacts is of course its success. That is, they derive legitimacy from their output, their performance. If parties experience that such agreements are successful in the sense of furthering their goals – be it a reduction of unemployment, industrial recovery or budget consolidation – they will obviously be more inclined to continue on the road taken. In this sense central corporatist concertation can experience a spiral of positive reinforcement.

This has clearly been the case in the Netherlands and Ireland. The very positive economic performance of these countries over the last five years has, certainly in the Netherlands, changed the public perception of corporatist concertation. Up to 1995 a dominant stream in the political discourse associated corporatism with stalemate and sclerosis. A turnabout came when foreign newspapers in 1995 started to point to the strong economic performance of the country, and linked it to its institutions of consensual bargaining. Thus quickly the dominant stream in Dutch political discourse came to perceive these institutions proudly, first as the Dutch 'deltamodel', and subsequently as the 'poldermodel' (van Waarden 1995). This change to a positive perception has popularized concertation within socio-economic policy-making, but also in other policy fields.

Of course positive experiences can come from the country and parties themselves, but also from neighbouring countries. In that sense, modelling and imitation can and do also foster the conclusion of central social pacts. The positive experiences of countries like the Netherlands and Austria have induced others, e.g. the Mediterranean countries or Germany, to try hard to be successful with such an approach as well.

Situation

The willingness of social partners and the state to engage in centralized corporatist concertation and to agree to central social pacts has certainly been enhanced if not occasioned by a jointly shared sense of crisis, of imminent and escalating problems which threaten to run out of control. The variables that imbued a direct sense of crisis have been different to different actors. For the state it was a fiscal crisis: rising expenditures for welfare state and other social programmes, declining income due to falling growth rates, resulting in escalating budget deficits. For the unions it was rising unemployment and declining membership. For the employers it was a loss in competitive strength and declining profit rates. The important thing was that parties realized that these could be 'traded', and/or that the different problems had similar roots: a slow-down in growth, industrial restructuring, loss of competitive position. Such a realization was facilitated by sudden changes or shocks and by a joint national sense of vulnerability. Many of those countries experimenting with social pacts again have traditionally felt such a sense of vulnerability, owing to an openness to international competition. Belgium, the Netherlands, Finland, Denmark, Switzerland and Ireland all have rather open economies. In earlier times this has led to a sense of shared responsibility to withstand the 'foreign enemy'. In the immediate postwar years this was a very strong sentiment in Dutch socio-economic policy networks for example. This thesis of a link between openness of the economy and corporatist concertation, originally formulated by Katzenstein (Katzenstein 1985), seems to hold again for the new wave of social pacts.

An extreme and interesting case has been Finland, which experienced a sudden shock around 1990 with the loss of the traditionally important Russian export markets, following the political and economic revolutions there. This led to a strong concerted and unified response of the whole society, which also found expression in a very active industrial policy, focusing all state and societal resources on reducing its dependency on forestry and developing the ICT sector (Nokia!).

Institutions and culture

The capacity and willingness of actors to engage in centralized corporatist concertation is also influenced by the political institutions and the political culture of a country. The institutions set the rules of the game, and thus they facilitate or hinder the conclusion of central social pacts.

This is most clearly seen for the government as actor. Its capacity to enter into centralized negotiations with comprehensive interest associations, to bind itself in such negotiations and to deliver upon its promises is clearly determined by its political room for manœuvre. In a political system with many checks and balances on the power of the government this capacity is obviously reduced. Thus institutions like federalism, judicial review, a strong dualism between government and parliament, or a referendum set limits to the conclusion of central social pacts. Such institutions filter and correct decisions and reduce the capacity of the state to deliver upon its promises.

What is helpful on the other hand, are legal and political instruments that allow governments to threaten credibly with intervention. Thus the legal *Tarifautonomie* of social partners in Germany, which limits the power of the state to intervene in wage negotiations, does not really aid the state there to provide a credible 'shadow of hierarchy'.

Also important is some measure of political stability and continuity of governments and their political composition. Such stability reduces the options for social partners to wait for a new government, perhaps more positively inclined to their interests, which may even overturn decisions of the present government deemed undesirable, and thus postpone the conclusion of central social pacts.

However, a state should also not be too strong and centralized, because then it may decide to go it alone, in particular when it finds only relatively weakly organized social interests in civil society. This has been the case in France, where legal government intervention, for instance, regarding the weekly working week, has now further eroded the possibilities of interest associations to demonstrate their usefulness to their rank and file, thus undermining further their already weak power position.

Also conducive to concertation are institutionalized channels for contact and concertation, like formal advisory councils to the government, and the constitutional possibility for governments to involve interest associations in public policy. The continued existence of the Social Economic Council in the Netherlands, but also of a myriad of other policy or sector specific councils, boards, committees, in which the social partners and government officials frequently meet – often with the same people meeting again for different purposes in different arenas – has certainly aided the revival of centralized concertation in that country.

Finally, the importance of political culture should not be underrated. It makes quite a difference whether actors trust each other; are capable and willing to have some understanding for the opponents' interest and are willing to take account of this; have some tolerance towards the opponents, rather than vilifying each other as much as possible (either seriously or as part of the game); and are used to compromise and looking for consensus, rather than going for 'winning all or nothing'. That is, cultural values that emphasize consensualism as against adversarialism, tolerance as against intolerance, trust as against distrust, collectivism as against individualism, pragmatism as against legalism, tend to facilitate the conclusion of compromises, including central social pacts.

The development and maintenance of such cultural values do not come as 'deus ex machina' in political arenas. They have developed over long periods of time and found expression in political, legal and administrative traditions and institutions, which in turn continue to support such cultural values. Thus a majoritarian political system in which the 'winner takes all', and the frequent use of a legal system (high litigation ratio) that in the end identifies a winner and a loser, both tend to further an adversarial culture, also in the relations between interest associations and between them and the state. Conversely, a political system based on proportional representation and cooperative federalism condemns political actors to each other, condemns them to build coalitions. Such a system is first of all already an institutional expression of a culture that values tolerance for minorities and compromise; in turn it tends to support the continued existence of such a culture. In the relation between the state and organized interests the presence of many institutionalized channels and arenas in which actors meet is important. This does not only allow for generalized exchange, it also allows actors to get to know each other and develop some sense of basic trust. In such cooperative systems of labour relations actors may have developed provisions which give them an further interest in continuing their good relations.

An interesting example are the Dutch 'O and O funds'. Quite a few sectoral collective agreements contain stipulations that employers pay a certain sum per worker to these funds. The sectoral associations pay for the provision of sectoral collective goods (vocational training, health and safety at work, etc.) out of these funds; but increasingly they have also begun to secretly finance their own organizations out of this fund. The consequence is that both parties have acquired an interest in continuing their good relations, because only then can collective agreements be concluded and these funds continue to be filled.

The underdevelopment of the institutional and cultural dimension is a weak point of the otherwise interesting study of Visser and Hemerijck (1997) on Dutch corporatism. They emphasize that

> the Dutch trajectory of adjustment and reform was paved with many contingencies, such as a major recession, a change in the balance of power between capital and labour, a spiraling crisis of inactivity, and changes in the political landscape. ... There is no uniform institutional format for a common 'polder model' across policy domains. ... Likewise, there is no constant 'Dutch culture' of consensual decision-making, which only has to be mobilized in times of international danger and crisis to the nation. The breaking of the political stalemate of corporatist immobility required hard-won changes and slow learning processes, and success was not assured.
>
> (1997: 184)

They give a prominent place to what they call 'policy learning'. However, this concept appears a bit like a 'deus ex machina'. Why were actors willing to 'learn', and why could they? Why did they do so less in other countries? In other words, the authors cannot really explain why Dutch policy-makers were capable of such policy learning and why German or Belgian policy-makers, for instance were less capable. A comparative approach would have led them to ask questions that they did not ask in a case study of the Netherlands. Explaining the differences between countries requires recourse to differences in institutions and political culture. They may be right in emphasizing that corporatist institutions do not automatically produce consensual outcomes; it goes too far to conclude, as they seem to, that institutions do not really matter. It may be that they are not a sufficient condition, but they certainly may be a necessary – or perhaps better, conducive – condition for concertation.

Conclusion: national room for manœuvre for change/reform

Interest associations have often been seen in the literature as constraints on governments, as additional checks and balances in the political system, limiting the room for manœuvre of the state further, and threatening to produce stalemates. In systems with many checks and balances, interest associations have also used these to block or seriously delay government decision-making when this served their interest. The clearest case is that of the USA. American interest associations have used all the possibilities that the American dualist political system, its federalism and the elaborated and fragmented 'politicized' legal system (with its judicial review and high uncertainty of decisions (van Waarden 1993)) offer to block or frustrate decisions, either in the phase of policy formulation, or in that of policy implementation. An adversarial political culture, reinforced by adversarial and 'winner takes all' institutions has further reinforced this. But also European governments have been confronted with the power of interest associations. A major political strike by British miners, unions forced a government out of power and paved the way for the tough, adversarial and impositional tactics of the Thatcher governments. Something similar had also happened earlier in France. In the smaller continental European countries powerful comprehensive associations have also produced stale-mates in institutions of centralized corporatist policy formation. Thus for some years the Social Economic Council, whose Dutch acronym is SER, came to be called 'Sociaal Economische Rem', meaning 'socio-economic brake'. This was enhanced by a temporary adversarial political culture, stemming from the revival of class conflict in the 1970s.

Increasing technical, economic, political and legal internationalization gave policy-makers the idea that dangers were imminent, and that countries had to adapt faster to the changing international environment, that they had to be more flexible in policy-making, that they needed more room for manœuvre. Interest associations and institutions of corporatist concertation were considered hindrances to this for a while. Hence both policy-makers and observing social scientists expected that international-ization would be a threat to corporatist concertation. And indeed, it seemed to be so for a while.

However, a revival turned out to be just around the corner. Confronted with still powerful comprehensive interest associations some governments decided that they could actually increase their room for manœuvre by again integrating and committing social partners to intended reform measures. Some political elites came to the conclusion that they would have greater chances for realizing reforms by gradually building a consensus base among powerful interest groups. There have even been cases where governments used agreements with social partners to break stalemates in the political arena. And as we have argued, rather than internationalization and globalization being a threat to such concertation, they actually turned out to be motors and motives for it. Many recent central social pacts were occasioned by the need of governments to satisfy the EMU-entrance criteria.

Once some countries had success with this approach, others followed the model provided. However, not all countries could equally successfully adopt this approach. A major condition for success was a capacity of the state to bind itself in central negotiations with interest associations. This leads to the paradoxical conclusion that corporatist concertation has been most successful in countries that may need it least. Assuming that concertation actually increases a government's room for manœuvre, governments who have less of that would be in greater need. However, governments that are already less 'burdened' by many political and legal checks and balances, that have already relatively more room for manœuvre, find it easiest to further enlarge their room for manœuvre by engaging in corporatist concertation. Those governments who already experience important institutional limitations to their room for manœuvre also find it more difficult to conclude successful central social pacts which are meant to increase their room for manœuvre.

Note

1 [A reform-government ought to radically change the Chamber system, should distance itself more rigorously from functionaries collecting double and triple salaries, should end the corrupt entanglements between politics and the social security system, and should initiate drastic substantive reforms. Most of all: the political parties ought to change themselves – and become more modest and efficient. But will the many Chamber and trade union functionaries, used to benefices and privileges, accept that?]

References

Alber, Jens (1982) *Vom Armenhaus zum Wohlfahrtsstaat. Analysen zur Entwicklung der Sozialversicherung in Westeuropa*, Frankfurt am Main and New York: Campus.

Bernstein, Marver H. (1955) *Regulating Business by Independent Commission*, Westport, Conn.: Greenwood Press.

Ehrmann, Henry W. (1968, orig. 1961) 'Interest Groups and the Bureaucracy in Western Democracies', in Reinhard Bendix (ed.) *State and Society. A Reader in Comparative Political Sociology*, Boston: Little, Brown, pp. 257–76.

Esping-Andersen, Gosta (1990) *The Three Worlds of Welfare Capitalism*, Princeton: Princeton University Press.

Friedrich, Carl J. (1968) *Constitutional Government and Democracy. Theory and Practice in Europe and America*, 4th ed., Waltham, Toronto and London: Blaisdell.

Iverson, T., J. Pontusson and D.W. Soskice (eds) (2000) *Unions, Employers, and Central Banks: Macro-Economic Coordination and Institutional Change in Social Market Economies*, Cambridge: Cambridge University Press.

Katzenstein, Peter J. (1985) *Small States in World Markets. Industrial Policy in Europe*, Ithaca: Cornell University Press.

Keller, Bernd (1995) European Integration, Workers' Participation, and Collective Bargaining: A Europessimistic View', in Brigitte Unger and Frans van Waarden (eds) *Convergence or Diversity? Internationalization and Economic Policy Response*, Aldershot: Avebury, pp. 252–77.

Lazare, Daniel (1996) *The Frozen Republic. How the Constitution is Paralyzing Democracy*, New York, San Diego and London: Harcourt Brace and Co.

Lehmbruch, Gerhard (1967) *Proporzdemokratie: Politisches System und politische Kultur in der Schweiz und in Oesterreich*, Tübingen: Mohr.

Lehmbruch, Gerhard (1998) *Parteienwettbewerb im ` Bundesstaat: Regelsysteme und*

Spannungslagen im Institutionengefuege der Bundesrepublik Deutschland,   2nd revised ed. Opladen: Westdeutscher Verlag.

McConnell, Grant (1966) *Private Power and American Democracy*, New York: Knopf.

Mitnick, Barry (1980) *The Political Economy of Regulation*, New York: Columbia University Press.

Peters, B. Guy (1989) *The Politics of Bureaucracy*, New York and London: Longman.

Pierson, Paul (1994) *Dismantling the Welfare State? Reagan, Thatcher, and the Politics of Retrenchment*, Cambridge: Cambridge University Press.

Schmitter, Philippe C. (1979, orig. 1974) 'Still the Century of Corporatism?', in Philippe Schmitter and Gerhard Lehmbruch (eds) *Trends toward Corporatist Intermediation*, London and Beverly Hills: Sage.

Schmitter, P. (1989) 'Corporatism is Dead! Long Live Corporatism', *Government and Opposition*, 24/1: 54–73.

Schmitter, Philippe C. (1997) 'The Emerging Euro-Polity and its Impact upon National Systems of Production' in J. Rogers Hollingsworth and R. Boyer (eds) *Contemporary Capitalism: The Embeddedness of Institutions*, Cambridge: Cambridge University Press.

Streeck, Wolfgang (1992) 'From National Corporatism to Transnational Pluralism: European Interest Politics and the Single Market', in Tiziano Treu (ed.) *Participation in Public Policy-Making. The Role of Trade Unions and Employers' Associations*, Berlin and New York: De Gruyter, pp. 97–126.

van Waarden, Frans (1993) 'Verwaltungskultur im Vergleich. Wie lassen sich unterschiedliche Verwaltungsstile und Verwaltungskulturen erklären?', in Hans-Georg Wehling (ed.) *Politische Kulturen* Vol. 43, Stuttgart: Landeszentrale für politische Bildung en Kohlhammer Verlag, pp. 70–80.

van Waarden, Frans (1995) 'Breekt Nederland zijn dijken door?', *Economisch-Statistische Berichten*, 80/3993: 52–7.

Visser, Jelle and Anton Hemerijck (1997) *A Dutch Miracle'. Job Growth, Welfare Reform and Corporatism in the Netherlands*, Amsterdam: Amsterdam University Press.

Wilson, Graham K. (1985) *Business and Politics. A Comparative Introduction*, London: Macmillan.

Part II

Countries with traditions of corporatist concertation

2 The resurgence of Dutch corporatist policy coordination in an age of globalization[1]

Anton Hemerijck

Introduction

The 'Dutch model' today occupies a prominent place for progressive European politicians pondering the possibilities of a new model of capitalism with a human face in an era of economic internationalization. Foreign politicians, central bankers and union leaders alike praise the combination of fiscal conservatism, wage moderation, consensual welfare reform, job creation and the maintenance of overall social security. They highlight the extraordinary proportion of Dutch people, male and female, in part-time jobs, the sustained policy of wage moderation by the trade unions; the success in holding the course for EMU and the absence of social unrest. Best of all, they observe, the Netherlands is the only EU member state to have more than halved its unemployment rate during the past decade, from 13-plus per cent in 1983 to 5 per cent in 1998. Its annual growth rate in jobs of 1.6 per cent is four times the European average, and as good as the American 'job machine', but without the US's sharp increase in earning inequality and life-chances.

Although it attracted international attention only in the 1990s, the Dutch 'job miracle' has its basis in policy changes in the early 1980s. Over the past three decades we can observe four consecutive policy reversals across four different policy areas. The shift to a hard currency regime in macro-economic policy was made in the wake of the breakdown of the system of Bretton Woods and became firmly established in 1983. In 1982 the social partners agreed to resume a cooperative strategy of wage moderation. In the late 1980s and the early 1990 a series of reforms in the system of social security took place. From the mid-1990s, finally, the adoption of an active labour market policy stance together with additional reforms in labour market regulation gained political currency.

The purpose of this chapter is to analyse the lengthy and delicate process of renegotiating the Dutch welfare state over the past two decades. I will demonstrate that the shifts in macro-policy, wage formation, social security and labour market policy were 'sequentially' related. I will show how, over time, policy reforms across different policy areas created the conditions and the demand for one another, and that neither of these domain-specific policy changes could have been successful on their own account. As the sequence of policy reforms were practically all conditioned by the larger political institutional surroundings of consociational democracy and corporatist business–government relations in the Dutch political economy, the evolution of policy adjustment in the Netherlands is best characterized as a process of 'negotiated change'.

The chapter is organized into eight parts. First I will present a short overview of recent labour market performance in the Netherlands. In the next section I develop a number of theoretical considerations for exploring the sequential and composite character of policy adjustment. The emphasis is on important interaction effects between interdependent policy areas over time. In the following four sections, I will employ these insights for the empirical analysis of sequential policy adjustment in the Netherlands across the policy areas of macroeconomic policy, industrial relations, social security, and labour market policy. In the concluding section I will explore the political conditions under which the Dutch welfare state was able to overcome the pathology of 'welfare without work', so typical of a continental welfare regime, through a lengthy and cumbersome process of negotiated change.

Labour market performance

The miraculous employment performance of the Netherlands reveals a clear departure from the current unemployment malaise in the European Union and the Dutch recent past. Where there are so few examples of strong job growth in Western Europe, and so few signs that it is possible to consensually adjust the institutional, social and mental pattern of a passive welfare state, the Dutch example does invite closer scrutiny. Table 2.1 compares the performance of the Netherlands with the European Union average on six broad measures: real GDP growth, private consumption, investment, employment, unemployment and net labour force participation. We observe that in the 1990s the Netherlands did better on each of these indicators. This has been achieved while bringing down the budget deficit to 2.2 per cent of GDP in 1996, well within the 3 per cent norm of the Economic and Monetary Union (it was 3.8 per cent in 1970, 7.2 per cent in 1980). The collective expenditure quote has fallen for four years in a row and with it the GDP share of taxes and social charges. In 1996 this share was 44.4 per cent (47.3 per cent in 1970, 57.2 per cent in 1980), which is still a respectable sixth place in the European Union, behind Denmark, Sweden, Belgium, Finland and France. The total public dept has decreased to 78.5 per cent in 1996 while inflation averages under 2.5 per cent for the last decade.

If we concentrate on labour market performance, the Dutch experience clearly contradicts the continental pathology of 'welfare without work'. Dutch job growth was four times the average for the European Union

Table 2.1 Economic performance of the Netherlands in comparison to the European Union, in percentages

	Netherlands	*European Union*
(Average growth per year, 1991–6)		
GDP	2.2	1.5
Private consumption	2.3	1.5
Investment	1.3	−0.2
Employment	1.5	−0.5
Unemployment level	6.2	11.1
Employment/population ratio	64.2	60.6

Source: DNB (Dutch Central Bank), Annual Report 1996, Amsterdam, 1997, p. 24; and OECD, Employment Outlook, Paris, various years.

between 1983 and 1993, and thereafter still double the EU average (see Table 2.2). Unemployment has come down from an all time record in 1984 to 3.3 per cent in 1999, while the EU average remained at over 9 per cent (see Table 2.3). Since 1995 it has also been higher than the famous American jobs machine. However, in contrast to the latter, Dutch job growth is less associated with a sharp increase in earnings inequality. Inequality has increased, but the Netherlands has been able to maintain a middle rank between Germany and Scandinavian countries on the one hand, Britain and the US on the other.

The extraordinary growth of part-time jobs has contributed to the massive entry of women in the labour force, and the replacement of older workers by younger, cheaper and possibly more flexible and skilled

Table 2.2 Employment growth in the Netherlands, the European Union and selected OECD countries, 1983–2000, in percentages

	1983–93	*1994*	*1995*	*1996*	*1997*	*1998*	*1999*	*2000*[a]
Netherlands	1.8	0.8	2.4	2	2.5	3.3	3.0	2.5
EU	0.4	−0.7	0.5	0.3	0.6	1.5	1.6	1.5
Belgium	0.5	−0.7	0.3	0.4	0.3	1.2	0.9	1.4
Germany[b]	0.7	−1.8	−0.3	−1.2	−1.3	0.4	0.3	0.5
France	0.1	−0.4	0.9	0.0	0.3	1.1	2.0	2.3
Italy	0.0	−1.7	−0.6	0.4	0.0	1.1	1.2	1.5
Denmark	0.2	1.2	1.6	1.3	2.3	2.1	0.8	0.8
Sweden	−0.6	−0.7	1.6	−0.9	−1.0	1.5	2.2	1.9
UK	0.6	1.2	0.8	1.1	1.7	1.2	1.0	0.9
USA	1.8	3.2	1.5	1.4	2.2	1.5	1.5	2.1

Source: OECD, Employment Outlook, Paris, July 1996, July 1997 and June 2000, Table 1.2

Notes:
[a] Projections
[b] Until 1993 West Germany only.

Table 2.3 Unemployment in the Netherlands, the European Union and selected OECD countries, 1983–99, in percentages

	1983	*1990*	*1993*	*1994*	*1995*	*1996*	*1997*	*1998*	*1999*
Netherlands	9.7	6.2	6.6	7.1	6.9	6.3	5.2	4.0	3.3
EU	9.2	8.1	10.7	11.1	10.7	10.8	10.6	9.9	9.2
Belgium	11.1	6.7	8.9	10.1	9.9	9.7	9.4	9.5	9.0
Germany[a]	7.7	4.8	7.9	8.5	8.2	8.9	9.9	9.4	8.7
France	8.1	9.0	11.7	12.3	11.7	12.4	12.3	11.9	11.3
Italy	7.7	9.1	10.2	11.2	11.6	11.7	11.7	11.9	11.4
Denmark	–	7.7	10.1	8.2	7.3	6.8	5.6	5.2	5.2
Sweden	3.9	1.8	9.1	9.4	8.8	9.6	9.9	8.3	7.2
UK	11.1	7.1	10.5	9.6	8.7	8.2	7.0	6.3	6.1
USA	9.6	5.6	6.9	6.1	5.6	5.4	4.9	4.5	4.2

Source: OECD, Employment Outlook, Paris, July 1996, July 1997 and June 2000, Table A.
Notes:
[a] Until 1993 West Germany only.

workers. With some delay, the Dutch trade unions have come around in support of these changes and taken a positive attitude towards part-time employment and flexibility. The share of part-time work has surged from less than 15 per cent in 1975 to 35 per cent in 1994, a share well above that of any other OECD country. Of all part-time employment, 75 per cent of part-time jobs are held by women: 55 per cent of all female workers are employed part-time. The incidence of part-time work among men is at 12 per cent the highest among OECD countries (see Table 2.4). The Netherlands has the highest rate of part-timers among young people in Europe (25 per cent). This suggests that entry into the labour market is commonly channelled through part-time work.

The growth of female participation is perhaps the most revolutionary development in the Dutch labour market. Female labour force participation has been extremely low in the Netherlands in comparison to most OECD countries. Over the last decade participation of women in the labour market increased from under 35 per cent in 1983 to 61 per cent in 1999 (see Table 2.5). The growth in labour force participation is concentrated among women who are either married or cohabiting: they now represent a quarter of the active labour force. The majority of working women find employment in the commercial and non-commercial service sectors. The demand for a flexible workforce in the service sector agrees with a general preference of women to work part-time. As a consequence of the increase in labour market participation of women, there is also a growing interest among men for part-time work, so as to combine gainful employment work with unpaid family care.

Table 2.4 Incidence of part-time employment in the Netherlands and selected OECD countries, by sex, 1983–99, in percentages

	1983	1990	1996	1997	1998	1999
Men						
Netherlands	6.8	13.4	11.3	11.1	12.4	11.9
Belgium	2.0	4.6	4.8	4.8	4.9	7.3
Germany[a]	1.7	2.3	3.7	4.1	4.6	4.8
France	2.5	4.4	5.7	5.9	5.8	5.8
Italy	2.4	3.9	4.7	5.1	4.9	5.3
Denmark	6.5	10.2	10.2	11.1	9.8	8.9
Sweden	6.2	5.3	6.7	6.5	5.6	7.3
UK	3.3	5.3	7.7	8.2	8.2	8.5
USA	10.8	8.3	8.4	8.3	8.2	8.1
Women						
Netherlands	49.7	52.5	55.5	54.8	54.8	55.4
Belgium	19.7	29.8	32.1	32.3	32.2	36.6
Germany[a]	30.0	29.8	29.9	31.4	32.4	33.1
France	20.1	21.7	24.1	25.2	25.0	24.7
Italy	9.4	18.2	20.9	22.2	22.4	23.2
Denmark	43.7	29.6	24.2	24.2	25.4	22.7
Sweden	45.9	24.5	23.5	22.6	22.0	22.3
UK	41.3	39.5	41.4	40.9	41.2	40.6
USA	28.1	20.0	20.2	19.5	19.1	19.0

Source: OECD, Employment Outlook, Paris, July 1997 and June 2000, Table E.

Note

[a] Until 1993 West Germany only.

It should be emphasized that with the increase in part-time and temporary work, and the surge of female market participation, average annual working hours per worker have come down significantly since 1973 (see Table 2.6). Notwithstanding the overall increase in labour market participation rate (Table 2.5), the participation rate for older men (in the 55–65 age bracket) came down in the first half of the 1990s from 50 per cent in 1983 to 40 per cent in 1996, after which it started to rise again. This reflects a return from the early retirement policy (Table 2.7).

The Dutch job miracle represents a significant departure from the scenario of 'welfare without work', so typical for the continental welfare states. However, all that glistens is not gold. The present state of nearly full part-time employment may be judged a second-best solution only. The low unemployment rate of 3 per cent does not reflect the true state of slack in the Dutch labour market. The level of structural inactivity, although

Table 2.5 Employment/population ratios by sex in the Netherlands, the European Union and selected OECD countries, 1983–99

	1983	1990	1996	1997	1998	1999
Men						
Netherlands	69.1	75.2	75.7	77.9	79.6	80.3
EU	75.8	74.7	70.3	70.4	71.3	72.0
Belgium	70.4	68.1	66.8	67.1	67.0	67.5
Germany[a]	76.6	75.7	72.9	72.2	72.5	73.1
France	74.4	69.7	66.7	66.2	66.5	66.8
Italy	76.6	72.0	65.3	65.0	66.7	67.1
Denmark	78.4	80.1	80.5	81.3	80.2	81.2
Sweden	84.7	85.2	73.2	72.4	73.5	74.8
UK	78.7	82.1	76.3	77.4	78.1	78.4
USA	78.9	80.7	79.7	80.1	80.5	80.5
Women						
Netherlands	34.7	46.7	54.8	56.9	58.9	61.3
EU	42.9	48.7	50.3	50.7	51.6	53.1
Belgium	36.6	40.8	45.6	46.7	47.5	50.2
Germany[a]	47.8	52.2	55.5	55.4	56.0	56.5
France	49.7	50.3	51.7	51.5	52.3	52.9
Italy	34.9	36.4	36.1	36.2	37.1	38.1
Denmark	65.2	70.6	67.4	69.4	70.3	71.6
Sweden	75.5	81.0	69.9	68.9	69.4	70.9
UK	55.3	62.8	63.3	64.0	64.2	64.9
USA	57.7	64.0	66.3	67.1	67.4	67.6

Source: OECD, Employment Outlook, Paris, July 1996, July 1997 and June 2000, Table B.

Note
[a] Until 1993 West Germany only.

Table 2.6 Average annual working hours per employee in the Netherlands and in selected OECD countries, 1973–99

	1973	1979	1983	1990	1996	1997	1998	1999
Netherlands	1724	1591	1530	1433	1374	1365	–	–
Germany[a]	1804	1699	1686	1562	1523	1524	1531	1535
France	1771	1667	1558	1539	1608	1605	1604	–
Italy	1842	1748	1724	1694	1577	1577	1575	–
Sweden	1557	1451	1453	1480	1623	1625	1628	1634
UK	1929	1821	1719	1773	1738	1736	1731	1720
USA	1896	1884	1866	1936	1951	1966	1955	1976

Source: OECD, Employment Outlook, Paris, July 1997, and June 2000, Table G.

Note
[a] Until 1993 West Germany only.

Table 2.7 The unemployment and employment/population ratios for men, 55 to 65, 1983–99

	1983	1990	1996	1997	1998	1999
Employment/population ratio						
Netherlands	50.5	44.5	40.7	43.0	46.2	48.8
EU	58.5	53.2	47.5	47.7	47.9	48.3
Belgium	47.7	34.3	32.2	32.2	32.1	35.1
Germany[a]	57.4	52.0	48.0	47.9	47.6	48.0
France	50.4	43.0	38.6	38.4	37.9	38.9
Italy	55.3	50.9	42.1	41.5	41.5	40.8
Denmark	63.1	65.6	58.4	61.0	58.5	59.9
Sweden	73.9	74.4	66.0	64.7	65.8	67.1
UK	62.6	62.4	57.0	58.6	58.3	59.4
USA	65.2	65.2	64.7	65.5	66.2	66.1
Unemployment						
Netherlands	6.7	2.8	3.5	3.2	1.8	2.1
EU	6.9	6.2	9.2	9.3	8.6	8.4
Belgium	5.8	3.1	4.7	4.8	5.3	4.5
Germany[a]	9.0	9.9	12.8	14.1	13.7	12.8
France	6.0	7.3	8.6	8.6	8.3	8.7
Italy	1.5	1.7	4.3	4.6	4.7	4.6
Denmark	6.2	5.2	6.0	4.4	4.2	3.2
Sweden	4.0	1.3	9.4	9.4	7.8	7.3
UK	10.6	8.4	9.5	7.8	6.8	6.4
USA	6.1	3.8	3.3	3.1	2.8	2.7

Source: OECD, Employment Outlook, Paris, July 1997 and June 2000, Table C.

Note
[a] Until 1993, West Germany only.

declining in absolute and relative terms, including all unemployed and inactive persons of working age receiving a social security benefit and persons enrolled in special job creation programmes, remains high at 20 per cent of the current labour force. New jobs have gone predominantly to younger and better-skilled recruits to the labour market and many are part-time, sometimes for a limited number of hours only. The share of long-term unemployment may have decreased to 43 per cent in 1999, and is even low by European standards, but is still high in absolute terms (Table 2.8). Unemployment remains a huge problem for unskilled and immigrant workers, with unemployment rates two to three times the national average. In short, the success of the employment and labour market performance of the Netherlands is relative, to be set against the background of the dismal

Table 2.8 Long-term unemployment in the Netherlands and in selected OECD countries, percentage unemployed longer than 12 months, 1983–99

	1983	1990	1996	1997	1998	1999
Netherlands	48.8	49.3	50.0	49.1	47.9	43.5
EU	–	48.6	49.3	50.1	49.1	47.5
Belgium	64.8	68.7	61.3	60.5	61.7	60.5
Germany[a]	41.6	46.8	47.8	50.1	52.6	51.7
France	42.2	38.0	39.5	41.2	44.1	40.3
Italy	58.2	69.8	65.6	66.3	59.6	61.4
Denmark	44.3	26.5	26.5	27.2	26.9	20.5
Sweden	10.3	12.1	30.1	33.4	33.5	–
UK	45.6	34.4	39.8	38.6	32.7	29.8
USA	13.3	5.5	9.5	8.7	8.0	6.8

Source: OECD, Employment Outlook, Paris, July 1997: Table H and June 2000: Table G.

Note

[a] Until 1993, West Germany only.

experience of the recent past, on the one hand, and the lacklustre performance of most neighbouring European countries on the other. There is no full employment yet and the present state of nearly full part-time employment should be judged a second-best solution only.

The sequential logic of policy adjustment

The theoretical argument of this chapter builds on five propositions. First, social and economic policy adjustment is a fundamentally dynamic process. Second, policy adjustment impinges on a wide variety of policy areas. For our purposes, the most important are: macro-economic policy, industrial relations, social security and labour market policy and regulation. Third, trajectories of policy adjustment are paved with interaction effects between policy choices adopted in different areas and ongoing changes in the international economic environment. In the face of interaction effects and cumulative changes in the international political economy, fourth, policy makers have responded by making sequential adjustments in different policy areas, usually by addressing one policy problem in one policy area at a time. Policy responses adopted in one policy area subsequently impinge on other policy domains, which in turn, encourages policy-makers to make additional policy changes that follow from earlier choices made elsewhere. Fifth, the extent to which policy interdependencies are the object of explicit institutional coordination and the degree to which non-state corporate actors participate in processes of policy adjustment are crucial institutional variables in the process of sequential policy adjustment. Together, changes in the international economy, interaction effects across policy areas and time, and efforts at cross-sectoral policy coordination shape the pace, scope, character and direction of policy adjustment.

Policy interdependencies

Ever since the late 1960s, the economic environment of the advanced welfare states in Europe and North America has been subject to substantial and continuous change. The challenges brought on by accelerating inflation, stagflation problems associated with the collapse of the Bretton Woods system, the two oil crises, the resurgence of mass unemployment, the liberalization of capital markets, path-breaking advances in the process of European integration, the fall of the Berlin Wall and the crisis in the European Monetary System, have triggered a variety of highly diverse trajectories of policy adjustment across different economically advanced welfare states. In the process, many European welfare states have been gradually recasting their once stable policy repertoires of macro-economic policy, industrial relations, social security and labour market policy commitments.

How are we to make sense of the great variety of trajectories of policy adjustment across the economically advanced welfare states in response to dramatic international economic changes over the last quarter of the twentieth century? It is my contention that for an adequate analysis of policy adjustment it is necessary to draw together in a single study a wider range of policy areas than has generally been thought relevant in comparative political economy research. Under conditions of baffling change, we should focus on the composite character of policy choices adopted across different policy areas. Trajectories of policy adjustment are paved with interaction effects between policy choices adopted in different policy domains. For the analysis of national patterns of policy adjustment, I consider four interdependent policy domains. These are macro economic policy (including monetary and fiscal policy), industrial relations (including labour market regulation), social security policy and labour market policy.

During the Golden Age of postwar prosperity, these four policy areas developed as relatively autonomous, functionally separated, policy domains, each with their own sector-specific methods of provision and regulation. Although fundamentally engaged in the tasks of meeting and stabilizing the material needs of citizens, the four policy areas vary in substantive policy content and are governed according to different rules of policy making. Macro-economic policy designates the role of the state in helping to stabilize the macro-economic policy environment and facilitate economic development. The domain of industrial relations structures the relationship between the trade unions and the formal employing organizations of the labour market, and regulate, under labour law, procedures of collective bargaining, working conditions, hiring and firing legislation, and patterns of consultation, representation, cooperation of the two sides of industry.

Social security regulation is politically disengaged from the regular labour market, serving to protect the non-working population – the aged, the sick, the unemployed – by providing them with sources of income, social security and public assistance. The fourth domain of labour market policy entertains a tenuous position between those inside and outside the labour market. The 'right to work', difficult to uphold in a capitalist economy, is commonly anchored in public commitment to pursue full employment by way of an active labour market policy.

In the Golden Age of postwar capitalism, different advanced political economies achieved relatively stable, coherent and functional clusters of macro-policy, industrial relations, social security, and labour market policy. These different 'golden age' policy repertoires, in retrospect, displayed a high degree of 'goodness-of-fit' over the prolonged period of postwar prosperity, political stability and social inclusion. However, we should not exaggerate the degree of harmony among separate policy areas. The relatively benign economic environment of the 1950s and 1960s made practically every national social and economic policy repertoire equally successful in securing high growth rates, full employment, price stability and the expansion of the welfare state. Since the early 1970, stagflation, low growth and the resurgence of mass unemployment have come to unsettle these once stable repertoires of social and economic regulation. In addition, in the 1980s the class compromise that originally supported the policy formats of the postwar decades crumbled under the shift in the balance of power from left to right, unleashing various conservative attacks on the welfare state in different countries (Hall 1999).

Over the past quarter century, dramatic international economic and related domestic political changes have resulted in a substantial reconfiguration, to different degrees in different countries, of the basic policy repertoire around which the welfare state is organized. Under conditions of rapid international economic integration successful policy responses increasingly depend on the capacity of policy-makers and producer groups to swiftly adjust to changing economic conditions. For a better understanding of the process of policy adjustment I wish to draw special attention to interaction effects between different policy decisions adopted in different policy areas. The interdependencies between the policy areas of macro economic policy, industrial relations, social security and labour market policy, in the context of international economic integration are fairly obvious. In the open economy generous standards of social protection depend heavily on and in turn affect substantially the competitiveness of the economy to create the wealth, jobs, and the tax and contribution bases for high-quality welfare provision. As a consequence, policy responses executed in one policy domain are likely to shape and constrain options for reform in a neighbouring policy area. Although sectoral policy actors are often unaware of the interdependencies between policy areas, they usually respond to unanticipated spillover effects by way of local adjustment to previous choices adopted in other areas of social and economic regulation. Spillover effects not only constrain the range of policy options in the affected policy areas, they also create the opportunities for the realization of much desired policy changes that have heretofore been blocked.

Sequential character of policy adjustment

By drawing the policy areas of macro-economic management, industrial relations, social security and labour market policy together in a single analysis, we are able to bring out the composite character of policy adjustment. As efficiency gains won in one policy area are likely to incur efficiency losses elsewhere, which are likely to gain political salience in a next cycle of reform, patterns of social and economic policy adjustment seem to follow a temporal or sequential-diachronic logic. Over time, spillover effects in another area create additional problems of adjustment in a neighbouring area of social and economic regulation. By the same token, policy continuity in one area, in the face of ongoing changes in the policy environment, can affect policy changes in other policy domains. Initial choices are especially important in shaping the content and scope of consecutive reform efforts. From this, it follows that when countries adopted different policy solutions to tackle the crisis of stagflation in the late 1970s, they may unintentionally have created additional problem loads in other policy areas. The composite effects of these temporally interrelated policy choices subsequently interacted with novel changes in the international economic environment. Moreover, it should be emphasized that national policy responses are not wholly independent from other national responses. National policy choices in macro-economic policy will be influenced by macro-economic policy choices made elsewhere. To be sure, towards the end of the 1980s the Bundesbank increasingly came to delineate the space for monetary policy choices in the majority of European political economies.

To give an example: the Swedish choice of a soft currency response to the fall in aggregate demand, resulting from the first oil shock, helped to restore the competitiveness of the Swedish economy, while maintaining high levels of employment. When solidaristic wage bargaining eventually broke down in the face of a revolt from metalworking employers, Swedish policy-makers were unable to contain inflation. Rising interest rates resulted in a loss of competitiveness. When capital controls were lifted in the second half of the 1980s and when the Swedes finally decided to peg the krone to the German mark in the early 1990s, a radical surge in unemployment could no longer be avoided. The Scandinavian recession was exacerbated by the high interest rates policy of the Bundesbank in response to the Chancellor Kohl's decision for a one-to-one conversion of East German marks into D-marks over unification.

The Dutch followed a distinctly different adjustment route. The basic choice of a hard currency in response to the second oil crisis resulted in the early 1980s in a loss of competitiveness, rising public deficits and massive increase in unemployment. This predicament persuaded the social partners and state officials, after a long period of policy stalemate, to resume a concerted strategy of wage restraint in order to recoup corporate profits, investments and jobs. Fiscal discipline and wage restraint in the Netherlands ultimately paid off in terms of revolutionary job growth in the second half of the 1980s when growth picked up in the world economy. Furthermore, low wages and increased demands for Dutch exports in the new German Länder helped the Netherlands to successfully weather the global recession of the early 1990s.

Failure-induced policy learning

Policy adjustment seems to take place by trial and error. Necessity often is the mother of invention. Following the canons of organizational theory, it could be argued that processes of policy adjustment follow a pattern of 'failure-induced search' (March 1994; Cohen and Sproull 1996). When policy performance falls below acceptable targets, i.e. when inflation, unemployment and public deficits reach double-digit figures, search activity is increased. No consistent policy repertoire can maintain a severe discrepancy between targets and aspirations for very long. In periods of sustained poor performance, even the most entrenched policy-makers come to understand that standard rules of procedure are no longer adequate. The focus of policy adjustment under pressure brings out the central role of policy actors, willing to learn from experience and able to change policy and innovate the institutions within which they operate. Accumulated policy failures provoke a readiness for learning, engendering an 'unfreezing' process, in which old policy paradigms are shaken and new ideas are accommodated (Hall 1993).

Under conditions of faltering performance, many elements of the existing policy repertoire may be up for grabs, but again, given the limited attention spans of policy-makers, not everything can be attended to all at once. And as the political economy of the welfare state is made up of interdependent policy domains, policy failure is likely to produce a struggle for political attention between different problem areas. Macro-economic policy-makers may draw attention to accelerating inflation as the root cause of all evil, whereas social policy-makers argue that growth should be stimulated to fight unemployment through demand stimulation. Policy changes, prioritizing full employment over price stability and vice versa, more often than not depend on temporary political disequilibria, which allow certain policy actors to impose their definition and diagnosis of policy failure and its appropriate solution on the rest of the policy repertoire.

Policy reform is contingent on social and political support. Powerful actors are able to stimulate research and mobilize resources for tackling the problems they find most pressing. With the passing of time, as a consequence of sectoral spillover, the locus of problem attention and policy action is likely to shift to yet again another policy area.

Organizational theorists emphasize the role organizational slack in processes of organizational change (Cyert and March 1963). Slack accumulates in good times, can serve as a buffer in bad times. In the face of organizational decline, managers discover ways to decrease slack by cutting costs and through organizational restructuring. However, in the world of policy and politics, especially welfare policy, aspirations adapt to performance. The Golden Age of economic prosperity, full employment and rising expectations saw the institutionalization of generous social benefits and entrenched price-wage indexation clauses, which over time became appreciated by target groups as inalienable rights. If wages are sticky, as economists argue, than generous social rights and tough hiring and firing regulations, enshrined in law, are probably even more so. This makes it extremely difficult for policy-makers to simply rationalize on social rights, collective bargaining and labour market regulation in hard times. Given the importance of employment and social security in the lives of many citizens, to be sure, the politics of 'dismantling the welfare state' is not an attractive ticket for political competition (Pierson 1994). By its very nature, the process of adjustment implicates the polity, bringing the distribution of power, institutional structures and styles of decision-making, together with patterns of interest representation, to the centre of an analysis of policy responses. Effective policy responses must be functional, politically viable, socially acceptable and institutionally feasible, preferably all at once. The options for welfare retrenchment depends on the degree to which former political commitments embodied in prevailing social rights are resilient or vulnerable to political attacks. Are entrenched social rights supported by strong political forces, institutional constraints and ideological foundations? Do they offer credible policy solutions to problems at hand? Have cumulative policy failures undermined their status in political discourse? The more resilient received social rights are, the more difficult welfare retrenchment will be. The more vulnerable they are, the easier it is to renege on former social and political commitments. However, it should be emphasized that the mere ease of reform does not imply that effective policy solutions are up for grabs. Boundedly rational policy actors face important cognitive constraints that may prevent them from adopting and implementing effective policy responses. And even economically sound policy solutions which result in declining living standards are likely to provoke political protest and electoral shifts which can disrupt the adjustment process.

So far, little attention has been given to the composite, temporal and failure-induced character of national patterns of policy adjustment. The institutionalist literature, bent on identifying rather uniform national responses, provides little basis for understanding the interactive dynamic of policy adjustment. In particular, those studies which merely focus on single policy areas, such as industrial relations or social protection, are not able to offer an apt understanding of policy adjustment. The prevalence of interaction effects makes it practically impossible to isolate the independent effect of central bank independence, peak-level bargaining, payroll social security and active labour market policy (Regini 1999). Moreover, as policy actors, engaged in processes of sequential policy learning and problem displacement, call important aspects of the established rules of the game of policy-making into question, institutional parameters lose their portent as explanatory variables.

By drawing attention to policy change rather than institutional continuity, I am not advocating a radically indeterminist approach to the study of policy adjustment. I would not like to dismiss many of the important insights gained from the institutionalist literature. The great achievement of corporatist scholars like Crouch, Lehmbruch, Schmitter and Streeck and the contribution of Esping-Andersen to comparative welfare states lies in their having brought a large degree of coherence back into the idiosyncrasies of advanced political economies. However, policy legacies and institutional parameters are not impervious to policy change. To be sure, the options available to policy-makers at any point in time are not independent of resilient institutions and policy choices made in the past. Many of the stark differences in pattern of policy adjustment are indeed directly related to the specifics of the prevalent historical configurations of the four policy areas at the time of the closing of the Golden Age of postwar prosperity, which is the basic reference point for any analysis of policy adjustment.

Policy repertoire, interaction effects and political institutions

In the postwar era the Dutch economic and social policy repertoire developed around a cluster four interrelated features. These are: (1) restrictive macro-economic policy priorities; (2) highly coordinated patterns of collective bargaining at the sectoral level; (3) conditional employment-related arrangements of social security, and, last but not least; (4) a policy legacy of a distinct lack of active labour market policy priorities.

(Macro)economic policy priorities

Macro-economic policy-makers in the Netherlands endorse the policy priorities of stable prices and hard currencies. The Dutch central bank, De Nederlandsche Bank, is independent from the government and constitutionally committed to price stability. Ever since the collapse of the Bretton Woods system, as a standard rule of procedure, Dutch monetary authorities follow German monetary policy choices, in order to ensure that inflation and interest rates do not diverge too far from German levels.

Coordinated sectoral industrial relations

In the industrial relations literature, the Netherlands is usually grouped under the label of 'intermediate bargaining systems' (OECD 1996: 63; cf. OECD 1994). The level of union organization in the Netherlands is fairly moderate by international standards. About 30 per cent of Dutch workers are member of a trade union (Visser 1987, 1992). By contrast, Dutch employers are very well organized (Traxler 1995; van Waarden 1995). Collective bargaining predominantly takes place at the sectoral level (OECD 1994: 175–7). The coverage of collective bargaining is high, while coordination between trade unions and employers' associations at the peak level is considerable. Invariably, collective agreements have a legally binding status. The level of industrial conflict is low and if strikes occur, they are highly organized. State intervention has traditionally been very strong in Dutch industrial relations.

Conditional employment-related social security

Following the canons of comparative welfare studies, the Netherlands are usually grouped, together with Austria, Belgium, Germany, France and Italy, under the label of the regime-type of the continental, 'Bismarckian', conservative or Christian democratic welfare state (cf. Kersbergen 1995; Esping-Andersen 1990, 1996; Huber and Stevens 2001). Continental social policy is based on the principle of industrial insurance against occupational risks, financed by earmarked payroll contributions from employers and workers. Employment-related social security programmes revolve around income replacement and are targeted at the (male) breadwinner in order to safeguard traditional family patterns. As important financiers of the system (through premiums and contributions), the social partners are strongly involved in the management, administration and implementation of social security provisions.

Passive labour market policy priorities

The status of labour market policies is strongly correlated with the overall character of social security. Whereas the Scandinavian welfare states are well known for their strong emphasis on active labour market policy, the continental welfare states seem to have placed 'welfare before work'. Also public sector employment is modest compared to the Nordic countries. In the Netherlands, the public employment ratio even declined from 7.2 to 6.2 per cent between 1977 and 1995.

The productivity whip and the inactivity trap

For the Dutch experience, the particular combination of disinflationary macro-policy, coordinated sectoral bargaining, payroll financing of the system of social security, and the lack of an active labour market stance, has had important consequences for the road of policy adjustment travelled in the Netherlands. In particular, the intimate ties between sectoral industrial relations and payroll social security served in the 1970s and 1980s as an institutionalized support structure, allowing the social partners to externalize the costs of economic adjustment onto the social security system (Hemerijck and Manow 2001). The interaction between a hard currency regime, sectoral industrial relations and payroll social security, has put a virtuous Schumpeterian 'productivity whip' – due to the considerable non-wage costs imposed on workers and employers in the form of social insurance contributions – on organized industry in the Dutch economy. However, in due course this has given rise to a vicious 'inactivity trap' – due to the various pathways into non-employment that the continental welfare state, lacking any form of active labour market policy commitment, so generously provides for. A stylized account of the interplay between sectoral industrial relations and payroll social security contains the following features: under increased competitive pressure, firms in high-wage economies can only survive if they are able to increase labour productivity. This is most commonly achieved by way of raising the productivity levels of workers through high-quality vocational training and education, labour-saving investments and/or by laying off less productive or 'too expensive', mostly elderly, workers. Under the principle of traditional breadwinner family dependence, the latter strategy drives up taxes and payroll social security contributions. The Schumpeterian productivity whip, in turn, puts pressure on wage costs, which provides new ground for reassessing the remaining workforce in terms of their level of productivity, most likely leading to another round of dismissals. Hereby a virtuous cycle of productivity growth could run into a vicious cycle of high wage costs, exit of less productive workers, rising social security contributions, requiring further productivity increases in competitive firms, eliciting another round of reductions in the work force. In the absence of political intervention, this dynamic engenders a pathological spiral of 'welfare without work'. Jobs disappear in sectors where productivity increases stagnate and prices of goods and services cannot be easily raised. The overall labour markets effects of the interplay between sectoral industrial relations and payroll social security are: low employment and high structural unemployment; low female participation rates; declining participation of older workers; underdevelopment of part-time jobs; and a below-average job growth in the service sector, because comparatively high wages and non-wage labour costs block job-creation in the low-productivity segment of the labour market. In turn, low employment, high levels of inactivity, short working times, high (non-wage) labour costs and unfavourable population dependency ratios have important repercussion for the welfare state.

The interaction of the productivity whip and the inactivity trap points to the possibility that national economies may be perfectly able to maintain and restore their international competitiveness through high productivity strategies of 'diversified quality production'. However, with the passing of time, they prove unable to defend welfare state objectives of high levels of employment and social protection. Moreover, the self-regulatory character of social security administration seems to reinforce the already existing insider-bias in the continental welfare state. There is a distinct possibility that export-oriented 'productivity coalitions' will be formed between employers and employees at company and sectoral levels, which further limit the opportunities of low-skilled groups of ever getting a job.

During the 1980s the Dutch welfare state, like many other continental welfare states, was trapped in a pathological vicious cycle of what Esping-Andersen called 'welfare without work' (Esping-Andersen 1996). While in Germany early retirement provided for the main labour market exit route, in the Netherlands generous and lenient sickness and disability insurance served this purpose.

Political institutions: consociationalism and corporatism

Policy adjustment cannot be explained by a dominant system logic of spillover and interaction effects between different policy areas over time. Political institutions provide important constraints and opportunities for political intervention in the policy repertoire, especially when it engenders pathologically perverse effects.

The political system of the Netherlands is traditionally considered as one of the clearest manifestations of consociationalism (Lipset and Rokkan 1967; Lehmbruch 1967; Lijphart 1968, 1984; Daalder 1974). Central to consociational democracy, the ideal-typical alternative to the majoritarian Westminster model, is that various party elites cooperate in a spirit of non-competitive acceptance in both government and parliament. In his seminal theoretical case-study of Dutch politics, *The Politics of Accommodation* (1968), Lijphart delineates consociational democracy in terms of four character-istics: proportional representation, power sharing by grand coalitions, mutual veto rights and subgroup autonomy. In the Netherlands usually three to four parties, representing confessional, social-democratic and liberal subgroups, are represented in oversized coalition governments. In the second half of the 1960s the Dutch segmented or pillarized cleavage structure system began to disintegrate. This process of depillarization challenged the traditional elitist and confessional authority structure of Dutch society, which in turn led to more unstable and less effective government coalitions in the late 1960s and throughout the 1970s.

The Dutch political economy usually ranks high as a corporatist political economy. It is furnished with a firmly established apparatus of bi- and tripartite boards for nation-wide social and economic policy-making. For the purpose of wage policies the most important is the Foundation of Labour (STAR, Stichting van de Arbeid). STAR is a private body, founded in 1945, owned by the central union and employers organizations, and intended as their meeting place. Twice every year, in the spring when next year's budget is prepared, and in the autumn, when a new round of wage negotiations is about to begin, the Foundation meets with a delegation from the Cabinet (van Bottenburg 1995). The Social Economic Council (Sociaal Economische Raad, SER), founded in 1950, is a tripartite organization. Since its recent reorganization in 1995, employers and unions each have eleven seats, the other eleven are occupied by crown members appointed by the government, usually professors of economics, the President of the Central Bank, the Director of the Central Planning Bureau and, recently, some ex-politicians. In the first twenty years of its existence its role in setting the targets for wage policy and advising the government on the expansion and organization of the welfare state was very important. As the foremost economic forecasting agency, the Central Planning Bureau carries much weight as the key supplier of 'commonly observed facts' of the state of the Dutch economy, on the basis of which the social partners define their collaborative strategies of collective action.

Together consociationalism and corporatism delineate the institutional opportunity set of Dutch policy-makers for policy adjustment. As policy-making is critically dependent upon the agreement of different coalition parties and important measures of consensual support from the social partners who participate in policy decision-making processes, cabinets are constrained to respond autonomously to external pressures and demands. The institutional parameters of consociationalism and corporatism forge policy actors on to an adjustment path of negotiated change.

In the next four sections I will trace the progressive reconfiguration of the Dutch welfare state. I will show how the shift to a hard-currency regime, the resurgence of organized wage moderation and path-breaking social policy and labour market policy reform were sequentially related, and what role consociationalism and corporatism played in the Dutch endeavour to reverse the immanent crisis of 'welfare without work'.

The Dutch disease

The collapse of the Bretton Woods system in 1971 and the first oil price shock of 1973 accelerated domestic inflation, flattened effective demand and squeezed corporate profitability in the Netherlands. Given the strong Dutch commitment to trade liberalization, macro-economic policy-makers chose to let the Dutch guilder follow the German mark within the European snake mechanism. Pegging exchange rates on the DM changed the hierarchy of macro-economic targets from a balanced consideration of price stability in relationship to growth and employment to a more narrow consideration of exchange rate stability *'tout court'* (Jones 1995). The first oil price shock of 1973 undermined whatever political consensus remained among state officials and the social partners over Dutch social and economic policy. The leftist Den Uyl administration (1974–7) responded with mandatory wage, price and energy controls. True to the government's political credo of 'redistribution of wealth, knowledge, and power' and its belief that 'the strongest shoulders should carry the heaviest burdens', the crisis measures were couched within policies favouring the low-paid and privileging the trade union movement. Impressed by the rapidly deteriorating economic situation, the trade unions accepted a wage intervention measure in late 1973, by means of the special enabling act (Machtigingswet, 1974), without much discontent. In 1974 the controversial decision was taken to link the minimum wage and, indirectly, the related social security benefits, to contractual wage developments in the private sector. The minimum wage itself was indexed to wage developments in order to ensure that everybody would participate in real income improvement. At this time virtually all private sector contracts contained automatic price escalators, which made them inflation-proof. The result of this system was that, when new contracts were negotiated between unions and employers in the private sector, government costs went up automatically. The same applied to the salaries of an increasing number of civil servants, various semi-public employees of the welfare state and the increasing number of social security recipients. Together, the growing volume of benefits and their linkage to inflation and pay rises in the private sector led to higher costs that were insufficiently met by either social charges or taxes. It might have seemed to the governments of the 1970s that the linking of benefits to wages was a necessary condition for wage restraint and would provide a built-in brake on rising claims of and rivalry between different groups. However, when tripartite bargaining over wage restraint floundered throughout the 1970s, the linking system spurred social security expenditures. Moreover, it made the government the prisoner of the outcome of negotiations and tactical games between unions and employers (Hemerijck 1995).

In 1976, Wim Duisenberg, Finance Minister under Den Uyl, put on the brakes and formulated his so-called 1 per cent norm or rule that total public expenditure should not rise with more than 1 per cent of the net national income per year. This was a considerable revision of the projected 2.4 to 3 per cent at the time (Van Zanden and Griffiths 1989). The Central Bank joined in to pursue a restrictive monetary regime in order to retain parity with the German mark. The restrictive macro-economic policy shift played an ambiguous role in the Dutch economy – making it at the same time more austere and less competitive (Jones 1995). After 1976, the restrictive macro-policy response began to appear in declining profitability, weak private investment, capital flight, rising unemployment and increasing current account deficits, leading to the infamous 'Dutch disease'. The windfall benefit of huge gas resources turned out to be a blessing in disguise. The inflow of wealth from natural gas was used to pay for rapidly rising social transfer payments. As this stimulates consumer demand for goods and services, it invariably puts upward pressure on salaries and wages. Gas exports also led to the appreciation of the guilder and thereby caused a worsening of the terms of trade for import competition and put Dutch export at a disadvantage. Although the Dutch central bank succeeded in mitigating inflation by sticking to the German currency, this only exacerbated the problem of export competitiveness in the Netherlands. The rise in interest rates, starting in the late 1970s, finally resulted in the mid-1980s a massive burst of corporate bankruptcies and a massive surge in unemployment.

The years between 1976 and 1982 are characterized by a protracted policy stalemate in both corporatist industrial relations and consociational party politics. The new centre-right administration (1977–81), led by Andries Van Agt, was a weak coalition, internally divided, in particular within the newly formed Christian Democratic party, and had hardly a majority in Parliament. The Van Agt administration followed the policy legacy of Den Uyl with respect to wage policies and the linking of social benefits. It was unable to bring public finances under control (Toirkens 1988) and was locked in internal fights (Hemerijck 1995). In 1978 the government announced a further reduction in spending and a series of small curtailments in the index for calculating civil servants' salaries and social benefits, to be implemented in small steps until 1981. But because of internal obstruction from spending departments, little support in parliament and no support from the unions, little was accomplished (Toirkens 1988). An internal cabinet clash between Finance Minister Mr Andriessen and the Minister of Social Affairs Mr Albeda escalated in the second half of 1979. When the so-called 'almost accord' of 1979 between the central organizations, so carefully arranged by Albeda, failed, Andriessen clamored for an extended wage freeze for a period of two years. As this demand was considered outlandish, even by his Liberal coalition partners, Andriessen rapidly lost support in parliament and had to resign from the cabinet in early 1980. The commitment to concertation had triumphed over the objective of fiscal restraint, but not for long. When the second oil crisis of 1979 hit the Netherlands much harder than the first and left the country's economy and public finances in a much greater disarray. Albeda had no option but to apply the Wage Act and impose a wage freeze.

The crossroads at Wassenaar

The 1981–3 recession was exceptionally severe, by international standards and in the light of the post war history of the Netherlands (van Zanden and Griffiths 1989). National income declined during eight consecutive quarters and the net investment rate, which had decreased from 7 per cent in the decade before the first oil crisis (1973) to 4.6 per cent in the second half of the 1970s, slumped to a mere 2 per cent. The predicament of rising unemployment, increasing public deficits, declining competitiveness, relative to Germany, and falling growth rates forged a remarkable shift in policy orientation.

Public finances and unemployment were singled out as the most pressing problems of the day. The 'financing deficit', calculated as the difference between government revenue and expenditure, minus the amount paid on long-term loans, which had decreased to just over 4 per cent in 1977, rose dramatically to 10.7 per cent in 1983. Between 1981 and 1983 300,000 jobs were shed, mostly in industry. Unemployment soared at a rate of 10,000 per month to a record 800,000 in 1984 and seemed unstoppable. Meanwhile, the trade unions lost 17 per cent of their members and of the remaining membership nearly one-quarter was out of work, on social benefits or in retirement. Union density plummeted and stood at a mere 25 per cent by 1987, compared to 35 per cent before 1980.

A growing awareness of the causal relationship between high real wages, unemployment and unstable public finances shifted the attention of policymakers away from demand stimulation toward supply-side measures for policy adjustment. Although the 'hard-currency policy' provided for greater macro-economic stability, it also meant that changes in the international political economy had to be answered for by voluntary wage moderation and/or productivity increases. After the government brought inflation under control, wages and the welfare state became the prime targets for policy adjustment.

The general elections of 1981 resulted in a patched-up coalition between the Christian and Social Democrats, but the new administration immediately fell back into policy immobilism. The government lasted only nine months, from September 1981 to May 1982. The fall of the cabinet, again led by van Agt (CDA) and with PvdA leader, Den Uyl, as Minister of Social Affairs, raised the level of drama and ended the political basis for a Social Democratic management of the crisis.

Politically, 1982 is a turning point. New elections brought to power a true 'no nonsense' austerity coalition, led by Ruud Lubbers, and relegated the Social Democrats to the opposition for nearly the whole duration of the 1980s. The new coalition of Christian Democrats (CDA) and Liberals (VVD) commits itself to a three-track strategy of, first, a drastic reorganization of public finances in order to reduce the 'financing deficit', lower interests and inflation; second, economic recovery through improved business profitability, lower labour costs, industrial restructuring and less regulation; and, third, work-sharing without extra costs to business in order to alleviate the unemployment problem. Unveiling its plans on 22 November 1982, the new cabinet declares that 'it is there to govern'. Eight years of centre-right rule provoked a break with corporatist immobilism as the Lubbers government – no longer committed to full employment as a primary policy objective – disengaged itself from critical dependence on corporatist bargaining. A major goal was to guarantee that collective bargaining outcomes would no longer have a direct effect on government expenditures. The government achieved this by severing price indexation and breaking the statutory couplings between wage increases in the market and those in the public sector, and between wages and social security benefits. This put the trade unions in a tight corner. With unemployment soaring at a postwar record, the trade union movement was in no position to wage industrial conflict. After a decade of failed tripartite encounters, based on Keynesian presuppositions, the new coalition's entry into office was crowned by a bipartite social accord in December 1982.

With the Accord of Wassenaar, the unions recognized that for a higher level of investment, essential for the creation of more jobs and the fight against unemployment, a higher level of profitability was required. This path-breaking accord marked the resurgence of corporatist adjustment on the basis of a commonly understood 'supply side' diagnosis of the crisis (Visser and Hemerijck 1997). The path-breaking 'Wassenaar Accord', named after the hometown of VNO chairman Chris van Veen, at whose house the agreement was prepared, marked the resurgence of corporatist adjustment in the political economy. The accord encouraged proliferation of cooperation between the social partners based on: (1) in terms of policy content, the exchange of wage moderation for a reduction in working hours to fight unemployment and help restore the profitability of industry; and (2) in terms of institutional structure, a process of 'organized decentral-ization' in the Dutch system of industrial relations. Weakened but in a political environment of unquestioned institutional security and semi-public status, they returned to the consensual policy style which had characterized Dutch corporatism in the early postwar years. It was helpful that the (by now dysfunctional) institutional framework of a concertation economy was still there and did not have to be invented. For employers, on the other hand, an agreement with the unions is a means to forestall government intervention, because they feared political interference in the form of a statutory and uniform reduction of the working week.

The response to the Wassenaar agreement was swift. Although negoti-ations over shorter hours proved cumbersome, in less than a year two-thirds of all collective agreements were renewed, mostly for two years, during which the payment of price compensation was suspended and a 5 per cent reduction of the average annual working hours was to take place. By 1985, cost-of-living clauses had virtually disappeared; less than 10 per cent of all collective agreements included a fully paid escalator clause. Average real wages fell by 9 per cent in real terms. The share of labour in the net enterprise income, still 89 per cent in 1982, fell to 83.5 per cent in 1985 (Visser and Hemerijck 1997: 105).

Assured of restraint, the government had its hands free to get control over public sector finance. In the spring of 1983, preparing the Budget for 1984, the government decided to play its card as the country's largest employer and step up restraint. The unveiling of its plan to reduce public servants' salaries, minimum wages and benefits by 3.5 per cent in January 1984 caused an uproar among the public sector unions. Later in the year they organized their largest-ever postwar strike, only to find out that they had become isolated. 1982 is also the start of the unlinking of private and public sector wages and the development of autonomous labour relations in the public sector. In 1985 parliament approved new legislation ending the 'trend-following' mechanism in the subsidized sector. In principle, employers and unions were free to negotiate wages, as in the private sector, but within limits set by the Cabinet. In the next ten years labour relations in the government sector were normalized: while civil servants lost most of their special privileges with respect to pensions and dismissal protection, civil servants' unions gained the right to strike and to collective bargaining. The conclusion is that the private sector can no longer be taken hostage and that the government has gained more authority if it wants to cast a 'shadow of hierarchy' over private-sector wage bargaining.

The Wassenaar Accord inaugurated an uninterrupted period of wage restraint up until the late 1990s. All agreements since 1982 have reconfirmed the need for wage restraint. Nominal wage increases have fallen to zero and since the 1980s the anticipated increase in inflation has been the basis for sectoral negotiations. Only in 1992 and 1993 did the average negotiated wage increase exceed the inflation rate by half a percentage point. Estimations are that over 40 per cent of job creation in the last decade must be attributed to prolonged wage moderation. The return to wage moderation contributed to job-intensive job growth in three ways. First by helping to restore profitability of business it created a necessary condition for investment and job growth. Initially, employers tend to recapture profits in order to improve corporate balance sheets rather than to step up investment strategies. The pattern of Dutch recovery shows an early growth in exports, with a more gradual increase in employment, investment and consumption. Second, wage moderation contributed to the sale of manufactured goods and tradable services in foreign markets, raising net exports and growth in the exposed sectors of the economy. Third, it helped to keep more people on the payroll. As a corollary, labour productivity per hour, although very high by European and American standards, increased less than in other countries. Wage restraint has had a favourable effect on employment in sectors that produce mainly for the domestic market, making low-wage, labour-intensive production more profitable.

While wage restraint in itself helps to preserve and create jobs, an additional pay-off was required to make corporatist adjustment tangible for trade union rank and file. Over the last decade the average working week has been brought down from 40 to 37.5 hours. In those sectoral agreements in which a reduction of the working week was negotiated wage increases have been smallest. The process of across-the-board labour time reduction has now come to a halt as concertation shifted gradually towards part-time work as the main tool for redistributing work. In 1990s there a shift in issue-linkage at the macro-level, whereby wage restraint was increasingly compensated by reductions in taxes and social security premiums, made possible by improved public finances and a broader tax base through the creation of more jobs in domestic services. This allowed real net incomes to rise, even in the absence of gross wage increases, and thus helped to maintain spending power and boosted domestic demand.

Although the appreciation of the guilder (pegged to the German mark since 1983) has made exports more expensive, the overall decline in wage costs has been capable of compensating for competitive losses due to changes in the exchange rate. The strict exchange rate policy seem to have had some additional disciplinary influence on wage developments. On the other hand, moderate wage developments have enabled the Dutch central bank to stick credibly to its policy target.

Institutionally, the corporatist agreements have evolved from comprehensive package deals to so-called central framework agreements that generally voice non-binding recommendations to be filled out in more detail at the sectoral level. The accords therefore embrace the freedom of sectoral collective bargaining and the primacy of self-regulation in industrial relations. These new principles have been politically recognized. Since the Wassenaar Accord there has been no political intervention in wage setting. The role of the peak organizations of capital and labour is now basically confined to redirecting sectoral contracting parties towards tacit, economy-wide wage restraint. Central consultation in the Foundation of Labour – the central bipartite corporatist institution (Stichting van de Arbeid) – allows the centrally bargained deals to be passed on to sectoral negotiators. The higher the level of consensus at the central level, the smoother bargaining takes place at the meso-level (Heertum-Lemmen and Wilthagen 1996). The inclusion of sectoral bargaining in the central agreements is an example of 'organized decentralization', which stresses sectoral bargaining with an effective input from the central level (Traxler 1995). Although the state plays a considerably less dominant role in collective bargaining, there is still extensive political power. Based on pre-war laws, the Minister of Social Affairs and Employment has the authority to declare collective bargaining agreements legally binding for all workers and employers in a certain branch of industry, whether they are unionized or not. This provision remains a treasured policy instrument and is crucial for securing economy-wide wage restraint. Employing a so-called 'shadow of hierarchy' (Scharpf 1993), governments have been effective in encouraging labour and capital to reach agreements that concur with their central policy goals.

So far, the regained practice of corporatist adjustment in the Netherlands has proven to be robust, but not entirely without conflict. In 1993, consensus was under pressure, as economic conditions rapidly deteriorated and unemployment increased. And it was not until the government threatened to intervene directly in the process of wage-setting that a new accord was reached. Again the success of this accord was contingent on a large measure of decentralized commitment to the central recommendation and the politically strategic use of the shadow of hierarchy.

Reversing the spiral of 'welfare without work'

Organized capital and labour, under the shadow of hierarchy, managed to find a responsible and mutually rewarding solution to problems of economic adjustment during the 1980s. However, prolonged wage moderation and industrial reconstruction were perversely compensated for through the welfare state, via a generous labour exit route for less productive, mainly elderly workers.

The Dutch postwar compromise in social security revolved around an implicit political exchange between the state and the social partners, whereby the state was granted primary control over wage policy for the reconstruction of the Dutch economy in exchange for a bipartite execution and administration of the system of social security. This has had major consequences for Dutch social security reform. In terms of policy design, the Dutch social security system has both universalistic schemes (e.g. the flat-rate public pension) and social insurances (e.g. for unemployment, sickness and disability). The universalistic schemes are solidaristic, financed via general taxation, and geared towards supporting non-working citizens with a minimum income. Social insurance provides earnings-related benefits to workers and employees, financed through compulsory payroll taxes, and eligibility depends on contribution years. They are administered by Industrial Boards (Bedrijfsverenigingen), which consist of the representatives of the unions and the employers' organizations. The Boards collect contributions and decide on benefits. Because of their quasi-monopoly in social security the bipartite Industrial Boards have a high degree of institutional power, independent of the state, over social policy in general. The third tier, public assistance, provides the public safety-net for those whose benefits under the other tiers have expired. Public assistance is tax-funded and administered by local authorities. Until the 1960s the expansion of social protection in the Netherlands lagged behind most advanced European countries. In the 1970s and 1980s the take-up of social security in the Netherlands bypassed the level of the majority of the European welfare states, except Sweden (Flora 1986).

The political crisis of the Dutch welfare state revolved around the disability scheme that increasingly became an instrument for early retirement and industrial restructuring. Four features established the idiosyncrasy of this scheme (Aarts and De Jong 1996). First, the scheme did not make a distinction between different causes of disability. The risk of disability was defined as a social rather than solely an occupational risk. Second, the so-called 'labour market consideration' provision stipulated that in assessing the degree of disability the diminished labour market opportunities of partially disabled persons should be taken into account. As a consequence, disability as the basis for entitlement was redefined as a worker's particular incapacity to find a job similar to his former job. If the probability of not finding an 'appropriate' or 'fitting' job was evaluated to be high then the degree of disability would also be determined as high. Third, disability and sickness benefits were closely related, to the extent that a person would first receive sickness benefits during the first full year and then would qualify for the disability scheme. The funding of the schemes, however, is dissimilar. Sickness pay is primarily financed by employers, while disability benefits were entirely financed by the contributions of employees. Workers' contributions were set at uniform nation-wide rates and were unrelated to the particular risk factors in different industrial branches. Most firms supplemented sickness benefits up to 100 per cent of former earnings and many even supplemented disability benefits to a comparable level for a year or longer.

The broad definition of disability, the incorporation of labour market opportunities into the calculation of the degree of disability, and the high replacement rates are not per se unique features of the system. The most distinctive property of the Dutch programme concerned the institutional organization of responsibilities and control. Sickness pay and disability benefits were administered by the Industrial Boards. These were largely responsible for examining the health of employees for whom their employers pay sickness contributions directly to the appropriate Industrial Board. However, there arose a remarkable deficiency in the transparency of medical assessments as well as economic incentives for employers to use the sickness and disability schemes as a convenient procedure for 'firing' redundant, particularly older workers and to avoid social friction at the same time. Paying a sickness benefit for one year and then letting the disability scheme take over was calculated as in many ways a much cheaper option than maintaining a redundant worker on the regular payroll. Medical doctors could interpret the labour market clause of the scheme generously, employees and the unions appreciated that the disability scheme guaranteed generous benefits until retirement and the government had found an additional early exit instrument. In fact, the combination of the low threshold for entitlement, the blurring of social and occupational risks, and the generous level and duration of benefits explains why the disability scheme became a major method for reducing the supply of labour.

The unanticipated yet inevitable result was, however, that a steep rise in the number of recipients would exhaust the scheme's financial resources. A scheme that was originally meant to support no more than 200,000 people was paying over 900,000 benefits in 1990. By 1986 among the age group 55–64 those who received a disability benefit already outnumbered those with a job. Estimates indicate that between 30 and 50 per cent of those receiving disability benefits should be considered unemployed. To the generous disability scheme early retirement facilities were added and these also rapidly became popular labour market exit routes.

The loss of jobs for manual (elderly) workers in industry, which occurred rapidly and massively, encouraged the use of sickness and disability legislation and early retirement in order to shed older, low-skilled males from the labour market before the normal age of retirement. The explicit objective of disability legislation to encourage revalidation and labour market reintegration was almost entirely discarded. Instead, the scheme became a harsh welfare trap: once officially recognized as partially disabled a worker acquired a permanent labour market handicap. The labour market consideration was interpreted by the relatively independent Industrial Boards in such a way that, if productivity was below the wage level, a worker would be considered fully incapable to work. It was assumed that discrimination in the labour market would prevent such a person from finding another job.

Political attempts were made to reduce the demand on the schemes. Stricter measures were introduced to curtail misuse and to cut back social spending. In 1984 the statutory minimum wage was reduced. Replacement rates were cut and nominal benefits were 'frozen' between 1984 and 1990. In 1987 the second centre-right Lubbers government enacted a structural reorganization of the system of social security. Replacement rates were cut down from 80 to 70 per cent, entitlements were restricted, indexation was cancelled, and the duration of disability and unemployment benefits was shortened. Moreover, the labour market consideration of the disability scheme was repealed. However, these and similar measures had little effect on spending because the number of social security beneficiaries continued to rise. One of the reasons for the failure of the reform is that the weak prominence of the state in the social security system prevented the mobilization of sufficient power to override the incentives to misuse the disability scheme for labour market reasons. As a result, policy adjustment stalled.

By 1989 the number of people receiving disability benefits was rapidly approaching one million and costs were exploding. Continuing the labour market exit strategy would necessarily end in disaster. This added to an already growing sense of emergency among most social and political actors, notably among social democrats who had entered a coalition with the Christian democrats. In a dramatic *cri de cœur*, Prime Minister Lubbers proclaimed that the Netherlands had become a 'sick country' and that 'tough medication' was required. In this context of predicament, the government proposed introducing a radical reform in order to discourage the misuse of sickness and disability benefits and to close off other labour market exit routes. In spite of the emergency and the widespread conviction that radical changes had to be made, the proposal was highly controversial, politically risky and met with stiff resistance. In 1991 nearly a million people demonstrated in The Hague against the reform in what was probably the largest protest demonstration ever. The Labour Party was internally divided, its party leader almost fell over this issue, and its members of parliament ambiguously defended the proposed changes. The costs were high for the Social Democrats as the party experienced a haemorrhage of its membership and of electoral support. The Social Democrats were largely held responsible for what the electorate saw as an attack on established rights. The party did not recover in time and at the 1994 elections it was punished with a historic defeat.

Notwithstanding popular resistance and obstruction by the trade unions, the reforms were enacted. The Act on the Reduction of the Number of Disablement Benefit Claimants (TAV, 1993) introduced a so-called 'bonus-malus' system for employers. A bonus will be received by an employer who hires partially disabled workers, while a financial penalty (malus) was to be paid into to the sickness scheme if an employee became disabled. However, political pressure from the employers has already forced the withdrawal of the measure. The reform of the disability programme included an age-related reduction of replacement rates, which left older workers largely unaffected (TBA, 1993). The duration of the benefit was substantially shortened. This especially affects employees with an income substantially above the statutory minimum wage. Benefits for persons aged under 50 at the time of the enactment of the new legislation were reduced and these now decline gradually over time to 70 per cent of the statutory minimum wage plus an additional age-related allowance. Finally, medical re-examinations of beneficiaries were undertaken on the basis of more stringent rules and the legal requirement for partially disabled employees to accept alternative employment was tightened. A new definition of disability serves to coerce beneficiaries to accept all 'normal' jobs. In 1993, the re-examination concerned 43,300 beneficiaries younger than 35 years of age. Little over 50 per cent maintained their benefit, 18 per cent had their benefit reduced, and nearly 30 per cent lost their benefit, while 2 per cent saw their benefit actually increased.

Under the new sickness leave scheme of 1994 (TZ, 1994) the first two weeks (for enterprises with fewer than sixteen employees) or six weeks (for all other enterprises) of sickness benefits were directly charged to the employer. By way of making employers bear part of the costs the measure attempted to stimulate employers and employees to reduce absenteeism. Employers were compensated by an average reduction of sickness benefit contributions of 4 per cent of gross wages. In addition, in 1994 the Amendment to the Working Conditions Act (ARBO, 1994) introduced the obligation of firms to buy the services of private health organizations for all their employees and to develop a firm-specific health policy, especially designed for the reintegration of sick workers.

The reforms encouraged the trade unions to circumvent the effects by demanding supplementary benefits to be included in the collective agreements. As a result, the costs of sickness and disability have now become part and parcel of the bargaining process itself. But this tends to reinforce the incentives to reduce absenteeism at the level of companies and industrial sectors where collective bargaining takes place as the relation between costs and benefits is more directly visible.

The reform endeavours of the coalition between Social and Christian Democrats were greatly enhanced by the results of a series of inquiries into the causes of the crisis of social security. These studies essentially revealed what everybody already knew, namely that social security was being misused by individuals, employers and firms, the Industrial Boards, the unions and local governments for purposes of industrial restructuring. In 1992, the National Audit Office (Algemene Rekenkamer) diagnosed major deficiencies in the design, administration and implementation of social security. Taking heed from the National Audit Office, the Social Democrats, despite resistance by the Christian Democrats, successfully promoted a committee of parliamentary inquiry into the causes of the disability debacle. Such a committee is the parliament's strongest instrument of control as it has extended legal authority in hearing witnesses. Its major recommendation was that the implementation of social security ought to be monitored by a government agency that could operate fully independently of the 'social partners' and their bipartite Industrial Boards. The Kok government (social democrats, progressive democrats and conservative liberals, i.e. the first government since 1918 without any of the religious parties) has reorganized social security in this vein and installed an independent body of control. The parliamentary committee has also advised that the Industrial Boards be replaced by regional agencies that closely work together with Public Employment Services in order to link passive and active labour market policies (see below).

The restructuring of the Dutch system of social security by the 'purple' coalition revolved around two dimensions of reform. These are the introduction of financial incentives through the partial privatization of social risks and the managed liberalization of social policy administration, and a fundamental redesign in the institutional structure of the administration of social security. The government has marketed the system of social security in an attempt to improve incentives and efficiency and to curb problems of moral hazard. The right to an unemployment benefit is now more conditional upon the willingness to accept a job offer or to participate in training programmes. The privatization of the sickness scheme became effective in 1996 with the Act on the Enlargement of Wage Payment during Sickness (WULBZ, 1996). Employers are now legally obliged to continue to pay their employees for a year, have a direct stake in reducing absenteeism and seek private insurance against this risk. The institutional change does not necessarily lead to a deterioration of protection. Replacement rates are 70 per cent of earnings and benefits are commonly upgraded to 100 per cent in collective agreements. However, the new institutional form of the sickness scheme led to quite a drop in absenteeism, while the anticipated negative effect of a greater reluctance on the side of employers in hiring persons with higher health risks is not clear yet. The possibility for employers to 'opt out' of the disability system and seek private insurance was introduced in 1998 and allowed for differentiation in contributions between sectors and firms according to occupational risks. Under the Act of Differentiation of Contributions and Market Compensation in Disability

Insurance (PEMBA, 1997), employers have two options. They can take full responsibility for the first five years of occupational disability, which oblige them to pay publicly guaranteed benefit levels and to ensure occupational risks with private insurers. Alternatively, they remain in the public insurance system, in which case they are confronted with a rise of premium payments dependent on the number of cases of (full or partial) occupational disability. This last reform which allows for a differentiation of employers' contributions was meant to encourage firms to develop responsive policies for health and safety at work, and to constrain the deployment of disability insurance for laying off less productive workers. As expected, these measures made employers more cautious in hiring workers with higher than average sickness and disability risks.

The most path-breaking reforms in the Dutch system of social security concern the changed status of the social partners in the administration of social insurance policy. In 1994 the Social Insurance Council (SVR) was dismantled. It was replaced by an independent control body, the Supervisory Board for Social Insurance (CTSV). A separate institution was created for the implementation of social security legislation, the Temporary Institute for Coordination (TICA), which remained tripartite. In 1997 the Industrial Insurance Boards were dismantled and the temporary TICA board was reorganized into the permanent National Institute for Social Insurance (LISV) and made responsible for contracting out the administration of social security to privatized delivery agencies. The trade unions and employers associations were granted an advisory status in the LISV. With the establishment of independent supervision and the introduction of market incentives in the administration of social security, the government believes that it has laid down the institutional preconditions for more effective social policy implementation in the spheres of sickness and disability insurance.

From fighting unemployment to increasing participation

Hard-won social security reform, initially opposed by the unions, and revived confidence in corporatist adjustment, embraced by unions and employers and supported by the corporatist infrastructure of the Dutch political economy, slowly but surely concurred with a shift in the problem definition of the alleged crisis of the Dutch welfare state. In the late 1980s, policy-makers came to realize that the low level of labour market participation was the Achilles' heel of the extensive but passive Dutch system of social protection. In 1990, the Netherlands' Scientific Council for Government Policy, an academic advisory board with a mandate to carry out future studies in those areas it sees fit, proposed to break with the past and advocated a policy of maximizing the rate of labour market participation as the single most important policy goal of any sustainable welfare state (WRR, 1990). Gradually, this lesson, though not the specific policy recommendations voiced by the WRR, which included a lowering of the statutory minimum wage, were embraced by the government.

When the Social Democrats regained office in the third Lubbers administration, policy adjustment took on a different tack. Economic recovery allowed for a partial restoration of the 'coupling system' which linked social security benefits to wages. Since 1982, Parliament had allowed the suspension of the application of the 1980s law on coupling (WAM). As a result, the gap between average earnings of employed workers and people dependent on welfare benefits increased by 12 per cent between 1983 and 1989. The restoration of the linkage system was an important precondition for the PvdA, headed by Wim Kok, to return to government. On the other hand, Prime Minister Lubbers needed the support of the Social Democrats for welfare retrenchment. In the meantime, the policy recommendations of the WRR inspired top civil servants at the Ministry of Social Affairs and Employment to design a new contingent system of coupling, which was enacted in 1992. The new linkage Law (Wet Koppeling met Afwijkingsmogelijkheid (WKA)) made full indexation between increases in the statutory minimum wage and social security benefits to average wage developments conditional on two counts. First, the government is no longer obliged to link benefits and wages if there is 'excessive' wage growth, that is, rises which exceed the anticipated increases in inflation and productivity. Second, if the number of social security beneficiaries increases to the extent that a significant increase of the rate of taxes and social security contributions is needed, the government has another reason not to increase benefits in correspondence with the rise in wages. In other words, the coupling of benefits is only guaranteed if the number of people claiming social security benefits does not increase relative to the working population, that is: if wage demands do not cause the volume of welfare recipients in whatever form to rise. For practical purposes, the two grounds for suspension have been combined in one formula, the so-called I/A or inactive/active ratio, measuring the number of benefit recipients as a ratio of the employed population. If the I/A ratio exceeded a predetermined reference level, the government can suspend the coupling mechanism. However, it must seek advice from the SER, whose recommendations the government is not obliged to endorse, as the SER is only an advisory tripartite council. At the introduction of the new linkage system, the reference level of the maximum I/A ratio was set at 82.8 per 100 employed workers. This was the level when the Lubbers/Kok administration took office in 1990. In both 1990 and 1991 minimum wages and social benefits were fully indexed. In 1993, 1994 and 1995 the government again froze the legal minimum wage and social benefits, because the I/A ratio rose from 81.4 in 1992 to 85.8 in 1994. In 1996 linkage was restored, reflecting a decrease in the I/A ratio under 82.6. For 1997 and 1998 the new linkage logic was also applied.

Changes in labour market policy, developed and adopted in the 1990s, cohere with the new policy priority of raising the level of labour force participation relative to the number of inactive citizens depending for their livelihood on the welfare state. Since the early 1990s the public employment service has been reformed twice. With the adopted of the 1991 Employment Service Act, the former dormant state placement monopoly was reorganized into a tripartite and regionally decentralized agency, independent from the government. While the de-monopolization of placement and the tenuous combination of functional and regional decentraliztion represented a major break in Dutch labour market policy, the high expectations in terms of performance were not met. Output increased, but the fragile institutional arrangement of the 1991 employment service was unable to develop a prominent position in Dutch social and economic policy. The shift from an 'active' to an 'activating' labour market policy gained absolute priority. Under the 1996 Employment Service Act the scope of the employment service was once again limited to a labour market provision service for weak groups in the labour market. However, there is a new policy window for issue-linkage. Unemployment benefit recipients are obliged to register with employment offices and actively seek to re-enter the labour market. Both the revision of the National Assistance Act (1996) and the new Social Security Act (2000) are designed to enhance co-operation between municipalities, industrial insurance associations and the regional employment offices, but so far the reforms stop short of creating a one-counter service.

Since the early 1990s, the Lubbers/Kok administration and the purple coalition have, in large part independent of the PES, taken steps to redress the balance between active and passive policies: these include 'labour pools', the 'Youth Guarantee Plan' and the so-called 'Melkert-jobs', named after the Minister of Social Affairs and Employment in the first Kok administration. The overall volume of these additional job programmes, geared toward the reintegration of the unskilled and low-paid workers, has been doubled from 1.5 to 3 per cent over the tenure of the purple coalition. Most of these additional employment measures are carried out by municipalities. Most recently, the government has introduced several kinds of employment subsidy schemes, which have significantly reduced employers' wage costs. Through a substantial reductions in taxes and social security contributions, instigating a decline in the tax wedge for employers who hire long-term unemployed, employment subsidies can add up to as much as 25 per cent of the annual wage (Opstal *et al.* 1998).

The success of negotiated social policy reform

In this chapter I have argued that composite interaction effects shape and drive the trajectory of policy adjustment. In the process, pressing policy problems, largely informed by policy failures, are on the whole considered one at a time. These theoretical considerations have helped me to describe and understand the sequential-diachronic pattern of policy adjustment in the Netherlands over the past twenty-five years. In a rather schematic form the interplay of macro-economic management, the system of industrial relations, social security and labour market policy provisions unfolded as follows.

1   In the wake of the collapse of the Bretton Woods system, wage costs soared, including social security contributions, as did inflation. Monetary authorities stepped in to contain the growth of domestic prices. In the early 1980s government had to confront spiralling deficit spending. The fiscal crisis of the state made budgetary restraint a political imperative for the incoming 'no-nonsense' centre-right Lubbers administration which came to office in 1982. Since 1983 the Dutch guilder has remained solidly pegged to the German mark, even after the crisis of the EMS in 1992 and 1993.

2   The basic policy choice for a tight money policy and fiscal constraint shifted a large part of the burden of adjustment from macro-policy to the system of industrial relations and the welfare state. The political conditions of the resurgence of corporatist wage restraints were provoked by a considerable weakening of the Dutch labour movement and the development of a more indirect but still persistent patterns of political intervention in the sphere of collective bargaining. A weakened trade union movement gradually accepted that increased profitability was a prerequisite for job growth. The stronger organizations of capital were willing to re-enter the existing corporatist institutions and accepted labour time reduction under the threat of political intervention by the government.

    The institutional rules of the game, within which the new policy consensus over external adjustment developed, shifted gradually from central tripartite encounters, with strong state leverage, toward bipartite organized decentralization under the shadow of hierarchy. The ultimate availability of hierarchical intervention and state ratification of agreements reached among the social partners helps to curb distributive conflict and limits the options of 'rent-seeking' and 'free riding' among the bargaining parties.

3   The resurgence of corporatist adjustment in the early 1980s laid a solid foundation for far-reaching social policy reform in the early 1990s. Eventually, as the crisis of inactivity spilled over into a general crisis of governability in the social security system, this prompted path-breaking policy changes, particularly in the sickness and disability schemes. A freezing of benefits in 1983 and an overhaul of unemployment insurance in 1987 could not halt the rise in inactivity. When the number of people receiving disability benefits was rapidly approaching one million, the centre-left Lubbers administration was able to introduce more radical measures to curtail the improper use of benefits and to close off some of the labour market exit routes of disability insurance

and sickness leave. In recent years the government, joined by most of the opposition, has partly succeeded in excluding the social partners from the administration and supervision of social security programmes, breaking the century-old corporatist legacy bipartite sovereignty in this domain. Most recently, the left-liberal government, headed by the social democrat Wim Kok, introduced far-reaching social policy reforms, setting the stage for managed liberalization of social security, while strengthening the role of the state in the supervision of the welfare state.

4   Successive changes in macro-policy, industrial relations and social security legislation and administration coincided in the early 1990s with a general shift in the problem definition of the crisis of the Dutch welfare state. The overarching policy objective was no longer to keep overt unemployment down by channelling people into other programmes. Instead, the Scandinavian preoccupation with maximizing the rate of labour force participation has become number one priority. Instruments like the I/A ratio have translated this priority into a new norm for wage bargaining and a policy instrument for the government in its management of minimum wage and benefit adjustments. With the tripartization of the Public Employment service, the Netherlands finally broke with the long tradition of passive, or absent, labour market policies. The Kok administrations have subsequently introduced a number of policy innovations geared towards the reintegration of unskilled and low-paid workers.

It is often argued that the continental welfare state is particularly dependent on high levels of employment, but is structurally unable to encourage domestic service sector job growth, because of the high social wage component that goes together with job creation. As this is true, the reverse may also hold. Wage moderation leads to job growth in the sheltered sector and curtails social wage costs, which eventually encourages more people to enter the labour market and thus pay into the social security funds. The Dutch experience represents a significant departure from the scenario of 'welfare without work' so typical of the continental welfare state.

The politics of adjustment has remained structured around regular consultations between consociational government coalitions and the 'social partners' participating in solidly entrenched institutions for corporatist concertation. The shift to a hard currency and the resurgence of corporatist wage restraint were part and parcel of a supply-side strategy of external adjustment to changing conditions in world markets since the early 1970s. The resurgence of wage restraint has to be credited to the social partners, although the threat of political intervention by strong coalition government played an important role. The political responsibility for welfare and labour market policy reform, geared towards raising the overall level of labour force participation, was shared all major political parties, from right to left. But it should also be noted that welfare reform, considered necessary for reasons of fiscal austerity, would perhaps not have been supported politically without the parallel increase in employment opportunities since the mid-1980s that resulted from the Accord of Wassenaar. Notwithstanding the overall positive appraisal of the sequential dynamic of negotiated social policy reform, it should be remembered that the Dutch trajectory of negotiated welfare reform was paved with a number joint-decision traps in all the four policy domains we have studied.

Note

1 Much of the work of this chapter was done while I was a visiting fellow at the Max-Planck-Institute for the study of societies in Cologne in 1997 and 1998. I am thankful to all the participants in the project 'The Adjustment of National Employment and Social Policy to Economic Internationalisation', and especially to its co-directors, Fritz Scharpf and Vivien Schmidt, and Philip Manow and Bernhard Ebbinghaus, for the many inspiring and helpful discussions we have had over these issues over the past year. For the empirical part of the contribution I continue to be grateful to Jelle Visser. Our collaborative endeavour in rediscovering the fascinating contingencies of Dutch political economy (Visser and Hemerijk 1997), upon which this contribution heavily relies, has immensely broadened my insights in understanding policy change.

References

Aarts, L. and Ph. De Jong (1996) *Curing the Dutch Disease*, Aldershot: Avebury.

Cohen, M.D. and L.S. Sproull (eds) (1996) *Organizational Learning*, Thousand Oaks, CA: Sage.

Cyert, R.M. and J.G. March (1963) *A Behavioral Theory of the Firm*, Englewood Cliffs, NJ: Prentice Hall.

Daalder, H. (1974) 'The Consociational Democracy Theme', in *World Politics*, 26: 604–21.

DNB (Dutch Central Bank) (1997) *Annual Report 1996*, Amsterdam: Dutch Central Bank.

Esping-Andersen, G. (1990) *The Three Worlds of Welfare Capitalism*, Cambridge: Polity Press.

Esping-Andersen, G. (1996) 'After the Golden Age? Welfare State Dilemmas in a Global Economy', in idem (ed.) *Welfare States in Transition. National Adaptations in Global Economies*, London: Sage.

Flora, P. (ed.) (1986) *Growth to Limits: The Western European Welfare States Since World War II*, Berlin: De Gruyter.

Hall, P.A. (1993) 'Policy Paradigms, Social Learning and the State: The Case of Economic Policy Making in Britain', in *Comparative Politics*, 25: 275–96.

Hall, P.A. (1999) 'The Political Economy of Europe in an Era of Interdependence', in H. Kitschelt, P. Lange, G. Marks and J.D. Stephens (eds) *Continuity and Change in Contemporary Capitalism*, Cambridge: Cambridge University Press.

Heertum-Lemmen, A.H. and A.J.C.M. Wilthagen (1996) *De doorwerking van de aanbevelingen van de Stichting van de Arbeid*, The Hague: SDU.

Hemerijck, A.C. (1995) 'Corporatist Immobility in the Netherlands', in C. Crouch and F. Traxler (eds) *Organized Industrial Relations in Europe: What Future?*, Aldershot: Avebury.

Hemerijck, A.C. and P. Manow (2001) 'The Experience of Negotiated Reform of the Dutch and German Welfare State', in B. Ebbinghaus and P. Manow (eds) *Comparing Welfare Capitalism. Social Policy and Political Economy in Europe, Japan and the USA*, London: Routledge, pp. 217–38.

Huber, E. and J.D. Stephens (2001) *Development and Crisis of the Welfare State: Parties and Policies in Global Markets*, Chicago: University of Chicago Press.

Jones, E. (1995) 'Changing the Political Formula: Economic Adjustment and Political Transformation in Belgium and the Netherlands', Dissertation Paul H. Nitze School of Advanced International Studies of the Johns Hopkins University, Baltimore.

Kersbergen, K. van (1995) *Social Capitalism. A Study of Christian Democracy and the Wefare State*, London and New York: Routledge.

Lehmbruch, G. (1967) *Proporzdemokratie: Politisches System und Politische Kultur in der Schweiz und in Oesterreich*, Tübingen: Mohr.

Lijphart, A. (1968) *The Politics of Accomodation: Pluralism and Democracy in The Netherlands*, Berkeley, CA: University of California Press.

Lijphart, A. (1984) *Democracies: Patterns of Majoritarian and Consensus Government in Twenty-One Countries*, New Haven: Yale University Press.

Lipset, S.M. and S. Rokkan (1967) *Party Systems and Voter Alignments*, New York: Free Press.

March, J. (1994) *How Decisions Happen? A Primer on Decision-Making*, New York: Free Press.

OECD (1994) *The OECD Jobs Study, Part II*, Paris: OECD.

OECD (1996) *OECD Economic Surveys 1995–1996: Netherlands*, Paris: OECD.

OECD (Various Years) *OECD Employment Outlook*, Paris: OECD.

Opstal, R. van, H. Roodenburg and R. Welters (1998) *Low Skilled Jobs Through Job Creation and Wage Subsidies*, CPB Report, The Hague: Central Planning Bureau.

Pierson, P. (1994) *Dismantling the Welfare State? Reagan, Thatcher, and the Politics of Retrenchment*, Cambridge: Cambridge University Press.

Regini, M. (1999) 'Between Deregulation and Social Pacts: The Responses of European Economies to Globalization', Working Paper 1999/113 Centro de Estudios Avazados de Ciencias Sociales, Madrid: Instituto Juan March.

Scharpf, F.W. (1993) 'Coordination in Hierarchies and Networks', in F.W. Scharpf (ed.) *Games in Hierarchies and Networks. Analytical and Empirical Approaches to the Study of Governance Institutions*, Frankfurt am Main: Campus.

Toirkens, J. (1988) *Schijn en Werkelijkheid van het Bezuinigingsbeleid 1975–1986*, Deventer: Kluwer.

Traxler, F. (1995) 'Farewell to Labour Market Associations? Organized versus Disorganized Decentralization as a Map for Industrial Relations', in C. Crouch and F. Traxler (eds) *Organized Industrial Relations in Europe: What Future?*, Aldershot: Avebury.

van Bottenburg, M. (1995) *Aan den Arbeid! In de Wandelgangen van de Stichting van de Arbeid, 1945–1965*, Amsterdam: Bert Bakker.

van den Toren, J.P. (1996) *Achter gesloten deuren? Cao-overleg in de jaren negentig*, Amsterdam: Welboom.

van Waarden, Frans (1995) 'The Organizational Power of Employers' Associations: Cohesion, Comprehensiveness and Organizational Development', in C. Crouch and F. Traxler (eds) *Organized Industrial Relations in Europe: What Future?*, Aldershot: Avebury.

van Zanden, J.L. and R. Griffiths (1989) *Economische Geshiedenis van Nederland in de 20e Eeuw*, Utrecht: Spectrum.

Visser, J. (1987) 'In Search of Inclusive Unionism: A Comparative Analysis', Dissertation, Amsterdam.

Visser, J. (1992) 'The Netherlands. The End of an Era and the End of a System', in R. Hyman and A. Ferner (eds) *Industrial Relations in the New Europe*, Oxford: Blackwell, pp. 323–56.

Visser, J. and A. Hemerijck (1997) *A Dutch Miracle: Job Growth, Welfare Reform and Corporatism in the Netherlands*, Amsterdam: Amsterdam University Press.

3 The societal and historical embeddedness of Dutch corporatism

Frans van Waarden

The resurgence of Dutch corporatist concertation in the 1990s, described in detail in the foregoing chapter by Hemerijck, cannot merely be explained by historical accident or by 'policy learning'. Why were the Dutch able to 'learn', why did they turn to this organizational strategy for welfare state reform, while other countries were less able or willing to do so?

A major part of the explanation is that corporatism has had broad and deep roots in Dutch history, and has in the course of time found expression in a great variety of institutions as well as in the political culture of the country. Corporatism may have been 'away' for a while, its quick return in popularity was no doubt facilitated by the strong roots that were still present.

The breadth of Dutch corporatism: its many organizational faces

Not only central wage bargaining

The international literature on corporatism has focused mostly only on macro-level institutions for bi- or tripartite bargaining over wages, working hours and other working conditions between peak associations of capital and labour. This holds for most of the economic literature (Calmfors and Driffill 1988; Soskice 1990a; Soskice 1990b; Layard *et al.* 1991; Boyer 1997; Teulings and Hartog 1999) on corporatism as well as for quite a bit of the political science literature (Schmidt 1982; Czada 1983; Cameron 1984; Katzenstein 1985). It also holds for the recent book on the Dutch model by Visser and Hemerijck (Visser and Hemerijck 1997). They explain most of the recent strong performance of the Dutch economy by wage moderation, reform of social security programmes, and the flexibility of the labour market due to the popularity of part-time and temporary work, all supposedly results of consensual macro-level bargaining between employers, unions and the state.

However, this is only one element of a much wider phenomenon. There has been and is more to Dutch corporatism than just macro-level bi- or tripartite bargaining. And important in this context is that these *broader* roots in society and the economy facilitated the re-emergence of macro-corporatist concertation in the 1990s.

Characteristic of this was the fact that much of the economy was regulated and organized by 'corpora', at all levels of aggregation and in many policy fields, not just industrial relations. Private associations engaged in various ways in self-regulation, which was tolerated, accepted, recognized or even authorized by the state; and/or they participated in the formulation and implementation of public policy, and to this end were equipped with statutory powers. The Dutch economy was permeated by institutions in which capital cooperated with capital; and in which labour cooperated with capital. In short, it was a coordinated or concerted economy in which private associations shared in public sovereignty.

Market institutions and regulation

Long before the advent of institutional economics, Dutch economic policy-makers recognized that markets need institutions in order to function. Economic transactions are more likely to take place if a number of conditions are present, such as a minimal reduction of uncertainty over property rights, trustworthiness of the transaction partner, discouragement of opportunistic behavior, enforceability of contracts, stability of the generalized means of exchange, quality guarantees for goods, etc. In addition, transaction partners, with less information or less economic power, such as consumers and/or workers need protection, in order for the economic system to acquire a wider legitimacy. These institutions can be provided by various principles of coordination and allocation: the market, the state, clans or communities, firm hierarchies and associations (Williamson 1975; Ouchi 1980; Streeck and Schmitter 1985). Although all principles of economic governance are found in the Netherlands, 'association' has been a dominant one, compared to other countries.

Market institutions have been provided both by the state and associations, and in the case where the state took the initiative, implementation has often been delegated to associations. The fundamental economic institutions, property, contract and corporate law, a stable currency, etc. have of course long been in place, and remained largely a state responsibility. The Christian Democratic and later also the Social Democratic governments added a whole set of social and economic public law. Much of the first social regulation dates from the post-First World War revolution scare. In the 1930s a whole host of economic regulations were initiated: agricultural crisis measures (later the example for EU agricultural policy, whose architect Mansholt came from Dutch agricultural circles), product quality regulations (originally more to support the reputation of export products than to protect domestic consumers), establishment licensing for small shopkeepers and artisans, regulation of shop closing hours, statutory support for collective wage agreements and cartels, price control of basic commodities, regulation of specific markets such as inward shipping, banking and insurance, taxis, the professions, and the introduction of arbitration schemes. After the Second World War more regulations of labour relations were added: a ban on lock-outs and on collective dismissals, a statutory minimum wage, statutory wage and price controls. When the latter were gradually loosened, they were replaced by institutionalized consultation, negotiation and concertation over prices and particular wages.

Trade associations and trade unions played a large role in the formulation and implementation of these policies. In addition, many special institutions were created to organize and channel class cooperation and market regulation.

Interest associations

The *organizational edifice* of corporatism consisted first of all out of about 2,000 voluntary employers' associations and trade associations on the entrepreneurs side (van Waarden 1992, 1995); and 338 unions on average in between 1951 and 1960 (Visser and Waddington 1996). Both categories were integrated in a more or less hierarchic system: associations cooperated first in peak associations at the sectoral level (e.g. associations for housing construction, road construction, well drilling, pipe laying, civil engineering, etc. in a peak association for the construction industry); and these in turn were integrated in national sector-unspecific peak associations. Up until the mid-1970s the system of peak associations was differentiated by pillar. On the trade union side there were three major peak associations: a Protestant (CNV), a Catholic (NKV) and a socialist one (NVV). In addition there were three smaller peak associations of white collar workers and/or civil servants. These did gain however in size and importance from the 1970s on. On the entrepreneurs' side there were many more. The larger firms were organized in four peak associations: protestant (VPCW), Catholic (AKWV) and two general-liberal ones: one that organized 'social' interests, i.e. the peak employers' association (VNW), and one that represented the economic, commercial and technical interests, i.e. the peak trade association (CSWV). Then there were also three peak associations – Catholic, Protestant and liberal – for small and medium-sized firms (SMEs) and three for farmers. Altogether hence six peak associations on the trade union side and ten peak associations for entrepreneurs. Of these however, two were clearly dominant: the NVV on the union side, and the VNW on the employers' side. In the last two decades they merged to two peak trade unions (FNV and CNV) and two peak employers' associations (VNO-NCW and MKB, the latter for small and medium business).

Institutions of cross-class cooperation

Second, there were the institutions for cross-class cooperation in which trade unions and employers' associations cooperated. Predecessors had already been founded in the early decades of the twentieth century. Thus the revolution scare shortly at the end of the First World War led to the creation of the High Council of Labour in 1919. The most important ones in the postwar period were the Foundation of Labour (Stichting van de Arbeid (STAR)) and the Social Economic Council (Sociaal Economische Raad (SER)).

The STAR was an organization under private law, founded at the end of the Second World War by the leaders of the former peak unions and employers' associations, who were together taken hostage by the German occupants in a camp in St Michielsgestel. It remained during the whole postwar period the place where the peak trade unions and employers' associations could and did meet amongst themselves, that is, in the absence of the government.

The STAR was joined in 1950 by the Social Economic Council (SER). It was created by the government – and got a position under public law – as the official advisory council for the government on social economic policy, and had a statutory right to be consulted on all such policy issues, before the government could take any measures. In addition, it became the peak organization and supervisor of the system of statutory trade associations (see below, p. 76). The SER was originally made up of forty-five members: fifteen representatives of the different peak trade unions (originally the white collar peak unions were, however, not represented; they had to stage a long fight for official recognition); fifteen members appointed by the various peak associations of business and agriculture; and fifteen members appointed by the state. The latter, the so-called 'crown members', were appointed for their expertise, and they were not supposed to represent the interests of the state.

Thus the SER embodied the two different principles of corporatism and technocracy. The underlying idea was to bring together the social partners with economic experts, so that the first could be confronted with the economic consequences/external costs of policy choices and wage demands, in the rightful expectation that this would moderate demands and policies. This worked well indeed. The political influence of economic expertise in policy-making in the Netherlands has been remarkable. Notwithstanding the fact that corporatism is basically a structure of representation of more or less particularistic interests, more or less interest-neutral ideas and knowledge have been important in the system. The judgement of economic experts was taken seriously and had to be countered with economic arguments by the social partners. In time this led them also to create their own economic expertise departments.

The STAR and SER were and are the major formal institutions for centralized bargaining between the social partners. In the first fifteen years after the war their influence was still rather limited, because wages, working hour, and working conditions were mostly fixed by the state in the person of the state-appointed College of State Intermediators. The increasing shortage on the labour market and the upward pressure on wages which this brought about (increasing distance between regulated wages and actual paid wages, wildcat strikes; the year 1964 saw a wage explosion) forced first a delegation to the level of the STAR (1958–63), and subsequently a 'decentralization' to the institutions at the sectoral level. Over time the influence of the state on wage formation decreased, although the Dutch social partners never had anything like the constitutionally guaranteed *Tarifautonomie* that their German counterparts had. And the government kept repeatedly interfering with wage bargaining through statutory measures.

The STAR and SER were only the peak organizations of a whole edifice of institutions of class cooperation. 'Below' them, at the sectoral level, there were similar institutions of class cooperation. Sectoral wage bargaining took place in the *vakraden* (trade councils), *bedrijfsverenigingen* (lit. trade associations) implemented workmen's compensation plans, and *bedrijfscommissies* (lit. trade commissions) supervised the implementation of the law on works councils. The works councils themselves embodied class cooperation at the firm level.

The STAR and SER were only concerned with general socio-economic policy. There were however more peak-level consultation, advisory and bargaining councils for other, more specific policy areas, in which unions and employers' associations participated. Many of these had, just like the SER, a statutory status and were official advisory councils to the government on specific policy fields. They existed for social security (Sociale Verzekeringsraad), for health and health insurance (Ziekenfondsraad), industrial policy, health and safety at work, product quality regulation, technical standardization, vocational training, environmental policy, health policy, public housing, transport and infrastructure, development aid, and even military procurement. All these institutions were ever so many channels in which the social partner leadership met, got to know each other well, and which also allowed for generalized exchange (Marin 1990) and complicated trade-offs.

Institutions of competitive cooperation: trade associations and cartels

In addition to institutions for class cooperation, there were also organizations that channelled and decreased the intensity of the competitive struggle. This was done first of all through the many trade associations. Many of these are quite well-developed, command large resources in terms of capital, staff and expertise, have privileged access to state agencies, form coalitions and joint ventures with other associations of customers, suppliers or workers, exert some control over members' behaviour, and furnish a multitude of activities. In addition to the usual activities such as providing services to members (information, advice) or negotiating agreements with associations of suppliers, they provide collective goods such as training for workers and entrepreneurs, organize and finance generic research and development, make collective propaganda for Dutch products at home or abroad (especially where it concerns bulk products without brand names, such as dairy products, horticulture, fruits and vegetables, civil engineering works, cement, sand, asphalt, bituminous roofing). They organized one annual exhibition and forbade their members to partake in any other in an effort to prevent competition from forcing up advertising costs. Associations of retailers have their own brand products and engage in collective purchasing and advertising. Other associations handle and implement decisions on investments in machinery on behalf of their members. In the cooperative sector associations used to control the books of the industry on behalf of the members of the cooperatives, the farmers. They have binding rules as to the behaviour of member firms during conflicts with unions, prohibit poaching of workers and have occasionally organized supply boycotts.

Prototypical for the Dutch 'concerted economy', however, were the many *cartels*, trade associations with the specific aim to mitigate competition. The country has been called a 'cartel paradise' (de Jong 1990) and the OECD still spoke in 1993 of 'the unusual Dutch case': 'Many sectors of the economy are enmeshed in a web of restrictive agreements, regulations and barriers to entry' (OECD 1993: 57). In 1992 the secret cartel registry still contained 245 market-sharing agreements, 267 price and tendering agreements, 202 distribution agreements, and 45 collective exclusive dealing agreements, the latter mostly of professional organizations which limit market entry. These were all agreements which would be illegal in most other OECD countries (OECD 1993: 60). Hence it is no accident that this European 'cartel paradise' has been a main target of interventions by the European Commission and Court of Justice. In the period 1970–90, of all Article 85 decisions of the ECJ rejecting nation-wide cartels, Dutch firms were involved in 40 per cent of them (de Jong 1990).

Neo-liberalism has changed this to some extent. Among the more important measures is the change in competition policy in 1998. A new law replaced the 'abuse' by the 'prohibition' principle, shifting the burden of proof from the state to business: business has to prove from now on that a specific cartel is beneficial to society, rather than government having to prove that it is harmful. Several cartel-types, such as horizontal price and quota cartels, have become outright illegal. For some other forms exceptions can still be allowed, e.g. when it can be proven that important non-economic interests are at stake, as in the case of the vertical price cartel for books. A new, semi-autonomous cartel office has been created to implement the new law.

State support: extension and statutory trade associations

For a long time the state provided support for this form of economic governance through associations: by tolerating them, providing access, extending private agreements and turning them into public law, and by even providing certain associations with statutory powers.

State support for associational governance went further than mere passive tolerance. It could also adopt private regulations, turn them into public law, and impose them upon the sector, including on the non-organized business firms, who were not bound by the agreements of associations, a procedure which is usually called 'contract extension'. In 1935 a law was enacted that allowed the state to do so with cartels, and in 1937 this possibility was also introduced for collective wage agreements. The procedure has only rarely been used for cartels, but many sector-wide collective wage agreements are usually extended to the whole sector.

The state went still further by not only giving regulations and agreements of associations public status, but by doing so for some associations themselves. The Dutch economy knows in addition to the many voluntary associations also a number of compulsory statutory trade associations. About a quarter of Dutch industry (notably agro-industry and artisan-like sectors) is organized in sectoral statutory trade associations (STAs), which were created at the same time as the SER, in 1950. The SER is the peak body of the STAs, and supervises them. Their creation was inspired by the comprehensive system of compulsory trade associations which the Nazi occupants introduced to organize the economy for the war effort. They differ however in a number of important respects. They are not imposed on industry. A sector who wants so can apply to have an STA. Some sectors have done so, others not. Furthermore, while the wartime associations were authoritarian, top-down, according to the 'Führer' principle, the STAs are in principle democratic.

These are comparable in legal status to provinces and municipalities. Whereas the latter embody territorial decentralization of the state, the STAs embody what is called in the Dutch constitution 'functional decentralization': decentralization of state power to bodies with specific functions. Their creation may have been facilitated by the presence of a precedent: the centuries-old hydraulic boards are also such statutory bodies of functional decentralization. Just as the inhabitants of a municipality are 'members' by virtue of their living in its territory, so 'inhabitants' of an industrial sector are members of an STA. They have similar duties and rights. Both kinds of inhabitants have to pay taxes to their municipality and/or STA. And in both cases there is 'no taxation without representation'. Citizens are represented in the city council through direct elections. In the case of STAs firms and their workers are indirectly represented through their voluntary trade associations and trade unions, which appoint the board members. Direct representation – as in the case of the Austrian *Kammern* which have a similar status – was considered back in 1950, but met with strong resistance from the established interest associations. The boards can decide to tax the firms in their sector. Just as with municipalities the income is used for collective goods, but now they are specific to the sector, such as vocational training, health services, collective research and development, quality control, generic advertising, buying-out of over-capacity, subsidy for continuity of work during winter months (in some construction sectors), etc. Furthermore, they implement government policy, such as EU agricultural policy, and distribute agricultural subsidies.

In addition to the STAs there are still the Chambers of Commerce and Industry, originally created by Napoleon, but changed in status and tasks since. They too have a public law status, membership is compulsory, and some 'taxes' are levied. They cover all firms, but have a rather limited task: register incorporation and represent regional business interests.

Thus Dutch corporatism has found expression in a large variety of formal organizations and at all levels of aggregation, macro, meso and micro. Typical is the formal character, also and in particular at the top. This distinguishes it from, for instance, the Austrian version. The Austrians may have also very elaborate formal and bureaucratic organizations such as the Wirtschafts-, Landwirtschafts-, Handwerk- and Arbeiterkammern; however, at the very top it is rather informal. The Paritätische Kommission is nothing like the Social Economic Council in terms of formal structure.

Typical of all these forms of market ordering is that they are rather moderate. In no sense do they eliminate markets and competition, they merely regulate markets and channel and lessen competition. In that sense, the Dutch institutions of the 'concerted economy' are an eclectic combination of the allocation and coordination principles 'market', 'state' and 'association'.

Administrative regulatory style

The same holds for state regulations. It may seem that the Dutch economy was encapsulated in a myriad of regulations; they were however flexibly applied. The Dutch public administration developed a regulatory style in line with corporatism and consensualism. The typical Dutch administrative style of policy implementation is flexible, pragmatic and tolerant, as in Britain, but unlike in Germany, France, or, for that matter, the US, which have a much stricter, more legalistic and more adversarial style of implementation (Vogel 1986; van Waarden 1999). Dutch inspectors are more willing to take account of specific circumstances and problems of the subjects of regulation, and they may enter into negotiations, offering to overlook certain transgressions in exchange for certain concessions. Feasibility and practicality are important criteria, and many regulatory agencies and inspectors have considerable discretionary authority to use them. Sanctions are rarely imposed and cases are not frequently brought to court.

Many rules allow citizens and businesses to apply for exemptions. A study of the National Accounts Office of 80,000 applications for exemptions on a diversity of rules showed that in only 2 per cent of the cases were such exemptions refused. Other rules have loopholes, which make them more acceptable to society. Since 1945 the country has had a legal ban on collective dismissals. Employers who want to lay off workers have to apply for permission from the director of the regional labour bureau. This rule is often quoted as a labour market 'rigidity', hindering flexibility and innovation. But does it really? For one, the procedure for the labour bureau is much less formal and time-consuming than a similar procedure in court would be (employees could challenge the decision in court, as they do elsewhere, e.g. in the US). Furthermore, permissions are easily granted. Blankenburg and Bruinsma (1994) showed that 95 per cent of 90,000 annual applications are granted. The legal requirement allows, however, for a phase of deliberation, in which employers might think over their decision once more. It is often feared that a strict ban on dismissals would make employers wary of hiring new people. The Dutch economy has, however, created a loophole. Employers may put people temporary to work who are formally employed by commercial temporary work agencies (*uitzendbureaus*). Dutch law allowed for this, while other European countries, such as Germany, did not. The practice of *gedogen* (see below) is of course another form of flexible, tolerant and pragmatic policy style.

Underlying general characteristics

These organizational forms of Dutch corporatism express four more fundamental characteristics typical of Dutch political, administrative and economic institutions: the importance of associations, subsidiarity, collegiate government and consensualism.

Associability

The Netherlands is still a real 'civil society' in the meaning of De Tocqueville: a society organized in a plurality of associations. The Dutch themselves call this *maatschappelijk middenveld* which means something like 'intermediary societal field', intermediary, that is, between the individual and the state. The percentage of the population which is organized in one or more associations is, after the Swedes and Danes, the highest in Europe (Table 3.1), and that holds also for the specific subcategory of political and social organizations. In the past, membership of unions, political parties and church organizations was very high. This has decreased with the depillarization of society, but in return the membership of public interest associations (such as Amnesty, Greenpeace) is the highest in Europe, as can also be seen in Table 3.1. The density ratio of trade unions may lie below the European average (in part a reflection of the fact that only 18 per cent of the Dutch still earn a living in industry); however, the public trust in trade unions is the highest in Europe.

Compared to, for instance, the British, the Dutch have a strong inclination to formalize such 'associational relations'. It has been said, mockingly, that wherever three Dutchmen meet, they found an association, and one becomes chairman, the second secretary and the third treasurer.

Table 3.1 Dutch associability compared to other European countries

	NL	B	D	A	UK	F	I	S	DK
Pct. of population member of one or more associations (> 15 yrs; 1998)	79	48	53	55	53	40	36	85	84
Pct. of population member of one or more social or political associations (1990)	74	54	57	–	61	42	38	–	86
Pct. of population member of a new public interest association (Amnesty, Greenpeace, WWF, Red Cross)	16.0	3.7	7.1	–	1.2	1.3	0.9	–	3.2
Density ratio of unions (1998)	30	54	28	42	38	9	39	97	89
Pct. population with trust in trade unions (>15 yrs; 1999)	62	39	37	–	41	36	30	–	51

Source: SCP 2000: 132-44; based on data from Eurobarometer, ILO, UEFA.

Thus we find still many trade unions, employers' associations, trade associations, artisan guilds, health care and social welfare associations, housing corporations, broadcasting associations, school associations, literary societies, playground-, aquarium-, soccer-, judo-, painting-, bicycle-, hiking associations, environmental and other public interest associations, and not to forget of course political parties. Three changes have taken place however since the heyday of pillarization and consociationalism:

1   The formerly separate Catholic, Protestant, socialist, and/or liberal associations have disappeared, usually through a merger.
2   This has enhanced more general trends of increase of scale and size of associations, and with that of professionalization of staff and leadership. A typical trade union leader is no longer a former factory worker, but a trained sociologist or welfare worker, who has been hired on to the staff of the union and has subsequently made a career of a leadership position in the organization.
3   This in turn has enhanced a more distant relation between members and their association. The latter plays a less dominant role in the life of citizens than before.

Subsidiarity

Many of these associations have still an autonomous sphere of 'jurisdiction', accepted if not guaranteed by the state. They can structure and regulate social life in their task and/or member domain. Often they are also involved in the preparation and implementation of public policy. They help formulate, administer and even enforce state regulations. This holds for many policy fields: the economy, social security, health, education, welfare, public housing, broadcasting, the environment, infrastructure and spatial planning, etc. Of course there have been changes here too. The most important is the increase in importance of many of these policy areas, an increase in the amounts of money and workers involved, and linked to that an increase in the involvement of the state in funding and regulating measures and provisions in these policy fields. This has in some cases reduced the autonomy of private associations somewhat, e.g. in social security. Periodically voiced political concerns over 'the primacy of politics' have once in a while led to a reassertion of the role of the state in some of these policy areas. However, often these changes were merely temporarily. They have not really reduced the importance of private associations in self-regulation and in the formulation and implementation of public policy.

Collegiate government

The Netherlands is still very much ruled by collegiate government, as distinct from monocratic government. Politics and society are permeated with councils, chambers, committees, boards, estates, colleges, commissioners. The formal state institutions are all collective bodies. So are advisors to the government, the executives of many state and semi-state agencies, the executive boards of private foundations, associations and corporations, of cultural institutions, and not to forget of the church. It can be no coincidence that the protestant church, the former official 'state church', is led – decentrally – by church councils, rather than by an individual, as is the case with the Catholic church. These councils do more than provide 'counsel', i.e. investigate, discuss, consider, advise: they do make the decisions themselves. Decision-making in the Netherlands is typically group decision-making.

Of course nowadays councils and boards are found in many societies and polities. What is, however, typical for the Netherlands is that these councils rarely have individual leaders. They do have chairmen or chairwomen, to be sure. But these are usually merely *primus inter pares*, first among equals. Typical is the role of the Dutch Prime Minister. He has much less authority in the Cabinet than, for instance, the American President, the British Prime Minister, or the German Bundeskanzler. The latter, for instance, has a formal Richtlinienkompetenz and can give instructions to his Cabinet ministers. Not so the Dutch Prime Minister. What holds for the Cabinet holds also for most other councils or boards. They are rarely dominated by strong leaders. The country is not known for charismatic political leaders such as Churchill or Bismarck. Its economy has no 'captains of industry', like Carnegie, Rockefeller, Krupp or Iacocca. If at all, dominant leaders in the economy have been entrepreneurial families, such as Van Heek, Ledeboer, Fentener van Vlissingen, Van Beuningen, Wilton, Van der Valk. That is, again groups, inter-generational groups. Companies led by these families were not driven by individualism, by the incentive to amass profit for the individual contemporary owner, but by what has been called 'familism' (van Heek 1945; van Schelven 1984), the temporary stewardship of family property to be passed on the new generations. Dutchmen seem to be always in groups. Even the country itself is in the plural: The Kingdom of the Netherlands. And thus it is known abroad: the lowlands, les Pays Bas, los Paises Bajos, Die Niederlande. And it is ruled in the plural, in councils. In a way, the country is a real 'soviet union', perhaps more so than the country that ever went officially by that name.

Consensualism

Collective decision-making has consequences for the style of decision-making. It requires usually consultation, discussion, negotiation, concertation, compromise and, if possible, consensus. This has been characteristic of the old consociationalism. With depillarization consensualism had to make way for more adversarial politics. However, this did not last. Adversarial politics declined again. The change must be situated between 1977 (the end of the Den Uyl Cabinet) and 1982 (the last great political strike, the start of the 'no-nonsense' business-like politics of the Lubbers Cabinet, and the by now almost mythical Treaty of Wassenaar between the social partners). Now politics is again practised largely according to the rules of consensual politics.

Conflict is avoided, in all walks of life. The American sociologist at the University of Amsterdam and keen observer of Dutch social life Derek Phillips wrote:

> Rather than risk a conflict with others in the group, someone whose ideas do not agree with the point of view of the group will tone down his own opinion and make it known in a mild and quiet manner. And in extreme cases may turn away from the group. Open conflict, opinions presented with much conviction, a high level of verbal aggression and emotional scenes are much less common in Dutch society than in the US.
>
> (Phillips 1985: 29)

The complement of compromise and consensus, proportionality, is still very much in place, whether in allocating positions for mayor or provincial governor, in allocating funds for broadcasting associations, or seats on advisory boards. There is a strong sense of distributional fairness. Municipal governments are again more and more proportionally composed, after majority governments had been popular for a while.

Secrecy may be less common than in the past, and is certainly less formal. However, much politicking does *de facto* take place in less visible arenas and depoliticization is frequently practised to allow for more flexibility in negotiations and consultations. It may be that there is more control now on policy-makers. However, much of it comes from consultants and policy evaluation researchers and is often more pragmatic and unpolitical ('what can we learn from past experiences, how do our policies work?') than adversarial and political. Most of the political institutions that 'condemn' politicians to consensualism have remained firmly in place. The old practices are introduced in new policy fields, such as environmental policy.

Pragmatic tolerance, closely linked to consensualism, finds expression in the persistent tradition of tolerant rule application, if that is considered to increase the effectiveness of reaching the policy goals. The Dutch use the term *gedogen*, a term difficult to translate in English. It is a kind of 'policy of the lesser evil'. A less serious transgression is tolerated in order to combat a more serious one more effectively. It is not an informal policy, not one only of *de facto* tolerating, as is also done in many other countries. No, in the Netherlands this is official policy, with institutional backing. The Dutch legal system knows the 'expediency principle', laid down in the Code of Criminal Procedure. It makes a distinction between that which the law formally requires, and what the directives of the public prosecutor in fact prescribe. In other words, the public prosecutor has some discretion to prosecute a case or not. He is empowered to refrain from bringing criminal proceedings if there are weighty public interests to be considered. This is quite different from, for example, the 'legalist' principle in German law, which obliges prosecutors to prosecute all cases known to them, and allows only the judge freedom to decide whether or not to penalize specific behaviour.

The famous example of *gedogen* is soft drugs. They are tolerated and regulated and can be sold in registered 'coffee shops' – which curiously enough do not sell coffee – in order to fight hard drug abuse more effectively. Prostitutes work in recognized brothels, checked by health inspectors, in order to fight AIDS and other sexually transmitted diseases more effectively. But it is also found in many other fields: the long-time tolerance of cartels, for example, or in environmental politics. A study of a few thousand violations of environmental law in 1986 found that only half of these had been checked by the municipal authorities, and of this half only 36 per cent were penalized.

In order to have an interlocutor and partner in regulating and fighting abuses, the authorities have recognized or even actively encouraged the formation of associations by the relevant 'industries'. Thus there are official business associations of brothels and of 'coffee shops'. Such associations try to control and prevent excesses, which could threaten their hard-won recognition or could precipitate state intervention. Thus the Coffeeshop Association forbids and tries to control the sale of hard drugs in the coffee shops or the sale of soft drugs to minors. And the Brothel Association has instituted a trademark for 'recognized' brothels which practise only safe sex, complete with 'recognized' signs to be posted on the door.

Typical of the persistent importance of consensualism and conflict avoidance are also some major characteristics of the Dutch legal system. This has always been, like most other continental ones, an inquisitorial one, rather than an adversarial (Damaska 1986). The search for 'truth' in the courthouse takes place still more through investigation and evaluation than through contestation between opponents, as in the Anglo-Saxon system. The judge does more than preside over the proceedings. He investigates and decides, whereas the latter is done elsewhere by a jury. What distinguishes the Dutch system from other continental European countries is the very low litigation rate and the average short duration of court cases. Many conflicts are handled out of court. That holds both for civil law and criminal law cases. People try to settle conflicts informally or through arbitration – there are many specialized arbitration bodies. When cases do come in court, they are handled flexibly. The Dutch judge has a relatively large discretion. In substantive civil law cases, the judge can circumvent a legalistic outcome by means of a general escape clause based on the principles of 'fairness and reasonableness'.

There is not yet anything even approaching what Kagan has called 'adversarial legalism' and which is so prevalent in the US. The contrast with the US is especially great, but also with neighbouring Germany. One example out of many: Kagan (1990: 10) compared the handling of damaged cargo from trans-Atlantic shipments in the ports of Rotterdam and New York and found that 'lawyers' bills are far higher if a legal dispute is processed in New York rather than in Rotterdam, even though the relevant substantive law in the two countries is essentially identical'. The differences in density of lawyers and in the costs of tort litigation as percentage of GNP is indicative. In the US the lawyer density was in the early 1990s ten times as high as in the Netherlands; in Germany it was five times as high (data about 1988; Lipset 1996: 50). Holland had ten judges and 1,550 court cases per 100,000 inhabitants; Germany 29 judges and 3,120 cases (data 1992: Blankenburg and Bruinsma 1994). Things are changing here as well. Thus the density of lawyers is increasing in the Netherlands, from 35 per 100,000 inhabitants in 1987 to 70 in 1999. But this is still well below that in most other capitalist-industrialized nations.

Historical roots

These underlying principles of associability, subsidiarity, collegiate government and consensualism seem to have all been with the Dutch since the inception of their state. As with so many other countries, early political values found expression in the first state institutions, including legal traditions, and these in turn have fostered and maintained a related political culture. The mutual influence and support between culture and institutions may explain their persistence over long periods of time.

Associability

The Dutch Republic, which existed between 1581 and 1795, was a well-organized civil society. The Republic was in fact a loose confederation of city republics, located on the trading city belt that has extended since the late Middle Ages, from the middle of England to the middle of Italy, and which still forms the economic heartland of Europe (also called the 'blue banana', after the blue glow visible at night from a satellite). It was one of the two axes which Stein Rokkan (1981) distinguished to categorize different European societies (the other axis was the distance to Rome, the centre of catholicism). These trading cities developed as the first in Europe a bourgeois society organized in many formal horizontal organizations: militias, corporations and limited liability companies (*compagnieschappen* and *rederijen*), guilds, charitable institutions, etc.

This republican tradition seemed to have come to an end with the Napoleonic wars and occupation. The edicts of 1798 and 1811, following similar measures in France, banned those guilds and other *corps intermédiaires* which had still survived the economic decline of the eighteenth century (Wiskerke 1938). A 'liberal intermezzo' (Maier 1981) followed, in between the French period and the onset of industrialization – which in the Netherlands was also a 'near absolutist intermezzo' – in which relatively few associations existed, albeit that they did not completely disappear. Immediately following the coalition ban, the Napoleonic state formed its own 'bridgeheads' in the economy, the regional Chambers of Commerce, which have persisted until this day. These were originally state agencies. Affiliation was compulsory and the executive board members were appointed by the state. But in 1848 this changed, and henceforth the board members were elected by the affiliated entrepreneurs. The Chambers kept however their public law status. Voluntary associations did not completely disappear in the 'liberal interlude'. Several still existing trade associations trace their origin to the beginning of the nineteenth century. A prominent example is the 'Association for the Promotion of the Interests of Bookstores'.

The old republican tradition of a well-organized civil society was reinvigorated by the bourgeois revolution and the liberal constitution of 1848, and the industrialization which took off after about 1870. These facilitated and/or sparked off several emancipation movements of disadvantaged social groups: Catholics, socialists and a new Calvinist revival movement among the lower middle class, the *kleine luyden*. Their emancipation required the development and consolidation of separate identities and the conquest of societal and political power. These in turn required: (a) the external distinction vis-à-vis the dominant strata of society, the liberals and Dutch reformed church; and (b) the internal organization and regulation of the group, including the provision of group-specific services, such as health care. Formal organization in associations was a major instrument of internal consolidation and regulation as well as the external conquest of power. In a relatively short time this led to a proliferation of associations, differentiated by class, religion, region, function and economic sector. Often, formal associations were created immediately. In other cases they developed stepwise out of more informal and *ad hoc* proto-organizations. Such was, for instance, the case with employers' and trade associations (van Waarden 1992: 474). Depillarization may have reduced their numbers, but has not broken the tradition of a well-organized civil society.

Subsidiarity

The societal organizations created in the Dutch Republic organized and regulated their own specific sector of society, and often performed tasks that sooner or later came to be considered state tasks in many countries. Whatever there was in terms of an embryonic state in the Republic did not only recognize the autonomy of these associations, but also delegated or rather left tasks to them. Citizens' militias provided internal order and security, guilds took care of economic ordering, charitable institutions provided some measure of social security. Even those most central state tasks, external security, defence and diplomacy, were in part 'privatized' under the Republic: the Dutch East India Company, one of the earliest limited liability companies, had the authority to engage in war and to conclude peace treaties on behalf of the Republic.

These are all indications that there was no real separation between state and society/economy and to some extent this is still characteristic of the Netherlands. The country may have inherited the distinction between public and private law from the French and the Romans; it is somewhat at a loss as to how to handle it. Therefore there are too many organizations and regulations at the interface of both. This was so at the times of the Republic; it has been reinforced by pillarization; and it is still the case. Private associations have under certain conditions been entrusted with state power and have sometimes even acquired statutory powers, including the basic rights of taxation, enactment of binding regulations, and enforcement and sanctioning. Conversely, public state bodies are formed out of organizations of civil societies. It is symbolic that the latter function as important recruitment areas for top civil servants, mayors, ministers, MPs, and even higher: where else on earth are prime ministers recruited from among trade union leaders (the former PM, Kok) or employers' associations (his predecessor, Lubbers)?

In so far as there is a primacy of one over the other in the relation between state and society/economy, the latter dominates over the former, certainly in the days of the Republic. This was quite unusual in those days.

Whereas in French mercantilism the economy was a means to increase state power, the political elite of the Republic formed out of merchant families considered state power an instrument to increase their economic power, something which has become a bit more common since.

The primacy of organizations of civil society reflected a distrust of a strong central state, akin to that found in the United States. It can be no coincidence that both countries had a similar history of state formation. Both emerged out of a revolt against a centralizing state power. The Dutch against the Spanish Habsburg King Philip II starting in 1579, the Americans against the British Tudor kings about two centuries later. This prompted the American revolutionaries to include a lot of checks and balances in their constitution, using the experience of the Dutch, and the teachings of the French political philosophers of the Enlightenment, like Montesquieu. The Dutch had to do without this experience and theory; but they also introduced federalism as well as a primacy of organizations of civil society to keep the central state power in check.

Collegiate government

For the same reason they preferred collegiate government over monocratic government. State sovereignty in the Dutch Republic was placed with councils, the provincial Estates, and not with 'the people' – as became later custom – or a monarch – as was the custom at that time – or even whatever there was of a 'central' state, the Estates-General. This may have been facilitated by the absence of a strong landed aristocracy. It was nevertheless unique for its time. Almost all organizations of the state and of civil society were governed by collectives: the municipal governments, the hydraulic boards (*heemraadschappen*, see next section), the church, the guilds, the militias, the philanthropic foundations for the poor, the elderly, the orphans, or the homeless, and the private corporations, up to and including the very first large 'multinational' companies, such as the Dutch East India Company (governed by the *Heren Zeventien*, the 'Lords Seventeen'), or the West India Company (the *Heren Negentien*). It is typical that the leading Dutchmen of those days did not have themselves portrayed as individuals, but in groups. The portrait galleries of the Rijksmuseum, the Amsterdam Historical Museum or the Frans Hals museum are full of them. How different the Prado or the Louvre. There we find individual kings, princes, emperors or royal families on the wall.

Consensualism

Collegiate government, together with the weak central state and the sovereignty of provincial, municipal and private agencies, implied a high dispersal of political power, pluralism and factionalism in the Republic. Particularistic interests came to be considered legitimate, but since no faction of the oligarchic elite dominated, practical cooperation between the various factions became a necessity. The earlier experience with religious strife up to the threat of civil war (between '*hoeksen* and *kabeljauwen*', '*remonstranten* and *contra-remonstranten*') may have added to the awareness of the need for consultation, cooperation and compromise. Such conflicts fostered the development of institutions and cultural values which could prevent conflict escalation. 'The need to adjust conflicting interests fostered a tradition of compromise and an acceptance of disagreement and diversity' wrote Daalder (1966: 189). He continued: 'Effective political power at the center depended on the ability to balance carefully widely varied particularist interests. . . . A climate of constant reciprocal opposition fostered a habit of seeking accommodation through slow negotiations and mutual concessions' (ibid.: 192). This was possible in the Dutch Republic thanks to the relative small size and cultural homogeneity of the oligarchy of politicians involved. Frequent personal contact made it easier to come to compromises and reduced the threat of free riders in the production of public goods.

An essential part of this early consociationalism was the acceptance of differences instead of attempts to win the battle or to smooth down such distinctions. This presupposed tolerance of dissidents, and in the long run their recognition and integration, if not cooptation. And just as the established merchant family elites integrated in time newcomers and adapted to new circumstances (Daalder 1966: 217; 1977: 360), so does the present political elite again try to integrate new dissidents, such as the environmentalists, in the political institutions. This flexibility of the elite provided for its continuity and broad influence, and also for its consensual culture.

Roots in early hydraulic society

It is not unimaginable that the tradition of self-organization, cooperation, consultation and search for consensus is still older. The Netherlands is, in the words of the historian Huizinga, a 'hydraulic society' and many of its characteristics – in trade, industry, society, polity and culture – derive from that. The early and permanent need to organize dyke maintenance and continuous drainage of low-lying land made cooperation, collective action and regulation of mutual obligations of utmost importance, and these values and phenomena are still very much present in political and economic life, as will be seen later. One could say that the physical conditions of survival condemned the Dutch from the very beginning to cooperation, consensus, compromise and the orderly settlement of conflict. But whereas in Asia hydraulic problems led to the formation of hierarchic, authoritarian state organizations (Wittfogel 1957), in Holland these hydraulic problems fostered the development of horizontal political organization. In the absence of an aristocracy who could have enforced such cooperation (especially in the areas lacking a nobility, West Friesland, Friesland, Groningen), such cooperation had to emerge on a voluntary and horizontal base.

Already in the eleventh and twelfth centuries the landholders in a prospective polder formed horizontal, more or less 'democratic' forms of organization to construct, guard and maintain dyke systems. They were called *heemraden* and *heemraadschappen*. Many of these still exist, although they too have merged lately. Dykes are prototypical collective goods, and dyke construction and maintenance is consequently fraught with the typical Olsonian problems of collective action. Informal organization did not suffice here. Formalization of the mutual obligations was a life necessity. Everyone had to contribute, and others had to be able to rely on that. Formal corporations were created, with compulsory membership for all those who owned or exploited land within the relevant territory. They had duties, but also rights. The regulations stipulated that they had to provide services in kind (in modern times, this has been changed into a tax, used to pay professionals to carry out the drainage work). In return they had the right to vote for board membership. These boards had a typically collegiate leadership. The agreements were enforced by active mutual social control, and only incidentally also by aristocratic authority where that existed, and then only in the background.

Horizontal collective action may have been facilitated by a combination of the seriousness of the threat, and the small scale of early 'polders' (territory surrounded by dykes). However, of equal importance was certainly the absence of a landed aristocracy, which could have provided monocratic leadership of hydraulic boards. Feudalism has never really existed in the country, at least in its political and economic centre, the western part. Again this seems to have been related to the 'water'. The threat of flooding and the high water table made arable farming difficult, and hence large land-holdings impossible or unattractive. At the time that it became possible, the classes of small independent farmers and merchants were so well-established that the development of a feudal aristocracy was no longer possible. This absence of an aristocracy has contributed in turn to the importance of values of collegiate government, equality, achievement and universalism.

The need to keep feet dry may be co-responsible for that curious typical Dutch combination of formalization and improvisation. Formalization of obligations of participation in collective action was necessary to ensure that everyone contributed his or her part for the sake of collective security. For the same reason, the implementation of regulations was strictly formalized. However, emergencies required sometimes also improvisation and hence a considerable degree of discretionary authority by those implementing regulations. These imperatives, already present in the fight against the water, have been carried over into political and administrative culture, and are characteristics of the Dutch policy style, both in public and in private bureaucracies, which is characterized by pragmatism, formalism, flexibility and search for consensus.

The same imperatives also made for a combination of individualism and collectivism. Tradition holds that rugged individualism developed out of dependence on nature, on water and wind, in keeping feet dry, in fishing, in trade. But it was always tempered, mitigated by the need to cooperate, first in the fight against the water, later in that against societal ills. It finds expression in the Dutch willingness to associate, and to be bound by the self-imposed regulations of one's own associations; but not in the form of an unquestioning acceptance of authority and of regulations and commands for their own sake. On the contrary: the early experience with successful horizontal cooperation has led to an absence of respect for authority and hierarchy for their own sake, quite unlike that, for instance, in Germany and Austria. This tradition was reinforced by Calvinism, which held individual conscience to be the ultimate authority, not some external agency. The obedience to authority of the Dutch under pillarization was only a temporary interlude, typical of a phase of emancipation. The quiet revolution of the 1960s, which undermined such authority again, can hence in retrospect be considered merely a return to an old tradition.

Roots in consociational ideologies

Dutch corporatism may trace its institutional and cultural roots to the early phases of state formation of the country: the period when the first hydraulic boards were established around 1100, and subsequently the period of the decentralized Dutch Republic (1581–1795). However, the principles were again revived and reconfirmed in the various ideologies of the societal pillars that emerged from the second half of the nineteenth century onwards. These fostered an ideology of a corporatist organization of the economy. Another distinguishing characteristic of Dutch corporatism is hence that it was explicitly and intentionally created out of two ideologies, Social Catholicism and Calvinist teaching, of which Catholicism was the earliest and the most dominant one. This was not so in Scandinavia and much less in Germany and Austria.

Catholic social teaching was particularly strong in the Netherlands. This Social Catholicism developed from the mid-nineteenth century onwards, starting with the work of von Ketteler in 1848 (Defourny 1942; Kothen 1945). It was codified in two papal encyclicals, Rerum Novarum of 1891 and Quadragesimo Anno of 1931. The encyclicals intended to develop a 'third way' in between socialism and capitalism. The Pope tried to prevent the defection of Catholic workers to socialism and socialist trade unions by criticizing the 'chaos' and 'social desintegration' of unregulated capitalism, by stressing that property brought not only rights but also social responsibilities to its owners (it was merely a temporary loan from God), by developing the idea of 'ordered' or regulated and organized markets, and by instigating Catholic leaders to create separate organizations for Catholic labour and capital (preferably in one organization, otherwise at least separate from non-Catholics). These should provide a home for Catholic workers, should be the institutional bases for class cooperation and consultation, and should organize and regulate labour and product markets.

Catholic social thinking combined a reactionary nostalgia for the passing of the medieval guild system with a forward-looking attempt to seek class harmony in the industrializing society. To this end, Catholic thinkers developed and popularized an organic theory of society which was borrowed from early nineteenth-century conservative Restoration thinking. This explains also the term 'corporatism'. It stems from the Latin root *'corpus'* or corpse, body. As many nineteenth-century social conceptions, the ideology made an analogy between society and the biological organism (see for an elaborated example Hollenberg 1941). The individuals in society were considered to be the cells of the organism. Just as the cells are first organized in functionally specific organs – like the skin, the nervous system, the blood-circulation system, the kidneys – which give life to the organism as a whole as well as the constituent cells through their division of labour and the coordination between them, so the individuals should also be organized in functionally specific organizations, allowing both society at large and individuals to live and thrive. These *corps intermédiaires* should bring together individuals engaged in the same productive activity. Historical models were the family, the army and especially the medieval guild, organizing artisans of the same trade. Such intermediary organizations should keep society integrated and prevent presumed social ills such as disorder, political chaos, revolution, secularization, and individual ills such as alienation and anomie (see also Durkheim 1960). Just as the various organs have their own functions which they can perform best, so the 'head' of the societal body, the state, should delegate specific functions to the *corps intermédiares* who can perform these best, and be itself only responsible for overall coordination and representation.

Structural conflict in capitalism, both the competitive and the class struggle, was seen as destructive and dehumanizing and had to be mitigated by organizations which would bring order through internal regulation and external bargaining and concertation with other associations. The competitive struggle should be reduced by organizations of industries and market-ordering rules like the medieval guilds used to have. How the class struggle was best contained was a subject of debate. The dominant view was that associations should bridge class distinctions, i.e. should include both capitalists and workers. By bringing together labour and capital in one association, it was hoped that class conflict would be replaced by a new loyalty to the function or profession, as it had been in the old guild system. In the end, however, most Catholic ideologists had to adjust to the reality that this was hardly feasible and that separate trade unions and employers' associations emerged. Class conflict would then be reduced through cooperation and bargaining between the associations of the different classes.

Social Catholicism has been particularly influential in the Netherlands (van Waarden 1980). When he celebrated the fortieth anniversary of Rerum Novarum with Quadragesimo Anno, the Pope actually complimented the Dutch Catholics for having developed the ideas of the 1891 encyclical to their strongest expression in their country. Dutch Catholics were, between 1860 and 1960, some of the most zealous Catholics around (Rogier and de Nooy 1953). There were several reasons for this. Two had to do with their status as minority group in a predominantly Protestant nation. First, being close to Protestants, they were infected with their puritanism and fundamentalism. As a matter of fact, the most 'puritan' Catholics were found in the northern part of the country, where they often lived in small enclaves in a predominantly Protestant region (in the south the Catholics were in the majority). Second, the Catholics had been secondary citizens since the days of the Dutch Republic. The liberal bourgeois revolution of 1848, which brought a constitution, constitutional rights and liberal governments, together with the formal equality of religions (including the reinstatement of the Catholic church hierarchy in the Netherlands) gave them the opportunity to embark on an emancipation drive, to improve their social and political status. This required the organization of a Catholic civil society in separate organizations. Social Catholic teaching provided an ideological support for this. This factor, minority emancipation, was lacking in predominantly Catholic countries such as France, Spain or Italy and in the predominantly Lutheran Scandinavian countries. This may explain why corporatism never caught on so much there (with the exception of Franco's Spain), or why it lacked this specific Catholic touch (Nordic countries). In the Netherlands, the papal teachings fell on fertile soil. The more so, a third reason, as the Dutch had a long tradition of a well-organized civil society, as has been mentioned before. The Catholics revived this tradition.

Dutch Catholic intellectuals spend a lot of effort in further developing Catholic social teaching. Many studies were written on 'economic ordering' and 'corporatism'. Doctoral theses were devoted to it, including studies that admired 'corporatism' as it was practised in Mussolini's fascist Italy since 1922, Salazar's Estado Novo in Portugal since 1933, Franco's Spain, and Austria under Dolfuss (e.g. Anema 1934; Koenraadt 1934; Romme 1935; Brongersma 1940). Up until the 1950s Catholic 'Handbooks of Sociology' appeared which were not what their title suggested, but were introductions in corporatist thinking (see Aengenent 1909 for a early one). This adoption of 'sociology' by Catholic social teaching explains, by the way, why the early real sociological chairs were called chairs in 'empirical sociology' in order to distinguish them from 'normative sociology', being the Catholic variety. Political pamphlets, church meetings and conferences of the Dutch society of economists, all were devoted to this topic. Up until the Second World

War, the word corporatism was frequently used. After the war the association of corporatism with fascism made the term unpopular and suspect, but not the ideas behind it. Instead, the Dutch began to use the term *overlegeconomie* (concerted economy), not unlike the euphemism of the Austrians, *Sozialpartnerschaft*.

The Protestants followed suit. Social Catholicism was influential in protestant circles. The Calvinist leader and ideologist Abraham Kuijper (prime minister at the beginning of the century) borrowed heavily from it when he developed his own Calvinist social philosophy. Catholic and Calvinist social ideology had much in common – which in fact subsequently facilitated cooperation in government. Both shared the ideal of a decentralized society. The Catholic principle of *subsidiarity* and the Calvinist one of *sovereignty in own circle* gave preference to self-organization of civil society (that is, themselves: Catholic and Protestant organizations). What civil society could do itself, the state should not do. However, in this the Calvinists were more extreme than the Catholics. In Catholic thinking, producer associations should, under the doctrine of subsidiarity, be licensed by the state to perform specific functions, like price and wage regulation, which would bring order to the competitive and class struggle. However, the state as licence-holder had the right to intervene when these regulatory functions were not performed well, or when other interests, especially those of the state itself, were at stake. The Calvinists stressed much more, the autonomy of sub-national units as church, family, charity, business firm and association, and were much more hesitant in allowing the state the right to interfere in these. This is what the term 'sovereignty' in 'own circle' (meaning: the Calvinists own organizations), referred to.

In this ideological environment, and in the context of consociational concertation, the social democrats developed their own variation of a corporatist philosophy, called *functional decentralization*. They too wanted to harness capitalism, but unlike their religious co-pillars they saw a much larger role for the state, as social democrats did also elsewhere. However, they found the other pillars squarely in their way in their attempts at state regulation of the economy. A case in point was the development of the Dutch welfare state. The Netherlands was relatively late with this, much later than, for example, Germany and Britain (Alber 1982; Flora and Heidenheimer 1982). The edifice got its boost only in 1957 with the general pension plan and 1967 with the disability plan. This was not because the Dutch attached less importance to social security – on the contrary. The Dutch have a high preference for reduction of risk and uncertainty in life, and attach also great importance to egalitarian values, i.e. more or less equal life chances for the unemployed, disabled, retarded or retired. Social security provisions were delayed because of disagreement over their implementation: by state organizations or by corporatist bodies. The first social security law, on disability, failed in parliament in 1899 because of disagreement on what kind of organizations were to implement it. And the first sickness compensation plan already passed parliament in 1913, but was not implemented until 1930 for similar reasons. Confronted with this resistance of the religious pillars against a large role of the state in the economy, the social democrats developed, in a typical pragmatic way, their own variation of corporatism: the state could delegate and/or decentralize specific functions to private or semi-public organizations. Thus in the end the old Dutch corporatism got three different ideological underpinnings, from three different pillars; ideologies that were developed within each of these pillars in the context of consociationalism: that is, the presence of neighbouring pillars with different ideas, and the need to find compromises.

These ideologies led, from the last quarter of the nineteenth century, to a virtual explosion of associational activity, first at the local level, and subsequently nationally. Hundreds if not thousands of trade associations, unions, or farmers' organizations were created as part of the emancipation movements and the so-called 'social question'.

Important for the development of the Dutch variety of corporatism was hence in a way the geographic location of the country: at the crossroads of Western Europe, at the heart of the two axes of Stein Rokkan's geo-political map of Europe (Rokkan 1981): right on the city belt, which had stretched, since the late Middle Ages, from the North Sea and the Baltic over the Alps to the Mediterranean; and just distant enough from Rome to be at the boundary between protestant Northern Europe and Catholic Southern Europe. The city belt provided the tradition of a well-organized civil society. The distance to Rome explained the mixed Protestant–Catholic population.

Conclusion

Dutch corporatism has both broad and deep roots in society. *Broad* in the sense that socio-economic concertation at the macro-level is but one manifestation of a much broader phenomenon, whose basic elements are: associability, subsidiarity, collegiate government and consensualism. These elements find expression in a multitude of phenomena:

- at different levels: from macro-level socio-economic policy formulation to meso-level industrial self-regulation in both voluntary and compulsory trade associations;
- in a diversity of policy fields: labour relations and wage policy, social security, health, education, welfare, public housing, environmental protection;
- and in different state institutions, including in the legal system and the policy styles in public administration.

Deep roots it has too. They can be traced back to different historical periods: to the period of industrialization and emancipation of Catholic and Protestant minorities and the ideologies they developed; to the Dutch Republic with its associational self-governance and consensualism; and perhaps even to the emergence of the first embryonic elements of the Dutch state, the early hydraulic boards that emerged in the eleventh century.

Hence it comes as no surprise, that the Dutch reverted back to corporatist institutions for the reform of the welfare state, notwithstanding the fact that these socio-economic institutions were themselves blamed by many for some of the problems and excesses of the welfare state. The broader societal and historical embeddedness of these institutions provided conditions for their successful application.

One implication may of course be that such corporatist solutions to welfare state reform, as chosen by the Dutch, are less easily transferable to other countries, which want to imitate apparently successful models, but lack the appropriate institutional, cultural and historical bases. Let us see in the other chapters how some of them have fared.

References

Aengenent, J.D. (1909) *Leerboek der sociologie*, Leiden: Stenfert Kroese.

Alber, Jens (1982) *Vom Armenhaus zum Wohlfahrtsstaat. Analysen zur Entwicklung der Sozialversicherung in Westeuropa*, Frankfurt am Main and New York: Campus.

Anema, A. (1934) *Grondslag en karakter van de Italiaans-fascistische staatsleer*, Kampen: Kok.

Blankenburg, Erhard and Freek Bruinsma (1994) *Dutch Legal Culture*, Deventer and Boston: Kluwer.

Boyer, Robert (1997) 'The Variety and Unequal Performance of Really Existing Markets. Farewell to Doctor Pangloss?', in Robert Boyer and J. Rogers Hollingsworth (eds) *Contemporary Capitalism: The Embeddedness of Institutions*, Cambridge: Cambridge University Press.

Brongersma, E. (1940) 'De opbouw van een corporatieven staat. Het nieuwe Portugal', dissertation. University of Utrecht.

Calmfors, Lars and John Driffill (1988) 'Bargaining Structure, Corporatism and Macroeconomic Performance', in *Economic Policy*, 6: 14–61.

Cameron, David (1984) 'Social Democracy, Corporatism, Labour Quiescence, and the Representation of Economic Interest in Advanced Capitalist Society', in John Goldthorpe (ed.) *Order and Conflict in Contemporary Capitalism*, Oxford: Clarendon Press, pp. 143–78.

Czada, Roland (1983) 'Konsensbedingungen und Auswirkungen neokorporatistischer Politikentwicklung', *Journal für Sozialforschung*, 23/4: 421–39.

Daalder, Hans (1966) 'The Netherlands: Opposition in a Segmented Society', in Robert A. Dahl (ed.) *Political Opposition in Western Democracies*, New Haven and London: Yale University Press, pp. 188–236.

Daadler, Hans (1977) 'On Building Consociational Nations: The Cases of the Netherlands and Switzerland', *International Social Science Journal*, 23: 355–70.

Damaska, Mirjan R. (1986) *The Faces of Justice and State Authority. A Comparative Approach to the Legal Process*, New Haven and London: Yale University Press.

Defourny, M. (1942) *De corporatieve gedachte bij de katholieke sociologen van de 19e eeuw*, Utrecht and Antwerpen: Het Spectrum.

Durkheim, Emile (1960) *Le suicide, étude de sociologie*, Paris: Presses Universitaires de France.

Fernhout, Roel (1980) 'Incorporatie van belangengroepen in de sociale en economische wetgeving', in Han Verhallen (ed.) *Corporatisme in Nederland. Belangengroepen en democratie*, Alphen aan de Rijn: Samsom.

Flora, Peter and Arnold J. Heidenheimer (eds) (1982) *The Development of Welfare States in Europe and America*, New Brunswick and London: Transaction.

Heek, F. van (1945) *Stijging en daling op de maatschappelijke ladder. Een onderzoek naar verticale mobiliteit*, Leiden: Stenfert Kroese.

Hollenberg, A. (1941) *De natuurlijke inrichting der samenleving als grondslag voor een nieuwe staatkundige en sociaal-economische orde*, Heemstede: De Toorts.

Jong, H.W. de (1990) 'Nederland: het kartelparadijs van Europa?', *Economisch-Statistische Berichten*, 75/3749: 244–48.

Kagan, Robert A. (1990) 'How much does Law Matter? Labor Law, Competition, and Waterfront Labor Relations in Rotterdam and US Ports', *Law and Society Review*, 24/1: 35–69.

Katzenstein, Peter J. (1985) *Small States in World Markets. Industrial Policy in Europe*, Ithaca: Cornell University Press.

Koenraadt, W.M.J. (1934) *Corporatieve staat, organische staat*, Credo, Vivo 3, Hilversum: De Boer.

Kothen, R. (1945) *La Pensée et l'action des catholiques 1789–1944*, Leuven: Em. Warny.

Layard, Richard, Stephen Nickell and Richard Jackman (1991) *Unemployment, Macroeconomic Performance, and the Labour Market*, Oxford: Oxford University Press.

Lipset, Seymour Martin (1996) *American Exceptionalism. A Double-Edged Sword*, New York and London: Norton.

Maier, Charles S. (1981) 'Fictitious Bonds . . . of Wealth and Law', in Susanne D. Berger (ed.) *Organising Interests in Western Europe*, Cambridge: Cambridge University Press, pp. 27–61.

Marin, Bernd (1990) 'Generalized Political Exchange: Preliminary Considerations', in Bernd Marin (ed.) *Generalized Political Exchange*, Frankfurt am Main: Campus.

OECD (1993) *OECD Economic Surveys. Netherlands*, Paris: OECD.

Ouchi, William G. (1980) 'Markets, Bureaucracies, and Clans', *Administrative Science Quarterly* 25: pp 129–41.

Phillips, Derek (1985) 'Het Nederlandse volkskarakter. Enige notities', in Derek Phillips (ed.) *De naakte Nederlander. Kritische overpeinzingen*, Amsterdam: Bert Bakker.

Rogier, L.J. and N. de Nooy (1953) *In vrijheid herboren. Katholiek Nederland, 1853–1953*, Den Haag: Pax.

Rokkan, Stein (1981) 'Territories, Nations, Parties: Toward a Geoeconomic-Geopolitical Model for the Explanation of Variations within Western Europe', in R.I. Merritt and B. Russett (eds) *From National Development to Global Community*, London: Allen & Unwin, pp. 70–95.

Romme, C.P.M. (1935) 'Inaugural Lecture', Catholic University of Tilburg.

Schelven, A.L. van (1984) *Onderneming en familisme. Opkomst, bloei en neergang van de textielonderneming Van Heek & Co te Enschede*, Leiden: Stenfert Kroese.

Schmidt, Manfred G. (1982) 'Does Corporatism Matter? Economic Crisis, Politics and Rates of Unemployment in Capitalist Democracies in the 1970s', in Gerhard

Lehmbruch and Philippe C. Schmitter (eds) *Patterns of Corporatist Policy-Making*, London: Sage.

SCP (Sociaal Cultureel Planbureau) (2000) *Sociaal en Cultureel Rapport 2000: Nederland in Europa*, The Hague: SCP.

Soskice, David (1990a) 'Reinterpreting Corporatism and Explaining Unemployment: Coordinated and Non-Coordinated Market Economies', in R. Brunetta and C. Dell'Aringa (ed.) *Markets, Institutions and Corporations: Labour Relations and Economic Performance*, New York: New York University Press, pp. 170–211.

Soskice, David (1990b) 'Wage Determination: The Changing Role of Institutions in Advanced Industrialized Countries', *Oxford Review of Economic Policy*, 6/4: 36–61.

Streeck, Wolfgang and Philippe Schmitter (eds) (1985) *Private Interest Government. Beyond Market and State*, Beverly Hills, London, and New Delhi: Sage.

Teulings, Coen and Joop Hartog (1999) *Corporatism and Competition. An International Comparison of Labor Market Structures and their Impact on Wage Formation*, Cambridge: Cambridge University Press.

van Waarden, Frans (1980) 'Corporatisme als probleemoplossing. Een "ideengeschichte" van het corporatief denken, met name in katholieke kring', in H.J. Verhallen (ed.) *Corporatisme in Nederland. Belangengroepen en Demokratie*, Alphen aan de Rijn: Samsom.

van Waarden, Frans (1992) 'Emergence and Development of Business Interest Associations. An Example from The Netherlands', *Organization Studies*, 13/4: 521–61.

van Waarden, Frans (1995) 'The Organizational Power of Employers' Associations Compared. Cohesion, Comprehensivenesss and Organizational Development', in C. Crouch and F. Traxler (eds) *Organized Industrial Relations in Europe: What Future?*, Aldershot: Avebury, pp. 45–97.

van Waarden, Frans (1999) 'Ieder land zijn eigen trant', in Wieger Bakker and Frans van Waarden (eds) *Ruimte rond Regels. Reguleringsstijlen vergeleken*, Amsterdam: Boom.

Visser, Jelle and Anton Hemerijck (1997) *A Dutch Miracle'. Job Growth, Welfare Reform and Corporatism in the Netherlands*, Amsterdam: Amsterdam University Press.

Visser, Jelle and Jeremy Waddington (1996) 'Industrialization and Politics: A Century of Union Structural Development in Three European Countries', in *European Journal of Industrial Relations*, 2/1: pp. 21–53.

Vogel, David (1986) *National Styles of Regulation. Environmental Policy in Great Britain and the United States*, Ithaca and London: Cornell University Press.

Williamson, Oliver E. (1975) *Markets and Hierarchies: Analysis and Anti-Trust Implications: A Study in the Economics of Internal Organization*, New York: Free Press.

Wiskerke, C. (1938) *De afschaffing der gilden in Nederland*, Amsterdam: Paris.

Wittfogel, Karl A. (1957) *Oriental Despotism: A Comparative Study of Total Power*, New Haven: Yale University Press.

4 Austrian social partnership

Just a midlife crisis?[1]

Brigitte Unger

Introduction

Since the late 1970s considerable changes have affected the economic, political and social conditions of social partnership action. Growing uncertainties related to an ever-greater intertwined world economy, the end of high growth rates, increased unemployment and the erosion of homogeneous interests have given new fuel to the question as to the decline of corporatism for some time now. Most recently, external incisive changes in social partnership are being underscored along with watchwords such as neoliberalism and globalization. Together with internal undermining tendencies of the system such as a new coalition government without social democrats, a calling into question the existence of chambers and the declining degree of the organization of labour unions, the question arises as to what survival potential and what future social partnership will have.

Forecasts as to the future potentials of social partnership have become relatively pessimistic, lately. Many sociologists, political scientists and economists, though for different reasons, all predict its decline. Crepaz (1995), for example, used the metaphor of the 'end of a dinosaur' in order to express the inability of social partnership to meet the sociological needs of post-modern time. According to his view the dinosaur called social partnership will die out because young people want a transparent system of decision making, a democratic way of making these decisions and equal and fair access possibilities for men and women, to give some examples. No more closed-door compromises by some old boys sitting around a green table, no more paternalistic decisions over people's heads would, indeed, mean, the end of social partnership, because non-transparency is one of its main characteristics and an important pillar for it to function. Divergent interests can only be harmonized into some sort of compromise between capital and labour if they are filtered internally within the associations. More democracy within the organization makes this filter process much more difficult.

Political scientists stress the fact that social partnership is designed for a system consisting of two large parties, which is progressively undermined by a third party or by more and more small parties. Consociationalism (*Proporz*) is easy when posts and jobs have to be shared among two parties and compromises have to be found between two groups, but it is no longer possible when there are many rival parties. And it is no coincidence that especially the third large party in Austria – the populist Austrian Freedom Party (Freiheitliche Partei Österreichs, FPÖ) – had already attacked social partnership most heavily before it came into power in April 2000, when the two conservative parties ÖVP and FPÖ formed a coalition government.

Economists, after all, claim the primacy of economics over politics. Economic forces such as the mobility of capital and the competition for the influx of foreign direct investment and multinational enterprises would force national governments and labour associations to give in to the demands of capital. No room for manœuvre would be left for national economic policy-making, according to this view. Neither for government nor for associations. The most prominent hypothesis of this kind of view is the neoclassical convergence theory (see Unger 1997). If the main economic variables, such as growth rates, interest rates, profits, wages and prices are forced to become alike, there is not much left for which to bargain and negotiate.

Even if it is not without a certain irony, when I as a woman endorse an institution set-up hardly accessible to women (to put it lightly), such as Austrian social partnership, I will claim in the following that social partnership is both economically and socially desirable, still exists and is worth maintaining.

Austrian social partnership was founded after the war (with, for example, the wage-price agreement in 1947, the Joint Commission in 1957) and is now some fifty years old. Though I agree with Crepaz (1995) that there is pressure from post-modern society, I want to stress the fact that dinosaurs took a while to die out. Rather than facing death like a dinosaur, Austria´s social partnership is undergoing a sort of *midlife crisis* which can be characterized in the following way:

1 the best times are over (one boasts of the past);
2 fears of faltering potency (in view of progressing internationalization one perceives one's own impotence);
3 these fears are glossed over by a flight forward (leaving the family and finding someone younger and more attractive in Brussels);
4 regretful comeback to the old partner if the rejuvenation kick failed.

The best times are over: changed conditions of action based on social partnership

I have reported in depth on the changed economic, social and political conditions of action based on social partnership in Hinrichs and Unger

(1990). The most important factors which we listed as contributing to a weakening of the side of the employees included:

1 Growing internationalization.
2 Greater uncertainty given the increased tempo of transactions.
3 Instability in the structure of branches, which makes collective bargaining agreements more difficult.
4 The 'end of mass production' making the markets more susceptible to fluctuations and increased flexibility demands directed to the employees.
5 New, quickly changing technologies, which makes plans of qualification demands and adequate formal training patterns ever more difficult.
6 Heterogenous manpower, which makes a (unified) labour union lobby and orientation to an 'abstract' employee (without professional and company identity) ever more difficult.
7 Weakening of the labour associations. Since business associations have always had a more heterogenous composition than labours associations and in many countries the entrepreneur associations only assume a consulting function in the development of collective wage agreements, the former are less affected than the latter.
8 Markedly lower growth rates which aggregate distribution conflicts, for which status quo oriented arrangements of partnership are less suited.
9 The departure from Keynesian economic policy – in part due to the emerging structural weaknesses of a purely demand-oriented policy represents a clear paradigm shift in the economic political scene. Monetarism and neoliberalism opt for a withdrawal of state and association interventions.
10 The departure from an offensive employment policy and the resulting growing unemployment implies a weakening of the position of employees in the corporatist negotiation processes.
11 The 'dissolution of the socio-moral milieu' and the 'individualization of life states and life stories'.
12 The growing split of the labour market in a 'core' of employees sitting on 'secure' labour and an increasing number of working persons whose employment stability and continuity is seriously endangered, has significantly contributed to a 'tighter' definition of collective interest.

For Austria the following items should be added to the list compiled at this time:

13 The decrease in employment in nationalized industry with companies that traditionally had strong labour unions has contributed to a lower degree of organization in labour unions. Furthermore, dismissed and frustrated workers from the nationalized industries were the optimal clientele for the FPÖ. (The last election's panel showed that 45 per cent of workers had voted for the FPÖ.)

14   The weakening of the two large parties and the emergence of a third large party which managed to come into power in 2000 in Austria can be interpreted as an institutional shock 'from within'. Social partnership was traditionally conceived for two parties – a big coalition – with strong ties of party members to their camp. Through the dissolution of ties to a particular political camp and the emergence of a third large party, such traditional patterns of negotiation are being rocked. It is no coincidence that precisely this third party tried to saw away at the columns of social partnership, as the abolition of obligatory membership in Austria's chambers, demanded by the FPÖ, in 1997 showed.

15   The new coalition government between the two conservative parties ÖVP and FPÖ tries to govern without social partners. Latest efforts to drain the chamber of labour financially, and efforts to pass bills without consultation with the social partners in parliament reflect the fact that labour is weakened both at an international and national level.

Fears of faltering potency: institutional shocks – the new challenges of the 1990s

In the 1990s the type of shocks with which systems based on social partnership are confronted has significantly changed. Whereas in the 1970s and 1980s, mainly the demand shocks (e.g. fluctuations in demand due to fluctuations in purchasing power) and the supply shocks (e.g. oil shocks) dominated, the social partners today are confronted with structural, organizational and institutional shocks. The creation of a European single market, the fall of the Berlin Wall, along with the opening up of Eastern Europe, the restructuring of companies from national to international firms and corporations, the liberalization of the capital markets which has resulted in greater speculation in the financial markets, are only a few examples. The growing importance of such new kinds of shocks represents a great challenge for existing institutional arrangements. Arrangements of social partnership are traditionally geared to absorbing demand shocks and have reluctantly gone from 'demand corporatism' to 'supply corporatism' (see Traxler 1996: 25). In this sense they have already ensured great adjustments. As Prisching (1996: 212) put it aptly, the legend of a 'political deficit of associations' is thus a legend 'since it borders on the inconceivable' of what social partnership has performed in the past decades. Recently, social partnership in Austria has been mainly confronted with two institutional shocks, one 'from without' and one 'from within'. The institutional threat 'from without' can be grasped with the watchword 'globalization', the institutional threat 'from within' is to be illustrated with the 'change in government' and 'the existence of the chambers'.

The spillover of conservative ideology has not just hit Austria but also many other European countries. In this sense no country can evade 'globalization' through the media and international policy. Nevertheless, the way problems are perceived in and the unanimous reaction of associations is unique in Austria.

The fact that given internationalization and globalization (almost) nothing can be done any more on a national level seems to be undisputed. Almost every interview with a politician, expert or journalist contains, in numerous ways, the explanation that under the sway of internationalization nothing can be done. Regardless from which party he or she (more rarely) being questioned comes, regardless of chamber he or she (which almost borders on the inconceivable) comes from, the arguments are almost identical. It is a sense of impotence among fifty-year-old men which becomes so clear in the Austrian debate.

Since non-transparency prevails in social partnership arrangements, a certain autonomy for the leadership of the association from the members must exist to be able to negotiate autonomously, that is to say, also few democratic base elements are included, since little experience with discourse and no willingness to enter into conflict exist, the institutional shock of the debate of the EU-membership and internationalization had to be processed as inconspicuously as possible. The fact that in Austria there was no counter-position to the EU on the part of labour, no fear of real wages being reduced or of traditional collective bargaining areas being dissolved, that the population was not informed of potential disadvantages of the EU, that is to say, there was a perfect EU-monologue of the large parties and associations, is unique in an international comparison.

This is to be explained on the one hand by the fact that when a line has been decided on this has to be doggedly adhered to. Why social partnership, and in particular labour, decided for the uncompromising recognition of the conditions of capital can be explained by the 'midlife crisis' sense of impotence. The 'constraints' accepted thus were presented to scientists, heads of staff councils, members, media, etc.: We are a small country that does not want to remain behind Hungary. Provide us with arguments in favour of the EU. Alternative positions will not be taken note of, reports on the social consequences will be locked up, EU-opponents will no longer be invited to discuss. Scientists can only think within the given framework of pro-EU, pro-budget consolidation, etc. Of course, the scope of action is very limited under such premises. It is also not very stimulating intellectually when the results of thinking are already pre-given. But it is still proof of the fact that Austria ranks top as a corporatist nation in international comparison. The institutional shock resulting from the preparation for the consequences of joining the EU had been assimilated in an exemplary way: unanimity and agreement among the social partners, stability, almost no conflict, just as if nothing had happened.

Globalization was seen as a given constraint. It was probably not analysed how much globalization and internationalization were now different from earlier years. That with the unanimous agreement to join the EU and the currency union, basic changes would take place in the balance of powers, was however, not acknowledged or addressed. With the issue of internationalization and globalization, the language of capital was also imported to Austria: efficiency instead of solidarity, economic site instead of welfare state, inefficiency of the public sector instead of important businesses and ancillary suppliers for the private sector, to elaborate a savings package instead of fighting unemployment. It was thus an ideology and not constraints that became rampant in the 1990s.

As a result of the perception nurtured by a sense of impotence ('there is nothing we can do about it anyway') the representatives of the employees anticipatingly and obediently defined away alternatives, which finally confirmed the thesis of globalization in a way of self-fulfilling prophecy.

Flight forward: the path to Brussels

If the best times are over and nothing can be done about it anyway, why not give up home and try to rejuvenate somewhere else? The speed and elan with which Austrian politicians, trade unions and other associations built their offices in Brussels was unique. In many countries 'Brussels' was used and still is abused as an excuse for domestic political impotence and failures. In Austria the EU-phoria was amazing, especially on the part of social democrats and labour associations.

For a very appropriate account of the view of the Austrian social partners, in particular of the position of the labour associations which differs substantially compared to other European countries, see Chaloupek (1995). The discussion in Norway and the opposition of Norwegian labour unions in comparison to the EU-monologue being conducted in Austria demonstrate various discourse options that exist even in social partnership arrangements. For a critique of Austria's EU-phemism see Weissel (1996).

The Austrian argumentation can be formulated as follows in exaggerated terms. Here the 'we' stands for 'Austria' in compliance with the Austrian diction which reflected a desire for consensus.

1   We became a member of the EU because we were actually already part of it. On the one hand, we have for a long time followed EU-guidelines, now we are able to help design them. On the other hand, international competition limits us this way or the other (Chaloupek 1995: 26).

2   We will join the European monetary union, since we are already part of it anyway. And since the European monetary union means really only two changes: it excludes high state deficits and devaluation of currency, that is, options the Austrian government and social partners never considered to begin with. It would thus make no sense to speak of a 'loss of autonomy' through joining the EU and the monetary union (ibid.). Sometimes this point was also legitimized in a different way. Through the monetary union nothing changes, since we already have

something like a monetary union through the hard currency policy with Germany. Note this false confusion of a fixed exchange currency system with a monetary union – a confusion which seems to exist only in Austria and even among economists and professors of international economics such as Breuss (1992). In a monetary union there is no possibility of using the exchange rate or the fear of devaluation as a disciplinary instrument. Even if Austria has not used this instrument for a while, it has always been a potential threat, a Damocles sword hanging above the heads of the social partners during negotiations. The shared fear of a devaluation of the currency imposed self-discipline both on capital (in particular export-oriented industries) and on labour in negotiations.

From the perspective of social partnership, there was unanimity with regard to the inventory and outline of its future prospects.

3   The future of Austrian social partnership lies in Brussels. Even if the social partners underscore their reduced influence on a national level, on an international or supranational level they seemed to feel stronger. In a more 'modest' vein, the social partners are envisioned 'as an extended arm of Austria, as an interest group representative of Austria in Brussels' (Nowotny 1994). In a more 'bold' vein, it is hoped that participating in the 'social dialogue' will allow Austria to influence the rest of the world in the direction of solutions based on social partnership (Chaloupek 1995: 27). Austria's social partnership as an emissary of the welfare state. In an 'omnipotent' form, some even toyed with the idea of a 'Eurocorporatism', that is an application of the Austrian model of social partnership to the rest of Europe (Marterbauer, no year). The future assessment of the Austrian social partners thus seemed to have something in common with what Sigmund Freud referred to as the Austrian psyche: a fluctuation between a minority complex and megalomania.

Such argumentation remained weak when it came to explaining how this strong influence of the social partners, weakened within the country, was to be exerted on an EU-level. Handler and Hochreiter (1996: 16), for instance, argued that a sort of adjusted model of social partnership could be deployed on EU-level based on the Austrian version, if adequate institutional conditions could be found for this. Authors such as Chaloupek (1995: 27) placed their trust in the likelihood of a 'development of the presently existing particularistic lobbyism at least in the direction of a certain centralization'.

Why Brussels was the false bride

The fact that corporatism needs some structural features which cannot be found in Brussels made it the false bride for Austrian social partnership, in particular for labour. To refer to a supranational level of a large scale and to hope to implement the low-scale political institutions there was doomed to fail.

The opening of borders within the EU gave capital much greater power than labour. Since neo-corporatism is a compromise between three actors (Schmitter 1985: 27) – the state which actually wants to regulate in an authoritarian way, the representatives of the enterprise who really prefer an allocation through the market, and the representatives of the employees who really want a redistribution of wealth – a certain balance of power is needed between them.

> Labor and capital must mutually back each other, each strong enough to uphold the other, through organized collective action, from asserting one's own interests directly through social control and/or economic exploitation and each too weak to assert his own interests indirectly through the state through one-sided manipulation of state authorities.
>
> (Ibid.: 36)

In Austria, in particular, the axis of state employee associations had become much weaker over time. This did not only happen during the new ÖVP–FPÖ coalition government, but started already during the big coalition government between the SPÖ and ÖVP. For instance, SPÖ chancellor Franz Vranitzky made declarations without consulting the labour unions, an act that would have been inconceivable in the Kreisky era. Also the ties between the SPÖ and labour unions were less intense than in the past. The compromise, however, was still possible, as the joint tying of the 'savings package' on budget consolidation showed. This package which involved great financial losses for the employees above all would have hardly been possible without the social partners.

Labour had been weakened already before the new conservative coalition government. The Austrian labour unions have had to accept a marked reduction in the degree of organization over the last decades. Whereas in 1970 (adjusted in terms of retirement) around 62 per cent of the workers were organized in labour unions, in 1990 it was only 46 per cent. In 1996, the degree of organization in labour unions was 49.5 per cent, which still ranked Austria in a top position of strong labour associations (see ÖGB 1996). But even today, despite further above-average losses in membership in international comparison, the Austrian labour unions show a high degree of organization and centralization. On a European level, a strong organization of the heterogeneous labour wage agreements is considerably less probable (Keller 1995).

While labour got weaker, capital gained power. In Austria the historically conditioned lack of large capital and the related weak capital side was a significant reason for organizing small and large companies in associations and for the willingness of the entrepreneurs to negotiate

(Traxler 1988). Management is considerably stronger elsewhere in Europe given the existing larger capital than in Austria. Big corporations regulate their work relationships themselves. At the European level, labour unions often lack management for negotiations (Traxler and Schmitter 1995). In Austria there are two organizations representing capital. On the one hand the economic chamber, where all entrepreneurs are obligatory members (Wirtschaftskammer Österreichs) and the association of industry (Österreichische Industriellenvereinigung). While artisans and small firms are represented by the former, only big firms are organized in the second.

In Austria, collective bargaining takes place between the economic chamber and the individual trade unions. At a European level, however, chambers with their compulsory touch are not recognized. Opposite views between the economic chamber and the association of industry with regard to regulations, the need to negotiate, etc., have become more open in recent years. The association of industry, for instance, wanted to do away with compulsory membership by suggesting that entrepreneurs should be able to opt either for membership of the economic chamber or of the association of industry. This statement was, however, retracted due to the protest of the economic chamber.

Altogether, the conditions for social partnership have worsened through the opening of borders. The chamber system came under attack, the balance of power shifted from the nation state and labour towards capital, and the feeling of 'being in the same boat', which was so important for Austria's compromises, got lost. Capital got the idea of escaping from the common boat and taking refuge in Brussels and international markets.

The new function of the social partners – compromise on the 'savings package'

Though paying much verbal attention to the false bride by expressing the will to implement social partnership arrangements at an EU-level, Austria's social partnership has, nevertheless, fulfilled enormous tasks of restructuring and adjusting at a national level. As Lehmbruch (1996) and Scharpf and Schmidt (2000) stressed, an important new function of social partners is to renegotiate the welfare state. Since the Keynesian welfare state broke down under the neoliberal wave of the 1980s and 1990s it had either to be sacrificed or to be renegotiated. Corporatist institutions have an important asset: they help to renegotiate the welfare state. The 'Dutch miracle' consisted of renegotiating the welfare state quite drastically, by regulating part-time jobs and pensions at a social partner level. The Austrian social partnership chose a much slower and more fossilizing, though also more stable and stabilizing, way of renegotiating the welfare state (see Hemerijck *et al.* 2000).

Though internationalization affected many countries in the same way, the Austrian response to it was unique. In Austria and in other countries as well the economic political goals have experienced a clear shift in recent years. The departure from Keynesian economic policy was accompanied by a pronounced shift of the political objectives. Whereas in the 1970s the primary goal was 'full employment', this goal became diluted to 'high employment' in the 1980s and to an 'increase in employment' in the 1990s. Whereas in the 1970s 'solidarity' was an important slogan, in the 1990s it was completely replaced by the notion of 'efficiency'. Whereas in the 1970s, in a time of full employment, one preferred to accept a budgetary deficit which was a few billion schillings higher rather than having sleepless nights because of greater unemployment, the generally accepted goal in economic policy has become 'budget consolidation'.

Labour and capital both agreed on a new social pact for reducing the welfare state without much public debate, strikes or excitement. How difficult this was for labour and for social democrats can be seen in the way in which this clear change in course taken by Austria's social partners was legitimized. If one reads the report (Bundesministerium fuer Finanzen 1995) compiled by the social partners on the consolidation of the budget from September 1995 (first version of the so-called 'savings package', the *Sparpaket*), one only learns that now is the right moment for consolidating budget because later is still later. We also learn a number of economic advantages of consolidation. Here there is the dilemma that all Keynesian arguments presented in the 1970s, for expanding the budget deficit had suddenly to be forgotten. Even if the conditions had changed, and Keynesian demand policy had become more difficult, the Keynesian theory still provided explanations for macro-relationships. Instead, arguments against high budget deficits had be presented. Hence, monetarist and neo-classical arguments of the 1960s had to be applied (also) by the (former Keynesian) social democrats.

They were suddenly arguing for economic liberalism, showed scepticism *vis-à-vis* the state machinery, much concern for efficiency and less concern for social issues. These arguments had been put forward by conservatives since the beginning of the 'Crowding-out' debate in the 1950s and 1960s. The left had countered with a 'Crowding-in' debate, arguing that in an open economy an increase in interest rates resulting from budgetary deficits was not possible because of sufficiently high liquidity from abroad, or that higher interests would even lead to desirable capital influx and pressure for revaluation. Furthermore, it was argued that inflation only appears when full employment is given. And last not least, Lorenz von Stein's century-old statement was cited to the effect that a state without state debt is either not doing enough for its future (when it does not build an infrastructure) or is demanding too much from today (if it makes the present generation pay the full tab, even if it is only the next generation which will benefit). The left also warned against consolidating the budget with the 'savings paradoxon' which one can find in any textbook on economics. If the state tries to cut expenditures, it depresses the economy, unemployment rises, state revenue declines and thus the state's tax income also shrinks. Paradoxically, because of tax losses in the wake of savings measures it can have a higher deficit than before (Kratena *et al*. 1988).

Instead, the report called for lower taxes so as to allow Austria to hold its ground in tax competition between the states for industries willing to settle in a given country. The list of advantages of budget consolidation culminated with the sentence 'a quickly and efficiently consolidated budget would ensure that Austria remains a promising future international 'enterprise' (Report: 11). Austria's social partners thus defined themselves as managers in a company! This, too, was part of a conservative turn in politics: the economization of all realms. Politicians now become managers.

With the savings package the social partners proved that they were able to perform their function of 'easing the burden of the state' in a very thorough way. No government had been able to legitimize and enforce such unpopular measures (such as a cut in the net income of some university professors by about one-third) without the backing of the social partners.

However, we have to ask ourselves, whether labour unions and social democrats are needed to opt for tax heavens, real wage cuts and redistribution of income from labour to capital. Is there anything left of social partnership which fights workers' interests? Is the *Sparpaket* a demonstration of the (continued) existence of corporatist arrangements or a demonstration of the failure of trade unions?

What became clear from the savings package was that the gate-keeper function had changed. It was the government who set the targets and the social partners who worked them out. While these new targets were welcomed by capital, they were definitely much less in line with labour interests.

Regret: Austrian social partnership lately

Already during the SPÖ–ÖVP coalition and more so since the new government coalition, capital has become stronger in Austria. Austrian entrepreneurs are suddenly toying with international capital. The fear of workers becoming radicalized has decreased since the fall of the Berlin Wall and opening of the East. Business is making more massive demands. For instance, entrepreneurs have demanded an extension of weekly working hours to 45 hours.

Hairdressers refused to close collective agreements between 1996 and 1998 (Interview, Legner 1996 and Interview, Kovarık 1998). Negotiations were also becoming increasingly difficult among metal workers. Metal workers are wage leaders in Austria. Usually, the metal industry workers start the collective wage negotiations, followed by the metal handicraft sector. Wage increases are the same in both sectors. In 1997 the business representative of the metal handicraft sector refused a collective agreement with the same wage increases as for the metal industry, claiming that they had lower productivity increases than the former. A joint strike of metal industry and craft workers finally resulted in the same wage increases. Since the new government has been in power, labour conflicts have increased. But even before, there was a trend towards increased labour conflicts. The number of court cases has increased by 40 per cent within the last ten years (Interview, Kovarik 2000).

The transition to monetary union also meant severe institutional changes in Austria. The exchange rate is no longer available as a potential instrument for averting crises. Even if none of the social partners in Austria ever wished devaluation, the exchange rate still served as a potential threat and a fill-in for crises. A threatening devaluation is a disciplinary instrument both for labour with its fear of inflation and real wage losses and for business with its fear of profit losses. In an economic and monetary union the exchange rate policy is no longer necessary. The budget consolidation demanded by Maastricht paralysed a second instrument for warding off crises: fiscal policy. Thus there only remained a third instrument for absorbing shocks: wage policy. The entire burden of adjustment was placed on wage policy.

A further 'debilitating element' of labour was the increase in illegal workers. Precarious and illegal employment conditions evaded collective bargaining agreements and increased the danger of wage dumping.

Since the new government has been in office, the already rough international wind for labour has been reinforced by domestic changes. First, the Ministry of Labour, Health and Social Affairs was split into separate parts. Among other things, the inspector of labour was transferred from the Ministry of Labour, Health and Social Affairs to the Economic Ministry. This seems unique in Europe: business associations checking whether firms fulfil working conditions properly!

Collective agreements are undermined. The Oesterreichischer Gewerkschaftsbund (ÖGB), which had originally refused to regulate working time arrangements collectively, has delegated this at a sectoral level. We now see a new trend towards including part-time arrangements in the collective arrangements of employees, for jobs of the 'new economy'. However, reality has overtaken trade unions. Precarious employment has increased in the last years, wages paid below the collectively agreed one have been arranged for firms in crisis, service sector jobs outside the traditional domain of trade unions have made the Austrian labour market much more flexible than is perceived from abroad (see Pichelmann and Hofer 1999).

The new government openly bypasses the social partners by setting important issues, such as the budget-accompanying law (Budgetbegleitgesetz, 2000), very late on the agenda. The social partners had only two days left to check on this proposal before it became a bill and found, anyway, the parliamentary majority of the two coalition partners. The fact that the social partners were not invited to consult on the latest pension reform was certainly the biggest affront.

While the economic chamber is more relaxed about this, since the proposals are in its favour, the trade unions are often completely left out.

Drastic changes in personnel to the disadvantage of SPÖ members take place in all institutions. Even the prominent former SPÖ Minister of Trade, Staribacher, had to quit the ÖIAG Aufsichtsrat. The ÖIAG, Austria's Industry Holding, is responsible for the privatization of the nationalized industries. Also in the Verbundgesellschaft, the electricity company, personnel changes took place, and government designated the new members. In television, in social security, in leading functions in the ministries, major personnel changes take place at high speed.

Austria's trade unions have started to regret the Europeanization that has reduced their influence significantly and has shrunk their clientele. However, the road down started with the breakdown of the nationalized industries. The elections of 2000, with 41 per cent of former social democrat workers voting for the (then not Europe-friendly) FPÖ showed that Europe might have been the wrong route for the Alpine status quo-oriented social partnership regime.

Social partnership is robust

It is difficult to foresee the near future. The sudden and undiscussed sales of public enterprises, and overnight reforms in social policy areas without consultation with the social partners, give rise to the idea that the end of social partnership has come. However, the author claims that this is only the deepest dip of the 'midlife crisis'. The new government, so far, has not really attacked the fundamentals of social partnership but only put it on ice. While Margaret Thatcher destroyed the trade unions the new government only plays with the old emotional hatred against the socialists, dating back to the civil war in 1934. This gives sometimes the impression that the old camps still exist. The Lager mentality between conservatives and social democrats, Austria's historical cleavage line, re-emerges in the public debate, in suspicions, in fears of being overheard by phone, etc. But, unlike 1934 the camps do not exist any longer, but the emotional feelings associated with them linger on.

One of the major institutions of social partnership are the chambers, for the Austrian chamber system is a central piece of social partnership and without obligatory membership there are no chambers. Every worker is a member of the chamber of labour, every self-employed person is a member of the economic chamber. To abolish this would amount to the end of the Austrian model of finding consensus. This existential threat to both systems came mainly from the FPÖ. Then FPÖ leader Haider questioned the legitimacy of the chambers so persistently, that in spring 1996 the members of the economic chamber and the chamber of labour were asked whether they support the maintenance of their respective chamber. The results clearly showed that the foundations of Austrian social partnership are not so easily shaken. In February 1996, 82 per cent of the members of the economic chamber voted in favour of the maintenance of the economic chambers with their guilds, committees, trade groups and professional associations as a common legal interest group for all entrepreneurs. The participation in the poll was 36 per cent, the same as at normal chamber elections.

In May and June of 1996 the members of the chamber of labour were asked: 'Are you in favour of the chamber of labour continuing to exist as a legal lobby for all workers?' The poll was a considerably more delicate matter, since the work done by the experts of this chamber for the members is less transparent. Eighty-seven per cent voted in favour of the maintenance of the chamber of labour. The participation on the part of the workers' chamber was clearly above normal. The participation in the vote of the chamber of labour was 29 per cent in 1994, whereas in the poll in 1996 it was almost twice as high, at 57.7 per cent (see Press Information of the Economic Chamber).

The realization of the poll in the chamber of labour shows that considerable forces were mobilized for it. In comparison to the chamber of labour elections it is striking that a large part of this poll was conducted in companies. This could also be proof that business was also interested in a high participation in the poll. Business, above all smaller companies, know that they need the chamber of labour for their concerns. Without the chamber of labour there is also no chamber of business. Business must have thus been interested in a positive outcome of the chamber of labour poll.

The new government tried to make the chambers again an issue. But this time more subtle. The government proposal foresees a 40 per cent cut in the compulsory chamber contribution (Kammerumlage). The chamber contributions are ear-marked pay-roll taxes. A 40 per cent cut would mean a loss of one billion schillings to the Chamber of Labour and, thus, reduce its financial means by almost one half. The Economic Chamber proposed a voluntary reform and to charge fees for services in order to support this government proposal. This indicates a big shift of the Economic Chamber's policy strategy under the new government.

The future of Austrian social partnership

Many of the latest changes towards neoliberalism started under the social democrats' umbrella in the large coalition government. The result was that the renegotiation of the welfare state took place much more slowly and much less radically than, for example, in the Netherlands. The budget cuts – though partly much more radical than in France and Germany – have passed without heavy strikes, since they were under the umbrella of the social partners.

The way in which the institutional shocks of the 1990s were handled by social partners shows thus that social peace is still the main asset provided by Austrian institutions. Lately, it has been recognized that the future of Austrian social partnership is not to be found in Brussels but only in Austria. Social partnership is a national arrangement and national realms of action will be used more in the future. On a supranational level, the disequilibrium of forces is too large for social partnership arrangements. As an 'emissary of the welfare state' they certainly have an important moral function in Brussels, but their political function is limited.

On the macro level the demands have become greater. In particular with regard to internationalization, the status quo-maintaining and fossilizing effects of social partnership, however, take on a new meaning for a small country. An upward movement in the wave of internationalization means growing uncertainty, greater fluctuations in output and employment, quicker reactions and more intense overreactions of the economic subjects given the greater mobility of financial capital, real capital and labour. This, however, also means that crises can appear too quickly and too drastically, which results in particularly high social costs. Social partnership can have a buffer effect on these excessively high and too quick fluctuations.

Social partnership structures thus become all the more important for a small country in the face of growing internationalization as they can protect it against extreme external shocks.

As the chamber polls showed, institutions prove to be considerably more stable than economic processes or governments in power. This means that at least on a mid-term basis the macro-economic, crisis-absorbing, stabilizing function of social partnership will be maintained. As compared to less corporatist countries, or those which have no corporatist culture at all, at least Austria's relatively advantageous position remains, in terms of a stable climate.

It is unlikely that trade unions will act in a more radicalized way or that trade unions will be able to organize their members. This seems to be less a problem for the workers than it is for the trade unions' organizations themselves, who have had no experience in organizing strikes in the post-war era.

It is more likely that business, in particular small business, will realize that negotiations can be cheaper than disorganized labour relations. Tensions within the ÖVP, tensions between the Economic Chamber and the association for industry, tensions even within the latter, indicate that not all business is willing to follow the aggressive neoliberal strategies of the FPÖ. The latest privatizations, which mainly resulted in mergers with German property (e.g. selling Austrian Banks and insurance companies to Germans), have split business.

From other countries we know that the abandoning of social partnership can be quite costly. The Agreement of Wassenaar in 1982 in the Netherlands is only one example of both labour and business recognizing the need for negotiations and compromise. Newly emerging social partnership arrangements in Ireland or in Denmark show that there is no clear trend towards abandoning compromise solutions.

Austria, might once again be a laggard. The consensual climate was certainly never as challenged in the postwar period as it is now, but there might also be some new learning on the part of the actors. What one can see from other countries is, however, that social partnership can change its function. The Dutch example showed that social partners eased the way to a more liberal road. The Austrian social partners might be forced to do the same.

Note

1 For valuable references and assistance I would like to thank Wilfried Altzinger Daniel Eckert, Georg Kovarik, Reinhard Pirker, Joseph Schmee, Berta Schreckeneder and Franz Traxler along with the friendly staff of the Österreichischer Gewerkschaftsbund (ÖGB) archives, Ms Scher and Mr Novotny.

References

Breuss, F. (1992) 'Was erwartet Österreich in der Wirtschafts- und Währungsunion der EG?', in *Monatsberichte des Österreichischen Institutes für Wirtschaftsforschung*, 65/10.

Bundesministerium fuer Finanzen (1995) *Gutachten zur Budgetkonsolidierung* (Sparkpacket), Vienna, September.

Chaloupek, G. (1995) *Entwicklung und Zukunft der österreichischen Sozialpartnerschaft*, Vienna: Arbeiterkammer Wien.

Crepaz, M. (1995) 'An Institutional Dinosaur: Austrian Corporatism in the post-industrial Age' *West European Politics*, 18/4: 64–88.

Handler, H. and E. Hochreiter (1996) *The Austrian Economy in the Wake of Joining the EU – Country Paper Austria*, Vienna: CEPS Economic Policy Group.

Hemerijck, A., B. Unger and J. Visser. (2000) 'How Small Countries Negotiate Change: Twenty-Five Years of Policy Adjustment in Austria, the Netherlands, and Belgium', in F. Scharpf and V. Schmidt (eds) *Welfare and Work in the Open Economy*, Oxford: Oxford University Press, pp. 175–263.

Hinrichs, K. and B. Unger (1990) 'Das 'Ende der Sozialpartnerschaft'? – Ein internationaler Vergleich der Entwicklung korporatistischer Systeme', *Kurswechsel*, 1/1990.

Keller, B. (1995) 'European Integration, Workers' Participation and Collective Bargaining: A Euro-Pessimistic View', in B. Unger and F. van Waarden (eds) *Convergence or Diversity?* Aldershot: Avebury.

Kovarik, G. (1996) Interview with the head of the Volkswirtschaftlichen Referats des ÖGB, Mag. Georg Kovarik, July 1996, Vienna.

Kovarik, G. (1998) Interview with the head of the Volkswirtschaftlichen Referats des ÖGB, Mag. Georg Kovarik, November 1998, Vienna.

Kovarik, G. (2000) Interview with the head of the Volkswirtschaftlichen Referats des ÖGB, Mag. Georg Kovarik, November 2000, Vienna.

Kratena, K., M. Marterbauer and B. Unger (1988) *Zukunftsperspektiven einer aktiven Budgetpolitik*, Vienna: Zukunfts- und Kulturwerkstätte.

Legner (1996) Interview with the federal secretary of the hairdressers' section of the HGT, July 1996, Vienna.

Lehmbruch, G. (1996) 'Die deutsche Vereinigung: von der Improvisation zum Lernprozeß', in B. Rebe (ed.) *Die unvollendete Einheit*, Hildesheim: Olms.

Marterbauer, M. (no year) 'Vollbeschäftigung ist machbar: Bedingungen und Maßnahmen einer beschäftigungspolitisch orientierten Wirtschaftspolitik in Österreich und Europa', in Gewerkschaft der Privatangestellten (ed.) *Der Countdown läuft*, Vienna: pp. 45–66.

Nowotny, E. (1994) 'Wirtschaftsordnung und Sozialpartnerschaft im internationalen Wettbewerb', *Wirtschaftspolitische Blätter*, 41/1994: 482–88.

ÖGB (1996) *Tätigkeitsbericht des Österreichischen Gewerkschaftsbundes*, Vienna: Österreichischer Gewerkschaftsbund.

Pichelmann, K. and H. Hofer (1999) 'Country Employment Policy Reviews: Austria', Symposium on 'Social Dialogue and Employment Success', Geneva: ILO.

Prisching, M. (1996) *Die Sozialpartnerschaft, Modell der Vergangenheit oder Modell für Europa? Eine kritische Analyse mit Vorschlägen für zukünftige Reformen*, Vienna: Manz Verlag.

Scharpf, F. and V. Schmidt (2000) '*Welfare and Work in the Open Economy – Diverse Responses to Common Challenges*', Oxford: Oxford University Press.

Schmitter, P. (1985) 'Neo-Corporatism and the State' in W. Grant (ed.) *The Political Economy of Corporatism*, Basingstoke and London: Macmillan, pp. 32–62.

Traxler, F. (1988) 'Das Ende des Österreichischen Weges? Optionen und Restriktionen einer korporatistischen Makrosteuerung des Arbeitsmarktes', in J. Feldhoff (ed.) *Regulierung – Deregulierung. Steuerungsprobleme der Arbeitsgesellschaft*, Nürnberg: Institut fuer Arbeitsmarkt-und Berufsforschung der Bundesanstalt fuer Arbeit (IAB), 139–72.

Traxler, F. (1996) 'Sozialpartnerschaft am Scheideweg. Zwischen korporatistischer Kontinuität und neoliberalem Umbruch', *Wirtschaft und Gesellschaft*, 22/1: 13–35.

Traxler, F. and P. Schmitter (1995) 'The Emerging Euro-Polity and Organized Interest', *European Journal of Industrial Relations*, 1/2: 191–218.

Unger, B. (1997) *Room for Maneuver – Choices Left for National Economic Policy*, Vienna: Vienna University of Economics.

Weissel, E. (1996) *Der große EUphemismus. Ein österreichisches Lehrstück der Manipulation*, Hamburg: Verlag Dr. Kovacs.

5 Nordic corporatism and welfare state reforms

Denmark and Sweden compared

Sven Jochem

Introduction

This chapter compares welfare politics and policies in Denmark and Sweden and attempts to provide an explanation for the diverging pathways and fates of corporatism in these countries from the 1980s until the mid-1990s. Why has it been possible to rebuild corporatist consensus in Denmark (Due *et al*. 1994; Albæck *et al*. 1998), and why has it withered away in that best-known example of Nordic corporatism, Sweden (Lewin 1994)? And what have been the consequences for the development of both welfare states?

The concept of corporatism has had a variety of different meanings. Here is meant the concertation of economic and social policies amongst interest associations and state actors. Three conditions for successful concertation have been distinguished. First, interest organizations involved should have some degree of representational monopoly, internal decision making should be centralized or at least coordinated, and they should have some disciplinary capacity in order to assure rank and file quiescence. Second, state institutions should enhance and ensure the integration of the interest organizations into the process of policy formation and implementation. Third, the strategies and actions of the collective actors should be directed towards coordination. A social partnership ideology and/or repeated experience of success with concertation by the actors involved is conducive to such strategies.

Theoretically, at least three possible causes of erosion or of challenges to corporatism can be distinguished (Garrett 1995; Schwartz 1998; Wallerstein and Golden 1997). First, globalization might undermine concertation in two ways. On the one hand, deregulated capital markets and rising exports and imports might diminish the capacity of governments to apply Keynesian policies, which has been seen as one specific condition for viable concertation. On the other hand globalization might change the strategies of the employers in the export-oriented sectors. The transaction costs of investing abroad have diminished and this could cause rising outflows of investment capital. Additionally, employers regard themselves increasingly as global players, and therefore the national systems of interest mediation might no longer be their main focus of interest.

Second, it is argued that modernization and socio-economic change are challenges to corporatism. A growing service sector and an expanding welfare state has brought new actors to the stage: white collar unions and unions which mainly operate in the public sector. These have undermined the hegemony of the traditionally dominant blue collar unions. This relationship between actors in the public and the private sector seems to have become a source of conflict, which has not been confined to wage bargaining (Shalev 1992).

Third, changing power resources and relations might undermine corporatism. Declining power of labour and – partly induced by globalization – rising power of capital might be conducive to breaking up the corporatist consensus and opening a struggle for a renegotiation of the institutional framework. Globalization, modernization and changing power relations pose challenges to the dominant institutions of the post-war era. Hence, a capacity to adopt the institutional framework consensually may be an important precondition for continued viable corporatism.

Which of the hypotheses might explain the diverging pathways of corporatism in the Nordic countries? Why has there been a corporatist renaissance in Denmark and, why, by contrast, failed concertation in Sweden? In order to answer these questions this chapter will proceed as follows. In the next three sections the historical foundations and the main characteristics of corporatism in Denmark and Sweden are presented and an overview of the comparative performance of both countries is given. The two subsequent sections examine the process of welfare state renegotiation in the 1980s. The last section concludes.

My main argument is that successful concertation and adaptation in Scandinavia rests not only on the different patterns of party competition, but also and mainly on the crucially important behaviour of the employers' associations. The Swedish Employers' Association, the SAF vehemently opposed concertation in the 1980s, whereas its Danish counterpart, the DA, successfully changed its own organisation and tried to rebuild effective cooperation between capital and labour. One reason for this divergent development, it is argued, is related to the differences in funding between these welfare states. As employers in Sweden bore most expenses of the welfare state, whereas in Denmark this is done mainly by the employees, the employers were less willing to compromise, and this undercut concertation and cooperation in Sweden.

Historical roots of Nordic corporatism

The Nordic countries, and especially Sweden and Denmark, rank high on several rank-orderings of corporatism (cf. the summarizing attempt of Lijphart and Crepaz 1991). Furthermore, it has been stated that there is a specifically Nordic variant of corporatism. In contrast to, for example, Switzerland (Armingeon, this volume), Nordic polities have a lack of political institutions which contain majority rule. There is no federalism. Central banks were – at least until the early 1980s – obliged to support the economic polices of the various governments, and from the 1960s to the 1990s there have been no cross-class coalition governments in Denmark and Sweden. In the absence of constraints on majority rule party competition prevails in the parliamentary arena (see the overview in Schmidt 1996). Hence, the broadly held view of the Scandinavian model is that it expresses compromise politics 'while at the same time the overall constitutional frame is of the Westminster type' (Lane and Ersson 1995: 255).

The foundations of Nordic corporatism were laid at the end of the nineteenth and early twentieth centuries. On the labour market, powerful organizations gained momentum and signed various accords regulating national labour relations. Denmark paved the way in 1899, when the labour market organizations signed the 'Septemberforliget' (September Compromise). This was the first such agreement in the world. In this accord the employers recognized the trade union confederation (DSF, later LO) as an equal partner in wage bargaining. Both confederations agreed to follow a consensual route in solving conflicts on the labour market. Although this was at times not easy, especially when in the 1920s labour market conflicts escalated (Elvander 1980: 68–71). Additionally, both peak confederations committed themselves to ensuring that agreements concluded were observed by their member constituencies. Thus, the compromise opened the road to consensual relations between both confederations and it strengthened the centralization of the trade unions and employers' associations. In Sweden, a similar development took place, but later. Only in 1938 could the treaty of Saltsjöbaden finally be agreed upon, with similar contents and functions as the September Compromise in Denmark. The lagging behind of Sweden had to do with the disastrous consequences of the great labour market conflict of 1909, which destroyed first attempts at consensual conflict regulation (Schiller 1967).

It is important to note that the major driving force behind these agreements in both countries were the employers' organizations. They repeatedly used multi-sectoral 'offensive' lockouts to force dissenting unions to follow the guidelines of the central trade union associations, and they took harsh action towards dissenting employers as well (Swenson 1992). Their main aim was to minimize wage competition between the domestic sectors – mainly the building industry – and the export-oriented sectors. This could only be achieved by centralizing both interest organizations and minimizing rank and file discontent. 'In alliance with labour interests, employers forced those reluctant unions to delegate authority upward to confederation leaders, primarily over the initiation and financing of strikes' (Swenson 1991: 517). At the same time they effectively centralized their own interest organizations.

This development was further strengthened by the political compromises negotiated between social democratic and agrarian parties in the 1930s (Castles 1978; Katzenstein 1985). In Denmark, the Kanslergade Agreement of 1933 initiated the position of the Social Democratic Party as the 'natural' party of government. The Agrarian Party backed the Social Democratic Party in its struggle against an employers' lockout, which tried to enforce a 20 per cent wage cut throughout the economy. The government, however, launched a job creation programme, large-scale agricultural subsidies and compensated the employers with a 10 per cent devaluation of the Danish crown (Esping-Andersen 1985: 74–5). In Sweden the Social Democrats became the major party in parliament after the 1932 elections and they could also rely on the backing of the Agrarian Party, which joined the government in 1936. As in Denmark, the red-green alliance in Sweden was based on a compromise of agrarian subsidies, deficit-financed employment programmes, and a devaluation of the national currency (Notermans 1993: 154–5). In both countries, left-centre governments intervened directly in the labour market to support the employers' goal of centralised labour relations and to prevent conflicts on the labour market. Additionally, labour market parties were increasingly incorporated into the process of policy formulation and implementation (Meijer 1967; Rothstein 1996). Additionally, unemployment funds in both countries were and still are managed by trade unions, which helps to explain their high density ratios (Rothstein 1992).

After the Second World War the welfare state in Denmark and Sweden expanded and the 'Scandinavian model' gradually emerged (Esping-Andersen 1985; Milner 1996). The first steps towards universalism were taken with the pension reforms of 1948 (Sweden) and 1956 (Denmark). Universal coverage and flat-rate benefits without means-testing were the cornerstones of these reforms. In 1959 Sweden added earnings-related benefits to the universalistic model of social security. The ATP pension plan, mainly designed by the LO, was the most controversial policy reform until the introduction of the wage earner funds in 1983 (see below, p. 123). Corporatist policy formulation crashed as the employers fiercely opposed the principle of collectively controlled pension funds. However, with the backing of a public referendum and because one Liberal Party member was persuaded to abstain from the final vote on the bill, the reform was finally ratified (Esping-Andersen 1985: 161–3). In the 1960s, the Danish LO proposed the introduction of a Swedish-style public superannuation scheme. However, it failed because the Danish Social Democrats lacked a political majority and were internally divided on this issue. The government then introduced generous tax provisions to encourage, in particular, salaried employees to invest in private arrangements. Indeed, from a Nordic perspective, the Danes actually spend most on private pensions (Kangas and Palme 1989; Overbye 1996). But in all Nordic countries, even in Denmark, this two-fold principle of social policy was extended to most other programmes such as sick pay, unemployment and accident insurance (Esping-Andersen 1985: 164). Hence, the main pillars of the Nordic welfare state – flat-rate security for all without means testing and on top of that earnings-graduated benefits – were erected in the 1960s.

Performance

In the 1970s, the 'dream of never-ending prosperity' ended nevertheless. Danish and Swedish governments tried – as governments in other countries did too – to bridge the crisis. However, at the beginning of the 1980s, governments in both countries decided to change their major policies. What they decided to do, how they tried to realize their goals and whether and how corporatist politics was able to adapt, is discussed on pp. 123–34. First an overview of the economic and political performance of both countries is provided.

The overall economic performance of both countries contains similarities as well as differences (Table 5.1). First, in respect of economic growth, both countries remain in the low-growth group of OECD countries, and until the early 1990s both countries had to struggle with low growth rates. However, in the 1990s, Denmark managed to improve its performance and is now in the upper half of the OECD-countries, whereas Sweden still suffers from low economic growth. In both countries, inflation was rather high in the period from 1960 until the late 1980s. In Denmark, the shift towards low inflation and – one should add – a hard-currency policy, was successfully achieved in the 1990s. In contrast, inflation in Sweden remains high, as significant wage increases fuel inflation despite high unemployment and the most severe economic crisis since the 1930s (for the reasons, see below). As to investments, both countries perform poorly throughout the whole period and Denmark especially suffered from low domestic investment in the 1990s: it recorded the lowest investment rate throughout the OECD. But in contrast to Sweden, Denmark did not have to tackle huge outflows of investment capital in the 1980s. The outflow of investment capital from Sweden was only exceeded by the Netherlands. Hence, taken as a whole, economic performance in both countries has not been impressive. Until the late 1980s, both countries combined low economic growth with comparatively high inflation and weak investment. In the 1990s, Denmark managed to significantly improve its performance on at least the first two indicators.

As can be seen further from Table 5.2, government consumption is high in both countries. In the early 1990s Sweden and Denmark had the highest government final consumption in relation to economic output among the OECD countries. On social security expenditures as a percentage of GDP Sweden is only surpassed by Belgium and the Netherlands in the 1990s. However, the trend in the Nordic countries had been upward in the decades before.

Table 5.1 Economic performance in Denmark and Sweden (in percentages)

	Denmark	Rank[a]	Sweden	Rank[a]
GDP–Growth				
1960–1972	4.4	15	4.1	19
1973–1982	1.7	21	1.8	20
1983–1989	2.4	18	2.5	16
1990–1995	2.1	10	0.4	22
Inflation (cpi)				
1960–1972	5.6	21	4.5	14
1973–1982	10.8	12	10.0	11
1983–1989	5.0	10	6.4	15
1990–1995	2.1	2	5.3	19
Domestic investments (as % of GDP)				
1965–1972	24.6	16	24.4	17
1973–1982	21.0	20	20.4	21
1983–1989	18.7	20	19.0	19
1990–1994	15.6	23	16.7	20
Investment flows (as % of GDP)				
Capital inflows				
1982–1993	0.5	14	0.8	8
Capital outflows				
1982–1993	0.9	8	2.7	19

Sources: OECD, *Historical Statistics*, various issues; IMF 1995; OECD 1995.

Notes

[a] Rank of the two countries in comparison to 20 to 23 OECD countries for which data is available. Rank No. 1 is for highest GDP growth, lowest inflation rate, highest domestic investment, highest investment capital inflows and lowest investment capital outflows.

As regards the funding of the welfare state both countries differ, especially in the importance of employers' contributions. In Denmark the financial burden placed on the employers is rather light. It has been the lowest in comparison to twenty-one OECD countries in the 1990s. In Sweden on the other hand the employers' share has increased significantly since the late 1970s and ranks in 1990 at the top of all OECD countries. In Denmark the greatest share has to be borne by the employees or is funded by taxes.

Performance on the labour market reveals a somewhat different picture. In respect of unemployment, Sweden performed well until 1990, whereas in Denmark unemployment had already begun to rise to a comparatively high level in the 1970s. But if we take the development of employment into consideration, the pictures changes. Here, Denmark's performance is very

Table 5.2 Public finances and the welfare state in Denmark and Sweden

	Denmark	Rank[a]	Sweden	Rank[a]
Government final consumption (% of GDP)				
1960–1972	17.3	3	19.1	1
1973–1982	24.9	2	26.8	1
1983–1989	25.6	2	27.1	1
1990–1995	25.4	2	27.2	1
Social security spending (% of GDP)				
1960–1972	9.3	9	9.8	8
1973–1982	14.7	9	16.3	7
1983–1989	16.9	7	18.5	5
1990–1995	20.2	7	22.9	3
Employers' social security contributions (% of GDP)				
1965	0.5	20	3.1	9
1970	0.4	20	4.7	8
1975	0.3	21	8.0	5
1980	0.3	21	13.5	1
1985	0.9	20	11.9	2
1990	0.3	21	14.5	1

Sources: OECD, *Historical Statistics*, various issues; OECD, *Revenue Statistics*, various issues.

Notes
[a] Rank of the two countries in comparison to 20 or 23 OECD countries for which data was available. Rank No. 1 is for highest government final consumption, highest social security transfers and highest share of employers' social security contributions.

good, and indeed, the high unemployment performance in Denmark was not caused by sharply shrinking employment, but by an increase in the labour supply in the 1970s and 1980s (Jochem 2000). In contrast, employment in Sweden decreased dramatically in the early 1990s, and the decline of employment was higher only in Finland. With these qualifications, Sweden performed better on the labour market until 1993. Thereafter the situations reverse. Unemployment decreased sharply in Denmark whereas in Sweden unemployment rates increased and seem to persist, and even now, employment is increasing slightly in Denmark and stagnating in Sweden.

Public sector employment has been high in both countries as has been spending on active labour market policies, but in Sweden, government employment decreased in the early 1990s – as a consequence of the policies implemented by the centre-right government – but remained fairly stable in Denmark even under centre-right governments. Taken together, it seems as if Denmark was able to accomplish a major transition on the labour market whereas Sweden lost its nimbus as the main model for the social democratic way to full employment.

Table 5.3 Labour market performance in Denmark and Sweden

	Denmark	Rank[a]	Sweden	Rank[a]
Unemployment rates				
1960–1972	1.7	8	1.6	7
1973–1982	6.5	16	2.1	7
1983–1989	7.5	12	2.4	4
1990–1995	8.7	14	5.4	6
Employment rates				
1960–1972	72.5	3	72.4	4
1973–1982	73.2	4	77.5	1
1983–1989	75.9	4	79.9	1
1990–1995	74.9	4	75.4	3
Government employment/total employment)				
1982–1995	30.4	2	32.1	1
Expenditure active labour market policies(/% of GDP)				
1985–1995	1.5	2	2.3	1

Sources: OECD, *Employment Outlook*, various issues, OECD, *Historical Statistics*, various issues.

Notes
[a] Rank of the two countries in comparison to 20 or 23 OECD countries for which data was available. Rank No. 1 is for lowest unemployment rates in commonly used definitions, highest employment share in % of population between 15 and 64 years, highest share of government employment in relation to total employment and highest spending for active labour market policies in relation to GDP.

Political relations and resources in the 1980s and 1990s

Finally, a short overview of the development of the distribution of political power resources and external challenges will be given (cf. for details Jochem 1998). As mentioned, conservative parties were in the position, for the first time since the Second World War, to lead coalition governments in both countries: between 1982 and 1993 in Denmark and between 1991 and 1994 in Sweden. However, the absolute decline of the social democratic parties was only modest in the 1990s, and they were again able to increase their share of the vote and form governments in Denmark after 1993 and in Sweden after 1994.

Trade union density ratios are exceptionally high in both countries. In Denmark, the density ratio declined somewhat in the 1980s but remained nevertheless at a high level. In Sweden, density ratios increased in the 1980s and even in the 1990s (SCB 1997: 335). Hence, the labour movements in both countries have not experienced a significant decline of their power resources. However, the labour movement has become more heterogeneous. The main blue collar confederations have lost their monopoly in the trade union movement (Lange *et al.* 1995), while white collar unions and professional associations have gradually been able to increase their share of organized labour since the 1970s. As a result, an internal shift of resources in the labour movement has occurred in both countries. The traditionally dominant blue collar unions had to tackle declining represent-ation on the labour market. However, overall the labour movement still commanded large power resources, despite increasing globalization. As Swank (1998) shows, in all four Scandinavian countries the trend towards globalization – measured by capital mobility and international financial integration – increased in the 1980s and the Nordic countries in fact followed the international trend.

Changes in government marked the beginning of new political eras in both countries. In Denmark, a conservative Prime Minister – the first since 1920 – was elected in 1982. In total, Poul Schlüter led five bourgeois coalitions up to 1993, all of which, however, lacked a parliamentary majority. Following this, Poul Nyrup Rasmussen formed – for the first time since the early 1960s – a cross-class coalition covering the Social Democrats and three centre parties. However, the Kristelig Folkeparti left the government in 1994, as did the Centrum Democraterne in 1996. Since then, and after the election in 1998, the Social Democrats govern together with the liberal Radiakale Venstre without a parliamentary majority. In Sweden, the Social Democrats were able to regain power in 1982 after six years of bourgeois governance. Olof Palme – and after his assassination in 1986 Ingvar Carlsson – governed until 1991, and the conservative Prime Minister Carl Bildt led a coalition government until 1994, which was replaced by a Social Democratic minority government, led by Ingvar Carlsson and after 1996 by Göran Persson.

Nonetheless, both countries started from different points of departure and policy inheritance was in reality quite different. In Denmark high and persistent unemployment in combination with high inflation, high and rising public debt and a serious deterioration in the balance of payments in the 1970s created a sense of crisis. The attempts of the various Social Democratic governments to strengthen policy coordination failed and wage growth accelerated by up to 20 per cent per annum. As a consequence and in order to regain competitiveness for the Danish export industry, Danish governments resorted to a series of devaluations. Between 1976 and 1979, the Danish currency was depreciated in total by around 26 per cent in relation to the German mark (Nannestad 1998). Hence, the centre-right government which came into power in 1982 announced its intention to break up the vicious cycle of economic failures. However, Prime Minister Schlüter did not try to achieve the major goals '*tutto et subito*' but he adopted the catch phrase of 'the long, thorough haul' (cited by Nannestad 1998).

In Sweden, the centre-right coalitions of the 1970s and early 1980s did not even try to retrench the welfare state or implement major deviations from the Social Democratic policy inheritance. Quite the opposite, welfare policies followed the Social Democratic mould: to manage the economic crisis of the late 1970s, the centre-right governments implemented counter-cyclical fiscal policies, increased active labour market policies, depreciated the Swedish currency several times, and did nothing to cut back public employment or social spending. The result was low unemployment but high inflation and rise in public debt, as the governments refused to increase taxes in order to finance the rising public spending (Esping-Andersen 1985; Scharpf 1991; Milner 1989).

Swedish corporatism in crisis

Wage bargaining

The incoming Swedish government in 1982 launched a policy of the 'third way' (Feldt 1991; Pontusson 1992b) which stood between the reflationary experiences of France in the early 1980s and the deflationary strategy in Great Britain at the same time. This policy of the 'third way' was introduced with a major devaluation in 1982. This measure was intended to improve the profitability of the export industry which in turn was dependent on continual wage moderation.

However, already by 1980 the fragility of the hitherto consensual wage bargaining system was demonstrated, as a great labour market conflict paralysed the economy. The competition between public and private sector unions undermined the role of LO and SAF as pace setters in the wage bargaining process (Elvander 1988: 50–4). To assure labour quiescence, the Social Democratic government implemented wage earner funds – despite opposition within the party – with the backing of the Left Party (Pontusson 1992a: 186–219). These funds initiated the collapse of corporatist policy making – for the first time since the pension reform of 1959 (Fulcher 1991: 281). SAF opposed the wage earner funds, seeing them as the first step towards socialization of the private economy (De Geer 1992: 174). The increasing tensions culminated in the break-down of centralized wage bargaining in 1983. For the first time since 1956, no central wage agreement could be reached. Actors in the manufacturing industry accepted moderate wage growth, but this was undermined by high wage increases in the public sector. In 1985, the government cut back its efforts to coordinate wage bargaining, as the so-called 'Rosenbad Agreements' had proven to be ineffective in curbing wage growth.

As can be seen from Figure 5.1, annual wage growth accelerated after 1985, and in the late 1980s wages rose by more than 10 per cent per annum. Indeed, the gains from the devaluation in 1982 melted away, and the LO clamoured for a further depreciation of the national currency in the late 1980s, but in contrast to 1982, the government refused to correct excessive wage growth this way (Mjøset 1996: 23). In globalized financial markets the leeway for using the national currency as a policy instrument

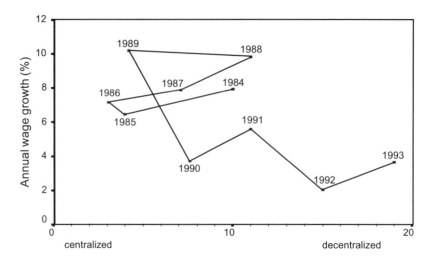

Figure 5.1 Wage growth and centralization of the wage bargaining system in
        Sweden, 1984–93.

Sources: Iversen 1996b; SAF 1996, own calculations.

Note: The degree of wage bargaining centralization is adapted from Iversen (1996b), who
provides data only until 1993.

has been reduced, and hence, large wage increases of the 1980s were one
major cause of the sharp decline of employment in the early 1990s (Jochem
2000).

Partly as a consequence of this, Swedish employers vehemently opposed
centralized wage bargaining in the late 1980s. In 1990, SAF shut down its
bargaining and statistics unit, which made it impossible to coordinate wage
bargaining on the employers' side, and withdrew its representatives from
the corporatist bodies of policy formulation and implementation (Iversen
1996a: 422; Pontusson and Swenson 1996: 229). Rothstein (1994), however,
was rather optimistic that this step would not have been the final death
blow to corporatism in Sweden, as representatives of the employers were
still engaged in corporatist bodies, albeit not as representatives of the SAF.
In fact, in 1997, an attempt to minimize labour market conflicts was made
(EIRO Observer 2/1997: 8), but wages are still highly volatile. Annual wage
growth in the mid-1990s was high from a comparative point of view and
wage drift remained a major problem (SAF 1997a: 29–37; OECD 1996:
35). This, despite the most serious economic crisis and the highest unemployment records since the 1930s, and in spite of a pronounced decentralization of wage bargaining (Figure 5.1)

As a result, the powerful SAF (van Waarden 1995) managed successfully to
dismantle coordinated wage bargaining and corporatist policy implement-

ation. It has been trying further to achieve its goal of a radically de-institutionalized labour market (SAF 1997b), which in turn provoked fierce opposition from the labour movement. At the time of writing, only a few attempts to reach a new *modus vivendi* between labour and capital can be discerned (Wallerstein and Golden 1997; Iversen 1996a). On the labour market, SAF could successfully dismantle corporatist consensus.

Welfare state reform

Social policies in the 1980s followed the main trajectories of the Swedish welfare state but welfare spending was consolidated at a high level. Public employment stagnated until 1990, and social spending increased only slightly (Table 5.2). There was an agreement between the Social Democratic government and the LO that the welfare state had reached its limits in the 1980s and that no further expansion would be aimed at (Stephens 1996: 44). However, in the light of the economic crisis that followed, things changed dramatically. In the first half of the 1990s many reforms were implemented.

Table 5.4 lists the most important social policy changes in Sweden between 1982 and 1997. Most changes occurred in the early 1990s in connection with the currency crisis. The centre-right government and the Social Democratic opposition agreed on several crisis packages in order to relax tensions on the capital markets. The overall direction was to cut benefits, introduce waiting days – as in the field of sickness and unemployment insurance – and to increase the share of employees in the funding of welfare state programmes. Both centre-right and Social Democratic governments cut social spending in most branches. However, after 1994 the Social Democrats increased spending on higher education – partly in order to take the pressure off the labour market – and they extended unemployment benefits despite criticism by the employers and the opposition. The overall amount of welfare state reforms is quite impressive. Lindbeck states that the 'Swedish Model has been in a state of great flux during the last decade'. He reports that over 300 rules of the social insurance system were changed between 1991 and 1996 (Lindbeck 1997: 1314). Can we conclude from this that the Swedish welfare state showed a high capacity to adapt, and have these reforms been made through concertation? As I will argue below, the many reforms of the Swedish welfare state have been the product of stop-and-go policies, and of increased party competition without effective corporatism.

The pension reform was the most impressive change in the Swedish welfare state initiated in the 1990s. The Social Democratic government had already appointed an Official Commission to investigate possible policy reforms in 1984. The final report was published in 1990 and identified various problems, for example the weak link between contributions and benefits which undermined popular acceptance. However, it could not

Table 5.4 Major welfare state reforms in Sweden

	Year	Reform
Pensions	1991	Abolishment of early retirement for labour market reasons by Social Democrats
	1992	Reduction of base amount and as a consequence reduced pension transfers
	1993	Reduction of employers' contribution by 4.5 percentage points
	1994–1999	Major pension reform of supplementary old-age pension (ATP), many new dimensions (cf. text below)
Unemployment	1991–1994	Reduction of unemployment benefits (from 90% to finally 75%), introduction of five waiting days by centre-right government
	1994	The centre-right government introduced obligatory unemployment insurance which was to be administered by the state and not by the trade unions – the Social Democratic Government reversed this reform the same year
	1994	Employees have to contribute to the financing of unemployment insurance
	1995	Changed funding of unemployment funds, the state covers nearly 100% of total costs
	1997	General and unified unemployment insurance (enhanced integration for those who are not members of the unemployment insurance funds); trade unions still administer the unemployment insurance funds; upgrading of unemployment benefits to 80%
Sickness/health care	1990	Reduction of sickness benefits by Social Democratic government
	1992	Introduction of one waiting day and significant reduction of transfers (throughout the 1990s); the employers have to bear the costs of the first fourteen days of sickness which is compensated for by a significant reduction in employers' social contributions
	1993	Employees have to contribute to the financing of the National Health Service (expanded in 1996 and 1997)
	1993	Introduction of family doctors
	1997	The employers have to cover the costs of the first four weeks of sickness, only partial compensation by reduced contributions

Table 5.4 (continued)

	Year	Reform
Education	early 1990s	The Social Democratic as well as the centre-right governments extended the leeway for private schools
	early 1990s	The centre-right government reduced the efforts for adult education, existing schemes to be targeted to the labour market
	1994	The Social Democratic government introduced a significant extension of higher education, huge increase of transfers to universities after 1994

Sources: Edelbalk *et al.* 1998; NOSOSCO, various issues; Ploug and Kvist 1996; Schludi 1997; SOU 2000.

present any concrete policy proposals. The Bildt government set up a new committee in 1991, made up only of representatives from parties in parliament. Labour market organizations were explicitly excluded from the negotiations (Andersen 1998: 19). The major economic crisis forced the Social Democratic opposition – despite internal pressures to defect from the committee – to participate and finally to support the reform. This introduced four major changes. First, ATP benefits would be based on lifetime earnings instead of the best fifteen years. Second, pension contributions would be split evenly between employers and employees, Third, benefits were to be linked to economic growth instead of inflation. Fourth, pension rights would be shared by spouses and pension points could be earned for military service, care of small children and higher education. The reform was approved by the Riksdag in 1994 but implementation was delayed until 1999. The trade unions opposed the reform, mainly because of the principle of life-time earnings, which, as was argued, discriminated against women who took time off to care for children and against white collar workers with longer education periods. Employers were more or less satisfied, but demanded that employees should contribute more to their pensions and complained that the reform might fuel wage growth, as the reform proposal stated that employees should be compensated for their contributions by increased wages. As the pension contributions should be in total 18.5 per cent, the employers would be expected to raise wages by 9 per cent, which was forcefully opposed by the SAF (Anderson 1998; Gould 1997; Stephens 1997; Swank 1998). Taken together, the Swedish pension reform was a departure from the Swedish Model. Party competition and fragile cross-class alliances, not corporatism, enabled such a reform. The window for reform was opened up by the economic crisis, and by the strategy of the Social Democratic Party, which backed the reform in the face of criticism from the trade unions. Hence, politics was rooted in party competition and could prove to be rather volatile – as can also be seen from the reforms of unemployment insurance.

Until the recession in the early 1990s unemployment insurance had not been a target for reform. Unemployment was quite low and the unemployment funds – administered by the trade unions – were financially sound. However, with the rise in unemployment the financial situation of the funds deteriorated. The bourgeois government reacted with benefits cuts, the introduction of waiting days and delayed adjustments of benefits. Against the opposition of the trade unions, the centre-right government relied on the backing of the Social Democratic party to cut benefits. However, the Bildt government also wanted to diminish union power and therefore tried to end union monopoly over unemployment insurance funds. A commission – without the participation of interest groups – prepared the dismantling of this major pillar of trade union strength in Sweden. With some modifications parliament passed the reform bill in 1994 with the support of the populist New Democracy. Trade unions and the Social Democratic Party forcefully opposed the reform and SAP promised to reverse this legislation if returned to office, which it actually did in 1994, immediately after the change in government. Concurrent with the reform bill in 1994, the centre-right government restricted the possibility of re-qualification for benefits through participation in active labour market schemes. In collaboration with the Left Party the new Social Democratic government returned to the 'old system' even in this perspective – true to the 'never-ending carousel'.

Despite all this, a reform of unemployment insurance was still on the political agenda. In 1995 coordination between the government and the Left Party broke down in a dispute over restrictions of benefits for young people. Subsequently the Social Democratic government collaborated with the Centre Party, the first cross-class collaboration since the 1970s. This created room for further reforms. In 1995, the labour market fund was abolished, unemployment benefits are now nearly totally financed out of tax revenues, and the SAP has declared that unemployment insurance should be a 'temporary adjustment insurance', i.e. benefits should not be paid indefinitely. SAP formed an Official Commission of Inquiry – the ABROM commission, which was in fact a one-person operation, headed by Birgitta Isaksson-Perez – which was to evaluate options for reform. In October 1996 the report was published. LO opposed the limitation of benefits to 600 days, and TCO opposed stricter qualifying rules and restricted benefits for university students. Consequently, the government created a new commission, now with both LO and Centre Party representatives – but without those of TCO or SACO, the white collar unions. This new commission came up with a half-hearted compromise: benefits were to be upgraded to 80 per cent of qualifying income and the time limit would in principle remain, but would not be implemented until another commission worked out specific proposals. This could first occur after the year

2000. Thus, cooperation between SAP and LO was far from being intact, as LO was able to block a major policy reform successfully and SAP only agreed to postpone the reform, hoping that an improvement in the labour market might reduce the saliency of that issue (Anderson 1998).

Taken together, the re-regulation of the unemployment and pension insurance systems have both been major issues in the 1990s. Several changes have occurred, but as exemplified in 1994, party competition is the major determinant of policy formulation and implementation. Interest organisations are in most cases excluded from policy communities, and if this is not the case, the governments are very selective about who gets access to the process of policy formulation. The centre-right governments relied mainly on the employers, the Social Democratic government mainly on the LO. Hence policy reform is a matter of power mobilisation within the various political camps. There have been only a few attempts to include interest organizations from both labour and capital. Given the Westminster type of the Swedish state, party competition is the major game in town and the outcome may be volatile policies. On the labour market, interest organizations from capital as well as labour could not successfully rebuild a peaceful *modus vivendi*. The employers still oppose coordinated wage bargaining and the funding system of the Swedish welfare state. Hence the welfare state itself has become a major cause of declining concertation, and SAF is a driving force in attempts to retrench the Swedish welfare state.

Danish corporatism – from crisis to success

Denmark entered the 1980s with huge problems: unemployment was over 10 per cent, public debt had soared and the current account of balance of payments was in the red. To counter these, the incoming centre-right government announced major policy changes. In the first place the government pegged the Danish crown to the German mark and announced that the government would not implement further devaluations in order to correct for wage increases. Second, in order to contain inflation, the government first suspended and then abolished automatic cost of living adjustments for wages and for some social security transfers in 1986 (Table 5.5, below). In doing this, the government followed the Danish employers' federation's (DA) line, drawing harsh criticism from the trade unions. Third, to contain public debt, the government launched several initiatives to cut public spending. However, in this case, only modest reductions were achieved and after 1986 public spending increased again slightly. Fourth, the government began to deregulate the Danish capital market. As a member state of the EU, several steps had already been undertaken in the 1970s, but in the 1980s it became a major goal of the government to actively abolish restrictions on the capital market (Mjøset 1996).

Wage bargaining and incomes policy

By far the most controversial issue was incomes policy. The suspension of the indexing clauses and the overall uncertainty about the future of the Danish welfare state instigated the trade unions to protest against the centre-right government. Several strikes were organized by private and public sector unions. In 1985 the most comprehensive strike since the Second World War blocked the whole economy. The LO tried to reach a central agreement which the DA rejected. Eventually the government intervened and imposed minor wage increases by law on the whole economy until 1987. As a supplementary bonus the working week was reduced to 39 hours. Trade unions reacted again with fierce strikes as they now saw their bargaining autonomy challenged. However, this could not prevent state intervention and in the end the trade unions stepped back. This conflict can be considered a watershed in the history of the Danish labour market. In the second half of the 1980s the wage bargaining system was gradually decentralized and, thus, the DA could finally reach its goal. As can be seen from Figure 5.2, wages declined significantly after 1986 and the wage bargaining system was decentralized step by step.

The interventionist incomes policy coincided with a downturn in the Danish economy. After 1985 the 'Schlüter-Boom' (Mjøset 1996: 15) faded

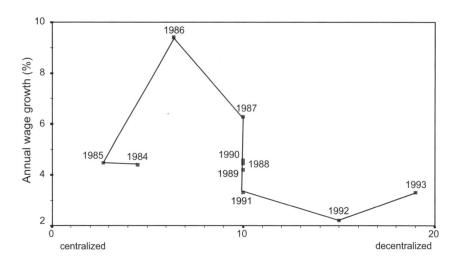

Figure 5.2 Wage growth and centralization of the wage bargaining system in Denmark, 1984–93.

Sources: Iversen 1996b; SAF 1996, own calculations.

Note: The degree of wage bargaining centralization is adapted from Iversen (1996b), who provides data only until 1993.

away and the government reacted with contractive measures, the so-called 'potato-cure' (Nannestad 1998). The government introduced green taxes, reduced the lending leeway for private banks, and implemented a comprehensive personal income tax reform which was passed with the consent of the Social Democrats in 1987. In this reform package the government reduced marginal tax rates, broadened the tax base and reduced the tax-deductibility of interest on private loans and mortgages. The last measure caused severe problems on the housing market, as the owners of new buildings were confronted with higher interest payments. However, the government was able to stop the 'financial bonanza' (Mjøset 1996: 21) – caused by the deregulation of the Danish capital market and the upswing in the international economy in the early 1980s – at an early stage. Hence the Danish government successfully changed the fundamental policy targets early in the 1980s. A hard-currency policy, a low inflation policy and a tight fiscal policy were the corner-stones of a so-called 'norm based' economic policy in Denmark.

Despite the upsurge in conflicts in 1985, the politics of compromise came to be rebuilt and – perhaps surprisingly – the employers took the first step. The Danish employers interpreted wage drift as the main problem in wage bargaining. In order to minimize such wage drift the employers in the metal industry supported more internal coordination in their camp. After a power struggle the Metal Industry Employers and the Industrial Trades Association merged and formed the Industrial Employers (IA). This new association represented nearly 50 per cent of the wage sum of DA's member organizations, which caused a 'major shift in the balance of power in DA' (Due *et al.* 1994: 204). The organizational system was further centralized when in 1991 the IA merged with the Industrirådet, which represented the economic interests of Danish employers. This centralization of the associational system of employers in the early 1990s went hand in hand with an increase in the density ratio of employers (Jochem 1998). Indeed, the Danish employers followed a strategy of 'Centralized Decentralization' (Due *et al.* 1994) or 'Organized Decentralization' (Traxler 1995; Schmitter and Grote, this volume). A decentralization of the wage bargaining system was combined with internal centralization, which enhanced the capacity of employers to bind their member-associations and member-firms to agreements. This desire was the driving force behind centralization; as one actor stated: 'The parties [on the labour market] must not only be capable of concluding collective agreements; they must also be capable of ensuring that the agreements are duly observed' (cited in Due *et al.* 1994: 210).

With some delay the trade unions reacted in a similar vein. In the late 1980s and early 1990s a major restructuring occurred in the trade union movement. The unions in the export-oriented sector took the first steps. Several unions amalgamated and the bargaining units were reorganized. Bargaining was henceforth divided over several cartels. This enabled viable coordination despite an official decentralization of wage bargaining

(Due *et al.* 1994: 211–21). Thus the strategies of employers and trade unions helped to minimize wage drift and paved the way for moderate wage increases (OECD 1997a: 25).

Welfare state reforms

The centre-right government avoided open conflicts after 1985. Instead, it launched several programmes to re-strengthen consensus on the labour market (Amin and Thomas 1996). Furthermore it implemented a major reform of the public sector (Mjøset 1996: 21) and expanded public spending moderately after 1986. Only minor cut-backs in social programmes were made beyond the changed indexations (Table 5.5, below). The most drastic change, the abolition of the automatic cost-of-living adjustments, already occurred in the early 1980s. In later years the government followed again an expansionary policy. It extended early retirement schemes in the late 1980s to dampen the pressure on the labour market. And it began to invest more in education and training, which further reduced labour supply.

In the late 1980s the Social Democratic opposition set up several commissions with participants from both capital and labour (Amin and Thomas 1996). Their main goal was to find ways to strengthen Danish industry and to enhance investment. Hence, when the Social Democratic Party regained power after 1993 in coalition with othere centre parties, the new government could build on wide experiences in trying to combine divergent goals and strategies of trade unions and employers' organizations.

One of the first measures was an encompassing labour market reform in 1994 (Lind 1994; Loftager and Madsen 1997). This covered four aspects: First, employees and – with a minor share – employers had henceforth to contribute to funding labour market policies. Second, active labour market schemes were expanded and mainly targeted at long-term unemployed. Third, the benefit period was initially limited to seven and after 1996 to five years (OECD 1997b: 31). It was divided into a so-called 'benefit period' – originally the first two years, which was stepwise reduced in the next years – and an 'activation period', in which the unemployed had the right to get and the obligation to take further training and education. Fourth, the reform introduced three paid leave schemes, which were extensively used after 1994: child care leave, educational leave and sabbatical leave. Danish women lengthened their maternity leave with child care leave, and, consequently, many women left the labour market after 1994. From 1996 on, the government reduced financial transfers from 80 per cent to 60 per cent of unemployment benefits, partly as a consequence of the success of the paid leave schemes. Hence, until the end of the 1990s, participation in these schemes declined gradually (OECD 1999: 29). Overall, the labour market reform was a major reform project, coming out of the work of the 'welfare commissions' in 1993 and 1995, which reached a broad consensus to – as it is called – 'activate' social policy.

Table 5.5 Major welfare state reforms in Denmark

	Year	Reform
Pensions	1984	Expansion of early retirement schemes
	1984	Introduction of means testing in pension schemes for those aged between 67 and 70
	1986	Further expansion of early retirement scheme (part-time retirement)
	1988	Regulation of transfers in accordance with wage developments for workers
	1994	Old age-pension became dependent on other income (introduction of means-testing for all pensioners)
Unemployment	1982–1986	Adjustment of transfers to cost of living developments suspended and finally abolished
	1988	Regulation of transfers in accordance with wage developments for workers
	1989/1993	Employers have to bear the costs for the first day/the first two days of unemployment
	1993	Encompassing labour market reform and introduction of three leave schemes (cf. detailed description in the text)
Sickness/health care	1982–1986	Adjustment of transfers to cost of living developments suspended and finally abolished
	1988	Regulation of transfers in accordance with wage developments for workers
	1990	Employers have to finance first two weeks of illness alone, reduction of benefit period, expansion of rehabilitation measures
Education	1989	Upgrading of adult education and training, extension of grants to compensate for earnings losses
	1993	'Education for all' – strategy introduced which focuses mainly on vocational training for the youth
	1994	Enhanced expansion of universities and further upgrading of student grant system
	1996	Compulsory education for unemployed youths without vocational education

Sources: Albæck *et al.* (1998); Andersen (2000); NOSOSCO (various issues); Ploug and Kvist (1996).

A second pillar of this activation policy was an extension of educational opportunities. First steps had already been undertaken in 1989, when the centre-right government expanded adult education and training. However, after 1993, the 'education for all' strategy (*Uddannelse Til Alle*) was launched. Vocational training was expanded and in 1994 so was university education. The centre-left government increased direct transfers towards the universities and upgraded the grant system. Denmark now has one of the most extensive grant systems in the OECD area, in which roughly 70 per cent of all students receive government loans (OECD 1997a: 88). As a consequence, between 1985 and 1995, the number of students enrolled increased by 79 per cent. These measures reduced the pressure on the labour market via an impressive reduction in the labour supply. In addition, the agreement of the social partners on such an active strategy might in the long run help to increase labour market chances for the participants. Indeed, Denmark has – in a comparative perspective – gone a long way on the 'social investment strategy' road (Esping-Andersen 1996: 14).

Taken together, the Danish reforms represent a clear case of consensual adaptation of institutions and policies. Changes on the labour market have been quite impressive. Decentralization of wage bargaining was coupled with increasing coordination within the capital and labour camps, which diminished wage competition. After 1993, major labour market reforms successfully reduced unemployment – to a great extent by a reduction of the labour force supply. However, the welfare state remained relatively unchanged. Neither the centre-right nor the centre-left government introduced major cutbacks of welfare state programmes. On the contrary, after 1985 programmes were even expanded. And as Scharpf (1996: 135) points out, in contrast to other Continental European countries, Denmark has not had a *Standortdebatte*. How can this be explained? Why has there been no major welfare state retrenchment in Denmark?

One reason could be that party competition in Denmark did not exclude cross-class coalitions, which may have induced rather consensual reforms (cf. Green-Pedersen 1999). Further, employers in Denmark bear only a minor share of welfare state funding and so their willingness to cooperate in welfare state reforms may have been higher than in Sweden. In other words, unlike in Sweden, employers did not see the Danish welfare state and its funding system as obstacles to minimizing wage growth or to a reorganization of the wage bargaining process. That might explain why the welfare state did not become a target for retrenchment in Denmark.

Conclusion

What happened to Nordic corporatism and welfare state programmes in the 1980s and 1990s? Denmark and Sweden followed different paths. In Sweden, policy concertation between capital, labour, and the state decreased, whereas Denmark experienced a corporatist renaissance. Apart from the fact that cross-class alliances in Denmark were promoted through minority coalitions in the 1980s, which had to rely on collaboration with the major opposition party (the Social Democratic Party), the difference between both countries may be further explained by the different strategies of the employers' associations. Danish employers reorganised their associations and were able to increase internal coordination, which might well be a decisive precondition for cross-class concertation. By contrast, Swedish employers not only dismantled corporatist institutions, but also suffered from declining internal cohesion. This manifested itself in 1990 as the SAF closed down the wage bargaining unit and moved towards becoming a powerful pressure group, which no longer saw itself as an organization for disciplining employers. Hence, seen over a longer period of time, the employers' strategies have been decisive both in the early and in the late twentieth century.

The origins as well as the adaptations of concertation in both countries were initiated by reforms of the labour market. In Denmark the centre-right government successfully changed economic policy after 1982. It was able to modify some of the fundamentals and sources of conflict in the Danish welfare state, such as the cost of living adjustments for wages and social transfers. This policy was strongly opposed by labour, and, hence, these reforms were carried through only after major social conflicts. After 1985 no further social policy retrenchment occurred and the centre-right government actively tried to re-affirm cross-class collaboration. In accordance with the employers' strategies several proposals and reform projects were prepared. These changed relations allowed the subsequent Social Democratic government to introduce and expand a social policy of labour market 'activation'. The labour market reform of 1994 and the growth of education are the most prominent examples of this strategy.

Thus, the Danish case has indeed been like a 'bumblebee': The 'Danish welfare state is a theoretical impossibility that nevertheless does fly' (Albæck *et al.* 1998: 1). Despite the international trend of welfare state retrenchment, the Danish welfare state has changed only little and is still rather comprehensive – and expensive. Actually, the reforms of the 1990s have even expanded welfare state programmes. As argued in this contribution, the system of welfare state funding may have been of crucial importance. In Denmark employers bear only a moderate share of the costs of welfare state programmes – quite unlike Swedish employers, who from a comparative point of view bear the highest share. Hence, Danish employers opposed not so much the welfare state as they did the wage bargaining system, because of its inflationary performance. After the change to the foundations of the wage bargaining system the employers mounted no major opposition to welfare state programmes. However, discontent might come from the electorate and from the increasingly influential right-wing populist parties which attack the huge tax burden of Danish citizens.

In Sweden the reverse happened. The employers' social contributions and wage bargaining were major issues throughout the 1980s. Swedish employers not only wanted to deregulate the wage bargaining system – here they were successful – but also to retrench welfare state programmes, in order to minimize unit labour costs. The more so as the Social Democratic governments did not accept a change in the funding system in the 1980s – the employers' share increased even. This different funding system thus became a major source of opposition for Swedish employers.

In contrast to Denmark, in Sweden, major aspects of the welfare state changed after 1992, but cross-class collaboration has come to an all-time low. The reforms have not been subject to corporatist concertation. On the contrary, Swedish social policy has been determined largely by conflicting party competition. Given the frequent changes in government composition this has made for high volatility in social policy. The pension reform of 1994 might have been an exception but, as argued, even this reform was the outcome of party competition. It could only be carried through because of the major economic crisis in the early 1990s, which – for a short period of time – enabled cross-class cooperation between the Social Democratic and the Conservative Party. Interest organizations were not integrated in policy formulation.

What have been the causes for the shifting strategies of employers, and which one of the three possible explanations mentioned in the introduction might explain the developments in both countries? Globalization may have had some impact. The deregulation of the capital markets, a new hard-currency policy, increasing competition on world markets, and changing management philosophies may have induced employers to change their strategies. Given that large, export-oriented firms dominate the Swedish economy, this had a greater impact in Sweden than in Denmark, where small firms shape the industrial structure. However, as currency devaluations were no longer options for enhancing cost-competitiveness of export industries, employers in both countries tried to reduce the growth of unit labour costs. In Sweden this meant both wages and social security contributions, in Denmark, however, it meant only wages. Hence, Danish employers did not challenge the welfare state as much in order to adapt to the new incentives arising from increased globalization, whereas in Sweden employers challenged both centralized wage bargaining and the welfare state programmes. Because the Social Democratic governments of the 1980s refused to take action on these issues, corporatist concertation was undermined.

Globalization as a common trend for both countries was mediated by changing actor constellations and by the forms of party competition (Green-Pedersen 1999). The cleavage between public and private sector actors in Denmark was blocked by government interventions already in the early 1980s, whereas in Sweden this cleavage was a source of conflicts throughout the 1980s and 1990s. Additionally, the forms of party competition help to explain the divergent adaptations. While the bourgeois government in Denmark – because of its minority status – had to rely on collaboration with the Social Democratic Party, Swedish politics was shaped until the end of the 1990s by intense conflicts between the two political camps. Hence, taken together, the common challenges of globalization were differently tackled in Denmark and Sweden. Because of governmental interventions, cross-class party collaboration and the specific nature of funding the Danish welfare state, actors could more easily adapt and renegotiate the pillars of corporatism. It was a success story, which was much more difficult to imitate for Swedish actors. In fact, from the perspective of corporatist politics, Sweden seems to have moved towards politics and policies more common in countries belonging to the Westminster model, albeit with a still powerful labour movement.

References

Albæck, Erik, Leslie C. Eliason, Asbjørn Sonne Nørgaard and Herman S. Schwarz (eds) (1998) *Negotiated Adaptation: The Survival of the Danish Welfare State*, in press.

Amin, Ash and Damian Thomas (1996) 'The Negotiated Economy: State and Civic Institutions in Denmark', *Economy and Society*, 25: 255–81.

Andersen, Jørgen Goul (2000) 'Welfare Crisis and Beyond. Danish Welfare Policies in the 1980s and 1990s', in Stein Kuhnle (ed.) *Survival of the European Welfare State*, London and New York: Routledge.

Anderson, Karen M. (1998) 'Organized Labor, Policy Feedback, and Retrenchment in Swedish Pension and Unemployment Insurance', paper presented at the Eleventh International Conference of Europeanists, Baltimore, 26–28 February, 1998.

Armingeon, Klaus (1998) 'Globalisierung als Chance. Zwei Wege zur wohlfahrts-staatlichen Reform in den OECD-Ländern', Diskussionspapier für die Drei-Länder-Tagung in Wien, Juni 1998.

Castles, Francis G. (1978) *The Social Democratic Image of Society. A Study of the Achievements and Origins of Scandinavian Social Democracy in Comparative Perspective*, London: Routledge and Kegan Paul.

De Geer, Hans (1992) *The Rise and Fall of the Swedish Model. The Swedish Employers' Confederation, SAF, and Industrial Relations over Ten Decades*, Chichester: Carden.

Due, Jesper, Jørgen Steen Madsen, Carsten Strøby Jensen and Lars Kjerulf Petersen (1994) *The Survival of the Danish Model. A Historical Sociological Analysis of the Danish System of Collective Bargaining*, Copenhagen: Jurist og Økonomforbundets Forlag.

Edebalk, Per Gunnar, Ann-Charlotte Ståhlberg and Eskil Wadensjö (1998) *Socialförsäkringarna. Ett samhällsekonomiskt perspektiv*, Stockholm: SNS.

EIRO (European Industrial Relations Observatory) Observer 2/1998, internet version, <http://www.eiro.eurofound.ie/>, February 1998.

Elvander, Nils (1980) *Skandinavisk arbetarrörelse*, Stockholm: Liber.

Elvander, Nils (1988) *Den svenska modellen*, Stockholm: Allmänna Förlaget.

Esping-Andersen, Gøsta (1985) *Politics against Markets: The Social Democratic Road to Power*, Princeton: Princeton University Press.

Esping-Andersen, Gøsta (1996) 'Positive-Sum Solutions in a World of Trade-Offs?', in Esping-Andersen (ed.) *Welfare States in Transition. National Adaptations in Global Economies*, London: Sage, pp. 256–67.

Feldt, Kjell-Olof (1991) *Alla dessa dagar . . . i regeringen 1982–1990*, Stockholm: Norstedts.

Fulcher, James (1991) *Labour Movements, Employers, and the State: Conflict and Cooperation in Britain and Sweden*, Oxford: Clarendon Press.

Garrett, Geoffrey (1995) 'Capital Mobility, Trade, and the Domestic Politics of Economic Policy', *International Organization*, 49: 657–87.

Green-Pedersen, Christoffer (1999) 'Welfare State Retrenchment in Denmark and the Netherlands 1982–1998. The Role of Party Competition and Party Consensus', paper presented at the 11th SASE Conference, Madison, Wisconsin, 8–11 July 1999.

Hermansson, Jörgen (1993) *Politik som intressekamp. Parlamentarisk beslutsfattande och organiserade intressen i Sverige*, Stockholm: Norstedts.

IMF (International Montetary Fund) (1995) Y*earbook of Financial Statistics*, Washington DC: IMF.

Iversen, Torben (1996a) 'Power, Flexibility, and the Breakdown of Centralised Wage Bargaining. Denmark and Sweden in Comparative Perspective', *Comparative Politics*, 28: 399–436.

Iversen, Torben (1996b) 'Wage Bargaining, Hard Money, and Economic Performance: Theory and Evidence for Organized Market Economies', unpublished paper.

Jochem, Sven (1998) *Die skandinavischen Wege in die Arbeitslosigkeit. Kontinuität und Wandel der nordischen Beschäftigungspolitik im internationalen Vergleich, 1984–1994*, Opladen: Leske & Budrich (in press).

Jochem, Sven (2000) 'Nordic Labour Market Policies in Transition', *West European Politics*, 23/3 (July 2000): 115–38.

Kangas, Olli and Joakim Palme (1989) *Public and Private Pensions: The Scandinavian Countries in a Comparative Perspective*, Stockholm: Swedish Institute for Social Research.

Katzenstein, Peter J. (1985) *Small States in World Markets. Industrial Policy in Europe*, Ithaca and London: Cornell University Press.

Kjellberg, Anders (1992) 'Sweden: Can the Model Survive?', in Anthony Ferner and Richard Richard (eds) *Industrial Relations in the New Europe*, Oxford: Blackwell, pp. 88–142.

Lane, Jan-Erik (1995) 'The Decline of the Swedish Model', *Governance*, 8: 579–90.

Lane, Jan-Erik and Svante O. Ersson (1996) 'The Nordic Countries. Contention, Compromise and Corporatism', in Josep Maria Colomer (ed.) *Political Institutions in Europe*, London: Routledge, pp. 254–81.

Lange, Peter, Michael Wallerstein and Miriam Golden (1995) 'The End of Corporatism? Wage Setting in the Nordic and Germanic Countries', in Sanford M. Jacoby (ed.) *The Workers of Nations. Industrial Relations in a Global Economy*, Oxford: Oxford University Press, pp. 76–100.

Lehmbruch, Gerhard (1984) 'Concertation and the Structure of Corporatist Networks', in John Goldthorpe (ed.) *Order and Conflict in Contemporary Capitalism*, Oxford: Clarendon Press, pp. 60–80.

Lehmbruch, Gerhard (1996) 'Der Beitrag der Korporatismusforschung zur Entwicklung der Steuerungstheorie', *Politische Vierteljahresschrift*, 37: 735–51.

Lewin, Leif (1992) *Samhället och de organiserade intressena*, Stockholm: Norstedts.

Lewin, Leif (1994) 'The Rise and Decline of Corporatism: The Case of Sweden', *European Journal of Political Research*, 26: 59–79.

Lijphart, Arend and Markus M.L. Crepaz (1991) 'Corporatism and Consensus Democracy in Eighteen Countries: Conceptual and Empirical Linkages', *British Journal of Political Science*, 21: 235–56.

Lind, Jens (1994) 'The Labour Market Reform in Denmark: Background and Perspectives', *Transformation of European Industrial Relations*, 1: 175–99.

Lindbeck, Assar, Per Molander, Torsten Persson, Olof Peterson, Agnar Sandmo, Birgitte Swedenborg and Agnar Thygesen (1993) 'Options for Economic and Political Reform in Sweden', *Economic Policy*, 17: 220–63.

Loftager, Jørn and Per Kongshøj Madsen (1997) 'Denmark', in Hugh Compston (ed.) *The New Politics of Unemployment. Radical Policy Initiatives in Western Europe*, London: Routledge, pp. 123–45.

Lundberg, Erik (1985) 'The Rise and Fall of the Swedish Model', *Journal of Economic Literature*, 23: 1–36.

Madsen, Per Kongshøj (1996) 'Popular Acceptance for Danish Leave-Schemes – But do they Work?', *Nordic Labour-Journal*, 1/1996: 16–20.

Meijer, Hans (1969) 'Bureaucracy and Policy Formulation in Sweden', *Scandinavian Political Studies*, 4: 103–16.

Milner, Henry (1989) *Sweden. Social Democracy in Practice*, Oxford: Oxford University Press.

Milner, Henry (1994) *Social Democracy and Rational Choice. The Scandinavian Experience and Beyond*, London and New York: Routledge.

Mjøset, Lars (1987) 'Nordic Economic Policies in the 1970s and 1980s', *International Organization*, 41: 403–56.

Mjøset, Lars (1996) 'Nordic Economic Policies in the 1980s and 1990s', paper presented to the Tenth International Conference of Europeanists, Chicago, 14–16 March.

Nannestad, Peter (1998) 'Keeping the Bumblebee Flying: Economic Policy in the Welfare State of Denmark, 1973–94', in Erik Albæck, Leslie C. Eliason, Asbjørn Sonne Nørgaard and Herman S. Schwarz (eds) *Negotiated Adaptation: The Survival of the Danish Welfare State*, in press.

NOSOSCO (Nordic Social Statistical Committee), various issues, *Social Security in the Nordic Countries. Scope, Expenditure and Financing*, Copenhagen: NOSOSCO.

Notermans, Ton (1993) 'The Abdication from National Policy Autonomy: Why the Macroeconomic Policy Regime has Become so Unfavourable to Labour', *Politics & Society*, 21: 133–67.

OECD (various issues) *Employment Outlook*, Paris: OECD.

OECD (various issues) *Historical Statistics*, Paris: OECD.

OECD (various issues) *Revenue Statistics*, Paris: OECD.

OECD (1995) *OECD Review of Foreign Direct Investment: Finland*, Paris: OECD.

OECD (1996a) *Economic Survey Sweden*, Paris: OECD.

OECD (1996b) *Economic Survey Denmark*, Paris: OECD.

OECD (1997a) *OECD Economic Survey Denmark*, Paris: OECD.

OECD (1997b) *Making Work Pay. Taxation, Benefits, Employment and Unemployment*, Paris: OECD.

OECD (1999) *Economic Survey Denmark*, Paris: OECD.

Overbye, Einar (1996) 'Pension Politics in the Nordic Countries: A Case Study', *International Political Science Review*, 17: 67–90.

Pestoff, Victor A (1995) 'Towards a New Swedish Model of Collective Bargaining and

140   *Sven Jochem*

Politics', in Colin Crouch and Franz Traxler (eds) *Organized Industrial Relations in Europe: What Future?*, Aldershot: Dartmouth, pp. 151–82.

Ploug, Niels and Jon Kvist (1996) *Social Security in Europe. Development or Dismantlement?* The Hague, London and Boston: Kluwer.

Pontusson, Jonas (1992a) *The Limits of Social Democracy. Investment Politics in Sweden*, Ithaca and London: Cornell University Press.

Pontusson, Jonas (1992b) 'At the End of the Third Road: Swedish Social Democracy in Crisis', *Politics & Society*, 20: 305–32.

Pontusson, Jonas and Peter Swenson (1996) 'Labor Markets, Production Strategies, and Wage Bargaining Institutions. The Swedish Employer Offensive in Comparative Perspective', *Comparative Political Studies*, 29: 223–50.

Rothstein, Bo (1992) *Den korporativa staten. Intresseorganisationer och statsförvaltning i svensk politik*, Stockholm: Norstedts.

Rothstein, Bo (1994) 'Modellen är död – leve modellen!', in Bertil Holmlund (ed.) *Arbete, löner och politik. Essäer tillägnade Nils Elvander*, Stockholm: Nordica, pp. 186–224.

Rothstein, Bo (1996) *The Social Democratic State. The Swedish Model and the Bureaucratic Problem of Social Reforms*, Pittsburgh and London: University of Pittsburgh Press.

SAF (Svenksa Arbetsgivarföreningen) (1996) *Wages and Total Labour Costs for Workers. International Survey 1984–1994*, Stockholm: SAF.

SAF (1997a) *Fakta om Sveriges ekonomi*, Stockholm: SAF (internet version).

SAF (1997b) *En arbetsmarknad utan AMS*, Stockholm: SAF.

Scharpf, Fritz W. (1991) *Crisis and Choice in European Social Democracy*, Ithaca, NY: Cornell University Press.

Scharpf, Fritz W. (1996) 'Politische Optionen im vollendeten Binnenmarkt', in Markus Jachtenfuchs and Beate Kohler-Koch (eds) *Europäische Integration*, Opladen: Leske & Budrich.

Scharpf, Fritz W. (1997) *Employment and the Welfare State: A Continental Dilemma*, MPIfG Working Paper 97/7, Köln: Max-Planck-Institut für Gesellschaftsforschung.

Scheuer, Steen (1992) 'Denmark: Return to Decentralization', in Anthony Ferner and Richard Hyman (eds) *Industrial Relations in the New Europe*, Oxford: Basil Blackwell, pp. 168–97.

Schiller, Bernt (1967) *Storstrejken 1909. Förhistoria och orsaker*, Göteborg: Akademiförlaget.

Schludi, Martin (1997) 'Kürzungspolitik im Wohlfahrtsstaat: Deutschland und Schweden im Vergleich', Diplomarbeit, University of Konstanz.

Schmidt, Manfred G. (1982) *Wohlfahrtsstaatliche Politik unter bürgerlichen und sozialdemokratischen Regierungen. Ein internationaler Vergleich*, Frankfurt and New York: Campus.

Schmidt, Manfred G. (1996) 'When Parties Matter: A Review of the Possibilities and Limits of Partisan Influence on Public Policy', *European Journal of Political Research*, 30: 155–83.

Schwarz, Herman (1998) 'Social Democracy Going Down or Down Under', *Comparative Politics*, 30/3: 253–72.

Shalev Michael (1992) 'The Resurgence of Labour Quiescence', in Marino Regini (ed.) *The Future of Labour Movements*, London: Sage, pp. 102–32.

SOU (2000) *3: Välfärd vid vägskäl*, Stockholm.

Stephens, John D. (1996) 'The Scandinavian Welfare States: Achievements, Crisis, and Prospects', in Esping-Andersen (ed.) *Welfare States in Transition. National Adaptations in Global Economies*, London: Sage, pp. 32–65.

Swenson, Peter (1991) 'Bringing Capital back in, or Social Democracy Reconsidered. Employer Power, Cross-Class Alliances, and Centralization of Industrial Relations in Denmark and Sweden', *World Politics*, 43: 513–44.

Swenson, Peter (1992) 'Managing the Managers', *Scandinavian Journal of History*, 16: 335–56.

Therborn, Göran (1987) 'Does Corporatism Really Matter? The Economic Crisis and Issues of Political Theory', *Journal of Public Policy*, 7: 259–84.

Therborn, Göran (1992) 'Lessons from 'Coporatist' Theoretizations', in Jukka Pekkarinen, Matti Pohjola and Bob Rowthorn (eds) *Social Corporatism: A Superior Economic System?*, Oxford: Clarendon Press, pp. 24–43.

van Waarden, Frans (1995) 'The Organizational Power of Employers' Associations: Cohesion, Comprehensiveness and Organizational development', in Colin Crouch and Franz Traxler (eds) *Organized Industrial Relations in Europe: What Future?*, Aldershot: Dartmouth, pp. 45–97.

Velstand og Velfærd – en analysesammenfatning, 1995, edited by Kommissionen om fremtidens beskæftigelses- og erhvervsmuligheder, København.

Wallerstein, Michael and Miriam Golden (1997) 'The Fragmentation of the Bargaining Society. Wage Setting in the Nordic Countries, 1980 to 1992', *Comparative Political Studies*, 30/6: 699–731.

6 Welfare state adjustment between consensual and adversarial politics

The institutional context of reform in Germany

Gerhard Lehmbruch

The trajectory of German welfare state reform looks paradoxical. When Helmut Kohl came to power in 1982, the programme of the conservative-liberal coalition led by him ostensibly emulated the neo-conservative agenda of Margaret Thatcher and Ronald Reagan. But – notwithstanding initial successes in consolidating public finance – the U-turn (*Wende*) proclaimed by the new majority did not really happen. Some minor deregulation of the labour market took place, the monopoly of the public service radio was abolished, and some steps toward privatization and deregulation of the public telecommunications monopoly were taken. Later, the process of Europeanization triggered more far-reaching deregulation and privatization of public services, which was largely decided with opposition support. But the core of the welfare state was left intact. Restrictions in social security benefits had already been initiated during the years since 1975, under the social-liberal government of Helmut Schmidt, and neither these nor further cuts after 1982 amounted to dismantling the traditional German *Sozialstaat*. The reform of the old age pensions law, passed in 1989 with the support of the social-democratic opposition, did not fundamentally affect the basic elements of the system. Still more, the launch in 1993 of nursing care insurance, pushed through after difficult bargaining processes with the opposition and considered as one of the major achievements in social policy in the early 1990s, was clearly indebted to the tradition of the Bismarckian welfare state. And warnings that it would eventually run funding risks comparable to those that might be faced by the old age pensions system were disregarded by most political actors.

The mood, however, changed at the end of the 1980s, and controversies about an institutional crisis of the German welfare state became conspicuous around 1990. But this incipient discussion was for some time eclipsed by the unexpected and dramatic process of German unification. It was not until the mid-1990s that core institutions of the German welfare state such as the institutional framework of the labour market and the systems of social security were widely regarded as being in jeopardy, and the complex system of public finance also became a critical issue. On 26 April 1997, seizing a rather odd opportunity, the inauguration of a new luxury hotel in Berlin (the Adlon), Federal President Roman Herzog in a carefully staged speech deplored 'the loss of economic dynamics, the inflexibility of society, an incredible mental depression', and pathetically called for a reform effort to overcome the 'congestion of modernization' (*Modernisierungsstau*).[1] This eloquent compilation of well-known topics of the new crisis rhetoric met an amazing resonance in public opinion. And a particularly significant aspect of this rhetoric was that Germany now appeared as a reform laggard compared to other, more advanced OECD countries.

To be sure, the controversies of the 1990s about a crisis of the German welfare state came not out of the blue. Since the second half of the 1970s, after the breakdown of the 'Keynesian consensus', the West German welfare state was viewed with a critical eye by the proponents of supply-side oriented policy change. But although the Kohl government itself defined its mission in similar terms, this debate did not result in radically transforming the political agenda. The conviction that the 'German model' (Markovits 1982) had successfully mastered the crises of the 1970s was still widely shared. *Modell Deutschland* was originally an electoral slogan invented under the chancellorship of Helmut Schmidt and claiming that Germany was distinguished by its exemplary economic and social achievements. And even after Schmidt's fall this confidence remained fairly robust. Most political actors apparently still considered the welfare state as solidly entrenched and were reluctant to seriously discuss the new challenges. Admittedly, such confidence was somewhat shaken by the substantial rise of the unemployment rate, from about 4 per cent in 1980, to about 7 to 9 per cent in the period 1985 to 1990. But this increase was not perceived as a serious political threat since structural unemployment hit peripheral groups in society rather than the traditional qualified core of the workforce. Moreover, the 'social net' appeared solid enough to cushion such job losses. Since 1982 the Kohl government had been quite successful in consolidating public finance and reducing the public debt, and at the end of the decade the social security systems were in relatively good shape. Hence the chances of the 'old' Federal Republic coping with the much discussed challenges of globalization seemed quite propitious (Czada 1998). How do we then explain the stereotype of institutional deadlock and crisis becoming so popular in the 1990s? Quite obviously the exogenous pressures which confronted the political economy of 'old' Federal Republic were magnified by the unexpected shock of German unification. This was a challenge which finally overtaxed the adaptive capacity of the traditional 'German model'. The original euphoria over German unification gave way to concern about the resulting strains on public finance and to the systems of welfare. And the further increase of the unemployment rate to 12 per cent and even more – largely resulting from the massive layoffs in East Germany – did much to heighten the sense of crisis. It was against this background that the failure of the conservative-liberal majority to tackle new and more radical reforms was widely seen as symptom of political exhaustion, and that the defeat of Helmut Kohl in the federal election of 27 September 1998 appeared as a logical outcome.

The costs of German unification

One of the consequences of German unity was a critical impairment of the resources of the welfare state. West Germany's leaders chose to grossly underestimate the redistributive challenge of integrating East Germany. According to an assessment of the EU Commission in February 1990, preventing large-scale westward migration would have required a transfer of the order of (initially) about 10 per cent of West German incomes to raise East German incomes to about two-thirds of the West German level.[2] Among the West German public, however, such a direct redistributive intervention would probably have been so unpopular as to endanger the legitimacy of German unity altogether. Hence West German leaders preferred a mixed strategy for financing unification: on the one hand, they set up an extra-budgetary fund for the reconstruction of East Germany (*Aufbau Ost*) which was refinanced by borrowing on the international capital markets, and on the other, a straight extension of the West German social security systems to East Germany permitted to *de facto* pay health, unemployment, or old age-benefits out of the contributions of the West German members of these systems instead from taxes. But since the optimistic projections of an economic upswing in East Germany proved utterly unrealistic the strategy chosen for the financing of German unity – together with the unexpected net loss from the privatization of the East German industries – inevitably resulted in a massive increase of the public debt. On the other hand, the massive social transfers endangered the reserves of the social security systems, exacerbating the worries about the old age pension system which (in Germany as elsewhere in Europe) was already threatened by demographic trends. The ensuing rise of contributions had the additional effect of raising the labour costs to employers.

Moreover, the unification strategy consisted in the wholesale transfer of West German institutions to East Germany. And since that was based upon the supposition of their undeniable superiority the discussion of welfare reform was shelved for several years. Those in West Germany who regarded the process of unification as a 'window of opportunity' for reform and wanted, for example, to preserve the state-run public health system of the former GDR, were soon silenced in order not to endanger the West German consensus on uniting Germany.

The first *Bündnis für Arbeit* and its fiasco

A corporatist strategy for coping with the crisis in the labour market was first put on the agenda on 1 November 1995 by Klaus Zwickel, leader of the metal workers' union (Industriegewerkschaft Metall) in a speech at the congress of his union. He offered to abandon the traditional high wage strategy of the unions in an 'alliance for jobs' (*Bündnis für Arbeit*), exchanging wage moderation for the guarantee of new employment. At that time his proposal had a considerable echo, and *Bündnis für Arbeit* remained a key reference in political semantics, competing for public attention right away with *Wirtschaftsstandort Deutschland*, a slogan which stood for the supply-side platform of Kohl's conservative-liberal coalition government.[3] The public appeal of this formula was indicative of widespread normative expectations favouring a strategy of corporatist consensus building between labour and business. One central element of this proposal (dubbed *Bündnis für Arbeit*, as mentioned above) was a decisive reduction of overtime work in favour of new jobs. From the outset the initiative got strong public acclaim – including from the government which did not hesitate to usurp the slogan *Bündnis für Arbeit* for its own strategic purposes.

The chancellor could not but welcome Zwickel's offer of a labour strategy of wage moderation, and for the first time openly blamed business leaders for their reticence. But the government had its own agenda on which the rising costs of the social security system had begun to rank very high. One of the most controversial aspects of the social policy of the last two decades was the increasing trend to solve employment problems by increasing use of early retirement and so shifting the loads from labour market policy to the old age pension system. Large firms, in particular, had turned to rejuvenate their workforce at the expense of the old age pension system in close co-operation with labour representatives. When demographic projections led to increasing concern over the future financing of the public pension system it became more and more clear that this practice could not be continued. But since it had become extremely popular with industrial workers the co-operation of labour unions for any change was indispensable. In a *Kanzlergespräch* of 12 February 1996 (with no more than thirteen participants) business and labour leaders finally agreed on the gradual phasing-out of the established practice. Two days later, this extra-parliamentary agreement was ratified by the cabinet, and soon after by parliament. This extraordinary pre-emption of the legislative channel constituted the temporary climax of a corporatist strategy where the government took the initiative.

Meanwhile, however, negotiations over the *Bündnis für Arbeit* proposal had stalled. Zwickel apparently had not sufficiently pondered the premise of this approach, namely, sufficient authority of employers' associations to make their member firms comply with an agreement about additional jobs. In particular the union's demand for strong limits to the use of overtime by employers who might wish to avoid new hirings met staunch opposition: many employers regarded overtime as an essential element of flexible management, and the employer associations dragged their feet. The political basis for an eventual corporatist reform strategy shrunk still more after the liberals achieved an unexpected comeback in several state elections. The liberal opposition FDP now successfully urged the chancellor to modify his course of striking deals with organized labour in favour of greater concessions to business demands. The breakdown of the negotiations followed when Kohl, in an apparently ill-considered U-turn, sided with the employers' quest for strong cuts in sickness pay. For organized labour this issue was of high symbolic importance: until the mid-1950s, blue-collar workers had been subject to a three days waiting period before receiving statutory sickness pay whereas by tradition white-collar employees continued to receive their full salary. This unequal treatment was successfully abolished in 1956, when the metal workers union in Schleswig-Holstein won a breakthrough after a strike which, lasting 114 days, was the longest in German post-war history. The settlement that was finally achieved, full payment of salaries by employers in the first six weeks of sickness, had not only been enshrined in many collective agreements but also in a federal law on sickness pay introduced in 1970 by the social-liberal coalition. Because of this history, in the eyes of labour the sickness pay rules had a high symbolic value. And when a 20 per cent cut in sickness wages was included in a government bill as part of a packet of budgetary economies (*Sparpaket*), the unions exited from Kohl's bargaining table.

In a first phase, this turn appeared to strengthen the position of the 'anti-corporatists' on the employers' side. Representatives of traditional bargaining were increasingly on the defensive, and the new president of the Bundesverband der Deutschen Industrie (BDI, Federation of German Industries), Hans-Olaf Henkel, became the most prominent advocate of a fundamental change in labour relations. He vigorously pleaded for the abandonment of traditional centralized collective bargaining (*Flächentarif-vertrag*) in favour of company-level bargaining, something which employers' associations had long regarded with strong reservations. The zenith of the conflict was reached when the metal employers association (Gesamtmetall) advised its members to cut sickness pay in line with the legal changes recently introduced with the *Sparpaket*. This recommendation violated – according to most legal experts – existing collective agreements,[4] and in the eyes of unions it ran contrary to the tradition of *Tarifautonomie* where social partners are expected to resolve their differences by way of contract without state interference. When the management of Daimler-Benz, one of the largest firms in the industry, announced its intention to implement immediately the association's recommendation it had obviously not expected the strong emotional reaction of its workforce. The union, on the one hand, accused the management of abandoning a long and successful tradition of social partnership, but on the other hand it was able to organize a series of work stoppages that in the end cost Daimler-Benz about DM200 million worth of lost production volume. This conflict spread to many other firms in the industry, and its mobilizing impact among workers was so immense that it overwhelmed even the union leadership. The Daimler-Benz management finally capitulated, and employers were left in profound disarray. Many were extremely disturbed by the quite unanticipated extent and intensity of workers' protest, and the desire to preserve the system of *Tarifautonomie* and peaceful labour relations led them into new reflections about their strategy.

Before the outbreak of this conflict, some important business leaders believed that under present labour market conditions corporatism was no longer needed for industrial peace. This was reconsidered after the unions demonstrated their power to mobilize workers even in periods of rising unemployment. However, much damage had already been done since the confrontation resulted in a stiffening of the position of labour leaders who found their space of manœuvre reduced by the strong mobilizing effects of the conflict. The ultimate reason, however, for the breakdown of this first attempt of negotiated retrenchment of the welfare state was the dominance of the electoral calculus in the chancellor's strategy. Until then, Kohl had most of the time taken care not to alienate important social groups such as organized labour. Now, however, the continuation of Kohl's majority depended on the electoral survival of his small liberal coalition partner the FDP, which wanted to demonstrate to its clientele that it was the indispensable guardian of free-market principles. Cutting sickness pay was one of the victories which the FDP might claim in their quest for staying alive. Competitive party politics, guided by a majoritarian logic, thus won the upper hand over the corporatist strategy of adjusting the welfare state.

The 'reform gridlock' as a political issue

Kohl's leadership style, guided above all by the quest for maintaining power in a bipolar party system, proved too inflexible to cope with the new problems of welfare reform, and the conflicts arising from this strategy did much to fuel the debate on a 'reform congestion' (*Reformstau*) which commentators and political orators liked to deplore in the 1990s. In 1990 the social democratic opposition had won a majority in the Federal Council (Bundesrat), the representation of the member states of the federation, and thus was able to veto important government bills. Kohl's dependence upon the small liberal coalition partner, however, prevented him from negotiating the compromises that would have been necessary for governing in such a situation of 'divided government'. Hence 'institutional gridlock' became another topic in the crisis rhetoric, alongside the ostensible rigidities of the labour market. To be sure, President Herzog – himself formerly an experienced negotiator as state representative in the Federal Council – had been careful not to join such reproaches in his 1997 'Adlon' speech. Much more outspoken, however, was BDI chairman Hans-Olaf Henkel in blaming an ostensible deficit in institutional reform and in demanding sweeping changes. He denounced the institutions of the German *Verhandlungs-demokratie*, a system based on continuous and complex negotiations both in the federalist and corporatist arenas, and the traditional political culture with its 'consensus sauce' for thwarting vital radical innovations. This amounted to the plea for extending deregulation to the traditional core institutions of the German welfare state, to labour relations with their strong corporatist elements, and to the systems of social security.

There was an evident bias in similar stereotypes of persistent institutional rigidities, attributed either to the veto power of organized special interests or to mechanisms of institutional gridlock. Indeed, at the end of the 1980s public opinion had begun to take the globalization issue seriously, and traditional elements of the political-economic framework were successfully challenged. Among others, a fairly broad consensus developed about the privatization and deregulation of public services, especially telecommunications and the railways. Although telecom deregulation was of course strongly encouraged by the initiatives of the European Union, the moves toward privatization of public services had important domestic sources. To keep the telecommunications and the railway system competitive in a changing international environment, more entrepreneurial flexibility was obviously needed, and the considerable investments that were required could no longer be shouldered by the state budget. So even the social democrats co-operated in these moves, in spite of persistent protests from the postal workers' union. Today the deregulation of the telecommunications sector is more advanced in Germany than in most other European countries, and the deregulation of the electric utilities is well under way. Similar changes contradict the notion of an immobile German society and politics nurtured by some commentators and polemicists und suggest that the capacity of this system for adapting to the challenges of globalization is much larger than pessimistic scenarios would make us believe.

Schröder's corporatist strategy

The electoral victory in 1998 of Gerhard Schröder gave a new turn to this discussion. The social democratic chancellor proclaimed the fight against unemployment as the central issue of his platform. As key strategy for achieving this purpose he relaunched the idea of a *Bündnis für Arbeit*. However, widening the label into *Bündnis für Arbeit, Ausbildung und Wettbewerbsfähigkeit*, i.e. 'alliance for jobs, (professional) training, and competitiveness' he indicated his intention to transcend the narrow focus on a labour market policy bent upon redistributing work. The accent put on competitiveness introduced a supply-side element which was meant to increase the attractiveness of a corporatist strategy for the business community.

Schröder's *Bündnis für Arbeit* aimed at a variant of corporatist 'concertation' familiar from the 'social pacts' as they had been concluded in the 1990s in some smaller European countries. Whereas in the 1970s consultations involving government and the peak associations of business and labour aimed at supporting Keynesian macro-economic policy by a bargained incomes policy oriented toward stabilization, this time wage policy and conditions of work should be tied together, in a series of sequential negotiations, with consensus-building on reforms of the systems of social security. Such a linkage of issues would differ considerably from those earlier instances of 'political exchange' where wage concessions on the part of organized labour might eventually be rewarded with compensations in social policy. What was at stake this time was a far-reaching and eventually painful re-adjustment of the welfare state under conditions of shrinking resources and pressures emanating from global competition. On the agenda was no longer corporatist demand management but corporatist supply-side policy (cf. Traxler 1995: 210). In Germany such a strategy is subject to peculiar institutional constraints which we will explore in this chapter.

The architecture of the second *Bündnis für Arbeit*

Schröder's *Bündnis für Arbeit*, though in constitutional terms no more than an informal discussion between government and the labour market peak associations, has a highly formalized architecture. Its apex is formed by the *Spitzengespräche* (peak talks) where the chancellor and the ministers of finance, economy, labour and health have so far met about every three months with the presidents of the four peak associations of business and of the German Federation of Trade Unions and the four most important industrial unions. These meetings are prepared by a 'steering group' (*Steuerungsgruppe*) composed of parliamentary secretaries and top civil servants from the chancellor's office and the four ministries together with the general secretaries of the peak associations. The steering group, for its part, is assisted by a 'benchmarking group' (to which I will return), and the details are prepared and elaborated in eight working parties (*Arbeitsgruppen*) and expert groups covering policy areas such as tax policy, old age and unemployment insurance, the reform of public health insurance, working time, early pensions or professional formation. These working parties again include top civil servants from the ministries concerned and experts from the peak associations.

Three aspects of this architecture are noteworthy. First, it sets the *Bündnis für Arbeit* off from its predecessors, the *Konzertierte Aktion* of 1967–74, and the *Kanzlergespräche* undertaken by chancellor Kohl since 1990. The initiator of the *Konzertierte Aktion*, Karl Schiller, Minister of the Economy from 1966 to 1972, conceived of it not so much as a place for bargaining but rather as forum for a rational dialogue with the 'autonomous groups' (as the Council of Economic Experts called them at that time). Insight into the interdependence of macro-economic aggregates and of the resulting economic constraints (*Sachzwänge*) should lead the economic actors to voluntarily co-ordinated rational economic behaviour after information about the essential macro-economic parameters had been exchanged (Lehmbruch 1977). Since the professed aim of the talks was mutual information and moral suasion it made sense to invite a broad spectrum of organized interests to take part. Hence the number of participants continuously grew from about 50 up to 200. In retrospect, it has often been said that these proportions of the *Konzertierte Aktion* contributed to its relative inefficiency. Moreover, being a forum in the exclusive responsibility of the Minister of the Economy and hence not involving the chancellor, the commitment of the government could not be taken for granted.

When Helmut Kohl started the *Kanzlergespräche*, he had drawn his lessons from the weaknesses of the *Konzertierte Aktion*: from the very beginning the head of government maintained the initiative and the leadership of the talks, and he took increasingly care to restrict participation to the leaders of the most powerful associations of business and labour. The aim was not mere exchange of information to encourage the judicious action of the associations, but to commit the most powerful corporate actors in German society. Schröder's *Bündnis für Arbeit* follows this example, but differs from the predecessor's *Kanzlergespräche* in its high degree of formalization.[5] Quite obviously this is meant to underline the commitment of the government to the success of the talks and at the same time to put subtle pressure on the invited participants to reciprocate this commitment.

The second – and new – aspect of Schröder's *Bündnis* which is note-worthy is the 'benchmarking' approach borrowed from the techniques of business administration. On the suggestion of BDI president Henkel, Schröder established a 'benchmarking group' consisting of a handful of experts from the research institutes of business and labour and some high-ranking officials of the Chancellor's Office. Its aim is an 'unambiguous stocktaking of the *Wirtschafts- und Sozialstandort Deutschland* in international comparison'. This semantic reference to the *Standort Deutschland* varies a standard topic of supply-side policies by including the 'social' character-istics of Germany as a location for investments. But at the same time it is also a far cry from *Modell Deutschland*, that well-known slogan from the chancellorship of Helmut Schmidt. Henceforth Germany is no longer considered as distinguished by its exemplary economic and social achievements – it rather looks for inspiration from abroad. In recent years particular attention was directed to the *Modell Holland*, considered as the most conspicuous example of re-dimensioning an over-extended welfare state by building consensus between the large groups in society.[6] (Another model frequently referred to was 'New Labour', but not always did social democratic 'reformers' keep in mind that these two references symbolized rather different political strategies.)

Among the lessons drawn from these foreign models – and this is another important difference from the *Konzertierte Aktion* – is the ambition to cover a very broad range of issues and policy domains. 'Renewed emergence of tripartite concertation is due to the need to co-ordinate policies across policy fields' (Ebbinghaus and Hassel 1999). Elsewhere negotiated reforms of the welfare state quite often included labour relations and wage policy as well as taxes, unemployment insurance, health costs and old age pensions, because all these systems are both interdependent and under pressure to adapt. Hence the architecture of the *Bündnis* attempts to integrate them by a series of tripartite negotiations between government, organized business and labour differentiated according to sectors. The tripartite approach is of course the logical conclusion of an implicitly shared analysis according to which high labour costs play an important role in explaining the rise of unemployment. Labour costs, to be sure, not only include wages, but also the indirect wage costs resulting from social security contributions (*Lohn-nebenkosten*). And since part of these are borne by employers, in the tradition inaugurated under Bismarck, employer representatives participate in the self-administration of most social security systems and thus share the responsibility for, and an interest in, their financial viability. Hence an integrated bargaining approach to welfare state reform should *a priori* be highly attractive to employers' representatives. Remarkably, however, the tripartite approach of the *Bündnis* is so pervasive that other, functionally specialized peak associations within the respective policy domains are tacitly left out. Thus not even the medical associations and the public health insurance funds are included in the working party for the reform of health insurance (*Arbeitsgruppe 'Reform der Gesetzlichen Krankenversicherung und der Pflegeversicherung'*).

Indeed, the experience of small neighbouring corporatist countries seems to indicate that a consensus achieved by the peak associations of the 'social partners' can be decisive for the enactment of reforms in all these fields of the welfare state. It is doubtful, however, whether such experiences can serve as model. Austria's *Sozialpartnerschaft* after the Second World War – to take but this example – was traditionally distinguished by the clear dominance of two peak associations who were also closely linked with the two largest parties, the socialists and the conservative 'People's Party', that have so long dominated the Austrian party system. Organized interests and political parties thus formed a rather tight network linked at one central nodal point, and therefore bargaining processes over key policy decisions were facilitated by the small number of powerful participants (Lehmbruch 1985). These structures formed a strong contrast to the German case. First, historically the German welfare state was characterized by considerable institutional segmentation of the welfare policy networks. To be sure, today the interdependence between the system of collective bargaining, the mechanisms of labour market and unemployment policy, public health insurance and the old age pensions system is obvious and considerable. But since the growth of the welfare state was rather an additive process where sectoral systems were constructed one after the next, in each of these policy domains we now encounter a specific configuration of actors and their particular discourses and rules of the game, and often particular conflict lines have evolved that are not represented by the tripartism of government, labour and business. In consequence, these sectoral policy networks with their long traditions are often only loosely coupled with each other. Moreover, in some of these networks the power of leaders is limited by strong internal conflicts of sectional interests and deficits in member compliance. Finally, quite often in Germany the party system cannot serve as linkage mechanism between sectoral policy networks as may happen in Austria and other smaller corporatist countries because the arena of bipolar party competition may work at cross-purposes with the arena of corporatist negotiations. Hence, to comprehend the problems with which the *Bündnis für Arbeit* is confronted the sectoral variations in the governance of the German welfare state must be taken into account.

The governance of the labour relations system

It is often stressed that wage moderation on the part of organised labour is one of the conditions of success for the new social pacts concluded for negotiated welfare state reform (Visser and Hemerijck 1997; Hassel 1998). Therefore the role of collective bargaining is one of the focal points of the present controversies about the future of the German welfare state – the other being the crisis of the systems of social insurance. It is a matter of controversy to what degree high unit labour costs are directly attributable to union wage policy or rather to currency movements of the past years. In the past, such developments were taken calmly because high wages could be considered as a 'rationalization whip' that contributed to industrial modernization. In the view of organized labour, the resulting increases in productivity improved the competitive position of industry and helped it to grant higher wages and shorter working hours. As I have shown above, this strategic repertoire became important in the process of unification. But it lost much of its credit after the failure of the traditional strategies in East Germany. Also, employment clearly suffered when, reacting to high labour costs, German employers increasingly endeavoured to maintain their competitiveness on international markets by labour-saving restructuring. Moreover, the effective elimination of a low-wage sector is increasingly regarded as one of the causes of mass unemployment. These considerations have gradually persuaded labour as well as employers to look for more flexible approaches to collective bargaining acceptable to both parts of industry, and informal contacts at the peak level were under way for some time. Finally, however, these talks ended without tangible results, especially in the metal industry. And strong disagreements persist about some central questions. IG Metall in particular, the massive metal workers' union, doggedly stuck to strategies of social partnership practised in the 1980s, notably to the widespread practice of early retirement as a means to relieve the pressure on the labour market, which meanwhile resulted in massive goal conflicts between traditional employment policy and the continued viability of the old age pensions system. And union leaders strontly resisted all plans to expand the low-wage sector and thus to relieve the pressure on the labour market because they feared that this might undermine the existing system of collective bargaining.

Indeed, some of the most visible dissensions in Schröder's *Bündnis für Arbeit* were due to the reluctance of labour unions, and in particular IG Metall, to include wage moderation on the agenda of the peak talks. The ostensible reason given was the tripartite character of the *Bündnis*: in the view of labour, commitments made in this arena would amount to involving government in collective bargaining, and this would violate the principle of *Tarifautonomie* (autonomy of collective bargaining), the institutional centre-piece of German labour relations. Whereas in the systems of social insurance we observe an increasing intervention of government at the expense of the traditional paritary-based self-administration, the other component of the German welfare state, the system of labour relations, remains characterized by bipartite relationships from which government is largely left out. *Tarifautonomie* would indeed be incompatible with govern-ment interference in the form of compulsory arbitration as it existed in the Weimar Republic, or with its legal authority to declare collective agreements void (as in the Netherlands), but one may doubt that this would rule out informal understandings in a tripartite forum. Yet union reticence was certainly increased by the anticipation of internal tensions which any open commitment of labour to government-sponsored wage restraint might trigger. In Germany, where the German Confederation of Labour (DGB) has no jurisdiction over collective bargaining, industrial unions are the key actors in wage negotiations, and on this level disagreements about strategy are not uncommon. While some of the industrial unions (e.g. in the chemical industry and mining) favour an accommodative 'social partnership' approach of settling disputes with employers, others, and primarily the metalworkers' union (IG Metall), have traditionally preferred a more militant stance (Swenson 1989). And IG Metall, to be sure, has not forgotten how mis-calculated wage concessions made in the context of the original *Konzertierte Aktion* led to the spectacular wildcat strikes of 1969 and 1973 (Bergmann *et al.* 1975).

On the other hand, the importance of such strategic dissensions should not be overestimated. Indeed, the apparent decentralization of collective bargaining on the national level which some researchers found in West Germany (Cameron 1984) is to a considerable degree compensated for by techniques of informal co-ordination between industrial unions

(Soskice 1999), and on the industry level either outright centralization or strict harmonization of collective agreements is the rule. Also, *Tarifautonomie* has not prevented German unions from taking the impact of wage policy on economic growth and competitiveness into account. The corporatist character of *Tarifautonomie* became fully apparent in the 1960s when West German labour unions adopted Keynesian macro-economic views (Lehmbruch 1977) but did not pass with the decline of Keynesianism. Although the *Konzertierte Aktion* as an attempt at tripartite concertation collapsed after some years, *de facto* corporatist practices continued, and this not only in collective bargaining (such as 'productivity-oriented' bargaining). Moreover, they gained increasing importance in 'meso-corporatist' industrial restructuring. The basic rationale of this corporatist orientation can be defined as a large consensus over industrial modernization, where high wages and shorter working hours were considered as perfectly compatible with a competitive position on world markets, assured by a peaceful social climate and a highly qualified workforce. In recent years, however, unions have increasingly voiced their doubts about the expected employment effects of wage moderation, and also about a sincere commitment of business to the maintenance of high employment.

This discussion has shifted the focus to the organizational problems within organized business. The past success of corporatism in West German labour relations was attributable not only to the structure and the coordination techniques of labour unions but also to the importance and power of centralized employers' associations (Thelen 1991). And the recent crisis of corporatist labour relations is less due to the tensions within the labour camp (for these have always existed) than to the increasing dissensions within organized business. One aspect of these dissensions was the erosion of the authority of employers' associations over their rank and file. Another was the new rivalry between the functionally differentiated business peak associations, and in particular the sometimes quite vocal dissensions between the Bundesvereinigung der deutschen Arbeitgeber-verbände (BDA) and the Bundesverband der deutschen Industrie (BDI). For a couple of years, the BDI leadership had become attentive to the gradual erosion of its basis resulting from the ongoing structural changes in the West German economy. Being the peak association of industry but not including other sectors of business, its dominant position is in jeopardy because of the shrinking of its traditional industrial basis and the corresponding growth of the service sector. Under the chairmanship of Hans-Olaf Henkel (who as former chief executive of IBM Europe was less committed to the traditional folkways of German industry) the BDI began to look for opportunities for diversifying its activities, and one of the options which Henkel openly discussed was to shift the responsibility for collective bargaining away from such broad employer associations as Gesamtmetall (representing all employers of the large and heterogeneous metal sector) to the trade associations (which, incidentally, are organized under the umbrella of the BDI). Henkel linked this with some acid criticism of the co-operative attitude of BDA and Gesamtmetall. But finally the BDA leadership under its new president Dieter Hundt reacted vigorously to successfully affirm the traditional turf of the employers' associations.

Irrespective of the outcomes of such conflicts, however, it is rather likely that the traditional type of nation-wide and highly standardized collective agreements (*Flächentarifvertrag*) will undergo significant transformations. But this is not tantamount to a breakdown of the established system of labour relations. After all, the distinguishing feature of German labour relations remains the 'dual system' coupling co-determination and collective bargaining, and this system has in the past exhibited a remarkable adaptive capacity (Streeck 1979; Thelen 1991). Both tiers are rule-bound in a manner adapted to stable corporatist bargaining, co-determination being closely regulated by law, whereas the rules of collective bargaining have largely been written by the labour courts. Works councils were first established in the early Weimar Republic, but they have definitely taken root in West Germany in the course of several decades after the Second World War and have *de facto* become transmuted into an organizational support of unions which may even compensate for low organizational density. This institution provides for orderly plant-level communication structures with management and serves to defuse the potential antagonism between the sectional interests and the eventual militancy of shop-floor members and the larger strategic orientations of union leadership (Streeck 1979, 1982; Thelen 1991). To be sure, most employers have remained lukewarm as far as company-level co-determination is concerned. But they have discovered that plant-level co-determination by works councils offers a scope for flexibility and decentralization in labour relations, the absence of which they often deplore in collective bargaining. All in all, this institutional symbiosis has proved remarkably stable, and the consolidation of co-determination was confirmed by its successful transfer to East Germany.

Governance mechanisms of the German welfare state: the social insurance systems

For our purposes, the institutions that constitute the German welfare state are, above all, the different but complementary rule systems of labour relations and the social security systems. Both are historically closely intertwined. The different sectoral institutions can all be considered as variations of the basic model introduced with the social reforms of the 1880s initiated by Bismarck. He had the social security systems designed specifically to protect the working class, for purposes of political stabilization, and therefore the wage nexus was a constitutive element of their institutional architecture. But Bismarck was prevented by parliament from constructing social security as a state-financed relief system as he originally intended. Instead it was conceived according to the insurance model, and its central institutional features are compulsory membership (within demarcations defined by the legislator), the self-administration (*Selbstverwaltung*) of the insured members, modified by the liability of workers and employers to share the contributions, and the 'parity' (*Parität*) of representation of both sides of industry in the administration of these systems.

Parität is a key concept in German corporatism. It originated in a specific institutional strategy for coping with social cleavages, and one which distinguished the process of state-building in Germany from that of other larger European countries (Lehmbruch 2002). The religious peace treaties of the sixteenth and seventeenth centuries introduced the principle of the 'parity' of churches, constituted as corporate social groups to which representational monopolies had early been granted. Through historical learning processes, this institutional device later developed into a key element of a strategic repertoire for managing conflicts of interests between such groups. *Parität* can serve to regulate conflict between organized interests that have grown bottom-up over long periods, such as in labour relations and in the system of industrial co-determination where today it is a key formula. Here its pre-history dates back to the late nineteenth century (Feldman 1966; Teuteberg 1961; Rabenschlag-Kräusslich 1983). But the breakthrough came with the democracy of the Weimar Republic. *Parität* was one important element in the development toward corporatist labour relations that began with the integration, in 1916, of organized labour in the war effort (Feldman 1966), with the Stinnes-Legien agreement of 1919 over the establishment of the Zentrale Arbeitsgemeinschaft of employers and labour unions (ZAG) to cope with the post-war crisis (Feldman 1981; Feldman and Steinisch 1985), and with the law on works councils in 1920, in which the strategy of conflict management by *Parität* was first systematically extended to the relationship of labour and capital. As Franz Leopold Neumann (Neumann 1937, 1957) put it persuasively, the Weimar Republic was based upon a series of social compacts between the large forces of German society: 'Hence, the Weimar democracy rested to a decisive degree on the idea of parity – a parity between social groups, between *Reich* and states, and between the various churches' (Neumann 1957). The 'old Federal Republic' revived this idea, and it became a pivotal element of the corporatist repertoire of strategies. The programme of a *Bündnis für Arbeit* is the most recent manifestation of this strategic tradition.

But *Parität* can also be established in a top-down strategy by the state, as was largely the case in the social insurance systems since Bismarck. As will be shown below, in these systems *Parität* is employed to delegate the implementation to representatives of social groups constituted and empowered by statute, and one may speak of 'corporatization' as an administrative strategy (Döhler and Manow-Borgwardt 1992). Bargaining relationships between these partners are limited in their scope because essential parameters continue to be controlled by the state, and the state can intervene strongly in situations of crisis.

Whereas the origins of *Parität* can be traced back to the sixteenth century, the concept of 'self-administration' had its roots in the historical compromise struck by the monarchical bureaucratic state with the rising bourgeoisie in the reform era of the early nineteenth century (Heffter 1969). While the German bourgeoisie accepted the survival of the monarchy and its rather authoritarian hierarchical power structure, as a counterpart it was granted the institution of self-administration (*Selbstverwaltung*) for the government of cities, under the supervision of government but with considerable autonomy. This model of state-supervised self-administration was now transferred to the social security systems with the proviso that those who contributed to the system, workers and employers, were represented in the administrative bodies according to their respective share of these contributions. In practice the representation of these two groups was soon controlled by their organizations, trade unions on the one hand, employer associations on the other, and thus corporatism became a constitutive element of the governance of social security (for the old age pensions system, see Nullmeier and Rüb 1993: 303ff.). Being based on another historical compromise between antagonistic interests, this model acquired a remarkable resilience. However, the powers and duties of the *Selbstverwaltung* differ from one system to the other, and the powers of government – both of the supervisory administration and of the legislator – are also variable. Since their inception some of these systems had to be co-financed by the state, and therefore the role of government was by no means limited to supervising the self-administration. As stated above, top-down 'corporatization' can play an important role, especially in the health system.[7] These peculiarities explain the remarkable variations in the governance structure of the different sectors of the German welfare state. Yet one assumption is common to all: since workers and employers share the burden of contributions to the social security systems they should – at least in principle – also share an interest in the efficiency of the respective systems. Obviously this basic assumption does also play an important role in the tripartite arrangement of Schröder's *Bündnis für Arbeit*.

However, the parity-based representation of labour and employers in the governing bodies does not readily facilitate the coordination of the social security systems with the system of industrial relations. Labour and employer representatives are dispatched from the peak associations, the DGB and the BDA, which are not themselves involved in collective bargaining. The latter is the domain of industrial unions and industry-wide employer associations. Hence the policy communities do not really overlap.[8] In consequence, if for example IG Metall comes out in favour of an early retirement scheme, it does not have to defend such demands directly nor does it get direct feedback from labour representatives in the old age pension funds.

The *Parität* of workers and employers, moreover, does not reflect many of the conflicts of interests which now accompany the crisis of the social security systems, particularly the pension system and public health insurance. The character of the public pension system has undergone profound changes since its original inception. From a subsidiary old age insurance intended to supplement other possible means of subsistence, it has become an earnings-related wage substitute, indexed on the increase of average salaries. Of the original insurance scheme it has retained the legal entitlement of the beneficiaries, but capital-based funding gave way to a 'pay as you go' system based on levy from the present contributors. This is often euphemistically described as the 'contract between generations', but the 'generations' had of course no organized voice when old age insurance thus assumed the character of an instrument for intergenerational redistribution. This is fateful insofar as the German public pension system is undergoing the same demographic pressures as those of most other industrial democracies, resulting from the parallelism of declining birth rates and increasing longevity. With a progressively ageing population, the 'pay as you go' system inevitably leads to a latent distribution conflict between a shrinking population of young wage earners and a growing population of old beneficiaries. This latent conflict was for some time disguised by the policy, much favoured by unions and employers, of solving labour market problems (and at the same time rejuvenating the workforce) by the large-scale use of early retirement. But while this may in the short run have ameliorated the labour market chances of young people it increasingly puts on that same generation an increasing burden for financing the system. Moreover, the inclusion of new categories of beneficiaries who had not paid adequate contributions (among them, after German unification, the East German wage earners) aggravated the in-built tension between the principles of solidarity and of some sort of equivalence of contributions and benefits. All these changes find no adequate reflection in the formal governance mechanisms of the system. As in the origins before the First World War, old age insurance continues to be administered by decentralized institutions, on regional level for blue-collar workers, on the federal level for white-collar employees. According to the principle of self-administration, their managing boards consist of union and employers' representatives. But the discretionary powers of this self-administration are rather limited since both the level of benefits and the method of calculating the rate of contributions are uniform across the country and are determined by the federal legislator. And in the legislative process the 'social partners' play only a limited role because their parity-based representation is obviously not suited to mirror the central – namely, intergenerational – conflict lines by which today the system is distinguished. The position of labour unions is strongly biased toward the interests of the older generation of union members who are approaching retirement age and expect to retain the present level of benefits. There are some quite important

Sozialverbände that have developed out of former associations of war veterans and now make efforts to represent the heterogeneous clientele of social security beneficiaries, but they tend of course to represent the present generation of beneficiaries and their influence is essentially limited to lobbying. The interests of the wage-earning contributors are diffuse and difficult to aggregate through associational action, and the growing anxiety of younger people who face the perspective of higher contributions (to finance the benefits of the older generation) but clearly shrinking benefits in their own old age has no specific advocates in the old age insurance policy network. Thus it is the parliament, and hence the political parties, which in the final instance play the decisive role in the decision-making process of social security.

This is also true of unemployment insurance. This system is administered by a central federal authority, the Bundesanstalt für Arbeit (BfA), and is governed by an Administrative Board (*Verwaltungsrat*) and a Directorate (*Vorstand*) in which labour unions, employers and public authorities (federal, state and local governments) have each a third of the seats (*Drittelparität*). The members of these are not elected but appointed by the respective organizations. Again this mode of governance is referred to as self-administration, but the autonomy of the BfA is severely limited: Its budget, bylaws and directives must be sanctioned by the federal government. This means, in practice, that the government can impose cuts in entitlements even against the opinion of the *Verwaltungsrat*, and that it is parliament – and hence political parties – which in the final instance determine both the level of unemployment benefits and the range of contributors. Indeed, in the recent past unemployment insurance has been the object of frequent political interventions.

Multi-tier corporatism in the public health system

Infinitely more complex, moreover, is the governance of the public health system (Alber 1992; Alber and Bernardi-Schenkluhn 1992; Döhler 1990). Here, bargaining processes play a much larger role, and because of the considerable heterogeneity of interests stable exchange relationships are much more difficult to achieve. Although traditionally self-administration has a larger scope of autonomy, the intensity of state intervention has very much increased in the last two decades (Döhler and Manow 1997).

The complexity of this system results from the successive superimposition of several tiers, the health insurance system in a restricted sense, and the different providers of medical care. The system of compulsory health insurance (*Gesetzliche Krankenversicherung*, GKV) itself, since its introduction under Bismarck, is extremely decentralized and fragmented. Originally, only blue-collar workers were insured in the local health funds (*Allgemeine Ortskrankenkassen*, AOK), characterized by parity-based self-administration with elected representatives from workers and employers (similar to the public pension system). When white-collar employees were included in the system they could instead choose to get insured in the *Ersatzkassen*, which were equally self-administered, but without employer representation. (In a recent reform, this differentiation of access according to status has been rescinded, and all wage earners subject to compulsory insurance are now free to choose one of the different GKV health funds.)[9] The powers of the GKV self-administration are wider than those of the old age insurance system: although the benefits are largely determined by law, each AOK or *Ersatzkasse* is autonomous in establishing the rates of contributions (half of which are paid by the members, the other half by employers) and, eventually, in granting supplementary benefits to its members. Originally they were also autonomous in contracting with the providers of medical care; however, this power is now exercised by the associations of GKV health funds (again, there are separate associations of AOK and of *Ersatzkassen*), and it is restricted by the *Kassenarztsystem*.

The *Kassenarztsystem* is the second tier of the public health system. Since the introduction of compulsory health insurance, the medical profession had increasingly resented the increasing dependency of many doctors on the *Krankenkassen* (public health insurance funds). In this system doctors cannot bill their fee directly to the patient (who otherwise might simply have been reimbursed by the *Krankenkasse*) but were originally directly reimbursed by the health insurance funds. In consequence the latter gained a strong position in contracting with doctors which the latter resented not only for economic reasons but also regarded as detrimental to their professional autonomy. Early in the twentieth century, medical associations therefore started a campaign patterned after labour union tactics: they organized a series of doctors' strikes to substitute collective bargaining for free contracting of fees. Finally in 1913 the Imperial Office (ministry) of Interior – then responsible for supervising the system – intervened and helped to negotiate an agreement (Berliner Abkommen) between health insurance funds and medical associations. Characteristically, this agreement fell back on the strategy of conflict settlement by *Parität*. It introduced collective bargaining and established joint committees composed of representatives of health insurance funds and doctors which were responsible for admission to practice in the system and for developing standard contracts. In the Weimar Republic, this system was further developed by instituting specialized associations, the *Kassenärztliche Vereinigungen* (KV) organized on a regional level. Membership in the KV is compulsory for all doctors practising with *Krankenkassen*, and since about 90 per cent of the adult population are by law included in the GKV, only few doctors in private practice can afford to stay outside the system.

The *Kassenarztsystem* thus established as the second tier of the public health system constitutes another example of a historical compromise for settling a distributional conflict between organized interests on the basis of *Parität*. The KV do not only represent the medical profession in collective bargaining with the *Krankenkassen* but have also the monopoly for settling doctors' fees. This is a complex bureaucratic system where individual doctors settle the services rendered to patients according to a system of 'points', the value of which is negotiated between the KV and the *Krankenkassen*.[10] It is obvious that, combined with compulsory membership, this gives the associations considerable power over their members, and that it also entails a considerable conflict potential between different groups of doctors, such as general practitioners and specialists. For the organized medical profession, on the other hand, the system involves a mix of important obligations and privileges in relationship to the state: doctors in private practice obtained the legal monopoly for ambulatory care – which excluded hospitals or any institutions established by the *Krankenkassen*, from delivering outpatient services. But as counterpart, the *Kassenärztliche Vereinigungen* are legally bound to ensure the provision of medical services, and this is tantamount to renouncing the strike weapon. A central institutional link with the GKV funds is established by the *Bundesausschuss* (originally: *Reichsausschuss*) *der Ärzte und Krankenkassen* (Federal Committee of Doctors and Health Insurance Funds), a parity-based body which has gradually acquired important functions in defining standards of adequate and efficient health care which have binding power. However, the *Kassenarztsystem* includes only one segment of the providers of medical care, and the other segments remained long outside this corporatist bargaining structure.

Since the 1970s, rapidly rising health costs caused increasing political concern and led to government intervention. Much of the responsibility for this *Kostenexplosion* was attributed to the medical providers, in particular to doctors as the gatekeepers of the system. In 1977 a first attempt of the socialist-liberal coalition government to institute some interventionist controls was blocked by the veto power of the CDU opposition majority in the Federal Council (Bundesrat), and the Christian Democrats successfully introduced the counterproposal of establishing the 'Concerted Action in the Health System' (*Konzertierte Aktion im Gesundheitswesen*, KAG), modelled after the 'Concerted Action' in economic policy that existed from 1967 to 1974 (Wiesenthal 1981). The KAG was conceived of as a conference of the representatives of corporate actors in the field of medical care, meeting at regular intervals to negotiate guidelines which the health funds and KV were expected to take into consideration, with the aim of containing the rising health costs. Bargaining in the KAG was very much characterized by a corporatist 'logic of exchange' where the medical profession restrained demands for higher fees and as a counterpart expected, for example, measures to check the rising influx of young doctors into practice. Initially, these negotiations in the KAG had some modest results, but after several years the tripartite bargaining approach of the KAG proved less and less effective in checking the further rise of health costs. The establishment, in 1985, of an Experts Council attached to the KAG (*Sachverständigenrat für die*

Konzertierte Aktion im Gesundheitswesen) was already a symptom of the crisis of tripartite bargaining between the health insurance funds, the provider groups and the administration. Represented among its members were the most important corporate actors in the health sector, but it was also composed in such a manner as to specifically bridge the antagonism between the medical profession and the health economists (Perschke-Hartmann 1994). The *Sachverständigenrat* was hence not instituted to mobilize neutral expertise but to search for solutions fitting as basis for compromises (Döhler 1990). So, even when the direct bargaining process was deadlocked, the government might still be in a position to intervene on the basis of a common denominator of conflicting interests.

Indeed, in the 1980s the institutional logic of the system progressively made more direct government intervention unavoidable. Notwithstanding the change of government in 1982 and the profession of beliefs of the new conservative-liberal majority in the superiority of markets, a fundamental market-oriented reform of the health system had no chance of serious consideration (ibid.). To be sure, some measures such as limited co-payments by patients were introduced to check the 'moral hazard' inherent – according to the liberal diagnosis – in the system. But the effects of co-payments remained limited, and the primacy of bargaining between health funds and providers of medical care was upheld. But in its pursuit of cost containment the government, by hierarchical fiat, attempted to limit the scope of bargaining within the self-administration to the distribution of strictly limited increments. To simplify a complex development, it may here suffice to say that the aggregate sum of doctors' fees was capped, with the consequence that the value of 'points' earned by doctors could no longer be freely negotiated by the KV and was bound to decrease. A further consequence was that the distributive shares of that shrinking cake became highly controversial within the membership of the KV. Recently, the system was refined by defining a 'budget' for the health system and threatening doctors with making them financially liable for exceeding the budget limit. The immediate effect of this system was that an augmentation of services by individual doctors did not automatically lead to a higher aggregate income for the medical profession. The indirect effect, however, was an increasing distributional struggle among different categories of the medical profession (in particular, between specialists and general practitioners). Yet, given the impossibility of exit from the system of compulsory membership, this remained an internal problem of the medical profession and only indirectly concerned the government and the *Krankenkassen*. The medical associations of course strongly opposed this strategy, by which they not only felt financially trapped but which they also resented as interfering with their professional autonomy.

What reinforced the resentment of the medical profession was that other providers of care, notably the hospital sector, were, for a long time, left out of the corporatist system of cost containment.[11] As only providers of ambulatory care were included in the corporatist system of the GKV *Selbstverwaltung*, state-monitored corporatist controls could of course only be effective in the case of doctors in private practice. But the government too considered this as a serious deficit and began to extend 'corporatis-ation' (Döhler and Manow-Borgwardt 1992) to other medical providers. It is remarkable that the strategy failed in dealing with the pharmaceutical industry but succeeded much better in the hospital sector.

In the first case the premise of the corporatist approach was that the market-liberal alternative, increasing patients' co-payments for drugs, had only modest effects and was also highly controversial and unpopular with the electorate. However, in the pharmaceutical industry the government found no associational partner with sufficient authority to effectively commit its members. Its peak association, the Bundesverband der Pharmazeutischen Industrie (BPI) remained extremely reluctant to co-operate, not least because the impact of cost containment would hit the different branches of the industry in a quite unequal manner. The interests of the big firms engaged in pharmaceutical research were diametrically opposed to those of the manufacturers of generic drugs who were bound to profit. The government tried different approaches (Perschke-Hartmann 1994) – first by putting pressure on the health insurance funds and the pharmaceutical industry to negotiate a reduction of the price of drugs. When this failed, it repeatedly asked the industry to make a 'solidarity contribution' to the effort of cost reduction in the form of rebates for the health insurance funds. This was likewise to no avail. Hence the government finally choose a different approach by mobilizing the disciplining effects of the *Kassenarztsystem*. This was done by indirectly including the costs of drugs in the capping of doctors' fees: if drug prescriptions exceed the aggregate 'budget' for drugs the excess was to be deducted from the capped sum earmarked for fees. Although this technique could not automatically eliminate the element of strong 'moral hazard' in the practices of prescribing drugs, many doctors became indeed reluctant to prescribe expensive or unnecessary drugs. As a further consequence, however, the distributional conflicts within the pharmaceutical industry have reached such an intensity that the BPI as the peak organization of the entire industry has fallen apart.

But the federal government succeeded, after negotiations with state governments, with the 'corporatisation' of the hospital sector (Döhler and Manow-Borgwardt 1992). The legal status of hospital associations, formerly umbrella organizations with limited service functions, was enhanced to give them power for collective bargaining on behalf of individual hospitals. Together with a series of other measures this aimed at the containment of hospital costs, until now the most dynamic factor in the rise of health costs. But this did not eliminate the latent domain conflict between private doctors and hospitals. The steering capacity of parity-based self-administration as the basis for concertation in health policy remains limited, and state intervention is on the rise. All in all, the corporatist repertoire in the system of public health insurance (including strong monitoring by government) was thus steadily expanding in the last decade but it developed into a mode of governance where associations saw their scope for bargaining progressively restricted and found themselves transformed into reluctant executors of a policy of financial restraint which was formulated against their protests but which they were nevertheless legally obliged to implement.

Consensus politics against electoral calculus: Schröder's strategy of reform

In the first year of the new majority the *Bündnis für Arbeit* produced few tangible results. The government spent much time and energy upon clarifying its programmatic options, and it was torn between Schröder's pragmatism and the polarizing party chairman Oskar Lafontaine (who also held the powerful office of minister of finance). When the latter, who had become increasingly isolated with his belief in Keynesian recipes, spectacularly withdraw from all his functions, this leadership conflict was resolved in the chancellor's favour. Yet the collapse of the corporatist approach to welfare state retrenchment under Kohl's leadership had left a lot of distrust among the actors involved, and it needed patient labour to restore the goodwill required for a renewed attempt. But the slow progress of the new approach was also due to the specific institutional constraints of negotiated welfare state reform just described.

Gerhard Schröder's strategic situation was still further complicated by the loss of the majority in the Federal Council after the state elections of 1999. The Social Democrats lost control of the states of Hessen and Saarland after a polarizing campaign by the Christian Democrats against the red-green project for facilitating the naturalization of immigrants. This highlighted the ambivalent impact of the electoral calculus on the politics of reform. For many decades the party system had been dominated by 'adversary politics' (Finer 1975) and so did not play that supportive role which in other countries was an important condition for the success of negotiated adjustment of the welfare state.

Reacting to these experiences, Schröder developed a leadership style fundamentally different from his predecessor's. Whereas Kohl had finally deadlocked himself in a polarized party system, Schröder undertook to shift political decisions from the party arena to extra-parliamentary consensus-building, employing techniques familiar from smaller European countries. The *Bündnis für Arbeit* was the first and most visible of these deliberative bodies, but several others followed. Expert commissions were established to submit proposals for old age pensions reform and for reforming the legal status of foreigners, and care was always taken to include prominent maverick Christian Democrats who would not subordinate their independent judgment to the electoral concerns of the party leaders.

Parallel to this pursuit of expert consensus, Schröder developed a considerable proficiency in building cross-party coalitions in the Federal Council. Although the CDU had succeeded in breaking the red-green preponderance in that body, they lacked a *Bundesrat* majority of their own to thwart the legislative agenda of the government. However, the latter needed the decisive votes of some state coalition governments including liberals or Christian Democrats together with Social Democrats. Since in these states the coalition agreements provided for abstention in case of disagreements, opposition leaders were confident that such abstentions would be sufficient to stall controversial bills if these required the approval of a majority (*Zustimmungsgesetze*) of the members of the Federal Council.[12] And after the red-green majority in the Diet had passed a tax reform that was generally considered as a remarkable step forward, the opposition was certain that it could bring this bill down in the *Bundesrat*. But the chancellor developed hitherto rather unusual log-rolling skills to buy the decisive votes from some 'black-red' governments. The Christian Democrats in these states could not refuse the favours offered for their local labour market or budget, and the final vote of the tax reform by an absolute majority of the Federal Council thus amounted to an embarrassing setback for the opposition leadership. Half a year later the same scenario was repeated for old age pension reform after the CDU had left the bargaining table of consensus negotiations.

Faced with this two-track strategy of expert consensus and *ad hoc* cross-party bargaining the opposition felt increasingly vulnerable. CDU leaders obstinately refused to get caught in Schröder's 'consensus trap' (*Konsensfalle*). But this attitude largely condemned them to immobility and contributed only to undermine their own standing. After all, passed despite their opposition contained significant departures from established features of the supposedly rigid German welfare state, and so in the eyes of many observers the 'reform gridlock' regarded as the hallmark of the late Kohl era was finally overcome. Tax reform, among others, made it easy for banks to sell their industrial holdings, and this created the conditions for dismantling traditional features of German capitalism that were increasingly dysfunctional in globalizing financial markets, and it was welcomed by large parts of the business community. The same was true of an old age pensions reform that introduced mandatory private insurance (with broad options for consumer choice) as one future key component of the system.

Indeed, the salience of corporatist bargaining in renegotiating the welfare state cannot be analysed without regarding the role of the party system. In Western Europe, the new social pacts have often been struck on the initiative or with a strong participation of governing majorities. And as a rule, this presupposed consensus-oriented political coalitions which were apt to mediate the conflict between business and labour interests. In Germany, however, traditional adversarial party strategies tend to discourage the formation of such coalitions, and moreover in the legislative process divided majorities in parliament and in the Federal Council may under certain circumstances prove dysfunctional for consensus-building. Schröder has so far been successful in circumventing the potential deadlocks arising from the party system.

Notes

1 Cited from the web page of the Federal President (http://www.bundespraesident. de/n/nph-b/reden/de/berlin.htm?reden/deutsch1997.map)
2 See Czada (1998) for these details and for the following.
3 *Wirtschaftsstandort* means the local conditions for investments. The *Standort Deutschland* debate focused on maintaining Germany's competitiveness in a globalizing economy by the removal of disincentives for foreign and domestic investors.
4 According to the established jurisprudence, collective agreements have precedence over legal stipulations if they are more favourable to workers (*Günstigkeitsprinzip*).
5 An elaborate organizational chart can indeed be found on the special internet homepage <http:www.buendnis.de> presented by the Federal Press and Information Office.
6 Olaf Gersemann and Monika Dunkel 'Niederlande – Nachbar mit Mumm: Die Holländer demonstrieren, wie man den erstarrten Wohlfahrtsstaat zurückschraubt und zukunftstauglich macht', in *Wirtschaftswoche*, 20/2 (1997), 22.
7 Some authors however contest the description of the health system as corporatist (Perschke-Hartmann 1994).
8 On the policy community of old age pensions, see Nullmeier and Rüb (1993).
9 There are still other types of health funds within the GKV system, mostly for specific groups, such as the health insurance funds established by firms (*Betriebskrankenkassen*). Like all other GKV health funds they are now equally open to all wage earners. Civil servants are exempted from compulsory health insurance: about half of their health costs are directly reimbursed by the state, and for the rest they may take private insurance, similar to self-employed persons.
10 For details, see Alber (1992).
11 Including hospitals in cost containment was for many years difficult because the *Länder* (member states of the federation) were concerned about their jurisdiction over the planning of capacities and investments in the hospital sector. The escalation of costs has finally led them to reconsider their interests (Döhler and Manow-Borgwardt 1992).
12 This procedure applies to about two-thirds of all federal legislation, including most major tax laws. In all other cases, the Federal Council has a suspensory veto (that can in turn be overridden by the Diet), but for such a veto the CDU could not muster sufficient majorities.

References

Alber, Jens (1992) *Das Gesundheitswesen der Bundesrepublik Deutschland: Entwicklung, Struktur und Funktionsweise*, Frankfurt am Main: Campus.
Alber, Jens and Brigitte Bernardi-Schenkluhn (1992) *Westeuropäische Gesundheitssysteme im Vergleich: Bundesrepublik Deutschland, Schweiz, Frankreich, Italien, Großbritannien*, Frankfurt am Main: Campus.

Bergmann, Joachim *et al.* (1975) *Gewerkschaften in der Bundesrepublik: gewerkschaftliche Lohnpolitik zwischen Mitgliederinteressen und ökonomischen Systemzwängen*, Frankfurt am Main: Campus.

Cameron, David R. (1984) 'Social Democracy, Corporatism, Labour Quiescence, and the Representation of Economic Interest in Advanced Capitalist Society', in John Goldthorpe (ed.) *Order and Conflict in Contemporary Capitalism*, Oxford: Clarendon Press, pp. 143–78.

Czada, Roland (1998) 'Vereinigungskrise und Standortdebatte. Der Beitrag der Wiedervereinigung zur Krise des westdeutschen Modells', *Leviathan*, 26: 24–59.

Döhler, Marian (1990) *Gesundheitspolitik nach der 'Wende': Policy-Netzwerke und ordnungspolitischer Strategiewechsel in Großbritannien, den USA und der Bundesrepublik Deutschland*, Berlin: Sigma.

Döhler, Marian and Philip Manow (1997) *Strukturbildung von Politikfeldern: das Beispiel bundesdeutscher Gesundheitspolitik seit den fünfziger Jahren*, Opladen: Leske & Budrich.

Döhler, Marian and Philip Manow-Borgwardt (1992) 'Korporatisierung als gesundheitspolitische Strategie', *Staatswissenschaften und Staatspraxis*, 3: 64–106.

Ebbinghaus, Bernhard and Anke Hassel (1999) *Striking Deals: Concertation in the Reform of Continental European Welfare States*, MPIfG Discussion Paper 99/3, Max-Planck-Institut für Gesellschaftsforschung, Köln.

Feldman, Gerald D. (1966) *Army, Industry, and Labour in Germany, 1914–1918*, Princeton: Princeton University Press.

Feldman, Gerald D. (1981) 'German interest group alliances in war and inflation, 1914–1923', in Suzanne Berger (ed.) *Organizing Interests in Western Europe: Pluralism, Corporatism, and the Transformation of Politics*, Cambridge: Cambridge University Press, pp. 159–84.

Feldman, Gerald D. and Irmgard Steinisch (1985) *Industrie und Gewerkschaften 1914–1924: die überforderte Zentralarbeitsgemeinschaft*, Stuttgart: DVA.

Finer, Samuel Edward (ed.) (1975) *Adversary Politics and Electoral Reform*, London: Anthony Wigram.

Hassel, Anke (1998) 'Soziale Pakte in Europa', *Gewerkschaftliche Monatshefte*, 626–67.

Heffter, Heinrich (1969) *Die deutsche Selbstverwaltung im 19. Jahrhundert: Geschichte der Ideen und Institutionen*, 2., überarbeitete Aufl., Stuttgart: Koehler.

Lehmbruch, Gerhard (1977) 'Liberal Corporatism and Party Government' [revised edn], *Comparative Political Studies*, 10: 91–126.

Lehmbruch, Gerhard (1985) 'Sozialpartnerschaft in der vergleichenden Politikforschung', in Peter Gerlich *et al.* (eds) *Sozialpartnerschaft in der Krise*, Vienna: Boehlau, pp. 85–107.

Lehmbruch, Gerhard (2002) 'Quasi-Consociationalism in German Politics: Negotiated Democracy and the Legacy of the Westphalian Peace', *Acta Politica* 37: 175–94.

Markovits, Andrei S. (1982) 'Introduction: Model Germany – a cursory overview of a complex construct', in Andrei S. Markovits (ed.) *The Political Economy of West Germany: Modell Deutschland*, New York: Praeger, pp. 1–11.

Neumann, Franz (Leopold) (1957) *The Democratic and the Authoritarian State: Essays in Political and Legal Theory*, New York: Free Press.

Neumann, Franz L. (1937) 'Der Funktionswandel des Gesetzes im Recht der bürgerlichen Gesellschaft', *Zeitschrift für Sozialforschung*, 1937, 542–96.

Nullmeier, Frank and Friedbert W. Rüb (1993) *Die Transformation der Sozialpolitik: vom Sozialstaat zum Sicherungsstaat*, Frankfurt am Main: Campus.

Perschke-Hartmann, Christiane (1994) *Die doppelte Reform: Gesundheitspolitik von Blüm zu Seehofer*, Opladen: Leske & Budrich.

Rabenschlag-Kräusslich, Jutta (1983) *Parität statt Klassenkampf? Zur Organisation des Arbeitsmarktes und Domestizierung des Arbeitskampfes in Deutschland und England 1900–1918*, Frankfurt am Main: Campus.

Soskice, David (1999) 'Divergent Production Regimes: Coordinated and Uncoordinated Market Economies in the 1980s and 1990s', in Herbert *et al.* (eds) *Continuity and Change in Contemporary Capitalism*, Cambridge: Cambridge University Press, pp. 101–34.

Streeck, Wolfgang (1979) 'Gewerkschaftsorganisation und industrielle Beziehungen: Einige Stabilitätsprobleme industriegewerkschaftlicher Interessenvertretung und ihre Lösung im westdeutschen System der industriellen Beziehungen', *Politische Vierteljahresschrift*, 20: 241–57.

Streeck, Wolfgang (1982) 'Organizational consequences of neo-corporatist co-operation in West German Labour Unions', in Gerhard Lehmbruch and Philippe Schmitter (eds), *Patterns of Corporatist Policy-making*, London: Sage, pp. 29–82.

Swenson, Peter (1989) *Fair Shares: Unions, Pay, and Politics in Sweden and West Germany*, Ithaca, NY: Cornell University Press.

Teuteberg, Hans-Jürgen (1961) *Geschichte der industriellen Mitbestimmung in Deutschland: Ursprung und Entwicklung ihrer Vorläufer im Denken und in der Wirklichkeit des 19. Jahrhunderts*, Tübingen: Mohr.

Thelen, Kathleen A. (1991) *Union of Parts: Labour Politics in Postwar Germany*, Ithaca, NY: Cornell University Press.

Traxler, F. (1995) 'From Demand-side to Supply-side Corporatism? Austria's Labour Relations and Public Policy', in C. Crouch and F. Traxler (eds) *Organized Industrial Relations in Europe: What Future?*, Aldershot: Avebury.

Visser, Jelle and Anton Hemerijck (1997) ' "A Dutch Miracle": Job Growth, Welfare Reform and Corporatism in the Netherlands', Amsterdam: Amsterdam University Press.

Wiesenthal, Helmut (1981) *Die Konzertierte Aktion im Gesundheitswesen: Ein Beispiel für Theorie und Politik des modernen Korporatismus*, Frankfurt am Main: Campus.

7 Renegotiating the Swiss welfare state[1]

Klaus Armingeon

Introduction

Corporatism, the institutionalized co-operation of trade unions, employers and the state, played an important role in the expansion of state intervention and of social security in the 1960s and 1970s in the Netherlands, Austria and Belgium. In top-level tripartite meetings, important decisions about fiscal policy and social security programmes were made. In the 1990s corporatism has played an important role in the adaptation of the Dutch and Austrian welfare states to new economic and social requirements, an adaptation which has involved a major remolding of social and economic policy. In Switzerland, the situation has been different. Expansive fiscal policy has never been used in a encompassing way to tackle economic problems. Compared to that of other European countries, the Swiss welfare state emerged late. Judged by social security expenditures, it remained slim for a long time. It did not experience a dramatic expansion in the 1960s and 1970 as most other Western countries did. As a result, the need for retrenchment has been less felt in the 1990s. In the 1990s, the Dutch Wassenaar agreement was not matched in Switzerland nor was there a counterpart to the Austrian budget cuts of the mid-1990's, which were approved by employers and trade unions.

This does not mean that there is no Swiss corporatism. The Swiss state, trade unions and employers co-operate in various ways, although not by means of top-level bargains on wages, taxes and public expenditures. Since 1947, the Constitution gives trade unions and employers the right to be consulted before the passage of any implementing legislation in a field of concern to these organizations. In the everyday political process, this means that they are consulted before any economic and social policies are decided upon. In addition, the Constitution guarantees the development of the economic interest organizations and stipulates that interest organizations can be called upon to implement public policy. Due to its weakly professionalized political system (and in particular its national parliament), the Swiss government relies heavily on expert commissions for the development of policy. About 200–400 expert commissions exist at the federal level. The members are nominated by the federal government which pays special attention to the representation of labour unions and employers' organizations (Papadopoulos 1997: 69–78; Linder 1999, chapter 9; Kriesi 1982). Interest organizations can take over public functions, particularly in agricultural policy (Sciarini 1994; Halbherr and Müdesacher 1985), but also in vocational policy (Farago and Kriesi 1986; Farago and Ruf 1992). In foreign economic policy, interest organizations participate in both formal and informal ways (Wildhaber 1992: 137).

Why did this institutionally highly developed corporatism so clearly fail to bring about the outcomes observed in other small countries like Austria or the Netherlands? For some authors the answer is obvious: Switzerland is the case of a liberal capitalist, a liberal corporatist and a liberal welfare state (Katzenstein 1985; Esping-Andersen 1990). In this country, a liberal party is particularly strong. The social democratic left and the Catholic centre are weak, hence state intervention in the economy is limited and a large welfare state never developed. Since there was no large welfare state, corporatism could not contribute to its retrenchment. A second answer points to an institution peculiar to Switzerland, not found in neighbouring nations: direct democracy. Direct democracy is a major impediment to the expansion of taxation and state intervention (Kirchgässner *et al.* 1999; Obinger and Wagschal 2000; Wagschal 1997; Gilliand 1993; Obinger 1998: 141–2).[2] Although neither one of these explanations is incorrect, they are hardly adequate if taken as mono-causal explanations for the development of economic and social policy. In what follows, I argue that the unique impact of corporatism on economic and social policy-making in Switzerland is to a large extent explained by the interlocking network of bargaining arenas, of which the corporatist forum is only one. This makes it so different to some other countries with corporatism, where there is fewer or – in case of majority democracies – no bargaining between the major parliamentary parties and/or where there is no need or a reduced level of need to negotiate between central and state authorities.

The underlying idea has been developed by Lehmbruch (1976). In the case of decision-making within interlocked political arenas, he argues that policy development is likely to be stalled, if the decision techniques in these forums vary. One could add that even if all decisions are made through bargaining and mutual concessions, for rapid policy-making the dominant goals or power distributions in these different forums have to be similar. Since this is probably often not the case and since bargaining in different arenas has to be co-ordinated with bargains between arenas, reaching agreement on the final decision is time-consuming. It is also contingent on 'windows of opportunity' (Kingdon 1984), when decisions emanating from one bargaining round are tolerated or even accepted by the other centres of decision making. Due to the need for compromise, the final policy programme is often composed of elements from different – and sometimes even contradictory – policy manifestos. In addition, delayed policy-making gives rise to functionally equivalent private organizations, which are an institutional legacy once a public policy decision has been agreed upon. I argue that these hypotheses are more consistent with the development of Swiss social and economic policy-making, compared to mono-causal explanations relying on direct democracy, the weak left and the strength of the liberal party. Thus I am extending an argument by Gruner (1964: 63): according to him, the post-war configuration of the Swiss state and economy is due to 'this strange hybrid of state socialism and intervention by interest organizations, accompanied by a nostalgia for liberalism' (*jene seltsame Kreuzung von Staatssozialismus und Verbandsinterventionismus samt dem mitlaufenden Heimweh nach dem Liberalismus*).

In the next section, the major policy decisions in economic and social policy-making since the 1970s will be listed. The major questions relate to the components of these policies. Are they overwhelmingly liberal, as the hypothesis of liberal capitalism and liberal or decentralized corporatism suggests? Or do they contain quite different elements which plausibly can be traced back to concessions in and between bargaining arenas? In the following chapter, the major forums of economic and social policy-making will be identified. Examples will illustrate how these forums interact.

Social and economic policy in Switzerland since the 1970s[3]

Economic policy

Even in its heyday, Keynesianism had far fewer supporters in Switzerland than in other countries (Frey 1993: 17). There were attempts at Keynesian co-ordination, though. In the early 1970s, when the economy was over-heated, the federal government levied a tax on exports, to be paid back later. In 1971, in selected regions tearing down houses was forbidden in order to limit demand for the construction industry. In 1975–6, when Switzerland experienced its first major employment crisis – in 1976, the number of jobs had fallen by 9 per cent compared to 1973 – public sector demand was increased, amounting to more than 2 per cent of GNP. Even in the 1990s, when Keynesian techniques had been eliminated from the government's policy options in most OECD countries, Switzerland implemented 'impulse programmes', intended to stimulate economic activity by fiscal expansion. However, these programmes only muted the pro-cyclical development of public budgets (social security expenditures excluded); in Switzerland, they did not become anti-cyclical (Schwartz and Graf 1986; Saurer 1996; Frey 1993: 39). The federal government acquired the right to macro-economic steering – without prejudicing the budgetary rights of the cantons – in 1978, after a draft Constitutional amendment which would have reduced cantonal prerogatives had failed in a popular vote in 1975.

This muted anti-Keynesian stance of policy-making is due to the aversion of Swiss political elites and the Swiss people — as expressed in popular votes – to public debt and deficits. As early as 1958, a Constitutional amendment required the federal government to pay off its debts (Article 42*bis*). In 1974, the Swiss people voted in principle for a 'brake on public expenditures'. However this did not come into effect due to its linkage to a tax increase, rejected by the people in the same popular vote. In 1995, a similar proposal led to a new article in the Constitution (Article 88.2 and Article 88.3). In 1996, parliament imposed moderation on itself with regard to expenditures. In 1998 the people voted to accept another constitutional rule. As soon as the federal public deficit exceeds a certain threshold, austerity measures have to be taken. In April 1998, an informal 'round table' of political and societal elites agreed on a package of policies intended to reduce the federal debt and deficit.

Price, agricultural and cartel policy have not been liberal in the past. In 1972 when inflation was rising, price controls were temporarily applied, lasting until 1978. These controls found broad-based support from the population, which in 1982 – against the advice of economists and the wishes of the government and the parliament – constitutionally introduced price controls. Agricultural policy has strongly protected farmers. It is only in the 1990s that major reforms have been introduced under domestic and external pressure (Sciarini 1994). In contrast to EU-Europe, cartels are not forbidden in Switzerland. However, a new law passed in 1995 (Mach 1998) stipulates that agreements on prices in cartels are no longer legal.

Apart from muted Keynesianism and price controls, the business cycle policy directed towards the secondary and tertiary sector has primarily been monetary policy (Frey 1993: 17, 20).

Social policy

Judged by the date of introduction of the major compulsory social insurance schemes of the European welfare states and by the coverage of those schemes, Switzerland has been a welfare laggard for a long time (Alber 1987: 152; Schmidt 1998: 180). Social security expenditures have been below the EU average. In particular, the expenditures were much below that of countries with comparable wealth. In comparison to Western European countries, Swiss expenditures in 1993 for pensions and health are almost as high as one would expect from a regression of security expenditures on economic wealth. Transfers to families and for mothers, however, are much lower than the regression estimates predict (Gilliand and Rossini 1997: 141–55). Health insurance contributions are levied per capita and not per household or family; for a long time premiums have been completely independent of income. Since 1998, there has been a subsidy to smaller groups with very low income. This income-related feature varies by canton. Judged by these measures, Switzerland was a welfare laggard. It has not avoided welfare state regulations, though. In addition, developments since the 1970s have seen the addition of many important elements of conservative and social democratic welfare states to the respective Swiss schemes (Obinger 1998). In the 1990s, the size of the Swiss welfare state converged towards the average European welfare state. Partly this is due to increased revenues and expenditures of social security programmes, partly it can be explained by the different statistical treatment of certain welfare schemes, previously coded as private and now as public, and partly this is due to shortcomings of official statistics.[4]

In historical perspective and apart from the major social security schemes (pensions, unemployment and health insurance), Switzerland has been a forerunner in social policy. It belongs to the group of countries which introduced the right of association and the right to combine already in the middle of the nineteenth century. In 1877, one of Europe's most modern factory laws was introduced, regulating minimum age of workers (14 years), the normal working day (11 hours), and hygiene and accident prevention at work. In 1911, Switzerland was one of the first countries – if not the first – to acknowledge collective agreements (including their inalienability) as legitimate and binding (Armingeon 1994). The factory law and the regulations on collective agreements codified at the federal level were modelled on laws which had been established previously in some cantons (the factory law of Glarus and the law on collective agreements of Geneva).

During the inter-war years, the Swiss welfare state fell behind the average European nation; after the Second World War, it was catching up. The people endorsed old age pensions for all residents in 1947; compulsory unemployment insurance in 1976 and obligatory health insurance in 1994. Although these reforms came late and after several failed attempts (cf. Immergut 1992), they contained remarkable and innovative elements, partly due to the legacy of delayed reform and partly due to cross-concessions in the political process.

When obligatory old age pensions were introduced, a system of occupational pensions was already in place. Since these schemes were extensive and long-standing, the new pension system could not simply dissolve these older systems but had to co-exist with them. In contrast to Bismarckian Germany in 1883, reforms were not written on what amounted to a *tabula rasa*. In this way, the Swiss three-pillar system of old age pensions (a basic public pension, occupational pensions and private savings) came into being. The basic public pension is based on the contributions of the working population, which are transferred to retired people. Occupational pensions come from a fund which has been accumulated by the individual employee while he or she has been in employment. This structure relieves the Swiss pension system of problems, which occur in other countries due to the exclusive reliance on a single way of financing the scheme. A second characteristic of the pension system is the coverage: it is confined to residents, not just employees. Thus it creates a base line of social security for all elderly inhabitants. Third, the system is strongly redistributive. The ratio of maximum to minimum pensions had been settled at 3:1; in 1969 this was changed to 2:1. Where a pensioner is not entitled to a normal minimum pension, subject to certain pre-conditions, s/he can claim an additional pension. Hence the guaranteed income of elderly people cannot fall below the minimum pension. Fourth, the pensions are intended to provide a basic minimum standard of living. In comparative perspective, they are rather generous, particularly since the late 1960s. As of January 1999, the monthly minimum pension amounts to about US$720 (US $1,080 for a married couple); the maximum pension is $1,440 ($2,160 for a married couple). In addition to this basic income, from the so-called first pillar of the pension system, occupational pensions also provide income: these constitute the second pillar. Taken together, these two sources of income should correspond to about 60 per cent of the last monthly paycheck. In addition, citizens can save money, which is tax deductible and can be received only after retirement or for the redemption of mortgages (the third pillar). The third pillar is mainly of interest to high income groups among wage earners, since it enables them to avoid high marginal tax rates. The fourth characteristic of the Swiss pension system is that the administration of the basic pension and additional pensions is carried out by the cantons and municipalities.

In 1995 the people endorsed a major reform of the pension system. The retirement age for women was increased from 62 to 64 (the retirement age for men was and still is 65 years). In return, the pension entitlements of couples were split, so that both receive the same pensions.[5] This means that the spouse who worked mostly in the household and did the child rearing (usually the woman) has her own income in her own bank account, which is the same as that of the other partner. Even more important, now years spent caring for the children until they reached the age of 16 are considered equal to years of employment for the purpose of calculating the pension.

Hence the Swiss pension system combines an egalitarian and generous basic pension with a strongly income-dependent system of occupational pensions and an even more inegalitarian third pillar. In comparative perspective, the basic pension is particularly egalitarian with regard to gender, since years of child rearing are treated on a par with paid employment and since spouses who have not been wage earners are entitled to 50 per cent of the couple's pension.

Disability insurance was introduced in 1959. It was introduced late and has a modern structure (Tschudi 1986: 17): (1) the basic principle is that integration into working life is superior to sheer alimentation by way of paying pensions; (2) mental disability is treated the same as physical disability; (3) pensions for the disabled are the same as the basic pension for elderly, i.e. their income rises with the level of wages and inflation.

In 1911, the federal state took over responsibility for health insurance.[6] The law established subsidies to private health insurance companies. At the federal level, affiliation to one of these insurance companies had not been obligatory. Some cantons, however, made it obligatory. By 1990, less than 10 per cent of the population was without health insurance. The insurance companies are private non-profit making organizations (mutual funds). Contributions are paid per capita and not per family or household, thus large families spent considerable sums for health insurance. Insurance companies could reject the applicants and they could levy premiums according to risk. Different health insurance companies reimbursed expenditures for different types of medical treatments. There were two major incentives which prevented the insured from using medical care excessively: an annual flat rate, and a deductible, equally about 10 per cent of all costs, both of which have to be paid by the insured party.

A major problem of this scheme has been its failure to stem the rising costs of health care. As long as insurance companies could try to avoid 'bad risks' and as long as costs could be passed on to the insured via higher contributions, insurance companies had few opportunities or incentives to affect the development of health care costs. Fees for medical services were negotiated collectively between insurance companies and associations representing providers. In 1994 this scheme was reformed. The basic idea was to continue with the existing system of private insurance companies – which could hardly be abolished or changed into public insurance – but to change how insurers compete for members. The new law stipulated that each inhabitant has to be covered by the same basic health insurance, plan which reimburses costs of a broad range of medical treatments. In addition, insurance companies cannot reject an application for membership. Premiums for a given level of insurance coverage must not vary according to age, sex or health. A mechanism for inter-firm compensation was created, equalizing the competitive position of insurance companies with different age and sex structures. As a result, insurance companies now have few opportunities to improve their position by selecting lower risk members. On the other hand, insurance companies are allowed to negotiate directly with providers over fees for medical services. Hence the competitive situation of an insurer is mainly dependent on its ability to negotiate advantageous contracts with providers and to improve internal administration. In this way, an insurer can offer comparatively low premiums and rapid turnaround in reimbursing claims for medical care. Subsidies to low income groups have been another element of this reform. Below a particular and rather low threshold of income, citizens can claim a subsidy, intended to reduce the costs of their insurance premium.

The reform of 1994 retained many of the liberal principles of the former system. Premiums have to be paid per capita. They are not income-dependent (except for low income groups). The insured have to pay a deductible and the insurance companies are still private organizations. By allowing companies to negotiate directly with providers, market elements have even been emphasized. On the other hand, egalitarian and redistributive elements have been added. In the selection of members, the market has been abolished, since insurance companies can no longer reject applicants. Low income groups receive a means-tested subsidy. There is a equalization between companies to compensate for differences in the age and gender structures of their membership. Finally, since the reform, insurance has become formally compulsory in the whole federal state, although *de facto* there was hardly change, since nearly all citizens already belonged to a insurance plan.

Up until 1976 unemployment insurance was not obligatory.[7] Since the late 1930s, Switzerland experienced uninterrupted full employment and little need was felt to establish such a scheme. Voluntary insurance was run by associations and companies, which received limited federal subsidies. In the early 1970s about 20 per cent of wage earners were members of such schemes. In the 1960s and early 1970s, the federal administration had already developed plans to introduce obligatory insurance with particular emphasis on active labour market policy (Freiburghaus 1987). The major employment crisis of 1974–9 triggered the introduction of obligatory insurance. It was approved by the people in a popular vote in 1976. A 1977 preliminary law implemented that decision. In 1984, it was replaced by the permanent law on unemployment insurance. In international comparison, Swiss unemployment insurance combines generous rates (70–80 per cent of previous earnings) with tight controls on the unemployed (Schmidt 1995) and a short duration of benefits. A major reform was brought about in 1995. It introduced active labour market measures, which the OECD labelled revolutionary, ambitious and matchless in comparative perspective (OECD 1996: 124, 132). Activation of the unemployed is the basic idea. After 150 days (30 weeks) of receiving unemployment benefits, the unemployed have to attend courses offered by the cantons. Only if they participate in such measures of active labour market policies are they entitled to further payments from the unemployment insurance. After a total of two years of receiving unemployment benefits, the benefits run out. If the unemployed accept part-time jobs or jobs with much lower wage than their last job, they are entitled to wage subsidies from the insurance scheme. The unemployed have to accept any reasonable job offer; a reasonable job is defined as a job with a wage amounting to at least 70 per cent of previous earnings.

Hence Swiss labour market policy combines different elements. With regard to the late introduction of obligatory unemployment insurance, the tight control of the unemployed, the strict rules on participation in programmes of active labour market policy and the definition of reasonableness of a new job, it is reminiscent of a model liberal welfare state. On the other hand, the introduction of active labour market policies in the 1990s and the generosity of unemployment benefits are features of social policy regimes labelled social democratic (Janoski 1994).

Three interconnected rounds of negotiation

This review of major economic and social policies in Switzerland casts doubt on Switzerland's unequivocal classification as a liberal welfare state. Although the major elements point in that direction, certain rules are redistributive and interventionist, which are familiar from social-democratic or Christian-conservative regimes of social policy. Neither does the term liberal corporatism seem completely adequate (Katzenstein 1984, 1985). Although central tripartite concertation of wage and public economic policies has not been achieved or even attempted, massive state intervention occurs in economic regulatory policy. This does not correspond to the assumption of a largely autonomous partnership between labour and capital, which leaves the state in a marginal role.

How can this mixture of a liberal, social-democratic and conservative welfare state with an interventionist but non-Keynesian state be explained? I argue that these seemingly incoherent policy patterns are the result of complex processes of compromise building in three interconnected rounds of negotiations. In their policy formulation these rounds of negotiation are constrained by popular votes – decisions by majority rule – and also the policies of the Swiss Central Bank, which favours price stability.

Two limits

Direct democracy is frequently accused of being a major impediment to reform and adaptation (cf. Borner *et al.* 1994). The numerous rejections of social policy reforms in popular votes can explain some of the lateness and the liberal character of the Swiss welfare state (Obinger 1998; Obinger and Wagschal 2000; Kirchgässner *et al.* 1999). In principle, such rejections are quite likely. Whenever a federal policy is proposed, the federal state must obtain the constitutional right to legislate in this area. Constitutional changes must be approved by popular vote. Once the federal state has the competence to legislate in a certain area, the relevant implementing legislation may be put to a popular vote. Hence there are two veto points for opposing groups (cf. Bonoli 1998; Bonoli and Mach 1998). If they fail in the first round (approving the constitutional amendment), they have a second chance when the implementing legislation is drafted. The first veto point, approval of constitutional change, is unavoidable. The second point, a referendum against a specific law, is optional. Since the requirements for a referendum are low (50,000 citizens or eight cantons have to support a referendum), major laws are frequently submitted to a popular vote. Hence expansion and retrenchment of the welfare state could be institutionally strongly impeded. This only applies however, if the group which successfully petitions for a referendum is relatively large. Once a compromise of all major societal groups has been achieved and the opposing groups are marginalized, direct democracy loses its braking effect in most cases.[8]

Usually the people accept decisions based on broad elite agreement (Sciarini and Trechsel 1996). On the other hand, political elites are forced to compromise if they want to avoid the rejection of an intended reform by a successful popular vote against it (Neidhart 1970).

A second institutional limitation on social and economic policy-making is the Swiss Central Bank. In its day-to-day operation it is independent of government, political parties and interest groups in its policies.[9] The law of the bank stipulates that government and bank inform each other before decisions on major monetary or business cycle policy are made. Government and bank should co-ordinate their policies. Since the 1973, the bank has considered price stability as its ultimate goal and restrictive monetary policy as the appropriate means to achieve this aim. As a consequence, any encompassing counter-cyclical fiscal policy is, in all likelihood, doomed to failure since the bank will probably react with restrictive measures in order to avoid inflation and thereby offset the additional demand created by fiscal policy measures.

Both of these limits on economic and social policy imply that any reform has to be based on broad agreement between the major political and societal groups and that the proposed policy has no major inflationary impact. This does not imply that successful reforms have to be watered down. Rather, the need to compromise enhances the possibility of policy packages which represent the outcome of barter deals between the respective groups. The more complex this bargaining procedure is, the higher the chance of non-decision. In addition, once agreement is reached, the probability is great that it is composed of very different elements, emanating from multiple deals.

Three forums of negotiation

The Swiss bargaining process is complex, since it consists of three different and interconnected arenas or forums, each of which has a major say in economic and social policy-making: the corporatist, consociational and federal arenas. The corporatist arena is made up of trade unions, employers' organizations and representatives of the federal administration. Political parties and representatives of cultural-linguistic groups bargain in the consociational forum. In the federal arena bargains occur between federal and cantonal authorities and between cantonal authorities themselves.[10] These rounds are interconnected with regard to the problems to be solved and the policies to be designed and implemented. In addition, loose coupling occurs on the level of the actors: due to the small size of the Swiss economic and political elite, the actors know each other, meet frequently in different settings and some individual actors in the various rounds are the same: they are for example representatives of a canton in the federal arena and representatives of a political party in the consociational arena (cf. Kriesi 1980, 1982).

Apart from the ability to trigger a successful referendum against a given economic or social policy, the power of the actors in these forums lies in their strategic position in these policy fields.

The corporatist forum

In terms of resources and personnel, the Swiss central state is a weak state. It even lacks its own direct tax resources. The present federal tax is only a transitory measure. To fulfil its functions, the federal state has needed the co-operation of private organizations and the voluntary and part-time participation of citizens. This resulted in a large number of extra-parliamentary commissions. These 200–400 extra-parliamentary, federal commissions (October 1998) are overwhelmingly staffed by private experts and representatives of interest organizations, and a few representatives of parliament and the federal administration. Some are of marginal importance, such as the former commission for awarding prices for the best billy-goat. Others, like the commissions for the social security system or economic policy, however, are the place where far-reaching plans are developed. Frequently laws are drafted in these commissions, which are sometimes simply ratified later by Parliament.

Constitutional changes in 1947 incorporated interest organizations into the state by guaranteeing their development (Federal Constitution Art 31*bis*.5) and by stating that the organizations of the economy have to be heard before the passage of any implementing legislation of some concern to them. In addition the federal state has the right to call upon interest organizations for the implementation of public law (Gruner 1959).

These rules and the tradition of formal and informal consultation (Kriesi 1980) give interest organizations – in particular employers' organizations – a position that can hardly be circumvented in economic and social policy.

The consociational forum

Parliamentary political parties are by no means of marginal importance in the Swiss direct democracy. Most laws are not submitted to a popular vote. Between 1947 and 1995 parliament voted on 1,271 pieces of legislation which could be have been put to a popular vote. Of these, only 6 per cent (75 cases) went to a popular vote and only 3 per cent of the laws (32 cases) were rejected by the people. Hence for most policies, political parties in parliament have the final say (Sciarini and Trechsel 1996). Due to historical and cultural reasons (Lehmbruch 1967, 1996) as well as the institutional threat of a referendum, the four major parties are used to seeking compromise and making policies in such a way that none of them attempts to trigger a referendum (Neidhart 1970). One consequence of this is a government made up of the same four parties since 1959. It acts as a collegial and coalition government, i.e. as a administration based on many political parties and without a coherent programme based on a party manifesto or an ideology. The parties of government account for about 80 per cent of members of the house of representatives (Nationalrat). Another implication is the need for lengthy processes of compromise building in government and major political parties. Any policy is dependent on agreement between four different parties of comparable power. Hence in contrast to most other Western countries, trade unions and employers cannot strike a deal with one or two major political parties in government and parliament. Whenever interest organizations want to accommodate their policies with the state, this presupposes difficult processes of policy decision making between numerous actors in the legislative and executive branches of the state.

The cantonal–federal forum

The third forum of economic and social policy-making is composed of representatives of the cantonal and federal authorities. The power of cantons in a given policy field derives from three institutional rules.

1   Since the federal government has no administrative apparatus for implementation, it is dependent on the cantonal and municipal organizations for carrying out the federal laws. In implementing a seemingly specific federal law, there is often an astonishing room for manœuvre. (Linder 1988, 1999).
2   In addition, some economic and social policy prerogatives lie with the cantons and municipalities. This has an impact on the extent to which they can modify a federal rule. In active labour market policy, cantons decide how they structure their employment agencies and they can even chose to create fewer jobs in employment programmes; although they have to pay for that. Subsidies for the cost of health insurance depend on cantonal decisions. Some cantons rarely implement these subsidies, other are very active and generous, benefiting every third person in the cantonal population. Some economic and social policies are decided upon solely by the canton or municipality. This is true of social assistance after social security benefits have run out. For example, an unemployed person gets unemployment benefits for about two years. After that time he/she is entitled to unemployment support from the canton. This varies considerably. After cantonal unemployment support has run out, there is cantonal social support. In some cantons this is a certain percentage of the previous unemployment benefits; in other cantons – like Geneva – it is cantonal minimum income scheme.
3   Judged by total resources, the tax burden in Switzerland is low and most taxes go directly or indirectly to the cantons and municipalities.

The federal budget is small, measured as a percentage of total GDP. This has a crucial implication for policies of demand management. Scharpf has coined the term ' the degree of difficulty in pursuing fiscal demand management', which is the increase in the central government budget which corresponds to a rise of 1 per cent in total GDP (Scharpf 1987: 261–9). Performing this calculation for Switzerland reveals that Switzerland is the country in the OECD world which has to increase central budget much more than any other.

The implication for the federal government is that it can hardly administer Keynesian demand management on its own. The solution has been co-operation between the federal state, cantons and municipalities. In the typical Keynesian designs of the 1970s and 1990s, the federal government announced that it was willing to pay a certain amount of the costs of cantonal or municipal investment, mostly in the field of building construction. Hence the local or cantonal authorities had an incentive to make investments, since part of the cost would be paid by the federal government. In this way, federal demand management triggered a local or cantonal demand management, which taken together, amounted to considerable sums.

Table 7.1 Degree of difficulty in macro-economic steering and centralization of public finances, 1995

Country	Degree of difficulty (Scharpf)	Centralization (receipts of central government in % of receipts of general government)
Norway	2.3	93.2
Denmark	2.4	67.7
Italy	2.8	67.9
UK	2.8	80.5
Belgium	3.0	59.6
Finland	3.0	48.0
Sweden	3.0	44.7
Ireland	3.1	83.0
Greece	3.4	60.2
Netherlands	3.4	55.0
Austria	3.7	52.2
Australia	3.8	72.0
Spain	4.0	53.7
France	4.4	10.7
Canada	4.5	44.6
USA	6.4	43.0
Germany	7.0	30.9
Japan	7.1	38.8
Switzerland	9.0	34.9

Sources: OECD 1997, *National Accounts*, Paris: OECD.

Examples

There is hardly an economic and social policy which is not of relevance to each of these three forums. As a result, policy reform happens only if the results of negotiation in one forum are not opposed by the outcome in any other forum. At least tacit approval is needed. If a reform takes place, it is likely to be composed of different elements which are quid-pro-quos for concessions made.

This interpretation can explain why Swiss social and economic policy-making is composed of different, incoherent elements. Some examples of major policy developments which support this explanation follow.

In 1975 a new constitutional article was discussed, giving the federal government the right to intervene in the business cycle by Keynesian means. This reform was supported by employers' organizations, trade unions and the major political parties. However, it was opposed in the federal forum. The representatives of the cantons feared that the federal government would limit the regional politicians' room for manœuvre. It was argued that the new constitutional article was an attack on cantonal sovereignty. In contrast to the national parties, about half of all cantonal factions of the federal political parties advocated rejection of the article. In the ensuing popular vote, representatives of the cantonal interests won by a slim majority. Three years later, the article in question was accepted after reducing the federal influence on cantonal budgets to co-operation of the federal state with cantons and representatives of the economy in the draft.

In the 1994–5 the reform of the unemployment insurance was debated. There was a discussion between federal and cantonal representatives with regard to the number of jobs cantons have to provide in programmes for active labour market policy. Due to the opposition of the cantons, the chamber of cantons in the strictly bi-cameral parliament did not accept the draft which was developed by the chamber of representatives in co-operation with employers and trade unions. The deadlock was solved in a common meeting of representatives of the cantons, the chamber of cantons, the chamber of representatives, employers and trade unions ('The Compromise of Solothurn'). Trade unions accepted some retrenchment in passive unemployment insurance in exchange for active labour market policy. Cantons accepted that they were to provide a large number of jobs in the context of the active policy, in return for reduced contributions to an unemployment insurance fund and for more flexibility with regard to the absolute number of jobs.

In 1995 the reform of the system of basic pensions combined egalitarian gender policies with an increase in the age of retirement for women. The latter had been opposed by trade unions and the Social Democratic Party. Trade unions called successfully for a referendum on the law. In the event of its rejection in a popular vote, gender equalization in basic pensions would have been eliminated too. The Social Democratic Party considered equalization superior to avoiding the increase in retirement age and hence proposed to accept the law. In the end, 61 per cent of participants in the popular vote voted 'yes'.[11]

The interconnectedness of the three bargaining forums and the ensuing vulnerability of policy changes is obvious in the case of the 1996 labour law reform. In the corporatist arena, an agreement was reached for a new labour statute. It would abolish the former prohibition of night-work for women, as well as facilitating work on Sundays. On the other hand, night-work should be compensated by a reduction in total working hours. Parliament changed this compromise in favour of employers by not accepting the compensation for night-work. Thereafter the members of the four major parties in the Federal government could not agree on a common position. In addition, the introduction of more work on Sundays would have been dependent on supporting legislation in the cantons, subject to cantonal popular votes. The trade unions and Social Democrats successfully called for a referendum against this law, which led to its rejection. The corporatist and consociational bargaining rounds did not arrive at the same result, making the law an easy victim of the organizations on the left.

A good example of successful co-ordination of negotiation rounds is the attempt at improving the federal budget deficit in April 1998. The federal Minister of Finance invited representatives of the cantons, the four major parties, the trade unions and employers' organizations to a common meeting. The federal Ministers for Justice and for Domestic Affairs participated as well. Working through the night of 6 April 1998, they decided that in order to reduce the federal budget:

- transfers from the Federation to the cantons would be cut by 300–350 million Swiss Francs per annum;
- the indexation of basic pensions to prices and wages would be delayed for one year. Previously pensions were indexed every two years, in future this would happen each third year;
- a temporary special tax for unemployment insurance would be continued;
- defence expenditures would be cut by about 12 per cent within three years;
- subsides to railways would be cut;
- federal expenditures (amounting to 3 per cent of expenses) would be cut or delayed;
- opportunities for legal tax evasion would be reduced;
- the participants would abstain from certain demands which increase federal expenditures or decrease federal receipts.

These items represent concessions made by the various actors. Reports from the meeting emphasize that the representatives of federal and cantonal administrations, political parties and interest organizations insisted on a balanced distribution of costs among their respective clienteles. Once again, the corporatist arena has not been the most important, nor was it co-operating with a few governing parties. Rather, negotiations occurred in and between bargaining rounds.

Conclusion

The expansion of the welfare state in Switzerland has been delayed; hence there is less need for its consolidation or retrenchment. Direct democracy is a major cause of the delayed development. An important reason for the rather small welfare state expenditures in the past is the distribution of political power: a weak left and a strong liberal party. However this explains only a part of the Swiss welfare state and government economic intervention. Elements of the respective policies and policy changes are not purely liberal: they represent conservative and social democratic goals as well. This seemingly incoherent combination of different policy elements can be traced back to negotiations in federal–cantonal and consociational as well as corporatist arenas.[12] Each of these arenas is important for economic and social policy making. Without at least tacit acceptance in one arena of the negotiation results in the other two, failure of policy- making is likely. In comparison with other corporatist countries, consociational democracy and state autonomy in a federal system are probably most pronounced in Switzerland. This applies in particular to the combination of both political institutions. No European corporatism is faced with both a strong federalism and a strong consociationalism. In contrast to other countries, the corporatist negotiations do not produce results, which – on the part of the state – will be implemented by a governing coalition of one or two large political parties. Rather, the results of the corporatist bargains have to be accommodated to the results of governmental and parliamentary decisions of at least four large parties and the decisions of twenty-six autonomous cantons and their populations. This explains why Swiss corporatist institutions could never attain such a dominant position in economic and social policy-making as those in other countries did.

Notes

1 This chapter was written in the context of a research project on the room for manœuvre of nation states in the period of economic internationalization. It was supported by a grant from the Swiss National Science Foundation. I am grateful to Guliano Bonoli, Herbert Obinger and Juerg Steiner for comments.
2 Another explanation points to the absence of centralization in Swiss collective bargaining. Under these conditions, the prerequisites of macro-economic steering are not in place. Thus, it is even questionable whether Switzerland can be labelled a corporatist country (cf. the review of literature by Kriesi 1995: 338–42). Even if one accepts the idea of a corporatism *sui generis*, this might explain the lack of a Keynesian past; it does not, however, explain why a strong corporatism did not affect social policy as it did in other European countries

apart from the explicit bargains between wage restraint and social policy compensation.

3 For the development of social policy I rely in particular on the accounts by Gilliand 1993, Bonoli 1997, 1998 and Bonoli and Mach 1998. The description of economic policy is based on Linder 1983, Frey 1993 and Armingeon 1999.

4 For an analysis of the expansion – at least in statistical terms – of the Swiss welfare state in the 1990s, see Armingeon 2001.

5 Hence, technically, it is not the pension that is split between spouses, but the contributions paid by either of them while married. It can make a difference in the case of divorcees and people who marry late. This is even more egalitarian, because it is a *de facto* recognition of the value of the unpaid work performed in the household. One implication of this splitting is the right of the spouse to get her own pension on her own bank account.

6 This section is concerned with basic health insurance, which covers all the cost of usual medical care. Supplementary insurance exists for special treatments, for dentists, etc.

7 For labour market policies see in particular OECD 1996.

8 There are, however, instances when major actors have been in support of a policy and the people rejected it. This applies in particular to decisions on foreign policy and European integration.

9 There is, however, a council, composed of representatives of political parties and interest organizations which supervises the conduct of business by the bank and which proposes the members of the board of directors to be elected by the federal government.

10 The deals between cantons and municipal authorities represent another level of negotiation which for the sake of simplicity will not be dealt with here. An informative description of the two- stage accommodation between federal, cantonal and municipal level in Keynesian policies is given in Saurer (1996).

11 In a second attempt trade unions tried to cancel the decision in 1998. They failed again.

12 This explanation refers exclusively to economic and social policy making. A precondition for such deals in and between rounds of negotiations is the ability of actors gradually to make concessions or to sacrifice less important policies for more important ones. In the case of strongly polarized or 'ideological' issues, barter deals are less likely and hence deadlock is probable. The innovative Swiss economic and social policies and the immobility in foreign policy support this hypothesis.

References

Alber, Jens (1987) *Vom Armenhaus zum Wohlfahrtsstaat. Analysen zur Entwicklung der Sozialversicherung in Westeuropa*, Frankfurt am Main and New York: Campus.

Armingeon, Klaus (1994) *Staat und Arbeitsbeziehungen. Ein internationaler Vergleich*, Opladen: Westdeutscher Verlag.

Armingeon, Klaus (1999) 'Wirtschafts- und Finanzpolitik', in Ulrich Klöti, Peter Knoepfel, Hanspeter Kriesi, Wolf Linder and Yannis Papadopoulos (eds) *Hand buch Politisches System der Schweiz*, Zürich: Verlag Neue Zürcher Zeitung, pp. 725–66.

Armingeon, Klaus (2001) 'Institutionalising the Swiss Welfare State', *West European Politics* (Special Issue, edited by Jan-Erik Lane).

Bonoli, Giuliano (1997) 'Switzerland: Institutions, Reforms and the Politics of Consensual Retrenchment', in Jochen Clasen (ed.) *Social Insurance in Europe*, Bristol: Polity Press, pp. 107–29.

Bonoli, Giuliano (1998) 'State Structures and the Process of Welfare State Adaption', in Paul Pierson (ed.) *The New Politics of the Welfare State* (forthcoming).

Bonoli, Giuliano and André, Mach (1998) *The Adjustment of National Employment and Social Policy to Economic Internationalization: Country Report on Switzerland*, Manuscript.

Borner, Silvio, Aymo Brunetti *et al.* (1994) *Die Schweiz im Alleingang*, Zürich: Verlag Neue Zürcher Zeitung.

Esping-Andersen, Gosta (1990) *The Three Worlds of Welfare Capitalism*, Princeton: Princeton University Press.

Farago, Peter and Hanspeter Kriesi (eds) (1986) *Wirtschaftsverbände in der Schweiz. Organisation und Aktivitäten von Wirtschaftsverbänden in vier Sektoren der Industrie*, Grüsch: Rüegger.

Farago, Peter and Heinz Ruf (1992) 'Verbände und öffentliche Politik – Staatstätigkeit ausserhalb des Staates?', in Heidrun Abromeit and Werner Pommerehne (eds) *Staatstätigkeit in der Schweiz*, Bern, Stuttgart and Wien: Haupt, pp. 71–96.

Freiburghaus, Dieter (1987) *Präventivmassnahmen gegen die Arbeitslosigkeit in der Schweiz. Methoden der Wirkungsanalyse und erste Ergebnisse*, Bern: Haupt.

Frey, René L. (1993) 'Wirtschafts- und Finanzpolitik der Schweiz', in Gerhard Schmid (ed.) *Handbuch Politisches System der Schweiz. Band 4. Politikbereiche*, Bern, Stuttgart and Wien: Haupt, pp. 10–107.

Gilliand, Pierre (1993) 'Politique sociale', in Gerhard Schmidt (ed.) *Handbuch Politisches System der Schweiz. Band 4. Politikbereiche*, Bern, Stuttgart and Wien: Haupt, pp. 111–223.

Gilliand, Pierre and Stéphane Rossinni (1997) *La protection sociale en Suisse. Recettes et dépenses, 1948–1997. Comparaisons avec les pays de l'Union Européene*, Lausanne: Réalités Sociales.

Gruner, Erich (1959) 'Der Einbau der organisierten Interessen in den Staat', *Schweizerische Zeitschrift für Volkswirtschaft und Statistik*, 95: 59–79.

Gruner, Erich (1964) '100 Jahre Wirtschaftspolitik. Etappen des Interventionismus in der Schweiz', *Schweizerische Zeitschrift für Volkswirtschaft und Statistik*, 100/1964: 35–70.

Halbherr, Philipp and Alfred Müdesacher (1985) *Agrarpolitik – Interessenpolitik? Eine Untersuchung der Zusammenhänge zwischen Politik und wirtschaftlichen Interessen in der schweizerischen Agrarpolitik*, Bern and Stuttgart: Paul Haupt.

Immergut, Ellen M. (1992) *Health Politics. Interests and Institutions in Western Europe*, Cambridge: Cambridge University Press.

Janoski, Thomas (1994) 'Direct State Intervention in the Labour Market: the Explanation of Active Labour Market Policy from 1950 to 1988 in Social Democratic, Conservative and Liberal Eegimes', in Thomas Janoski and Alexander M. Hicks (eds) *The Comparative Political Economy of the Welfare State*, Cambridge, New York and Melbourne: Cambridge University Press, pp. 54–92.

Katzenstein, Peter (1984: *Corporatism and Change. Austria, Switzerland, and the Politics of Industry*, Ithaca and London: Cornell University Press.

Katzenstein, Peter J. (1985: *Small States in World Markets. Industrial Policy in Europe*, Ithaca and London: Cornell University Press.

Kingdon, John W. (1984) *Agendas, Alternatives, and Public Policies*, Boston and Toronto: Harper Collins.

Kirchgässner, Gebhard and Lars P. Feld *et al.* (1999): *Die direkte Demokratie. Modern, erfolgreich, entwicklungs- und exportfähig*, Basel, Genf and München: Helbing & Lichtenhahn, Franz Vahlen.

Kriesi, Hanspeter (1980) *Entscheidungsstrukturen und Entscheidungsprozesse in der Schweizer Politik*, Frankfurt am Main and New York: Campus.

Kriesi, Hanspeter (1982) 'The Structure of the Swiss Political System', in Gerhard Lehmbruch and Philippe C. Schmitter (eds) *Patterns of Corporatist Policy-Making*, London and Beverly Hills: Sage, pp. 133–61.

Kriesi, Hanspeter (1995) *Le Système Politique Suisse*, Paris: Economica.

Lehmbruch, Gerhard 1967: *Proporzdemokratie. Politisches System und politische Kultur in der Schweiz und Österreich*, Tübingen: Mohr (Siebeck).

Lehmbruch, Gerhard (1976) *Parteienwettbewerb im Bundesstaat*, Stuttgart, Berlin, Köln and Mainz: Kohlhammer.

Lehmbruch, Gerhard (1996) 'Die korporative Verhandlungsdemokratie in Westmitteleuropa', in Klaus Armingeon and Pascal Sciarini (eds) *Deutschland, Österreich und die Schweiz im Vergleich (Sonderheft der Revue Suisse de Science Politique)*, Zürich: Seismo, pp. 19–41.

Linder, Wolf (1983) 'Entwicklung, Strukturen und Funktionen des Wirtschafts- und Sozialstaats in der Schweiz', in Alois Riklin (ed.) *Handbuch Politisches Systems der Schweiz. Band 1. Grundlagen*, Bern and Stuttgart: Haupt, pp. 255–382.

Linder, Wolf (1988) *Politische Entscheidung und Gesetzesvollzug in der Schweiz. Entscheidungsprozesse in der schweizerischen Demokratie*, Bern and Stuttgart: Haupt.

Linder, Wolf (1999) *Schweizerische Demokratie – Institutionen, Prozesse, Perspektiven*, Bern: Haupt.

Mach, André (1998) 'Quelles réponses politiques face à la globalisation et à la construction européenne? Illustration à partir de la révision de la loi suisse sur les cartels', in *Revue suisse de science politique*, 4/2: 25–49.

Neidhart, Leonhard (1970) *Plebiszit und pluralitäre Demokratie. Eine Analyse der Funktionen des schweizerischen Gesetzesreferendums*, Bern: Francke.

Obinger, Herbert (1998: *Politische Institutionen und Sozialpolitik in der Schweiz. Der Einfluß von Nebenregierungen auf Struktur und Entwicklungsdynamik des schweizerischen Sozialstaates*, Frankfurt am Main: Lang.

Obinger, Herbert and Wagschal, Uwe (2000) 'Zwischen Reform und Blockade: Plebiszit und Sozialstaatstätigkeit', in Manfred G. Schmidt (ed.) *Wohlfahrtsstaatliche Politik. Institutionen – Prozesse – Leistungsprofile*, Opladen: Leske & Budrich.

OECD (Organisation for Economic Co-Operation and Development) (1996) *Arbeitsmarktpolitik in der Schweiz (Deutsche Uebersetzung der offiziellen französischen Ausgabe)*, Paris and Bern: OECD and Schweizerisches. Bundesamt für Industrie und Gewerbe.

OECD (1997) *National Accounts*, Paris: OECD.

Papadopoulos, Yannis (1997) *Les processus de décision fédéraux en Suisse*, Paris and Montréal: L'Harmattan.

Saurer, Peter (1996) 'Der Investitionsbonus 1993–1995, Schlussbericht, *Mitteilungsblatt für Konjunkturfragen*, 3: 3–16.

Scharpf, Fritz W. (1987) *Sozialdemokratische Krisenpolitik in Europa*, Frankfurt am Main and New York: Campus.

Schmidt, Manfred G. (1995) 'Vollbeschäftigung und Arbeitslosigkeit in der Schweiz. Vom Sonderweg zum Normalfall', *Politische Vierteljahresschrift*, 36/1: 35–48.

Schmidt, Manfred G. (1998) *Sozialpolitik in Deutschland. Historische Entwicklung und internationaler Vergleich (2. Aufl.)*, Opladen: Leske & Budrich.

Schwartz, Jean-Jacques and Hans Peter Graf (1986) *L'administration face au défi de la politique conjoncturelle. Les programmes de relance 1975/76,* Bern and Stuttgart: Paul Haupt.

Sciarini, Pascal (1994) *La Suisse face à la Communauté Européenne et au GATT: Le cas test de la politique agricole,* Genève: Éditions George.

Sciarini, Pascal; Trechsel, Alexandre H. (1996) 'Démocratie directe en Suisse: l'élite politique victime des droits populaires?', in Simon Hug and Pascal Simon (eds) *Staatsreform (Sonderheft der Revue suisse de science politique, Vol. 2, Heft 2),* Zürich: Seismo, pp. 201–32.

Saurer, Peter (1996) 'Der Investitionsbonus 1993–1995, Schlussbericht', *Mitteilungsblatt für Konjunkturfragen,* 3: 3–16.

Tschudi, Hans Peter (1986) *Die Sozialverfassung der Schweiz (Der Sozialstaat),* Bern: Schweizerischer Gewerkschaftsbund.

Wagschal, Uwe (1997: 'Direct Democracy and Public Policymaking', *Journal of Public Policy,* 17/3: 223–45.

Wildhaber, Luzius (1992) 'Aussenpolitische Kompetenzordnung im schweizerischen Bundesstaat', in Alois Riklin, Hans Haug and Raymond Probst (eds) *Neues Hndbuch der schweizerischen Aussenpolitik. Noveau Manuel de la politique extérieure suiss,* Bern, Stuttgart and Wien: Haupt, pp. 121–49.

Part III

Countries without historical corporatist traditions

8 'Bargaining Celtic style'

The global economy and negotiated governance in Ireland

George Taylor

Introduction

The political legacy of a decade or more of Thatcherism, Reaganism and Kohlism has for many, it seems, irreparably tarnished the image of institutionalised interest intermediation. It is not simply that this form of bargaining has fallen out of fashion rather, the argument runs, it is no longer compatible with the prevailing structures of global capitalism. In many ways this is reflected in the current lexicon of political science and public administration, replete as it is with concepts apparently antithetical to the machinations of macro-political bargaining: flexible labour markets, polyvalent work structures and competitive international markets. Add to this the mobility of trans-national capital and a purported 'hollowing out of the state' and it is hardly surprising that pessimism should envelop any future role for macro-political bargaining in the new global economic order.

The problem for those who casually dismiss a role for macro-political bargaining in the new global economy is not just that they tend to over-emphasize the level of rigidity within these institutionalized agreements but in so doing they appear to have been seduced by neo-conservative interpretations of alleged administrative failure; that the real problem facing west European capitalism has been an explosion in the institutional impediments to economic growth (Taylor 1996).

Not surprisingly, the central feature of this neo-conservative critique has been the call for a reduction in state intervention and a corresponding increase in the role of the free market (Habermas 1989). And yet, in Ireland, macro-political bargaining has formed the cornerstone of government policy for over a decade. Indeed, if the public pronouncements of EU officials are anything to go by then 'bargaining Celtic style' is viewed in the political corridors of Brussels as an exemplary form of economic development. While many Irish politicians were perhaps initially sceptical, few would now be willing to publicly decry the role performed by national level agreements in revitalizing the Irish economy. And what a transformation it has been. Economic growth has been so startling and prolonged as to border on the surreal. Like Christmas, give-away budgets now appear to come around quicker each time.

This chapter seeks to challenge, therefore, a political orthodoxy which rejects a role for national level agreements in the new global economic order. In particular, it cautions against the inclination to portray sectoral or decentralized forms of negotiation in a more favourable light, as if there is a natural complementarity between such forms of negotiation and the new, emerging structures of capitalism. It is also an approach which assumes *a priori* that such forms of negotiation are somehow better suited to the current 'needs' of capital. This problem is compounded by the failure to consider fully the complexity of the managerial function where there is a tendency to conflate the interests of individual businesses with business in general or, alternatively, to restrict the parameters of the managerial function simply to the issue of pay.

Debate has also been hamstrung by the tendency to associate national level agreements with demand management strategies, a passive welfare state and/or a social democratic project to reduce unemployment and poverty through state intervention. It is a limited focus, one which has precluded consideration of the contribution which national level agreements may make in restructuring the supply side of the economy. Indeed, what remains novel (and perhaps appealing) to bargaining 'Celtic style' is that it has been formed around an attempt to construct a new form of governance, one capable of delivering a 'world class economy', which retains a *modicum* of commitment to avoid social dislocation.

To those of a social democratic disposition the national agreements are viewed as little more than a 'sheep in wolf's clothing', Thatcherism without the accompanying rhetorical garbage of 'trickle-down economics'. To others, it appears quite the opposite; excessive state intervention, rescued only by the influx of American multi-national capital. It is this apparent paradox, the restructuring of the supply side of the Irish economy within an ambit largely framed by macro-political bargaining, which has so perplexed Irish political scientists and economists and which forms the basis for this chapter.

In order to explore these themes this chapter is divided into three sections. The first examines issues which relate to the role of macro-political bargaining in the new global economic order. As a prelude to a discussion of macro-political bargaining in Ireland, the second section examines a number of critical views on the impact of such agreements on public policy and labour markets. The final section draws together empirical data which highlight the principal arguments presented in this chapter.

National level bargaining in the global economy

Among contemporary political scientists it has become increasingly fashionable to question the efficacy of macro-political forms of bargaining. Streeck (1992), Lash and Urry (1987) and Gobeyn (1993), to name but a few, have all expressed reservations about the compatibility of macro-political bargaining arrangements and the prevailing global structures of capitalism. It is a view which has also found favour among those of a more conservative political persuasion where macro-political bargaining is regarded as an anathema to an entrepreneurially driven economy. National level agreements, they contend, generate rigidities in the labour market because of the excessive influence of trade unions in a style of decision-making associated with 'old fashioned corporatism'.

Appraisals from a wide variety of political commentators, then, have argued that capitalism has moved into a new, dynamic phase in which the flexibility of productive systems, personnel and organizational strategy is paramount. Business, it is argued, can no longer sustain the level of economic growth upon which both the welfare state and trade union influence upon public policy were predicated. The explosion in social and political rights which accompanied such bargaining both increased rigidities in the labour market and imposed institutional impediments to economic growth. Put simply, macro-political bargaining procedures are viewed as increasingly anachronistic structures within an era of flexible specialization (Taylor 1996).[1]

This is a theme explored in the work of Streeck (1992), who has questioned the viability of macro-political bargaining in the new, emerging global economic order. For Streeck, the decay of national corporatisms can be attributed to a qualitative change in an economic and social structure which served to undermine the structural and cultural foundations of corporatism (Streeck 1992: 212). The simple dichotomy between capital and labour, the central pivot on which neo-corporatist negotiations were secured, has become increasingly untenable in the new global economy. Volatile international markets, advances made in technology and new political cleavages have usurped the basis upon which the alliance between social democracy and the trade unions had been forged (ibid.: 213).

Such themes also resonate in the work of Lash and Urry who view corporatism largely as 'a matter for compromise between social classes in very much a national context of resource distribution' (Lash and Urry 1987: 233). In their view, the penetration of global capital has dislocated national economies, making an assessment of what is an 'appropriate sacrifice' in the national interest a precarious exercise (ibid.: 233–4). The internationalization of capital markets and a corresponding shift towards 'disorganized capitalism' has manifests itself in a widespread decline in national level collective agreements and a corresponding increase in company and plant level bargaining (ibid.: 5). The transformation in production techniques, the growth of the service sector and the internationalization of production have all impacted detrimentally upon those areas of the economy which formed the basis for the centralized bargain of neo-corporatism (ibid.: 234).

For Gobeyn, it is possible to identify at least four domestic and international economic factors which demand a more 'capitalist oriented' explanation of the decline of macro-political bargaining structures: the entrenchment of high levels of structural unemployment in those sectors of the economy which had high levels of trade union density; the increased mobility of capital; reductions in tariffs and international barriers and, finally, the expansion of capitalist investment opportunities. For Gobeyn, corporatism is being 'rendered obsolete' by interrelated trends which have weakened the bargaining powers of trade unions and, therefore, question the efficacy of 'extensive nationally based concertative linkages' (Gobeyn 1993).

There are clearly discernible similarities between the respective positions of Streeck, Lash and Urry and Gobeyn. All emphasize the importance to management of being released from the constraints imposed by macro-political bargaining structures, the deregulation of national and international labour markets, the internationalization of capital and the corresponding shift in the composition of workforces. However, this chapter remains more cautious, particularly with regard to the premise that decentralized forms of bargaining offer a more flexible response to the *rigidities* imposed by corporatist tendencies.

The central problem lies in the way rigidity as a concept is used. More often than not it is applied only to corporatist tendencies and presumably, therefore, denotes problems which are not experienced in a market-based response to crisis. As such, the term becomes laden with *negative* connotations. A more useful distinction, one, which does not carry the assumptions of efficiency implicit within the metaphors of rigidity/flexibility, would be to argue that both corporatist *and* a market-based response to crisis offer *opportunities* and *constraints*. Formulated in such a manner, the framework does not assume *a priori* that a market response is more flexible than a corporatist response to crisis.

In this vein it is more preferable to see market-based approaches as offering both *opportunities* and *constraints*. It may well be the case that a reduction in the size of the public sector offers the state an opportunity to depoliticize any programme of restructuring and avoid undue conflict in vulnerable areas. However, we need to acknowledge that, in the process of relinquishing responsibility, the state may also lose strategic control in certain key sectors. This may be compounded by a reduction in the state's capacity to provide collective goods which are in the long-term interest of the economy but which may not emerge from the rational decisions of individual firms in a free market (Taylor 1996).

A further problem implicit in the work of Streeck, Gobeyn, Lash and Urry is the tendency to assume that decentralized forms of wage bargaining are necessarily more efficient in responding to the needs of business. It is a difficulty exacerbated by the fact that such authors not only perceive this form of bargaining to be inherently more beneficial but that it is somehow recognized uniformly as such by management. There is, needless to say, little evidence in the UK to support such a sweeping conclusion (see Black 1994; Black 1993; Brown and Walsh 1991).

In managerial parlance such moves are often justified on the grounds that gains can be made from the flexible deployment of manpower, enabling management to establish a closer link between pay, performance and the local labour market (Purcell 1991). However, as Walsh's research shows, decentralized forms of bargaining agreements present management with alternative problems and any tendency to see them as inherently more 'efficient' should be resisted. In particular, she argues that decentralized wage bargaining procedures may actually generate intra-firm bargaining pressures, thereby reducing the possibility of securing productivity gains. Moreover, where productivity is determined by interdependent technologies, as opposed to employee performance, management may encounter obstacles to the introduction of individual incentive schemes (Walsh 1993: 416).

A further area of controversy often raised in debates about macro-political bargaining is associated with its alleged propensity to promote rigidities in the economy. Here, neo-liberal economists have been particularly vociferous in their condemnation of macro-level interest intermediation, attributing to it a number of fatal flaws. The first relates to 'obligations', which tend to accompany national level agreements. Here, they present a stark contrast between, on the one hand, governments who face pressure from trade unions to defend jobs and, on the other hand, managers who need to be released from their political masters to make 'tough economic decisions' in order to restructure companies.

In a subtle and far more persuasive fashion neo-liberal economists have also argued that it is not just that public sector industries suffered from poor management/union relations, but that the state imposes a series of institutional rigidities which are a burden upon *any* industry operating within an internationally competitive environment. Such a difficulty is compounded by the demands of a new global economic order where management are required to enact decisions in a shorter time frame, a function which cannot be performed within the straitjacket of political dialogue. A further theme, one mentioned only occasionally in the accompanying political rhetoric, was that involvement in macro-level negotiations allowed unions to secure wage increases above the market level, a situation which reinforced a 'rates for the job' consciousness and prevented management from reducing job demarcations (Dore 1988: 400).[2]

A second flaw identified by the neo-liberal critique of state intervention relates to the changing nature of citizenship in the post-war period. Here, objection centres on the increase of citizenship rights, which have altered the level of security assumed under the auspices of an expanded welfare state (Hayek 1960). It is not simply a question of the level of entitlements, although this in itself tends to raise the hackles of any committed neo-liberal economist, rather it is the very structure of those entitlements. From a neo-liberal perspective welfare benefits increase wage rigidities in the economy, creating a culture of dependency, which inhibits the emergence of an enterprise spirit. In short, it represents a fundamental threat to the underlying efficiency of the economy.[3] It is an argument which critics of the New Right have found difficult to resolve.

Dore's response has been to concede that the presence of such schemes has an inevitable impact on the take-up of low-paid jobs (Dore 1988). There is, in his opinion, a complex relationship between equity (the redistribution of productive resources) and efficiency in periods of high unemployment. This, he believes, can be resolved only through some form of macro-political bargaining which ensures specific levels of employment, thereby reducing the impact of 'unproductive rigidities' (income maintenance schemes) (ibid.).

On this issue Streeck remains far more circumspect. He has argued that in the absence of any internationally agreed form of self-restraint and/or Keynesian employment-creation scheme the institutions which once served the weak have become defences for those who are employed. Governments throughout Western Europe have manifestly failed to reduce the division between the employed and the unemployed (Streeck 1988: 415).

However, the existence of some forms of rigidity need not present an insurmountable problem, providing that there is a reduction in productive rigidities. As Streeck observes, in countries like the United States and Britain, for example, they have had a trade-off between the flexible access to the external labour market (hiring and firing workers to change the size and composition of their workforce) – and strong 'rigidities' with respect to internal deployment, redeployment and retraining (ibid.: 417). It is a position which contrasts sharply with that of Germany and Sweden, where unions have managed to secure rigid entitlements to long-term employment in exchange for high levels of internal shop-floor flexibility (ibid.: 419). Moreover, as Dore notes, measures which seek to improve employment security (a significant source of labour market rigidity) may actually motivate firms to adapt to market change through intra-company diversification. In addition, they may also serve to stimulate employers to pursue retraining programmes. Within such working environs, Dore believes that employees may be more receptive to the introduction of new technology and changing work practices (see Dore 1988: 401).[4]

These are issues which have attracted the attention of Rhodes who has also questioned the purported 'benefits' of a neo-liberal approach to labour market regulation. While conceding that the UK has been successful in its move away from a 'cluster of Southern European States with rigid labour markets', Rhodes is unwilling to accept that this has transformed the productive fortunes of the British economy (Rhodes 1998). It is certainly plausible to suggest that greater external flexibility (the hiring and firing of workers) has been achieved and that the breakdown of union control over the workplace may have induced more internal flexibility. However, he warns that such gains have been achieved without a corresponding increase in 'levels of trust (except in inward investing Japanese firms which, in some sectors, have revolutionised work organisation)' (ibid.: 8). Neither, has the associated fragmentation of employers and trade unions assisted in the 'provision of collective goods such as an effective training system', hampering any concerted move away from a 'low skill equilibrium'. The consequence is that while the relationship between external flexibility and internal flexibility has altered, the UK's regime is still a 'price-based' rather than 'quality-based' productive structure (ibid.). A pattern of high wages and rigid job entitlements is, however, unlikely to result from the enlightening forces of the free market. In such circumstances, social peace, worker commitment and high and flexible qualifications tend to be under-supplied if left to the rational decisions of individual firms. In other words, certain rigidities (collective goods which are in the long-term interest of the economy) are important prerequisites to the development of an arena in which enterprising firms are able to respond and diversify in quality competitive markets. Here, Streeck suggests that a system of wage deter-mination which keeps wages higher than the market would otherwise dictate may actually encourage firms to diversify and invest in training and retraining. Similarly, employment protection appears to enhance individual firms' awareness of the need to invest in training programmes to retain expensive skills (Streeck 1988, 1992).

There are two themes within this set of arguments, which are of particular relevance to this chapter. First, it presents a challenge to the dominant neo-liberal interpretation of what constitutes an enterprising firm. Second, it raises the crucial question of why certain rigidities imposed upon management 'force' innovation and others not? Why, for example, do the (alleged) rigidities imposed by macro-political bargaining arrangements not provide a stimulus towards innovation? There can be little doubt that Streeck is in agreement on the beneficial impact of *certain* forms of political regulation when he states that: 'political regulation not only need not be detrimental to economic success, but may constitute a central precondition for it' (Streeck 1988: 419). This is reiterated in his opposition to the neo-liberal perspective when he suggests that rigidities may well stimulate managerial innovation:

> A polyvalent organisation whose subunits are capable of flexibly cross-ing the boundaries of their assigned functions is expensive, and the return on investment in polyvalence is difficult to establish. This is why the de-Taylorisation of work organisation, profitable as it undoubtedly is for firms pressed for higher product quality and diversity, seems to proceed faster where there is an additional independent pressure for reorganisation of work, for other than economic reasons. In the same way in which institutionally imposed obligations to train improve firms'

skill base, legislation or industrial agreements mandating employers to enlarge and enrich job definition may contribute to operational flexibility. *In both cases competitiveness increases as a result of adjustments individual firms would or could not voluntarily have made.*

(Streeck and Schmitter 1991: 19; my emphasis)

It is a view which sits comfortably with his original stance that rigidity and flexibility are not mutually exclusive. However, on closer inspection 'beneficial political regulation' does not extend to macro-political bargaining. This apparent discrepancy is intelligible only when we realize that for Streeck, political regulation is beneficial *only* if it is directed toward the *supply* side of the economy, a role he feels macro-political bargaining cannot perform because it remains circumscribed by its function as a tool for demand-side change. Streeck's principal point, and for many it is a persuasive one, is that:

> Some sort of effective Keynesian expansionist capacity seems indispensable for the kind of corporatist concertation and social contract bargaining that was to stabilise non-American capitalisms of the 1970s. As much as these systems may otherwise have differed, under the rules of corporatist bargaining a state that cannot with any reasonable prospect of success promise to apply its fiscal and monetary tools to alleviate unemployment cannot possibly hope to gain concessions from unions or to influence settlements between unions and employers by, for example, offering to improve the terms of the bargain through corresponding economic policy.
>
> (Streeck 1992: 211)

In more general political terms, the rejection of macro-political bargaining (and a partial acceptance of the neo-liberal critique of the welfare state) is also (re)presented by reconstructed social democratic thinking as a dichotomy between passive and active policy paradigms. The politics of the 'third way' finds its leitmotif in the persistent call for the overhaul of an archaic, passive, universal welfare regime with which macro-political bargaining is often assimilated.

In a subtle, but nonetheless crucial, fashion the view of reconstructed social democracy distinguishes itself from the neo-liberal critique of welfare in the fact that we are no longer exclusively concerned with the role of individual self-responsibility. A policy paradigm which attributes the *cause* of unemployment to the failings of individuals (and subsequently constructs a neo-liberal safety net) has been supplanted with one which creates 'opportunities' and generates 'incentives' for individuals who 'possess' the capacity to actively respond to their predicament. This is a policy paradigm populated not by individuals *per se*, but by 'categories of individuals' whose membership is defined by their 'particular circumstance' and experience of unemployment (lone parents, the young unemployed or absent fathers).

We no longer have a 'catch all' experience of unemployment (or receipt of welfare) and consequently the policy response can no longer be diffuse. Rather, we have a series of 'unemployment experiences' where policy is tailored to 'categories of individuals'. Unemployment is no longer ascribed to the failure of individuals, neither does responsibility lie at the doorstep of the state. The active dimension to this welfare regime resides in the tension which exists between state support and individual responsibility. The state functions to create opportunities from which to assist those categories of individuals who 'wish' to respond to their predicament (this is the positive/possessive dimension).

That Streeck's work sits comfortably within reconstructed social democracy can be deduced from his use of the term 'beneficial political regulation'. Where political regulation is beneficial (employment protection and training) his vocabulary is infused with terms such as 'stimulate', 'encourage' or 'innovate'. These are positive, 'possessive' categories and, as such, are suited to an active policy paradigm. Where political regulation is not beneficial it is usually associated with income maintenance schemes or welfare benefits (demand management). The problem for Streeck is that this tends to assume that macro-political bargaining is synonymous with a passive welfare state. Again, I remain rather more cautious.

The intention has not been to reduce many of Streeck's succinct observations to a discussion of semantics, rather it is to highlight the fact that macro-political bargaining tends to be (mistakenly) equated with economic demand management strategies (and/or a passive welfare state). Neither has the objective been to downplay the importance of pressures emanating from the global economy, which pose significant problems for Ireland's form of negotiated governance. Clearly, the increasing penetration of multi-national companies in the Irish economy, and their capacity to rapidly relocate production in periods of volatile market conditions, raise difficulties for successful macro-level concertation (and any co-ordination of policy response). It would also be naive to assume that in such circumstances international capital will not seek more flexibility in the search for an optimal balance in labour market regulation. This chapter does, however, caution against the current tendency to view a neo-liberal approach to labour market regulation as necessarily 'better suited' to the prevailing conditions of global capitalism. In the short term it may deliver greater external flexibility, but this may fall short of providing the collective goods (training and education) or the political and economic stability from which to pursue that most elusive prize; a high tech, high wage economy.

The general thrust of this argument would appear to find support in Rhodes' recent work when he argues that 'successful economic adjustment, including greater flexibility in labour markets and the organisation of welfare states, may require, in turn, a flexible form of "market" or "competitive" corporatism rather than attempted moves in a neo-liberal direction' (Rhodes 1998: 1).

While I am generally sympathetic to this position I feel he fails to 'hit the nail on the head'. The principal source of our difference rests on Rhodes' belief that the success of recent negotiated forms of governance can be attributed simply to the introduction of pay flexibility at the local level. Thus, he states that

> in sum there are pressures for both a decentralisation and a centralisation (or in some cases a recentralisation) of industrial relations systems.[5] An 'optimal' solution would combine some form of incomes policy or national wage co-ordination with *pay flexibility within certain margins at the level of the firm*'.
>
> (Ibid.: 3; my emphasis)

As the discussion of local pay bargaining below indicates, flexibility in pay negotiations has been an important contributory factor in the success of macro-political bargaining in Ireland. However, I also want to suggest that the success of macro-political bargaining should not be attributed solely to the issue of pay flexibility. I am more than willing to concede, for example, that the existence of local clauses in macro-level negotiations allows consideration for the plight of individual companies during periods of volatile market conditions. It may also establish a closer tie between pay, performance and the local labour market. However, it should be recognized that such clauses also provide a focal point for both management and unions to negotiate changes in *work practices* and the *introduction of new technology*. In other words, the type of issues involved in national level agreements (and those include local clauses) extend beyond the parameters of pay (increases) to embrace a discussion about changes in the supply side of the economy. If they were simply about adding an element of flexibility to pay negotiations (without removing productive rigidities, as Streeck so usefully points out) then presumably they would increase wage rigidity over time (given the constant desire to seek competitive international advantage). Above all, we need to recognize that the success of national level agreements is due not simply to the introduction of pay flexibility (Rhodes), and neither to whether they are exclusively concerned with economic demand management and/or a passive welfare state (Streeck).

The case study below returns to these themes at an empirical level. It addresses at least three key arguments. First, that the rigidities normally attributed to macro-political bargaining agreements are not necessarily inherent and that, far from being a constraint upon management, macro-political bargaining agreements in Ireland have been invaluable in the restructuring of the supply side of the economy. A second argument is that analyses to date have focused predominantly upon the role of macro-political bargaining upon setting wage rates in both the public and private sectors. As such, they ignore the fact that in the Irish case, particularly with regard to the latest agreement, Partnership 2000, macro-political bargaining has not only assisted management in the restructuring of the supply side of the economy (both private and public sector industry) but is at the forefront of moves to introduce flexibility into public sector service provision.[6] The final section examines recent attempts to expand the experience of partnership and the role this performs in the construction of a new form of governance in Ireland.

Macro-political bargaining in Ireland: from the Programme for National Economic Recovery to Partnership 2000

The origins of Ireland's experience with macro-political bargaining are to be found in the negotiated institutional arrangements first mooted as a response to industrial conflict in the late 1960s. To many inside government the debilitating experiences of such industrial strife could be attributed to the particularities of Irish trade union organization, multi-union representation and a relatively weak level of centralization. In a concerted attempt to restore stability to wage negotiations, and subsequently reduce the incidence of strikes, the government prompted a series of national level wage agreements (NWA) and 'national understandings' (NU) with employers and trade unions during the 1970s. These agreements, which lasted between 1970 and 1980, involved negotiations over pay between employers and unions and a series of non-pay negotiations between unions and government (Hardiman 1988: 53).

During the 1970s the national wage agreements assumed an increasingly more structured format. Largely at the behest of the SIPTU (Services, Industrial Professional and Technical Union), one of the largest trade unions, attempts were made to develop a structure in which future negotiations would pursue social and economic policies in a more integrated fashion. The unions were fully cognizant of the fact that any wage increases secured in national agreements could easily be lost in budgetary policies which placed an unfair burden upon employees. Although greater success on this issue was achieved in later agreements, the strategy was severely hampered in the early 1980s as the combination of political instability and economic crisis led governments to abandon negotiations with the trade union movement.

Management had also become disenchanted with national level agreements, apparent in its concerted campaign to decentralize wage negotiations and tie pay increases to either local labour market conditions or the profitability of individual firms. However, the emergence of the Programme for National Recovery (PNER) in 1987 and the Programme for Economic and Social Progress (PESP, 1990) signalled a renewed enthusiasm for national level negotiations.

The PNER had been negotiated amid a crisis in public finances, with government debt peaking at 117 per cent of GDP. As such, a large part of its remit was directed toward reducing the debt/GDP ratio to 96.5 per cent by 1990 (O'Riordan 1996). However, the programme also delivered higher living standards for employees as modest wage increases were coupled with tax reforms. Not surprisingly, its success led to negotiations for a successor, the Programme for Economic and Social Progress.

As Table 8.1 illustrates, by 1992 the success of these programmes had ensured that national level wage negotiations, particularly in the manual and clerical sectors were, by now, the norm.

A crucial part of the success of PESP was based around its focus on 'restructuring' the supply side of the economy.[7] Here, the most important innovation was the introduction of a local bargaining clause (clause 3) which allowed management to tie negotiations to local labour market conditions, achieve changes in productive rigidities and yet retain moderation in wage demands at a macro-level. As Table 8.2 shows, clause 3 of PESP allowed management to secure concessions in a wide range of operating areas, a fact highlighted in research undertaken by the *Industrial Relations News* (*IRN*) which showed that management was successful in gaining significant concessions in almost half (48 per cent) of the ninety-six local bargaining deals recorded at the beginning of 1991 (*IRN*, 37, 1992).[8] The *IRN* study also made an important distinction between items such as 'agreements to cooperate with on-going change or the tightening up on tea breaks' with agreements on cashless pay, increased productivity or major re-organization/rationalization. What is significant is that when both of these

Table 8.1   At what level is basic pay determined?

	Managerial	*Professional*	*Clerical*	*Manual*
National/industry collective bargaining	33.3	39.9	55.1	71.0
Regional collective bargaining	0	2.2	6.5	8.0
Company/division	27.5	23.9	24.6	18.1
Establishment/site	15.2	17.4	17.4	13.0
Individual	39.9	31.2	16.7	5.8

Source: *Industrial Relations News* (*IRN*) 38, 1992.

Table 8.2   Breakdown of clause 3 agreements

3% with 'significant' trade-offs	48.0
3% with 'minor' trade-offs	25.0
3% without trade-offs	14.6
3% plus/radical change	6.2
Less than 3%	4.1
Other	2.0
Total	100.0

Source: *IRN*, 37, 1 October 1992.

broad categories (significant and minor trade-offs) are put together, the overall figure for companies where concessions were agreed in return for clause 3 came to a total of 79 per cent (ibid.).

The type of changes agreed by unions in a trade-off for payment of clause 3 included productivity improvements, rationalization/reorganization, regrading, cooperation with new technology/new machinery, the introduction of 'just in time' working practices (JIT) and, of course, the all-encompassing 'co-operation with on-going change' (*IRN*, 36, 1992). Clause 3 was not simply a local pay bargaining clause. Although it introduced an element of flexibility into macro-level negotiations (allowing management some latitude on pay), it also realigned discussions toward the issues of new technology, changing work practices and job demarcations. In other words, it engineered a situation which demanded consultation, negotiation and compromise.

In a more novel fashion, PESP also allowed clause 3 payments to be paid in phases, ensuring that delays could be sought in 'periods of financial stricture'. This latter element to the agreement, subject to approval from both the Labour Court and the Labour Relations Commission on the financial state of an individual firm, was particularly interesting since it allowed a 'breathing space' to emerge during volatile market conditions or a currency crisis. Although the data here is more limited, Table 8.3 indicates that while the majority of companies (55.5 per cent) paid clause 3 in a single phase, a phased payment was made in 27 per cent of cases, a process which became more prevalent as 1992 progressed.

More revealing perhaps is the breakdown of changes provided in Table 8.4. This table highlights two important themes. First, that despite the predominance of macro-political bargaining structures, Irish management was extremely successful in altering working practices among core employees. Second, that many of the changes which took place relate specifically to the status of employees. As column 1 of Table 8.4 shows, the type of responses

Table 8.3 How the 3 per cent was applied

Full 3% (starting date, phase II of PESP	53 (55.5%)
Full 3% on a phased basis (starting date, phase II of PESP)	26 (27%)
Full 3% (starting date before phase II)	5 (5.2%)
Full 3% (starting date after phase II)	3 (3.0%)
Deals in excess of 3%	6 (6.2%)
Interim deals	3 (3.0%)
Total	96 (100%)

Table 8.4 Has there been a change in the use of the following working
arrangements over the last three years (percentages)?

	More	*Same*	*Less*	*Not used*	*Don't know*
Weekend work	14.5	50.7	14.5	14.5	5.8
Shift work	15.2	54.3	8.0	15.9	6.5
Overtime	23.2	34.1	34.1	2.9	5.8
Annual hrs contract	4.3	17.4	9.4	50.0	1.4
Part-time work	31.2	26.8	4.3	26.1	11.6
Temporary	37.7	36.2	8.7	6.5	0.7
Fixed-term contract	37.7	29.0	4.3	19.6	0.7
Home-based work	1.4	4.3	–	70.3	0.7
Govt training scheme	13.0	29.0	–	36.2	2.2
Sub-contracting	36.2	29.7	3.6	20.3	0.7

Source: *IRN*, 38 October 1992.

associated with flexible strategies designed to increase an organization's
ability to adapt to volatile market conditions altered radically. The use of
part-time employees, temporary or casual workers, fixed-term contracts
and sub-contractors have all shown significant increases (Taylor 1996).[9]

Clearly, the incidence of such change reveals a significant disparity
between the rhetoric of national level employer organizations, which often
allude to the restrictive nature of macro-political bargaining agreements,
and the experience of such negotiations.

An additional (but nevertheless crucial), component to the success of
macro-political bargaining in Ireland has been the institutional apparatus
designed to resolve disputes between management and unions. As Tables
8.5–8.8 show, there has been a substantial reduction in both the incidence
of strikes, the level of unofficial strike activity and the number of days lost
in disputes. Indeed, a comparison between the period 1982–7 and 1988–93
provides stark evidence of the success of PNER and PESP in reducing the
level of strike activity in the economy.

Table 8.5 Number of strikes and work days lost during a six-year period of
decentralized wage bargaining, 1982–7

	Strikes	*Days lost*
1982	131	434,000
1983	154	319,000
1984	192	386,000
1985	116	418,000
1986	100	309,000
1987	80	264,000
Total	773	2,130,000
Average number of days lost per annum		355,000

Table 8.6 Number of strikes and work days lost during the six-year period of PNR/PESP (1988–93)

	Strikes	*Days lost*
1988	65	143,000
1989	38	50,000
1990	49	223,000
1991	54	86,000
1992	38	191,000
1993*	48	65,000
Total	292	758,000
Average number of days lost per annum		126,000

Source: Central Statistics Office/*Department of Enterprise and Employment.

Table 8.7 Number of strikes which commenced in the period 1987–91

Year	*Total*	*Official*	*Unofficial*
1987	76	54 (71%)	22 (29%)
1988	72	46 (64%)	26 (36%)
1989	41	28 (68%)	13 (32%)
1990	51	35 (69%)	16 (31%)
1991	52	39 (75%)	13 (25%)

Source: Department of Labour *Annual Report*, 1991.

Table 8.8 Days lost due to strikes in the period 1987–91

Year	*Total*	*Official*	*Unofficial*
1987	260,000	235,000 (90%)	25,000 (10%)
1988	130,000	123,500 (95%)	6,500 (5%)
1989	41,400	29,800 (72%)	11,600 (28%)
1990	203,700	196,000 (97%)	6,800 (3%)
1991	82,900	73,600 (89%)	9,300 (11%)

Source: Department of Labour *Annual Report* 1991.

While the data confirms the success of macro-political bargaining in reducing industrial conflict it is worth noting that industrial strife has not simply disappeared. Any success in macro-level concertation demands a conciliation service (accepted as legitimate by all parties) which provides an institutional setting in which antagonism may be resolved. Here, as Table 8.9 indicates, the combination of the Labour Court and the Labour Relations Commission has proved remarkably successful in resolving disputes between management and unions. Clearly, while national level agreements have contributed significantly to a period of sustained political consensus we have also witnessed an impressively high ratio of settlements through the institutional mechanisms designed to alleviate antagonism.

Table 8.9 Settlement of industrial disputes in the public and private sector

Year	No. of referrals	Meetings	Settled
1990	1474	2074	73%
1991	1880	2385	85%
1992	1935	2450	75%
1993	1844	2379	71%
1994	1551	2055	66%
1995	1692	2072	70%
1996	1487	1999	81%

Although most commentators were of the opinion that PESP had been an outstanding success, the latter stages of this agreement coincided with a particularly unstable European economic climate and a national interest rate crisis during 1992–3. While growth rates in the economy were significantly less than those achieved during the late 1980s and early 1990s the picture was far from disastrous since the levels attained were still above the European average and, in contrast to other EU states, Ireland achieved modest growth in employment. However, the legacy of high rates of long-term unemployment coupled with an above average rate of expansion in the labour force meant that it continued to struggle with the seemingly interminable problem of long-term structural unemployment. It was against this backdrop of uncertainty that the social partners embarked upon negotiations for a third agreement; the Programme for Competitiveness and Work (PCW).

In contrast to its predecessor, the PCW did not have the provision for local bargaining. The debilitating experience of currency instability in 1992–3 had a profound influence on the parameters struck for the PCW. As a result of the slow-down in economic growth employers were reluctant to concede wage negotiation at a local level over and above that agreed for the national level. (O'Riordan 1996). Thus, in terms of the basic pay negotiations, the PCW involved a series of staged payments to be made over a three-year period from 1994–6. Basic pay increases of 2 per cent in 1994, 2.5 per cent in 1995 and a 2.5 per cent in the first six months of 1996 were agreed. An additional 1 per cent would be made in the remaining six months of 1996.

From the outset the main objectives of the PCW were alleviating the burden of taxation on workers with low incomes and raising the income threshold at which higher rates of taxation would come into play. With regard to the first priority, the increase in the level of income exempt from tax as a result of the government's 1996 budget did give a real relative improvement to the very low paid. However, it did so only after an inadequate increase in the exemption limit in the previous budget. Not surprisingly, from the trade unions' perspective the overall experience of the PCW was disappointing. Little real progress had been achieved in reducing the burden of taxation on the low paid (ibid.: 6).

The principal reason for the Irish government's failure to meet its tax reform commitments resulted from its decision to over-fulfil the PCW's agreed fiscal policy objective. All parties to the PCW had supported a policy of maintaining the government deficit within the Maastricht ceiling of 3 per cent of GDP and by staying at 2.2 per cent the Irish deficit met that condition by a wide margin. In addition, all parties to the PCW were in agreement with meeting the other Maastricht guideline in respect of fiscal policy, namely that of making satisfactory progress towards a Debt/GDP ratio of 60 per cent (ibid.). And yet, during the period of the PCW the Irish economy experienced an unprecedented level of economic growth averaging 6.5 per cent between 1994 and 1996. The period of the PCW also witnessed a particularly low level of industrial strife and a record low of industrial disputes in 1994 with just 25,550 working days lost (see Table 8.10).

That pay should be considered as only one of a number of issues which are important to relations between management and unions is confirmed by the Labour Relations Commission's findings that pay and conditions were no longer the primary source of industrial strife in Ireland (LRC 1997). Rather, issues such as poor human relations between shopfloor and line managers, the absence of communications/consultation and the introduction of major change were now the most significant issues of contention. Indeed, the Commission was moved to remark that 'significant and constant change is the order of the day' reflecting the impact of new technology, deregulation in state industries, international competition and the changing nature of the workplace. Accordingly, its conciliation service was now increasingly concerned with disputes about new management/ production techniques and changes in work practices, particularly in the public sector (LRC 1994). What is more, the Commission also noted that while a relatively low level of disputes had been recorded on the disclosure of information and union recognition they had shown a 'notable increase'

Table 8.10 Industrial disputes: 1993–8

Year	Number of disputes	Number of firms involved	Workers involved	Total days lost
1993	48	48	12,789	61,312
1994	29	238	5,007	25,550
1995	34	34	31,653	130,300
1996	32	30	13,339	114,584
1997	28	28	5,364	74,508[a]
1998	34	62	8,060	37,374

Source: Central Statistics Office

Note
[a] This period falls under the Partnership 2000. A significant element of this figure is attributed to the Irish Life insurance company dispute, which accounted for 10,080 days.

(LRC 1997: 18). For the unions, it is an important issue, one likely to assume greater political visibility in the future.

What remains patently clear is that under the terms of the PCW (which had been far more narrow than PESP) management was able to pursue with continued vigour the restructuring of the supply side of the economy. Management's success in this regard has been confirmed in a recent study which shows that during the 1990s 75 per cent of firms introduced new plant and technology and over 60 per cent secured changes to working time arrangements, working practices and new employee involvement initiatives. In addition, payment systems and promotional criteria were revised or altered in nearly half of all workplaces. As the authors note, 'while it is difficult to estimate the depth of such change from these data, the level of workplace change and the range of issues addressed appear very significant. Evidently workplaces in the Celtic Tiger are indeed highly dynamic' (Roche and Geary 1998).

There can be little doubt that the conditions of political and economic stability fostered under PESP continued throughout the duration of the PCW. While unions were seeking better terms for their members, they were also acutely aware of the need to pursue a strategy which endorsed investment in new technology and capital. Keen to avoid the experience of unions in the UK, who had found themselves isolated from the wider decision-making agenda of public policy, the trade unions have been willing partners in the search for new investment and the introduction of new technology. This is confirmed in recent research undertaken by D'Art and Turner (1999), which shows that while a 'them and us' attitude to management/union relations may not have disappeared, there have been important developments in the 1990s.

For D'Art and Turner, the intensity of a 'them and us' attitude in management/union relations is significantly related to 'employee awareness of the need for firm survival, greater discretion in work, satisfaction with industrial relations procedures and a cohesive union organisation' (D'Art and Turner 1999: 112). Their research suggests that the presence of a strong and functioning union at firm level has the potential to address problems such as 'lack of trust between workers and management or the lack of institutional support from upper management'. In addition, they argue that collective bargaining allows workers to participate and negotiate for a share in the surplus of the firm, and increase worker confidence in dealing with management (ibid.: 113). These are certainly themes which attracted the attention of Irish Congress of Trade Unions (ICTU) in the early 1990s as it sought to actively encourage firm level participation (ICTU 1991, 1993).

Almost all parties to the macro-level negotiations concur that in the area of employment expansion the PCW was a qualified success. What remains in doubt is the adequacy of this achievement, given the inherited unemployment problem and the level of resources being used to tackle long-term unemployment (O'Riordan 1996: 7). Under the terms of the PCW the government was committed to establish a new community employment (CE) venture which would enable the unemployed to undertake work of public or social value while providing them with work experience and development training. In order to reduce any 'disincentive' to take up such opportunities the government agreed that secondary welfare benefits would be retained. As such, the government was committed to provide 40,000 places on a voluntary basis by 1994.

The PCW also required the government to have regard to the findings of the National Economic and Social Forum (NESF), a consultative body which embraced diverse interests such as the unemployed and women's groups. In June 1994, NESF issued a report on Ireland's long-term unemployed, which called for the development of an employment service, targeted at those registered as unemployed for more than six months. In January 1996, the government finally responded with four initiatives: 30,000 or 75 per cent of CE places would be allocated to those over 21 and unemployed for at least twelve months; 10,000 CE places (25 per cent) would be reserved for those over 35 and unemployed for three years or more; an additional 1,000 places would be provided on a pilot basis for those over 35 who had been unemployed for more than five years; and finally, the government would introduce a new scheme aimed at those who had been unemployed for six months who it felt were likely to become long-term unemployed. The attractiveness and subsequent success of this initiative resulted in a conflict between the government and unions. Although participation averaged 31,800 the figure of 40,000 had been surpassed by the end of the year, encouraging calls from some quarters for cutbacks. As far as the unions were concerned such programmes had been jeopardized by an over-zealous pursuit of fiscal rectitude (O'Riordan 1996).

In many ways the trajectory of the PCW reflected the dilemmas facing the Irish state as it sought to balance the political demands of the trade unions to increase the living standards of its members, and government's intention of creating an environment in which global capital would seek to reside. As such, the main tenets of the programme (as its title so eloquently reveals) were designed to engineer a consensus around the need to embrace more fully the 'realistic economic strictures of the global market'. In this sense, it represented a subtle, but nonetheless crucial, shift towards a more conservative economic outlook, one which had effectively abandoned any pretension to the social democratic ethos which may have permeated elements of earlier agreements.

If we avoid being seduced by the political rhetoric which surrounded the PCW, it remains patently clear that while it may have embraced the language of inclusion it did little to alleviate the vast inequalities which persist in Ireland. Neither did it contribute in any meaningful sense to addressing fundamental questions about industrial democracy. This latter issue, which has attracted the sobriquet of 'plant level partnership', was the subject of negotiations, which formed the basis of Partnership 2000 and is likely to figure in discussions for a successor agreement.

The issue of firm level participation is a crucial one. As Regini has succinctly observed, concertative efforts during the 1970s were characterized by political exchange and a compensatory role for the state. Whereas such relationships offered immediate and tangible rewards for the state (stability, legitimation and self-restraint), the 'reverse was almost never the case' (Regini 1996: 17). In other words, a tension emerges between, on the one hand, the insulation from rank and file pressures offered by the monopoly of representation and on, the other hand, the risk of a crisis of representation as union leaderships become distanced from their memberships. As Regini points out, contrary to the assumption of neo-corporatist theory, the recent Italian situation shows that 'concertation without explicit political exchange may succeed precisely when interest organizations become less centralized and insulated from rank and file pressures; and especially, when workplace representation acquires a greater role vis-a-vis the union bureaucracy (ibid.: 19).

Representation rooted in the workplace (and enhanced participation) may overcome a crisis of representation because it reaffirms the 'relevance of trade union activity' to the rank and file. In this context it seems plausible to suggest that local level bargaining clauses, such as clause 3, may have (unintentionally) resurrected the role of plant level union activity, providing a focal point for management union discussions and thereby reaffirming the relevance, value and (partial) success of a trade union presence.

Such developments provide tangible reasons for caution against those who see macro-political bargaining in terms of rigid, static structures, populated by actors implacable to the changing circumstances of the global economy. Negotiated forms of governance should therefore be seen in more dynamic terms, recognizing its capacity to change over time and in response to influences emanating from outside national borders.

The latest two agreements have more firmly embedded national agreements and 'partnership' within the Irish political psyche. Indeed, they have confidently proclaimed the basis for a new political architecture in Irish politics. They are no longer simply about compensatory state action or simply crisis management but, more crucially, involve the construction of a new form of social and political regulation. They do not remain circumscribed as incomes policies or pay agreements (although these remain integral) but are about providing the basis for new forms of policy-making. This was a shift from a concern with the exchange of resources, in order to secure political acquiescence (redistribution), to an allocation of economic policy authority (regulation) (ibid.: 17).

On this matter, O'Donnell has noted that while bargaining as a concept distinguishes social partnership from more liberal and pluralist approaches in which consultation is more prominent, it 'does not entirely capture the partnership process' (O'Donnell 1998: 102). For O'Donnell, partnership entails the 'players in a process of deliberation that has the potential to shape and reshape their understanding, identity and preferences'. This is an important theme, since it recognizes that identity (and presumably interests and strategy) 'can be shaped through interaction'. As such, he suggests that one of the more notable features of the partnership experiments has been the reluctance to engage on 'ultimate social visions'. Under such circumstances the social partners are more concerned with a problem-solving approach where consensus is no longer a 'pre-condition' as much as an ' outcome' (ibid.).

A further element of innovation, as far as O'Donnell is concerned, has been the shift away from Partnership being the exclusive preserve of the peak organizations. Social partners are no longer concerned purely with their role as representatives of given occupational groups but are now actively engaged in 'mobilising citizens who have problems that need to be dealt with'. Fixed functional roles have been supplanted by the need to co-ordinate between groups and extend the functions of public advocacy (ibid.: 103).

These new forms of social partnership have induced changes in the relationship between policy-making, implementation and monitoring in ways which place monitoring at the centre of policy (ibid.: 104). It is a set of arguments with which I have a good deal of sympathy, not least because it reinforces the view that macro-political bargaining structures are not necessarily rigid and static structures, but involve the dynamic (re-)construction of relationships aimed at forging political and economic stability.

Bargaining and the (re-)construction of the Irish welfare state

Any discussion of the manner in which the Irish state has forged political and economic stability demands an examination of the changing nature of its welfare state. In Ireland it is an area of debate where there remains a good deal of confusion. To those of a social democratic disposition there appears to have been a discernible reorientation in the priorities of the Irish welfare state, a shift away from a concern with the redistribution of wealth as the Irish polity embraces the strictures of neo-liberal economic policies. Indeed for some, it is reflected in the changing lexicon of Irish politics which appears increasingly redolent of the Conservative administrations of Mrs Thatcher: the handbag may be missing, but the metaphor of 'all boats rising with the new tide' has simply supplanted that of trickle-down economics.[10] And yet it is difficult to avoid the feeling that in this attempt to ward off the neo-liberal 'bogeyman' debate has all too often tended to excessively eulogize the period in which the KWS was in the ascendant.

To others, it appears quite the opposite; obtrusive state intervention and excessive welfare benefits have proved an increasingly onerous burden upon the Celtic Tiger.[11] It is an argument which, more often than not, revels in a 'straw man' account of the welfare state, that its labyrinthine bureaucratic structure has crowded out investment, created a culture of dependency and undermined the emergence of an entrepreneurial spirit. Yet, such political arguments have undeniably assumed greater prominence as the Irish polity confronts the 'novel' (almost incomprehensible) prospect of a tightening labour market while many remain in the category of the long-term unemployed. Of course, there is little mention of the nature of the 'available' work, its rates of pay or conditions. Needless to say it is an environment in which the clichés of tabloid journalism prosper. The incessant calls for more stringent eligibility to certain welfare entitlements simply echo the rhetoric, which often accompanied the policies of the Conservative governments in the UK during the 1980s.

To a large extent the sterility of this debate can be located in the fact that it has often been reduced to little more than discussions about the benefits (or not) of reductions in taxation or increases in welfare provision. Yet, the central issues remain more complex and deep-rooted, as the Irish state has occupied itself with an altogether more important political project. Indeed, what remains novel (and perhaps appealing) to bargaining 'celtic style' is that it has been formed around an attempt to construct a new form of governance, one capable of delivering a 'world class economy', which retains a *modicum* of commitment to avoid social dislocation.

It is by no means a simple task, as is evidenced by the fact that policies have been *ad hoc* and in many instances experimental. Confusion stems from the fact that if there has been a social democratic element to certain policies designed to ease the passage into the labour market (medical cards and area-based employment schemes spring to mind) there has also been a distinct neo-liberal tinge to the preference for more stringent criteria for eligibility to welfare entitlements, a predisposition to increase the use of fraud squads and the determination to resist increases in welfare payments above the rate of inflation. What remains patently clear, however, is that even where reform has been marginally inclusive its principal motivation rests firmly upon enhancing the flexibility of the labour market.

If we are to grasp more fully the nature of this political project it is essential we avoid the tendency to associate national level agreements with demand management strategies and/or a passive welfare state. What is more, if we are to understand the relationship between macro-political bargaining and welfare policies we need to avoid assuming that macro-political bargaining becomes ossified into a rigid political landscape. The trajectory of policy (as well as its attendant political discourse) is clearly shaped by the pervasive influence of the global economy and the changing political complexion of coalition governments (in the Irish case there has been a discernible shift to a conservative/neo-liberal position in the latter part of the 1990s). This chapter argues therefore that these negotiations have not been preoccupied simply with the issue of either pay or a social democratic vision to reduce inequality. Rather, they form part of a wider strategy concerned with constructing a political discourse which champions greater flexibility in the labour market, the construction of a more active welfare regime and redefining the relationship between the public and private sector.

It would be churlish to suggest that the growth in employment attained so spectacularly during the 1990s has not been beneficial to many elements of Irish society. However, it would also be misleading to deny that those who have gained most have been those in employment and those that have gained inordinately have been those on higher wages. It may well be the case that a prolonged period of unprecedented economic growth and an improvement in public finances has ensured that the type of calculated assault upon the welfare state witnessed in the UK during the 1980s has been largely absent, but few would brook argument that it remains incongruous, indeed obscene, that poverty persists in the era of the Celtic Tiger

While the social security cuts of the late 1980s now appear a distant memory, the percentage of households below poverty lines, calculated as proportion of average income, was generally higher in 1997 than in 1994 (Nolan 1999; see also Nolan and Whelan 1999). If, as Nolan observes, distribution-sensitive measures are taken into account, incomes which fall below the poverty line rose sharply between 1994 and 1997, having fallen between 1987 and 1994. However, the numbers below a 'fixed' poverty line set at 60 per cent of average income in 1987 and up, rated in line with prices rather than average incomes, declined sharply between 1994 and 1997. As Nolan points out, this

> reflects the fact that average incomes have risen substantially in real terms, that is ahead of prices, for those with incomes from work and those relying on social welfare. The latter, however, have lagged behind the exceptionally rapid growth in earnings and especially profits over the period'.
>
> (Nolan 1999: 4)

There have also been notable changes to those categories 'at risk' of experiencing poverty. For example, from the data gleaned from the 1997 Living in Ireland Survey Nolan points out that between 1994 and 1997

> the 'risk of falling below half average income rose for single-person households, particularly for those where the head was 65 or over, and fell for some types of households with children. The risk of households, which were headed by an unemployed person, remained high, a situation alleviated only by the increase in employment during this period'.
>
> (Ibid.)

Medical cards and area-based employment schemes

Changes to the eligibility for medical cards and the introduction of area-based employment schemes are two of the more prominent (active) policy changes which reveal a concern with the relationship between welfare policies and the labour market. In Ireland, access to free medical care is available only to those whose income is below a specific threshold and is a means tested non-cash benefit. It has long been argued that the cost of medical care is an important consideration for those unemployed who are presented with an opportunity to return to the labour market. Defending the interests of your family can be an uncomfortable and complex juggling act, where the decision to enter low-paid (and often insecure) work is countered by the 'potential threat' of high medical costs. It was certainly a view recognized by the Expert Working Group on Integrating Tax and Social Welfare, which observed that:

> The effect of the medical card on the incentive to work is generally accepted to be significant. This is particularly marked where recipients perceive that there is a high risk of illness for themselves or their families . . . recipients can understandably put a contingent value on the card much in excess of the value imputed from estimates and ... in these circumstances an unemployed person might be unwilling to take up a relatively well paid job.
>
> (Cited in Callan and Nolan 1999: 67)

In its interim report the group recommended that, irrespective of future income, those registered as long-term unemployed should retain a medical card on re-entering the labour market. It was a measure implemented in the 1996 budget with the period of retention being three years as opposed to the two years recommended by the expert working group. While it remains too early to ascertain the impact of such measures, Callan and Nolan (1999) have suggested that the survey material would appear to indicate that it is a policy measure 'likely to be important for only a small minority of the unemployed, but for that minority the impact could be quite substantial' (ibid.: 2).[12]

What remains of interest to the arguments of this chapter is that this is not simply a case of improving public finances affording an increase in the threshold for eligibility (a passive policy reaction). Rather, a relaxation in the rules governing eligibility has introduced a more dynamic element to policy so that those who are unemployed can now retain their medical card for a period of three years as they re-enter employment. It is a policy which clearly attempts to both overcome the vagaries of employment insecurity associated with low-paid work and increase flexibility in the labour market. It has also been one of the clearest indicators of a shift towards a concern with the relationship between (active) welfare policies and their impact upon the supply side of the economy.

In Irish public policy there are few areas more prominent in debates about the appropriate role of the state than in rural and urban development. It is not that the social dislocation associated with uneven development is a particularly recent phenomenon. Rather, the problem (in its new guise), and by definition the character of its political response, is shaped by debates which surround public policy in both a national and international setting.

Since 1991 Ireland has been engaged in an attempt to produce a series of innovative programmes aimed at alleviating long-term unemployment. As part of the Programme for Economic and Social Progress (PESP, 1990) the government initiated the development of twelve area-based Partnerships in urban and rural communities. Few would deny that the stimulus to such policy developments originated in the failure on the part of successive central administrations to resolve what appeared to be the intractable problem of long-term structural unemployment.[13] Indeed, for those such as Sabel these schemes are at the 'core of the experiment' to 'address issues of social exclusion in a more flexible, decentralised and participative way' (Sabel 1996: 3). In a similar vein, the National Economic and Social Council (NESC) has argued that local area-based initiatives which tackle marginalization and social exclusion should be developed as a 'potentially effective strategy' in promoting greater integration in social and labour market policies, and that the 'more closely involved' are local communities in the planning and delivery of area-based projects, the more they will reflect 'local needs and priorities'.[14]

While these partnerships remain independent organizations under Irish company law they consist of representatives of a set of divergent interests: the unemployed, the social partners (trade unions and business), regional representatives of social welfare, training and education and farming organizations (Sabel 1996: 4). Through this structure partnerships have had an extensive influence over a significant share of the local activities and resources of the agencies of both local and national government. For both NESC and the OECD, the novelty (and anticipated success) of these ventures rests firmly on their capacity to transcend the traditional dichotomies of advanced capitalist economies: the public and private, local and national and representative and participatory forms of democracy. Thus, for example, the OECD's report contends that these partnership initiatives have served as 'springboard' to an exploration of innovative responses to economic and social problems that may provide a possible channel through which to circumvent the social dislocation associated with the drive toward a modern flexible economy.

Within such partnership-based approaches it is possible to delineate at least two crucial, complementary themes, which are of particular import to this chapter. First, the forceful assertion that these schemes offer the basis from which to establish a new set of state civil/society relations in a flexible economy. Second, that partnership schemes are somehow capable of delivering economic regeneration in areas which had proved stubbornly resistant to the benefits of the Celtic Tiger.

It is not simply that these experiments offer new avenues through which the unemployed may participate in mainstream economic activity. Rather, their supporters anticipate, or at the very least envisage, a remodelling of the traditional relationship between the state and the unemployed as stakeholders. A considerable amount of debate has therefore been generated around the extent to which these schemes offer new participatory structures or enhance empowerment (see Curtin and Varley, forthcoming). However, there has also been a discernible shift in these schemes to 'put enterprise development high on the agenda of these partnerships' (Craig 1994: 114).

In this context, one of the features of the new schemes which has received considerable attention has been the manner in which they have encouraged the relaxation of rules governing eligibility for social welfare payments. For those such as Sabel, such adjustments 'make participation in these programmes broadly affordable and attractive', removing disincentives which may 'deter the most needy from exploring these possibilities' (Sabel 1996: 10; see also Craig 1994). The introduction of the Area Allowance (enterprise) scheme meant that long-term unemployed people could establish their own business while retaining their welfare benefits for one year. At the end of 1992, 223 had availed themselves of this benefit. By 1993 it had risen to over 740 (Craig 1994).

This desire to applaud moves to relax rules governing eligibility stems in part from the firm belief that such moves mark an important step in attempts to redefine relations between citizens and state bureaucracies and encourage enterprise. In a more sceptical light, it is possible to suggest that the optimism with which these schemes have been endowed needs to be tempered by the possibility that any short-term success may be simply the natural by-product of an economy in a period of boom and that at some future point such schemes may well perform a role in identifying the difference between the deserving and undeserving unemployed.

The area allowance (enterprise) scheme is but one of series of active welfare policies designed to introduce flexibility into the labour market and which find their origins in developments emanating from the EU. Following the extraordinary meeting of the European Council in November 1997, Member States have been obliged to introduce National Action Plans (NAPs) in response to unemployment. In Ireland, the National Action Plan contains a succession of active welfare policies targeted toward the long-term unemployed. The back to work allowance scheme (27,000 places), for example, allows for 100 per cent retention of welfare entitlements for those taking up self-employment. In a similar vein, the Job Assist scheme offers those long-term unemployed returning to work a tax allowance of 3,800 euros (plus £IR 1,000 per child) tapered over three years, with a double deduction for employers who employ them. Similarly, the introduction of the one-parent family payment in 1997 which enables lone parents to earn up to 7,600 euros per annum without affecting their entitlement to payment form part of an incentive structure being built into welfare entitlements which are designed to alter the relationship between welfare entitlements and the labour market.[15]

And yet, while many of these incentives could be interpreted as active, inclusive policies they have also been accompanied by more stringent criteria for eligibility to welfare entitlements and a marked predisposition to increase the use of fraud squads. The line drawn between a policy aimed at constructing a more inclusive society (and remains optional), and a policy which attaches punitive conditions, can often be very thin. In the Irish case, for example, the evident discord between the Ministers for Social Welfare and Enterprise and Employment revealed tensions over whether social welfare payments should be discontinued if a person fails to take up the offer of a training scheme.

In a period of economic prosperity it is all too easy for such issues to be marginalized, a feature of Irish politics which may in itself reflect a shift toward a more dominant neo-liberal political paradigm. As this chapter has argued, it is by no means inconceivable that in the determination to construct a new form of governance, one which champions a more flexible economy, that there will be losers. Political discourse, it seems, is concerned less with equity, redistribution and efficiency and more with the complicated process of organizing consent around new definitions of poverty and justifiable entitlement.

Housing

If the introduction of area-based unemployment schemes and changes to the eligibility criteria for medical cards is an example of intervention which display a concern with inclusivity, housing is one which clearly does not. In many ways this should surprise few, since housing policy in Ireland has always been predominantly focused toward private ownership. However, the gap between public authority housing and private sector housing provision widened considerably during the 1990s as the government opted, wherever possible, to reduce the role for public authority housing and subsidize an expansion in both private ownership and private sector provision of rented accommodation.

Since 1987 public housing construction has remained stubbornly below 10 per cent of all new houses constructed, despite an increase in the waiting lists and an escalation in the costs of private sector houses. It is also a figure which contrasts sharply with the norm in decades prior to the 1980s, where public housing occupied a range between 20 and 30 per cent. The lower level of construction in the 1990s has also been accompanied by measures designed to encourage the privatization of housing stock through tenant purchases, a succession of policies which ensured that the overall size of public housing has remained around 100,000 units (Fahey 1999: 4).

As the role of public housing has diminished during the 1990s, government policy, through a succession of tax reliefs, has also encouraged further expansion in private ownership and the private sector provision of rented accommodation. Despite fears of the type of house price 'bubble' which exploded in the British economy in the late 1980s, government policy has steadfastly refused to consider public housing as a potential avenue out of the impasse of escalating house prices. Indeed, the government's neo-liberal instincts have been clearly displayed in its preference for a private sector solution to the 'housing crisis'. In an attempt to create 'affordable housing', regulations are to be introduced which stipulate that any new private sector developments will have to have at least 20 per cent of housing in the 'affordable category' (a move likely to be vigorously contested in the courts by property developers).

Bargaining in the new millennium

The backdrop to Partnership 2000 was very different to the PCW. The unions sought radical tax reform to provide tax relief for public sector workers, a flexible pay agreement which would benefit the low paid and new initiatives designed to include profit sharing in companies. Local pay clauses were reintroduced and linked to productivity gains in the private sector and modernization programmes in the public sector. This latter element to the agreement was to prove one of its more novel features.

It is not that the agreement sought to appease the more conservative elements of the Irish media or its academe who have voiced continued opposition to the 'spiralling' public sector wage bill. Rather, the agreement acknowledged the 'imperative' to build upon measures, which had induced change in the public sector (*Partnership 2000* 1997: 68). With regard to this, Chapter 10 of the agreement represents the culmination of almost a decade of concern to reorganize public service provision in which a succession of policy developments have sought to engineer reform: Delivering Better Government; Shaping a Healthier Future: A Strategy for Effective Healthcare in the 1990s; Charting our Educational Future and the Strategic Management Initiative.

Reflecting the international trend toward the restructuring of civil services emphasis has been accorded to improving the 'quality of service provision, flexibility in the deployment of resources and the use of performance measurement'. Here, Partnership 2000 contains a local bargaining element which links 'on-going' discussions about new and more flexible working arrangements in public sector service provision. Indeed, the agreement explicitly stipulates that adjustments in pay (at the local level) will 'be conditional upon there having been verified progress to a satisfactory level on implementation of the modernisation programme set out in chapter ten of the agreement' (*Partnership 2000* 1997: 80).

Few would doubt that the overhaul of the Irish civil service was long overdue or that the reform thus far achieved was significantly assisted by national level negotiations. However, while many of these reforms are well under way, and a trajectory is well established, there remain important questions in some quarters over the 'detail and extent of change'. The Department of Finance, for example, remains sceptical, convinced that the reform programme is infused with aspirations but has so far delivered rather less in terms of tangible change.

Nevertheless, the Department of the Taoiseach's office remains confident that significant steps forward have been made, providing the basis for future change. Negotiations with the unions via the framework provided by national level agreements 'institutionalizes' the accepted need for change, allowing future revision of public sector working practices. However tentative these developments may have been they confirm the ability of national level bargaining to provide a framework from which to establish change in the supply side of the economy. They are also important in the government's capacity to assuage business that gains in efficiency made in the private sector will not be sacrificed at the 'altar of public sector inefficiency'.

One of the features which distinguished Partnership 2000 from previous agreements, was the emphasis accorded to increasing the role of plant level partnership in Ireland. In particular, the agreement implemented a new body, the National Centre for Partnership, designed to promote workplace partnership in both the public and private sectors. However as O'Dowd, joint Director of the Centre has acknowledged, while there is 'growing interest' in these ventures it has been practised only in a minority of cases (*IRN*, 31, 20 August 1998). This is confirmed by the study on workplace change undertaken by Roche and Geary which has argued that the incidence of partnership at the firm level was only 'very modest' in union-ised companies. At most, 20 per cent have established partnerships, and fewer have used this as a means for organizing change. Moreover, it is also generally limited to 'operational issues' and rarely forms part of the strategic decision-making of a business (Roche and Geary 1998: 17). The reluctance on the part of management to embrace partnership may, in part, be attributed to risks which are commonly perceived to be carried in such forms of negotiation such as; the capture of management decision making, delays in decisions being taken or the dilution of the managerial prerogative (ibid.: 18).

A further issue which has caused consternation among trade unionists about Partnership 2000, has been that of trade union recognition. Through-out the 1990s trade unions have been alarmed at the tendency (particularly among multi-national companies) to establish non-union organizations. However, while the negotiations for Partnership 2000 embraced the idea of union recognition it has become clear that it has not been resolved to the satisfaction of the unions. The Irish Business and Employers Confederation (IBEC), which has a significant proportion of members for which non-union HR policies are a core value, could not agree to a legally binding mechanism for union recognition disputes. As such, the High Level Group drafted a series of proposals which involve voluntary negotiations, taken in conjunction with the Labour Relations Commission, which would be concluded in a non-binding recommendation (see *IRN* 1998, no. 3).

Partnership 2000 also sought to widen the nature of partnership. It established a new partnership body (National Economic and Social Forum), and set about to explore policy approaches to social exclusion and inequality (O'Donnell 1998: 87). This was a response to a growing concern that macro-level agreements between the social partners had failed to deliver to the marginalized sections of Irish society. However, this attempt at expanding the number of participants in negotiations to include elements of the voluntary and community sectors has not been without its problems. As O'Donnell and Thomas point out, these groups tend to bring normative arguments to the negotiating table. While this may expand the range of issues, change the nature of debate and include alternative visions of economic development, it also produces strains between the 'old and new social partners' (O'Donnell and Thomas 2002: 24).

Some concluding remarks

The arguments presented here suggest that despite the presence of macro-political bargaining arrangements in Ireland, management has been proactive (and at least partially successful) in pursuing a programme of productive restructuring. In stark contrast to neo-liberal criticisms of such forms of interest intermediation, this chapter has argued that the very presence of such arrangements may have assisted in engineering an environment more conducive to constructive negotiations on flexible work practices, employee status and social organization.

Initially, at least, this would appear to suggest that the optimism embedded in Streeck's view that flexibility and rigidity are not mutually exclusive, is not misplaced. The problem for Streeck (and he is not alone on this matter) lies in the failure to appreciate the role macro-political bargaining can play in restructuring the productive (supply) side of the economy. It is not simply that management in Ireland has been able to trade off a particular clause of the wage agreement in exchange for the introduction of new working practices and technology (although this has clearly been an important element). Rather, such agreements have contributed positively to the creation of a stable environment in which management has been encourage to innovate and reduce productive rigidities. Social peace, worker commitment and the recognition of the need to encourage long-term investment in new plant and technology are all a part of the political dimension to managerial strategies, which are shaped by macro-political bargaining agreements.

If the sentiments expressed by the Taoiseach, Bertie Ahern, are any indication of the likely trajectory of policy, then Ireland will continue to pursue the type of negotiated agreements which have take place over the last decade (*Irish Times*, 15 July 1999). The political storm which accompanied a severe currency crisis in the early 1990s was weathered, political and economic stability maintained and the problem of long-term unemployment 'eased'. This is not to suggest that all will be plain sailing. With an economic boom in full swing the trade unions remain perturbed at escalating house prices and the failure to redistribute more evenly the economic gains of the 'Celtic Tiger'. What is more, the findings from the United Nations Human Development Report, which showed that Ireland's level of poverty was the second worst in the industrialized world, will have done little to alleviate anxieties ahead of a further round of negotiations for a successor agreement (*Irish Times*, 14 July 1999). There are also difficulties surrounding the extent of plant level partnership, the persistence (indeed expansion) of marginalized groups in Irish society and the thorny issue of trade union recognition. However, there are few politicians not willing to subscribe to the view that national level agreements have contributed significantly to Ireland's economic regeneration. It seems, therefore, that considerable though these hurdles may be, they are unlikely to prove insurmountable.

Notes

1 The term 'flexible specialization' has emerged as an umbrella concept encompassing a wide range of processes within contemporary capitalism. For those such as Piore and Sabel (1984) the mass production techniques of the long post-war boom have been replaced by a new paradigm in which flexibility in production and consumption becomes axiomatic. The concept has become extremely contentious. In general terms, however, the components of this new paradigm include changes in both product and labour markets, new forms of flexibility in the workforce (both numerical and functional), product diversification and the emergence of smaller production units operating for niche markets. For alternative views on what are the main features of this new, emerging era see Hirst and Zeitlin (1991), Jessop (1990).

2 This is not to suggest that wage rigidities do not lead to higher levels of unemployment, rather it is to argue that the issue of wage rigidities is more complicated than most neo-liberal economists are willing to concede.

3 An interesting comparative analysis of some of the complex themes associated with this type of argument has been undertaken by Pfaller and Gough (1991). They suggest that their findings *do not* prove that welfare statism is linked to diminishing economic performance.

4 Rowthorn (1992) argues that such wage-efficiency considerations have an important bearing upon the issue of centralization and decentralization of bargaining. Moreover, the issue is perhaps a little more complex that either Dore or Streeck acknowledge. For example, Calmfors notes that there are at

least two types of firm which would prefer decentralized forms of negotiation to decentralized forms of negotiation: strong wage-effort-profit firms, which require relative wages and those with a weak such link which want low wage relativities (Calmfors 1993).

5 This is similar to the position held by Calmfors and Driffill (1994) who accord a priority to either a centralized or decentralized approach.

6 It is plausible to suggest that Ireland is simply an exceptional case. However, there are a number of features of this case study which make it a good example to analyse the allegedly inherent rigidities of macro-political bargaining structures. As a small, open economy located on the periphery of western Europe the need to respond quickly to changes in international markets is particularly pressing. Rigidities which emerge as a result of such bargaining would presumably compound the perceived economic costs of peripheral location and relative underdevelopment.

7 Under the terms of PESP increases in pay at national level were divided into three years. Year one (4 per cent), year two (3 per cent) and year three (3.75 per cent) In addition clause 3 allowed local negotiations up to a ceiling of 3 per cent of basic pay.

8 The SIPTU report was based on 187 cases covering 749 companies. See *IRN*, 37, 1992.

9 It is important to add a note of caution here. While recent figures suggest that part-time work is common, it is only for a relatively small proportion of organizations who responded to the Price Waterhouse Cranfield Project. However, as an emerging feature it is common across organizational ownership (Irish, UK and US) see Gunnigle *et al.* (1994).

10 The metaphor was used by the Minister of Finance, Charlie McCreevy, to defend his decision to reduce the 'tax burden' on higher income earners with the budget, 2000.

11 The political furore surrounding the strike by Dublin Bus workers (March 2000) is an example of the clamour to celebrate the alleged virtues of the free market. It was a dispute about the low level of basic pay for drivers in Dublin. Alarmed by the ability of the unions to bring Dublin to a standstill, elements of the business community found in this situation an opportunity to vent their opposition to the public sector and endorse the need to privatize all that moves.

12 Callan and Nolan have cautioned against reading 'too much' into these early findings since the data may not 'fully capture the extent to which the medical card cover affects willingess to take up jobs'. This may occur either because some respondents felt there was no available work or because later discussions with family members may alter their perception of its import or because the reservation wage some people consider to be acceptable may alter in practice. For more detail see Callan and Nolan 1999.

13 This tentative governmental commitment toward local development schemes was extended in the National Development Plans (1994–9) and the Programme for Competitiveness and Work (1993–6).

14 See the National Development Plans of 1988–93, 1994–9 and the Programme for Competitiveness and Work for declarations on the fundamental role for local communities in realizing economic growth through political participation.

15 I would like to thank John Canavan for his insights on these issues.

References

Black, B. (1994) 'Labour Market Incentive Structures and Employee Performance', *British Journal of Industrial Relations*, 32/1: 99–111.

Black, W.A. (1993) 'The Contraction of Collective Bargaining in Britain', in *British Journal of industrial Relations*, 31/2: 189–200.

Brown, W.A. and J. Walsh (1991) 'Pay Determination in Britain in the 1980s: The Anatomy of Decentralisation', *Oxford Review of Economic Policy*, 7: 45–59.

Callan, T. and B. Nolan (1999) *Tax and Welfare Changes, Poverty and Work Incentives in Ireland 1987–1994*, Dublin: Economic and Social Research Institute.

Calmfors, L. (1993) 'Centralisation of Wage Bargaining and Macroeconomic Performance: A Survey', *OECD Working Papers, no. 131*.

Calmfors, L. and J. Driffill (1988) 'Centralization of Wage Bargaining', *Economic Policy*, 6: 14–61.

Craig, S. (1994. *Progress Through Partnership: An Evaluation Report on the PESP Pilot Initiative on Long-Term Unemployment*, Dublin: Combat Poverty Agency.

Curtin, C. and T. Varley (forthcoming) 'Community Empowerment *via* Partnership? The 'Local Community' in Rural Ireland's Area-based Development Regime' in G. Taylor (ed.) *Issues in Irish Public Policy*. Dublin: Irish Academic Press.

D'Art, D. and T. Turner (1999) 'An Attitudinal Revolution in Irish Industrial Relations: The End of "Them" and "Us"?', *British Industrial Relations*, 37/1: 101–16.

Dore, R. (1988) 'Rigidities in the Labour Market', *Government and Opposition*, 23/4: 393–412.

Fahey, T. (ed.) (1999) *Social Housing in Ireland*, Dublin: Combat Poverty Agency.

Gobeyn, M.J. (1993) 'Explaining the Decline of Macro-Political Bargaining Structures in Advanced Capitalist Societies', *Governance: An International Journal of Policy and Administration*, 6: 3–22.

Gunnigle, P., P. Flood, M. Morley and T. Turner (1994) *Continuity and Change in Irish Employee Relations*, Dublin: Oak Tree Press.

Habermas, J. (1989) *The New Conservatism*, Oxford: Polity Press.

Hardiman, N. (1988) *Pay Politics and Economic Performance in Ireland 1970–87*, Oxford: Clarendon Press.

Hayek, F. (1960) *The Constitution of Liberty*, London: Routledge.

Hirst, P. and J. Zeitlin (1991) 'Flexible Specialization Versus Post-Fordism: Theory Evidence and Policy Implications', *Economy and Society*, 20: 1–56.

Industrial Relations News, various dates.

Irish Congress of Trade Unions (1991) *Joint Declaration on Employee Involvement in the Private Sector*, Dublin.

Irish Congress of Trade Unions (1993) *New Forms of Work Organisation: Options for Unions*, Dublin.

Jessop, B. (1990) 'Regulation Theories in Retrospect and Prospect', *Economy and Society*, 19: 152–216.

Labour Relations Commission, *Annual Reports*, 1991–1997, Stationery Office, Molesworth Street, Dublin.

Lash, S. and J. Urry (1987) *The End of Organised Capitalism*, Cambridge: Polity Press.

National Economic and Social Council (1994) *New Approaches to Rural Development*, Dublin.

Nolan, B. (1999) 'Monitoring Poverty Trends', *Poverty Today*, Dublin: Combat Poverty Agency.

Nolan, B. and C.T. Whelan (1999) *Loading the Dice: A Study of Cumulative Disadvantage*, Dublin: Combat Poverty Agency.

O'Donnell, R. (1998) 'Social Partnership in Ireland: Principles and Interactions' in

R. O'Donnell and J. Larragy (eds) *Negotiated Economic and Social Governance and European Integration*, European Commission, Proceedings of the Cost A7 Workshop Dublin, 24 and 25 May 1996.

O'Donnell, R. and D. Thomas (1998) 'Ireland in the 1990s: Policy Concertation Triumphant', in Stefan Berger and Hugh Compston (eds) *Policy Concertation and Social Partnership in Western Europe. Lessons for the Twenty-first Century*, Oxford: Berghahn.

O'Riordan, M. (1996) 'Towards a European Social Pact: The Irish Experience' paper presented to European Trade Union Institute Conference, Brussels, 1996.

Partnership 2000 (1997) Department of the Taoiseach, Dublin.

Pfaller, A. and I. Gough (1991) *Can the Welfare State Compete? A Comparative Study of Five Advanced Capitalist Countries*, Basingstoke: Macmillan.

Piore, M. and C. Sabel (1984) *The Second Industrial Divide: Possibilities for Prosperity*, New York: Basic Books.

Purcell, J. (1991) 'The Rediscovery of the Management Prerogative: The Management of Labour Relations in the 1980s', *Oxford Review of Economic Policy*, 7: 33–43

Regini, M. (1996) 'Still Engaging in Corporatism? Some Lessons from the Recent Italian Experience of Concertation', paper presented at the 8th International Conference on Socio-Economics, Session on Globalisation and the Future of Corporatism, Geneva, 12–14 July.

Rhodes, M. (1998) 'Globalisation, Labour Markets and Welfare States: A Future of "Competitive Corporatism"?', in M. Rhodes and Y. Meny (eds) *The Future of European Welfare: A New Social Contract?*, London: Macmillan.

Roche, W.K. and J.F. Geary (1998) 'Collaborative Production and the Irish Boom: Work Organisation, Partnership and Direct Involvement in Irish Workplaces', working paper, *Centre for Employment Relations and Organisational Performance*, Dublin: UCD.

Rowthorn, R.E. (1992) 'Centralisation, Employment and Wage Dispersion', *Economic Journal*, 102/412: 506–23.

Rubery, J. and F. Wilkinson (eds) (1994) *Employer Strategy and the Labour Market*, Oxford: Oxford Univerity Press.

Sabel, C. (1996) *Ireland, Local Partnerships and Social Innovation*, Dublin: OECD.

Streeck, W. (1988) 'Comment on Ronald Dore, "Rigidities in the Labour Market"', *Government and Opposition*, 413–23.

Streeck, W. (1992) *Social Institutions and Economic Performance: Studies of Industrial Relations in Advanced Capitalist Economies*, London: Sage.

Streeck, W. and P.C. Schmitter (1991) 'From National Corporatism to Transnational Pluralism: Organised Interests in the Single European Market' in *Politics and Society*, 19: 133–64.

Taylor, G. (1996) 'Labour Market Rigidities, Institutional Impediments and Managerial Constraints: Some reflections on Macro-Political Bargaining in Ireland', *Economic and Social Review*, 27/3: 253–77.

Walsh, J. (1993) 'Internalisation v Decentralisation: An Analysis of Recent Developments in Pay Bargaining', *British Journal of Industrial Relations*, 31/3: 409–32.

9 The negotiator as auctioneer

Wage centralization and wage flexibility: a comparison of corporatist and non-corporatist countries

Coen Teulings

Introduction

In the United States, wage differentials have for many years been much larger than in most European countries. How can this be? Both world regions are highly developed and utilize similar technologies. Both regions have a highly educated labour force. Based on the usual theories of supply and demand, one would expect that the market mechanism would result in a comparable wage distribution in both regions. If no explanation can be found in supply and demand, the obvious step is to seek a solution in the sphere of institutions.

The institutions for wage formation in the United States and Europe are completely different. Despite the great variety within Europe, one difference dominates: in the United States wage negotiations are decentralized, often to the point where the individual employee must take on his employer directly, while in Europe, as well as individual negotiations, there exists a negotiation circuit on a sectoral, and sometimes even national, level. This double system of wage formation is known as 'corporatism'.

Empirical research demonstrates that the existence of these institutions goes a long way towards explaining the difference in wage dispersion between Europe and the United States (Teulings and Hartog 1998: Chapter 1). This chapter presents a theoretical explanation of the role of these institutions.

Popular opinion holds that in Europe everyone's salary is determined in central negotiations. The unions' role is to compress wage differentials, reducing them to less than is justified on the basis of supply and demand. However, this view is not without problems. After all, salary level is not just the result of agreements between unions and employers' organizations. Wages are also negotiated in other circumstances, such as during job interviews, on promotion and on the allocation of increments. Why should all those taking decisions on a micro level concern themselves with what takes place on a central level?

A good theory of corporatism should therefore be able to explain the working of a system in which decision making on the same matters takes place on several different levels. Such a theory will be set out in this chapter. The attraction of this theory lies in the fact that it is based on an image of labour relations which applies to both Europe and the United States. However, labour relations seem to be handled slightly differently in corporatist countries than on the other side of the Atlantic.

In order to set out this theoretical model, the following five 'misunderstandings' will be discussed in the course of this chapter:

- institutions are the opposite of markets;
- the model of the American company union is a good point of reference for a theory on European corporatism;
- wage contracts and collective labour agreements are primarily enforced by legal means;
- corporatism is the opposite of competition and flexibility;
- wage negotiations deal with the level of wages instead of the annual wage increase.

The chapter will end with an analysis of the political economy of corporatism. Why do the administrators of corporatist organizations behave as they do in practice?

Misunderstanding I: institutions are the opposite of markets

There is enormous confusion surrounding the precise definition of the term institution. It is sometimes taken to refer to bureaucracies ('the march through the institutions'), sometimes to laws (employment protection laws), and sometimes to something more elusive altogether ('the family' or 'the labour contract' as institutions).

One important school of thought regards all allocation mechanisms other than that of the market mechanism as being institutions. Barter trade on markets comes into existence in freedom, without interference from any parties other than those actually trading. All other transactions are in one way or another steered, regulated or restricted by 'institutions'. A striking example of this vision is the definition of Lazear (1994: 73):

> I define institutions as those constraints, either formal or informal, that operate outside the price system.

This is how institutions are thought of from a simple neo-classical perspective. Welfare economics teaches us that a market economy left to its own devices leads to efficient allocation. Every control, regulation or restriction results in sub-optimality. We are familiar with the 'institutional explanation' of unemployment which arises from this perspective: social security, employment protection and collective labour agreements are all institutions which undermine the smooth operation of the market mechanism and therefore lead to unemployment. A consequence of this vision is that institutions can only be maintained by means of *force*. According to welfare economics, at least one of the two parties benefits from a market relation. Only force can prevent the changeover to barter trade.

The vision of institutions at work here ties up with the ideas of North (1990) and with developments in modern game theory. In the world view emerging from the simple neo-classical model, everyone can trade goods or labour with an anonymous trade partner, to their own satisfaction. However, the very least that agents in an economy must know is where the trade in certain goods takes place, and how to make it known that you wish to buy or sell. If not everyone goes to the same marketplace, trade cannot take place, or only takes place with great difficulty. The common knowledge of all agents that transactions in an economy take place in a specific manner is therefore a crucial precondition for the functioning of a market economy. This type of common knowledge is what we refer to as institutions.

A characteristic of this interpretation of institutions is that they are only enforced to a very limited extent. The institution is *self-enforcing*. This clause, self-enforcing, is crucial: it is in no one's individual interest to behave in a way other than that prescribed by the institution. One person's behaviour depends on his *convictions* or *norms* regarding the behaviour of others. Norms and convictions taken as a whole can also be termed *culture*. At heart, institutions are shared, self-enforcing convictions on the way in which business is done in a certain country. Understood in this way, they are in no sense the opposites of markets.

Misunderstanding II: the American company union as point of reference

The analysis of the role of unions has a long tradition in economic science. The theory is based on a union which operates on a company level. This point of reference is particularly suitable for an analysis of the American situation. The model is often indiscriminately applied to the European system of consultation, where union federations and employers' organizations negotiate on contracts which apply to several companies collectively, as in the well-known analysis of Calmfors and Driffill (1988). At first glance, this analogy is obvious. However, it requires an assumption as to the power of corporatist organizations which greatly exaggerates their impact.

The standard model holds the union to be a monopoly of employees. By uniting, employees can increase their wages above the market level. The negotiating power of the union is limited by two forces: the negotiating power of the employee, and the loss of employment resulting from excessive wage demands. Such unions are hazardous to the efficiency of an economy. Imagine that the union succeeds in increasing wages to 15 per cent above the market wage, as is usual in the United States and Canada. The employer will then only retain an employee if his value added is 15 per cent above the market wage. An employee who is dismissed from a company as a result of these higher (union) wages and must work elsewhere for the market wage then has a drop in productivity of 15 per cent. In Europe, this union effect is generally considerably lower, an order of magnitude of 5 per cent (Blanchflower and Freeman 1990).

In order for this model to be applied to Europe, one crucial assumption must be made. Unions can only lift wages above the market wage by uniting the forces of all the *insiders*. These insiders have an interest in this, because it will lead to their receiving higher wages, for example, the 15 per cent wage surplus mentioned earlier. Outsiders, on the other hand, have an interest in breaking through this cartel. By closing a deal with the employer in which they agree to accept a lower wage surplus of 5 per cent, both the employer and the outsider are better off. To unite forces effectively requires the rigorous exclusion of outsiders, to the detriment of their interests. The outsiders will do their best to break this cartel. The larger the wage surplus, the more they will want to do this.

A company union can maintain the cartel quite easily. It knows where to find the company, and members within the company will be prepared to get rid of 'blacklegs' by gentle, and often not-so-gentle, means. The structure of American and British unions is specifically aimed at solving this problem. They have a strong organization, with union officials in the company to enforce the correct application of the collective labour agreement. These officials have a large influence in the actual operation of the company.

In European relations with collective labour agreements on an industry level, it is hopeless to enforce collective labour agreement in this way. Enforcement is only possible if it is based in part on the conviction of employers and employees that it is in everyone's long-term interest. New companies are constantly being established, particularly in the services sector. In many of these companies, no one is a union member. How can the union possibly know whether the collective labour agreement is being adhered to?

The union lacks information about what is taking place within each individual company. Naturally, they will attempt to enforce compliance with the collective labour agreement, but if none of the company's employees consider it worthwhile, they do not have a leg to stand on. As former outsiders, these employees may have very good reasons not to attach any importance to union pressure groups.

This problem will become more important when various job types exist within a company. The union must then have a precise insight into the job classification of each employee. After all, it is easy for the employer to classify a lathe operator as an assistant lathe operator in order to pay him lower wages. Complaints arise in union companies in the United States regarding suffocating job classification systems for precisely this reason. These systems prescribe exactly what a person must do or not do. This is an essential tool for the company union to enforce compliance with the American type of collective labour agreement. Naturally, this type of system removes all flexibility from the operation of the company.

The application of this model to European relations, where a union federation negotiates for a number of companies at once, assumes that this system functions because strict compliance with the collective labour agreement is enforced by the union federation. Every single wage contract and promotion requires, as it were, central approval. This requires enormous assumptions about the availability of information to the union. In short: the American union model simply cannot be applied to European labour relations.

Interlude: specific investments, market boundaries and flexibility

In a market with full competition, price is determined at the crossroads of supply and demand. With the exception of an auctioneer, no negotiator enters into the market. This is different in an employment relation between company and employee. Both parties have made *specific investments* in the relationship. There are many different aspects to these investments, from knowledge about the company's production process and moving house to be closer to your current employer, to knowing where the photocopier is and the friends you make in your new working environment. All these investments lose their value as soon as you leave the job.

This is illustrated in Figure 9.1. The lowest line indicates the minimum the employee should earn. If he gets less, then he can find a more attractive job elsewhere on the labour market. The line at the top reflects the maximum the company will pay. For more money, the company is better off recruiting someone else from the labour market. The continuation of the relation is viable as long as the maximum acceptable wage for the company is higher than the minimum acceptable wage for the employee. If the salary falls outside these boundaries, then continuation no longer makes sense for one of the two parties, and the relation will be terminated. These boundaries will therefore subsequently be referred to as the *market boundaries* of the employment relation.

In a market with full competition, the two market boundaries coincide so that the wage is completely fixed. This is one of the blessings of competition. In an employment relation, however, the competition is some distance away, because they must first make the specific investments before they can compete on an equal footing. The distance between the two market boundaries is therefore a measure of the extent of the specific investments. As long as the wage lies between the two market boundaries,

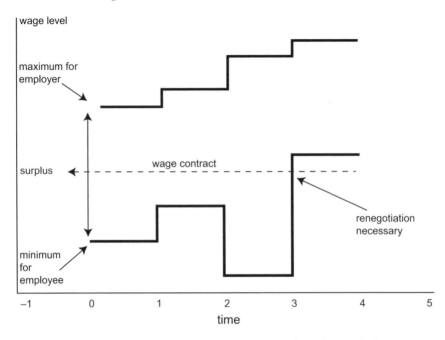

Figure 9.1 Positions on wage demands of employers and employees during negotiations.

the two parties are stuck with each other. If they do not reach agreement, then their specific investments will be lost. Neither party will want to break the relationship. Both have an interest in continuing the relationship. Precisely at what level wages will be fixed, then, is a matter of the bargaining power of each party.

In practice, it transpires that the partners in an employment relation will do anything possible to avoid negotiating with one another. This can be seen in the following example. In the Netherlands, an individual employee's wage rise can be divided up into three components. The initial component is periodically determined in consultations between unions and employers' organizations. The second component, annual increments, is laid down in the collective labour agreement for a longer period, on the basis of fixed pay scales. These two components are laid down in a contract for the individual employee. The third component is the incidental wage increases which may be granted to an employee. Negotiations on an individual basis only take place with respect to the incidental component. Table 9.1 reflects the distribution of incidental components in the Netherlands. In two out of three cases it equals zero. The wage increase of this group is therefore completely determined by fixed pay scales and the so-called initial wage increase. No negotiator is involved on a company level.

Table 9.1 The distribution of incidental wage increases in the Netherlands, 1991–2

Incidental wage increase in %	Share in %
<0	1.2
0	61.3
0–0.05	2.2
0.05–5	19.6
5–10	9.1
>10	6.7

Source: Author's calculations on the basis of data from the Wage Administration Service (LTD).

This is no different in the United States. Baker *et al.* (1994) drew up a similar table for an American company. Card and Hysop (1996) make similar calculations for the entire economy. There too, a large proportion of employees turn out not to receive any increase in wages, albeit to a lesser extent than in the Netherlands. Because the United States does not have a system of initial wage increase, and practically no fixed incremental increases, a large proportion of employees will receive the same sum this year as they did last year. This means a nominally equal sum, not a real equal sum. It follows, then, that in years of inflation a large proportion of employees is worse off. Evidently, there is a kind of unwritten law that wages should not be lowered. Because of the unwritten nature of this law, it is sometimes referred to as an *implicit* contract. It is not a contract in any legal sense, but woe betide anyone who departs from it.

Why do the company and the employee use this type of contract? A recent explanation offered by MacLeod and Malcomson (1993) centres on the *hold up* problem. When an employer takes on an employee, he will be cautious about making specific investments. After all, by making these investments he renders himself vulnerable. The employee is handed a powerful tool, because the employer's specific investments will be lost if he leaves. With this tool, he is in a position to rob the employer of part of the profits of that investment, in future wage negotiations, by threatening to leave. An employer can, of course, anticipate this problem. So his reaction is to postpone part of his investments. Less investment is made in specific training than is socially desirable. This problem also exists the other way round: an employee is sensible not to buy a house near his current employer, because it weakens his position in future wage negotiations. The company and the employee have a mutual interest in solving this problem. After all, by arranging matters in such a way that the employment relation functions as efficiently as possible, the total expected profit from the employment relation increases. If the pie is bigger, there are more slices to go round. Both parties ultimately benefit. The solution to the hold up problem is obvious. By fixing the future wage level at the start of the employment relation, prior to specific investments being made, the necessity for future negotiation is removed.

Figure 9.1 also offers some insight into the complex relationship between wage rigidity and flexibility. As long as the contract establishes the wage between the market boundaries of the employment relation, there is no problem. Wages are rigid in that case, as is often found in Europe as well as in the United States: see Table 9.1 and the figures of Card and Hysop (1996). Both parties have an interest in continuing the employment relation. The long-term contract, then, protects them for the hold up problem. However, as soon as one of the two market boundaries is pushed across the contract wage as a result of some unexpected event, continuation of the employment relation against the prevailing wage will no longer be rewarding for one of the two parties. If the contract is not adjusted, that party will wish to break the relation, even if it is still profitable. After all, the maximum acceptable wage for the company is higher than the minimum acceptable wage for the employee.

MacLeod and Malcomson (1993) show that in such situations the contract is renegotiated. The contract is adapted to the new conditions. One example is an impending bankruptcy. The employees accept wage reductions in order to keep the company operating, as occurred in the impending closure of aircraft manufacturer Fokker. Another example is the bonuses offered to information technology staff as a result of the shortage in this sector. One disadvantage of such renegotiation is that protection against the hold up problem disappears. However, this disadvantage does not outweigh the alternative, which is terminating the relationship. Something is better than nothing.

We arrive, then, at a paradoxical conclusion. If all is well, the long-term contract leads to wage rigidity: wages do not react at all to movements in the market boundaries of the employment relation. In that way the hold up problem is solved. However, if the movements become too large, adjustment will have to take place to prevent termination of the employment relation. The more rigidity is possible, the better the specific investments are protected against the hold up problem. However, this kind of rigidity does not mean no flexibility at all. The contract can always be adjusted by way of renegotiation if that is necessary to prevent termination of the relation. Flexibility here is not the ideal, it is an emergency measure.

Misunderstanding III: contracts, legal force or norms

The question now is why the company and the employer would stick to this contract. The traditional answer is that these contracts are enforced by legislation. Should one of the two parties breach the contract, the other will respond through the courts to enforce compliance.

This idea has little to do with actual practice. Going to court is an expensive and ineffective solution. The court lacks the knowledge on affairs within the company necessary to make a ruling. Furthermore, contracts often only stipulate the wage level. They do not prohibit an employee from leaving, any more than they offer the employee employment protection. One of the two parties can always threaten departure, a threat which the court cannot undo. Such a threat can be so credible that it forces adjustment of contract. The renegotiations discussed earlier, when the original wage contract meets the market boundaries of the employment relation, are based on that principle.

The question, then, is why the threat of leaving or dismissal is not continuously used to break open existing contracts. What is the force that precludes permanent renegotiation? The only difference from normal negotiations is that during these renegotiations there is a piece of paper on the table with a simple text reading: 'salary=X'. A piece of paper, no dissolution conditions; after all, that is all a wage contract is. Why would a party who could normally receive more than X by means of negotiation, allow himself to be fobbed off with such a document, without any further negotiation? MacLeod and Malcomson (1993) present an argument for this game full of theoretical subtleties. A practical approach, however, gives a reasonable feel for the essential nature of their argument.

Negotiations can be considered a kind of two-way hostage situation. The two parties have a *common* interest in agreement being reached. The two parties have a *conflicting interest* when it comes to dividing up the pie. Each dollar more for one party means a guilder less for the other. The outcome depends on nerves of steel. As a negotiator you should show as long as possible that you are willing to go for all or nothing. If the other party receives even the slightest hint of willingness to compromise you are finished. A small slip of the tongue is sufficient. Much depends on the credibility of the negotiator and, in particular, the credibility of his threats. It is for this reason that the outcome of negotiations is so sensitive to small details.

At precisely this point lies the role of that piece of paper which is sitting somewhere on the negotiating table, the wage contract. Assume that the employee has just made an offer. Without that piece of paper, the company now has two alternatives: it can accept the offer so that work can begin, or turn down the offer and propose a counter-offer so that negotiations drag on, and the work remains undone, in anticipation of agreement on the wage level. With that piece of paper, a third alternative comes into existence: the company can stick to the contract, and say that work must continue in the meantime. Now the ball is in the employee's court: either he refuses to continue working in anticipation of agreement on a new wage level, or he continues working and tries to renegotiate in the meantime.

The crucial point is that the piece of paper undermines the credibility of the threat of stoppage. Now that the alternative of following the agreement on that piece of paper is available, the short-term temptation will always be not to lose out on anything by interrupting the work. The temptation of continuity outweighs the threat of stoppage. This effect reinforces itself. If people work out that their threats are not credible, the threats will not be made. And where one party knows that the other party does not consider his own threat to be credible, the conclusion will be drawn that those threats will not be carried out. Etc., etc., *ad infinitum*. How a small piece of paper can have far-reaching consequences.

Negotiators, then, are constantly trying to calculate their optimum response. The outcome of that calculation, however, depends on the reaction expected from the other party. If everyone is aware that threats fall on deaf ears, they will not be made, because they are simply ineffective. Furthermore, because they are not made, they are also not complied with. This is precisely what is meant by social norms. They let people know three things: first, what they should do, second, what others will do if they don't do it, and finally, what they should do if others do not behave as they should. Ultimately citizens behave according to norms not because of their moral sense or because some union chairman or economist enforces these norms, but because they know that a breach will be punished by their fellow citizens. Norms are *self-enforcing*. They are maintained out of pure calculation, just like everything else in economic theory.

Such norms have come into existence over many generations as a tool for coordinating our behaviour. In wage negotiations in particular, there is good cause for this: as we are able to better estimate the value of the other party's negotiating stake, we are better able to prevent expensive conflicts, such as strikes. This is precisely what is meant by the well-known expression 'vested interests'. The norm prescribes that a party cannot unilaterally change a right. This norm is usually interpreted as a sign of rigidity. However, it serves a useful purpose. It contributes to upholding the wage contract. This in turn limits the hold up problem.

From here, it is a small step to the implicit contract (and therefore the implicit wage rigidity) seen in the United States. Why do you need a piece of paper anyway? Is it not sufficient to settle on an hourly wage at the start of the employment relation? The implicit contract is that this hourly wage is not changed unilaterally, but only with mutual agreement. That contract is implicit, because it is never even discussed. It is simply standard practice that things are done this way. The entire argument on the role of the written wage contract applies just as much to an implicit agreement.

This thought is confirmed by a nice piece of empirical research by Kahneman *et al.* (1986) into the meaning of norms in the economic process in Canada and the United States. They asked a group of citizens whether they found a certain course of action to be fair or unfair. Citizens have well-defined and broadly shared opinions on this. To an economist, those opinions appear completely irrational at first sight. They suffer from money illusion. Compare, for example, the following two scenarios:

1   There is high unemployment but no inflation. The company lowers nominal wages by 10 per cent.
2   There is high unemployment and 10 per cent inflation; the company leaves nominal wages unchanged.

In both cases, purchasing power drops by 10 per cent. In the first case, norms prohibit the cut in wages, but in the second case they do not require the increase in wages. The same applies for the car dealer who gives a standard discount of 5,000 dollars on his catalogue price of 25,000 dollars. If the demand for cars temporarily increases, this dealer can, according to the norms, eliminate his discount. The dealer who thinks all the song and dance with discounts is unnecessary, and immediately lists the standard price of 20,000 dollars in his catalogue, however, may not raise his price in times of shortage.

With the hold up model in hand, this type of strange result can be easily understood. Norms regulate distribution conflicts. The prescription how to behave when confronted with a distribution conflict prevents a situation in which citizens start to protect themselves by decreasing their specific investments. The norms which give least cause for confusion are based on money illusion: an hourly wage of three dollars remains an hourly wage of three dollars, no matter what happens. Agreements based on the real wage lead to enormous confusion: When do adjustments take place? How high should the adjustments be? Which inflation figure should be used?

The need for wage rigidity, therefore, is not typically European, but rather universal. What if we would have to renegotiate our wages every day? We would have no time left to work. In America, this need is given shape by making an implicit agreement on nominal rigidity: what is three dollars will in principle remain three dollars. In Europe, that need has, over the years, taken the form of a collective labour agreement. In both cases, the rigidities are self-enforcing: for the most part, the courts are never involved. It is now time to draw up the balance: which is the more flexible rigidity? That in America, or that in Europe?

Misunderstanding IV: corporatism is at the cost of flexibility

The model which has been discussed so far applies to both the United States and to Europe. Both types of economy have a need to prevent negotiation on wage level. The solution is the same in both cases: the company and the employee close a long-term wage contract, explicitly, as in Europe, or implicitly as in the United States.

In order to be able to understand the difference between Europe and the United States, it is necessary to distinguish two components in the unexpected shocks which force companies and their employees to adapt their contract to the market boundaries from time to time. The first component is *aggregate shocks*. These shocks influence the market boundaries of all employment relations in the same way. The second component is *firm-specific shocks*. These shocks only hit the market boundaries of one specific labour organization.

As the market boundaries are influenced by more and more extensive shocks, the chance that the contract wage which was established in advance is situated between the two market boundaries is obviously reduced. The chance of the contract needing to be renegotiated afterwards, therefore increases, as can be seen in Figure 9.2. In the top figure, a number of firm-specific shocks are depicted in the top market boundary without aggregated shocks; renegotiation is only necessary in instance 2. In the middle figure, an aggregate shock is placed on top of the specific shock. Now renegotiations afterwards are necessary in instance 5 as well as instance 2. And that was exactly what the market parties tried to prevent through the contract.

It would be profitable if contracts could be adjusted afterwards to the aggregate shocks. This part of the shocks could then be, as it were, filtered out. Consequently, the remaining shocks would be smaller, and there would be less chance of hitting the market boundary: see the bottom part of Figure 9.2. Renegotiations are only required in instance 2. However, adjustment of contracts after they have been made obviously requires a different form of negotiations. Here we can see the *fundamental dilemma* taking place:

> The wage contract serves to prevent future wage negotiations as far as is possible. If adjustment of the contract can only take place through negotiation, then the advantages of the contract are again lost.

The prospect of future renegotiations on the adjustment of the contract forces the employer and the employee to attend very carefully to their bargaining position. Once again, the hold up problem arises.

This is where the role of corporatist organizations enters into the picture. By delegating the task of negotiation on contract adjustment to higher level organizations at the start of their employment relation, an individual employee and his employer are able to avoid the hold up problem. After all, they cannot influence the outcome of such negotiations by postponing their specific investments. The wage negotiations are decoupled from the everyday situation.

In a corporatist economy, then, there are two types of renegotiation. The first type is renegotiation by corporatist organizations. These renegotiations remove the effect of aggregate shocks. The outcome of these negotiations cannot be influenced by individual companies or employees. This type has no equivalent in the United States. The second type is individual renegotiation, in those cases where 'corporatist' renegotiations do not have the desired result due to firm-specific shocks. These renegotiations in essence take place in the same manner in the United States.

The two types of renegotiation are expressed in the subdivision of the wage increase into the three components mentioned earlier: fixed increments are determined in advance, and are therefore not the result of renegotiation; the initial wage increase reflects the outcome of the corporatist consultation, and the incidental wage increase is the mirror image of

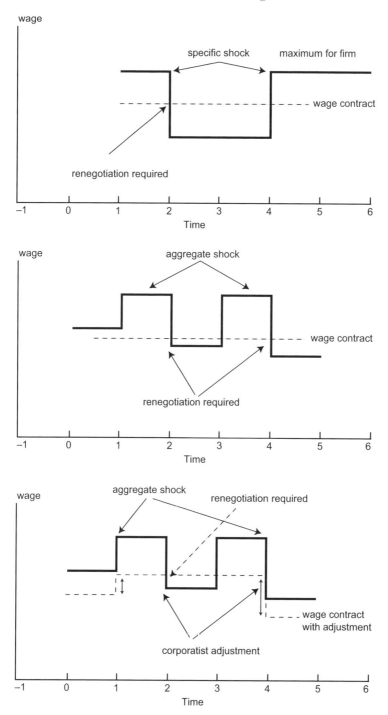

Figure 9.2 Specific and aggregate shocks and adjustments of the wage contract.

individual negotiations. Table 9.2 shows the extent of the various components under both systems. In the United States there are no corporatist organizations to take over the renegotiation of wage contracts. Initial wage increase does therefore not take place there. As a result, they have to rely on nominal rigidity there, but that is an inferior substitute. In Europe initial wage increase is a common phenomenon. Incidental wage increase takes place in the United States as well as Europe, but is more common in the United States. The reason for this difference is simple: aggregate shocks are absorbed by initial wage increase in Europe so it occurs less frequently that the remaining shocks exceed the market boundaries of the employment relation: see Figure 9.2.

The central idea, therefore, is that parties have an interest in decoupling wage negotiation from the everyday work situation. A good gauge is to find out how companies view the role of the works council in negotiations on primary labour conditions. The outcome of a number of interviews is remarkable in that respect. In only one of ten in companies interviewed did management negotiate with the works council on labour conditions. In all other instances, negotiation took place with the unions. Even though the Federation of Netherlands Industry (VNO) and the Netherlands Christian Employers' Union (NCW) sometimes suggest allocating to the works council a larger role in negotiations on the collective labour agreement, that opinion was only supported by one of the other nine companies. The rest of the companies were strongly opposed to this. An objection which was often mentioned was the fact that the works council was 'too directly involved' in the outcome of the negotiations.

A good example of this is the interview with a medium-sized business in the metal sector. Responding to the question about expectations for the future, the management answered that they had concluded from the newspaper that a further decentralization of wage negotiations would take place. In their opinion, this would lead to higher wages. To the question of whether the management found this decentralization desirable, they answered: 'As I said, our speciality is pipe-fitting. We don't know the first thing about wage negotiation.'

The model suggests that employers and employees will depart from the collective labour agreement when it is in both their interests to do so. Corporatist organizations, after all, lack the information to enforce com-

Table 9.2 Different forms of wage adjustment in economies with various institutions

	Corporatist (Europe)	Decentralized (the United States)
Only initial	Very often	Never
Nominally rigid	Never	Often
Incidental	Now and then	Regular

pliance with the collective labour agreement. This was only supported to a limited extent in the interviews. A number of quotes illustrate the employers' motives for not paying higher wages when an individual worker gets a better outside offer:

> When someone comes in saying that he can make more money elsewhere, I congratulate him.

> I only do that in exceptional circumstances. In practice it invariably means that after a while you have to give all his colleagues the same wage increase.

> If you do give someone a little bit extra, he or she will leave after a while anyway.

> I can't always see what happens in one branch or another, but if I do find out, that supervisor has to come up with a very good reason.

Companies turn out to have a large number of reasons to be very reserved in granting higher wage increases than those prescribed by the collective labour agreement, even if important employees threaten to quit. None of the companies, however, gave as a reason that the collective labour agreement did not permit it. Where employers do not follow the strict neo-classical model, it is not because the collective labour agreement prohibits this, but because they do not think that strict neo-classical behaviour is in their interest. A large number of more strategical reasons prevent them from breaking through their wage structure to keep an individual employee within the company.

This brings us to the fourth misunderstanding. Wages in the Unites States are more sensitive to firm-specific shocks; see Holmlund and Zetterberg (1991) and Teulings and Hartog (1998: Chapter 5). This is not a sign of flexibility, however. It is in fact precisely the opposite. While in Europe wages can be adjusted to aggregate shocks within the market boundaries of the employment relation, in the United States there is only a choice between wage rigidity and firm-specific adjustments. For this reason, the chance of firm-specific renegotiations being necessary as a result of these shocks increases.

A casual observer could easily jump to the wrong conclusion on the basis of this statistical information. He would see that wages in the United States are more sensitive to firm-specific shocks and would take this as a sign of greater flexibility. In actual fact, this is a sign of rigidity, because wages in the United States cannot be adjusted separately to aggregate shocks. The greater sensitivity of wages to specific shocks in the United States, is accompanied by a smaller sensitivity to aggregate shocks. This conclusion is confirmed by empirical research (ibid: Chapter 5).

Misunderstanding V: negotiations on the collective labour agreement are about the wage level

An important implication of all this is that corporatist organisations do *not* negotiate about *wage level*, as in the American union model discussed on pp. 227–8, but about the *wage increase*. Wage level is determined by the grading at the moment the employment relation starts. This grading is a matter of negotiation between employer and employee on a micro level. Negotiations on a macro level between corporatist organisations are concerned with the annual adjustment of wage contracts in percentage terms to the state of the economy, referred as the *initial wage increase*.

This implication links up with what takes place in practice. Many industrial collective labour agreement take the form of a minimum collective labour agreement, leaving companies the freedom to pay higher wages. As well as maintaining an individual pay scale within the company, there is the possibility of variation within that compensation system, by means of grading new staff. This grading also depends in part on the situation in the labour market. An important tool here is the entry wage of new staff, 'because they haven't settled in yet'. The room for this kind of policy is larger for graduates than for low-skilled staff. In addition, there is the possibility of some variation in job descriptions: a laboratory technician becomes a trainee laboratory technician.

Fluctuations in the relationship between supply and demand affect the payment of new staff through this channel. In case of excess supply of labour, employers will utilize entry wages to a larger extent than in a tight labour market. This shows the importance of this mechanism to flexibility in the labour market: it ensures that recruiting extra employees is more attractive in bad times and it ensures adjustment of the compensation structure to relative shortages on the market.

No matter how the actual wage level differs from that prescribed by the collective labour agreement, the initial wage increase is in all cases determined at the negotiating table of the collective labour agreement. This explains the misunderstanding. Negotiations on a collective labour agreement relate to the increase in wages in percentage terms, and not to wage level.

The political economy of corporatism

The average union official undoubtedly chose union work for idealistic reasons: elevating the working class or promoting the interests of your colleagues are honourable motives and excellent reasons for pursuing a career in union work. Even union officials, however, are only human. If you are up to your neck in problems, and it's either you or someone else, then idealism goes out the window. If the model described above is to function, then it must be resistant to this kind of self-interest. Just as applies to the power of every magistrate, the power of the union leader must be restricted, in order that he successfully fulfils his role in the social process. For politicians, of course, there is the threat of the coming election. Is there a similar process when it comes to union leaders? Trusting purely in their idealism seems to be asking a bit much.

The positive side of the corporatist system as it has started to function over the last decades is that it provides for the counter-forces which restrict the power of the union official. In a corporatist system, the power to adapt the collective labour agreements in the country to changed economic conditions is delegated to the unions. Unions can abuse that power in many different ways. At the start of an employment relation before the employer and the employee are bound by specific investments, both parties must decide whether they will indeed delegate the adjustment of their collective labour agreement.[1] The union will then undoubtedly promise to carry out that adjustment in good conscience. They will do this in such a way that the interests of both parties (the employer and the employee) are respected and that the mutual welfare of both parties is maximized. You could call this the *welfare maximizing strategy* or the *cooperative strategy*. Contracts are then adjusted with a view to having the production process take place as smoothly as possible. The cooperative strategy in fact maximizes the interest of outsiders beyond a level which would be feasible without corporatist organisations, because these organizations offer a solution to the hold up problem.

Once the union holds the power to adapt contracts, they can change their strategy without any objections. Instead of maximizing common welfare, they could, for example, pursue the objective of getting as many members as possible within the company. This can be achieved by negotiating as high a salary as possible for the employees within the company. In this case, the strategy changes from the surplus maximizing strategy to the *share maximizing strategy* or the *antagonistic strategy*. The contract is only adapted with the intention of maximizing the wages of current staff. Union members also appreciate this strategy. The employer, meanwhile, has committed himself, via specific investment, to the relation and it is difficult for him to dispose of the employee. Additional wage demands are almost certain to lead to higher wages. This is attractive for the union because satisfied members are prepared to make prompter and higher contributions. Despite all the promises to pursue the welfare maximising strategy, employers will always retain a fear that the union will be unable to resist pressure from its members (*the insiders*), and will switch to the share maximising strategy after they have bound themselves to the employees by way of specific investments.

The union, therefore, has a *commitment problem* or a *credibility problem*: they would like to rise above all suspicions so that all employers and employees trust the union and delegate the adjustment of the contract to it. However, the employer remains suspicious, and suspicion is a bad foundation for the delegation of authorities. Abuse of power must therefore be prevented. What guarantees does the employer have? On what can he base his confidence in a corporatist union?

The Dutch trade unions – fortunately – have a relatively small number of members. The trade unions organise only one in four employees, and negotiate the annual contract wage increase for one in four employees. The membership base is not only small, it is also highly dispersed. It is obvious that the trade union movement has a stronger position in some companies than in others. However, union members are to be found everywhere. For example, 6 per cent of employees in the retail trade are union members. Strangely enough, this dispersed membership provides considerable advantages to the union.

First, this dispersion provides the employer with a certain peace of mind. He knows that the power base of the union within his company is limited. Should the union ever consider shifting to the antagonistic strategy, then the employer can, if necessary, push the union out the door. The union will try to prevent such a confrontation out of fear of a negative outcome. This situation makes it easier for the union as a whole to maintain its market share in the 'contract renegotiations' industry. This is a paradoxical conclusion: the dispersed power base of the Dutch trade union movement increases its credibility as a cooperative bargaining partner. Because of this, the trade union movement has recently been able to improve its position in the banking sector, and steps forward also seem to have been made in the retail trade, information technology and temporary employment sectors.

That this is an important consideration is evident from the situation in the United States. After the war, the trade union movement there was in a very strong position. However, since that time, the unionization rate has steadily decreased to a mere 11 per cent of those currently in employment. The reason is not so much that the unions were thrown out of the existing companies. That is almost impossible, because in those companies for which the trade union movement conducts the wage negotiations, they reach a unionization rate of almost 100 per cent due to the antagonistic strategy. Such a power base is almost impregnable. The reason for the decrease in unionization rate lies primarily in the fact that some companies go bankrupt and other companies take their place. A union which loses members as a result of company closures, but gains no new members in newly established companies will obviously suffer in the long run.

Because they are known for their antagonistic strategy, however, the American trade union movement is unable to find new companies. New employees have little reason to delegate contract adjustment to the trade union movement. Prior to the specific investments they will have little need to put their fate in the hands of an antagonistic trade union movement. The antagonistic strategy maximizes the interest of insiders, and at present they are not insiders. If employees within a company wish to appeal to the union, the company will go to any length to ensure that they do not. Heavy pressure is exerted on both staff and middle management to prevent this ('union busting'). In those circumstances, it is extremely difficult for the trade union movement to get a foot in the door. For this reason, the antagonistic strategy is difficult to maintain in the long term.

Dispersed membership also helps the trade union movement in its relationship with its members. After all, members experience the same problem as the trade union movement itself. At the start of the employment relation it is in their interest to agree with their future employer that the trade union movement will negotiate on their behalf on adjustments to their wage contract, with the cooperative strategy as a point of departure. After the specific investments have been made, the employees, who have in the meantime been promoted to insiders, have an interest in exerting pressure on their union to shift to the antagonistic strategy, particularly when the company is doing well and they can demand higher wages as a result. A trade union organization which wants to pursue the cooperative strategy will have great difficulty in restraining its own members, particularly those in profitable companies.

Traces of this inherent tension between a union and its members can be found in the words of union executives:

> The first negotiations are those with your own members.

This tension between central (union) and decentral (company level) repeats itself within the union, as an opposition between a district executive and a union executive:

> A weak district executive is one of the type: you ask, we work.

As one union chairman stated:

> It is not acceptable to me that if we all agree on 2 per cent, some executive comes back having asked for 4 per cent.

Or, in a situation where insiders made higher demands:

> That was a case where a district executive did not have his union members under control.

One does not have to look far to find more of the same. Klandermans and Visser (1995) demonstrate that ideas like this can be traced back to the membership base of the trade union movement. A number of members are of the opinion that the trade union movement does not try hard enough to obtain the best deal in their specific situation.

Another indication of the cooperative attitude of the trade union movement is the state of affairs in the annual round of negotiations. The Dutch trade union movement formulates the bargaining position for the wage negotiations each year, and employers play only a passive role. Ideologically, the whole idea of coordination is not favourably thought of by employers. This suggests that employers' organizations have reasonable trust in the attitude of the trade union movement. If they did not, they would undoubtedly have formulated a stake themselves. Now that in most cases the stake of the trade union movement forms an acceptable point of departure, there is generally little need to formulate a stake, all the more so because this would in fact force the trade union movement to adopt a more radical standpoint.

Dispersed membership not only forced union executives to control insider power, but also provided them with the opportunity to do so. The employees of that single well-running company were always in the minority. As a result of the widely dispersed membership, there were also numerous companies in which business was not going so well, and in a minority things were going very badly indeed. The radical advocates for higher wage demands, mostly from the well-running companies, were buried amongst the large number of members from companies which were less successful. That large group had an interest in continuing the cooperative strategy and was therefore happy to support the officials in their goal of limiting insider power.

From the previous analysis roughly three possible equilibria of unionization and wage formation can be derived. The first equilibrium is observed in the United States and the United Kingdom. The trade union movement takes an antagonistic stand. The union therefore has great difficulties in finding new firms for which it gets delegated the task of bargaining on behalf of the workers. The market share of the union shrinks gradually.[2]

The second equilibrium is observed in the Netherlands, Austria, Germany and maybe France. There, trade unions with a relatively small membership bargain for a large majority of the workers. They can do so because they follow the cooperative strategy. The most important weakness of this equilibrium is the free rider problem of the workers: where the union bargains for all the workers anyway, individual workers have little incentive to pay their membership fees. In the Dutch case, there is special solution for this problem: a separate collective agreement stipulates that employers must pay a non-trivial amount of money to the unions. This money accounts for a large share of the total union budget. The government supports this agreement by mandatory extension of this contract, so that employers cannot evade their duties.

The final equilibrium is observed in most Scandinavian countries and Belgium, where the free rider problem is solved by giving the union a stake in social security. Where union membership is almost a condition for eligibility for social security, unionization will obviously be high. The danger of this system is that the union movement becomes too powerful, which threatens the stability of system. This might very well be what happened to Sweden.

In the theoretical model laid out in the previous sections, there was hardly any role for the government. As long as there exists a credible organization outside the firm the government does not need to enforce corporatist agreements. Employers and their employees will decide themselves that it is a good thing to delegate the task of renegotiating contracts.[3] However, the final analysis suggests that a corporatist/centralized system can only exist with some support from the government in solving the free rider problem, by giving trade unions a stake in social security, or by some other means. Solving the free rider problem might well be the most important role of mandatory extension. The clauses of collective agreement regarding wages are largely self-enforcing, see pp. 232–5. Extending these clauses is a largely symbolic act.

Conclusions

In this final section, two issues have to be considered. First, to what extent is this model able to cover the variation in institutional arrangements and factual outcomes between various countries, in particular within the corporatist league? Second, to what extent is the model applicable outside the narrow area of wage formation, in broader areas of economic policy such as social security, taxation and education?

Regarding the first issue, some remarks have been made in the previous section. As a first observation, the difference between decentralized economies (United States, Canada, Australia and the United Kingdom) on the one hand and the corporatist and so-called[4] centralized economies on the other hand is far more important than the institutional variation within the latter group of countries.

Second, though institutions may look different at first sight, they may in fact play a more or less similar role across these countries. Corporatism has not been designed on a drawing table. Institutions evolve in sequential process, where the solution to the one problem sets the institutional stage for the next problem. The political economy of corporatism gives a perfect illustration of this mechanism. The system of checks and balances that keeps the corporatism going is made up of all kind of strange arrangements. Starting from scratch, nobody would have designed the system as it operates now. All this institutional variation may therefore well reflect differences in the history of the system merely affecting the way checks and balances are organized, but less the actual labour market outcome. In particular, inter-industry wage differentials seem to vary mainly with the degree of centralization in wage formation.

Nevertheless, there are some differences in outcome between corporatist countries that cannot be ignored, that may or may not be temporary. An important example is the difference in real wage increases across countries. In recent years real wage increases in the Netherlands has lagged behind those in surrounding countries. Compared to Germany, the difference since the beginning of the 1980s amounts to 20 per cent. The increase in the average wage in the Netherlands is comparable to that in the United States. This difference is often attributed to the social partners and their willingness to accept wage moderation. This opinion implies a great trust in the corporatist model of wage formation. Apparently, it is possible to have the average wage level lag behind what would have been realised without wage moderation by a high percentage, for a considerable period of time.

It seems unlikely that such a large difference in wage increases between the Netherlands and Germany can be attributed to the willingness amongst the social partners to accept wage moderation. In the short term (up to a maximum of five years, see Broersma *et al.* 1998),[5] the willingness to accept wage moderation could lead to lower real wages. For instance, the radicalization of the trade union movement in the whole of Europe during the 1970s undoubtedly contributed to the increase of the labour share in that period. However, wage moderation cannot push the wage level below the equilibrium level for long, and certainly not by 20 per cent. The market mechanism calls up strong forces which quickly put an end to such aims. In that sense, the meaning of wage moderation is more restricted than is often thought. In the long term, wage level is determined by market forces and there is a close connection between labour supply and employment. The lagging behind of Dutch wages compared to other European countries can probably be explained by two factors: the sharp reduction in unemployment benefits and the rapid increase in female labour supply. The former led to a reduction in reservation wages and therefore in the wage rates actually paid. Broersma *et al.* (1998) estimate this effect to explain 8 per cent of the 20 per cent lagging behind of Dutch wages. The increase in female labour supply yields wage reductions in a standard demand and supply framework.

Simply because the *average* wage level adjusts reasonably well to the equilibrium level after some delay, does not necessarily mean that wages in *individual* companies and industry do the same. A comparison with countries which lack any form of coordination in wage formation, such as the United States and Canada, shows that wages are much higher in those industries where the negotiating power of insiders is large.[6] This leads to an inefficient allocation of labour: the industries with high wages employ too few people, and those with low wages too many. In a corporatist system, this insider power is restricted by placing negotiations on the initial wage increase outside companies. Pleas for wage moderation are a tool to restrict insider power. It is the verbal expression of the norms which keep the system going.

This interpretation of the pleas for wage moderation as a tool to restrict the insider power of employees in strong companies links up with the earlier analysis of the meaning of norms. The frequent use of the terms 'insiders' and 'outsiders' in the Dutch press is an example of this. They turn up all the time. The interesting thing here is that these terms were thought up by two European economists, Lindbeck and Snower (1988). In America these terms are much less popular. The study which most convincingly shows the effects of insiders on wage formation is that of a Canadian economist, David Card (1990), and relates to Canada. The terms 'insider' and 'outsider' do not appear in his article. There is no reference to the work of Lindbeck and Snower. Most North American economists follow the same line. While numerous studies suggest that insider effects are more of an American than a European phenomenon, people in America keep silent about them, while in Europe we never tire of talking about them.

This outcome is obvious when considered from the perspective of norm analysis. In Europe we maintain norms which are aimed at restricting the power of insiders as much as possible. One aspect of this is that the danger of abuse of power by insiders is constantly pointed out. This constant attention should make clear that abuse of power will not be tolerated. In America, it is standard practice for insiders to use their position of power. There is not much point in warning them against doing so. The warning would fall on deaf ears. Pleas for wage moderation therefore serve a useful function. Wage moderation cannot explain, however, why wages in the Netherlands remain some 20 per cent behind those in Germany. Other factors play a role in that.

Following Calmfors and Driffill (1988), who argued against the vagueness of the concept of corporatism and centralization, I have restricted the analysis strictly to the role higher level organizations play in wage formation. It is tempting to extend my analysis to other areas of the economy. Such approach would relate to the extensive literature on the civil society, stressing the importance of organizations which occupy an intermediate position between a government with political legitimation and atomized citizens at the market place.

However, one should be cautious about hasty generalizations. Most theories of corporatism do not really address the question as to how corporatist organizations are able to affect the outcome at a highly diverse micro level. Enforcement is usually taken for granted, regardless of the objections against this approach put forward earlier. The contribution of this chapter is that it shows how higher-level institutions can affect behaviour at the micro level without heroic assumptions about enforcement. The main impact of corporatist organizations is in the distribution of surpluses that arise due to the specificity of investment. In that case, the market mechanism does not operate, because of the absence of competition. Small institutional details can have large effects on the outcome.

The model of corporatism laid out in this chapter describes the way in which a large measure of discretion on the part of individual agents (firms and employers) at the micro level goes hand in hand with a large measure of influence of institutions which are not strictly enforced by the power of law. The large amount of discretion provides the flexibility needed for an efficient use of scarce resources in a highly diversified economy. The institutional alignment of individual behaviour provides a protection against wasteful distributional conflicts. The nice thing about the model laid out in the chapter is that the goals do not interfere with each other, as multiple goals usually do in economic theory.

This combination of flexibility in the application of scarce resources and rules of conduct for the management of distributional conflicts should therefore be the central characteristic of other areas where the model can be applied fruitfully. It requires a great deal of specificity (as in long-term employment relations). For example, it is hard to see how the model would be beneficial for the organization of child care facilities, which is one of the areas for which the benefits of corporatist institutions are often praised. Running a day care centre has mainly to do with having the child care workers there at the appropriate time and the appropriate place. Little distributional conflict is going on there, apart from the issue whether the worker or the firm has to pay. Corporatist organizations might have a larger role to play in the organization of on-the-job-training. There, the specificity is clear. However, one might doubt whether corporatist organizations have the information available to decide who has to take what training. My suspicion is that most corporatist training schemes provide a lot of rights to taking courses with only a limited pay off.

A similar reservation applies to the use of consultation by the government on general policy issues, often hailed as one of the main benefits of corporatism. In my view no hold up problem whatsoever is resolved by these consultations. Their main effect, and that is probably very important, is that they keep the unions and the employers' federation aligned to the general policy goals of the government. This helps to support the norms that induces unions to restrain insider power. Support for the general goals of the government helps to avoid the type of leapfrogging and insider wage setting that in the end pushes unions towards antagonistic strategy. This might be an important legitimation for consulting unions and employer federations on all kind of policies it is not saying that these policy as such become better designed and more warmly supported, as is sometimes claimed. In summary, applying the present analysis of corporatism outside the area of wage formation requires careful identification of the specific investment involved and the other relevant mechanisms. Simple hand waving and a loose reference to the importance of the civil society does not suffice.

Notes

1 In many new employment relations the choice will obviously be just a formality, because the other employees in that company are already a part of a collective labour agreement whereby the union negotiates on the annual wage increase. This is of particular concern, however, to new companies which were not previously included.

2 The situation in Canada is somewhat different. Contrary to the United States, membership rates have not been declining there. The most likely explanation for this divergence in historical development are some slight difference in the procedures for a union vote in a firm.

3 An exception might be the case where investment in search by workers and firms makes up for a large share in the specific investments, like in construction, cleaning and retail trade. Investments in search have to be made before players have the opportunity to solve the hold up problem by bargaining on a contract. Mandatory extension of collective agreements can solve this problem, see Teulings and Hartog (1998: Chapter 2).

4 The word 'centralized' probably reflects a far too rigid interpretation of the way in which the central negotiations in these economies affect the eventual labour market outcome. I suspect that the actual operation of these 'centralized' systems is not too much different from what I have described in this chapter.

5 Much damage could already have been caused in the meantime particularly due to the fact that the period is long enough for the unemployed to observe their qualifications decreasing. In order to speed up adjustment to worsened economical circumstances, pleas for wage moderation fulfil a useful purpose.

6 See Teulings and Hartog (1998: Chapter 5).

References

Baker, G., M. Gibbs and B. Holmstrom (1994) 'The Wage Policy of a Firm', *Quarterly Journal of Economics*, 921–55.

Blanchflower, D.G. and R. Freeman (1990) *Going Different Ways: Unionism in the US and Other Advanced OECD Countries*, ESRC, discussion paper no. 5.

Broersma, L., J. Koeman and C.N. Teulings (1998) *Labour Supply, the Natural Rate and the Welfare State in the Netherlands: The Wrong Institutions at the Wrong Point in Time*, working paper, Ministry of Social Affairs.

Calmfors, L. and J. Driffill (1988) 'Centralisation of Wage Bargaining and Economic Performance', *Economic Policy*, 13–61.

Card, D. (1990) 'Unexpected Inflation, Real Wages, and Employment Determination in Union Contracts', *The American Economic Review*, 669–88.

Card, D. and D.R. Hysop (1996) *Does Inflation 'Grease the Wheels' of the Labor Market?*, NBER Working Paper no. 5538, April.

Holmlund, B. and J. Zetterberg (1991) 'Insider Effects in Wage Determination: Evidence from Five Countries', *European Economic Review*, 1009–35.

Kahneman, D, J.L. Knetsch and R. Thaler (1986) 'Fairness as a Constraint on Profit-seeking: Entitlements in the Market', *American Economic Review*, 728–31.

Klandermans, B. and J. Visser (eds) (1995) *De vakbeweging na de welvaartsstaat*, Assen: Van Gorcum (in Dutch).

Lazear, E. (1994) 'Personnel Economics', Wicksell Lecture, Stockholm, March 1993; July 1994 draft, Stanford University.

Lindbeck, A. and D.J. Snower (1988) *The Insider-outsider Theory of Employment and Unemployment*, Cambridge, MA: MIT Press.

MacLeod, W.B. and J.M. Malcomson (1993) 'Investment, Hold ups, and the Form of Market Contracts', *American Economic Review*, 811–37.

North, D.C. (1990), *Institutions, Industrial Change and Economic Performance*, Cambridge: Cambridge University Press.

Teulings, C.N. and J. Hartog (1998) *Corporatism or Competition. An International Comparison of Labour Market Structures and their Impact on Wage Formation*, Cambridge: Cambridge University Press.

Part IV
European corporatism?

10 Renegotiating social and labour policies in the European multi-level system

Any role for corporatist patterns?

Gerda Falkner

Introduction

The forecast for corporatist policy styles[1] is usually dim. Sometimes even a general decline has been predicted for national corporatism. Alongside shifting powers at the EU level, mainstream scholarly thinking anticipates a development towards transnational pluralism. A closer analysis of recent developments at both levels, however, suggests some qualifications to these prognoses.

This chapter will first present the standard arguments as to the decay of corporatism in Europe. These will, after a brief outline of the relevant political science concepts, be contrasted with countervailing evidence. The conclusions will discuss the role and the impact of prevailing corporatist 'spots' within contemporary European governance.

Please note that parts of this text were written in 1995 and presented at the ECSA-USA Biennial Conference in South Carolina (11–14 May 1995). The full first draft entitled 'Corporatist Patterns of Decision-Making and Europeanisation: No Future in the Multi-level Game?' was presented at two conferences in early 1996 (EU Human Capital and Mobility Programme Network Conference, at the European University Institute, Florence; ECPR Joint Sessions of Workshops, Oslo). This is a revised and shortened version of the resulting print publication.[2] Later developments could not be included in very great detail for reasons of length, but they are referred to where essential for the argument.

Meanwhile, other authors have presented similar and/or further arguments on the persistence of the varieties of corporatism in Europe, most importantly Philippe Schmitter and Jürgen Grote. We agree on a number of crucial points, notably that the EU is no macro-corporatist system and will probably never develop into one; and that national corporatism is not dead but has changed in character, not least because of European integration. My specific point is that the EU is not in principle different from national political systems in that it employs, or tries to employ, a variety of governance patterns – including in some instances corporatist ones (but at a meso level). The patterns vary across policy areas and the mix can vary over time.[3]

The forecast: a fading out of corporatism?

For the *national systems*, some experts have predicted a decline of corporatism and convergence of industrial relations in the direction of disorganisation (e.g. Lash and Urry 1987). Three main arguments have been used to underline this trend (see overview in Traxler 1995a: 3f.): deregulation; decentralization of bargaining; and disorganization in the narrow sense, i.e. the decline in organizing capacities of the major interest groups. Windolf (1989) expected 'productivity coalitions' within single enterprises to replace corporatist systems at the macro and meso levels. The relevant background to such assumptions were changes in production patterns and the rise of the service sector, along with liberalization and increased competition in world markets.

For West European states, the progress in economic integration since the mid-1980s was expected to further the decline of national corporatism. First, Europeanization of previously national competences dismantled not only 'national sovereignty' (as vague as the concept may be), but also cut down the fields of possible social partner influence within national systems (e.g. Seidel 1989: 92; Wimmer and Mederer 1990: 208; Korinek 1994: 139f.). The effects of this were expected to be multiple, as a loss in bargaining chips could also hinder subsequent cross-sectoral log-rolling (Tálos 1994: 176f.; Falkner 1993b: 94).

Second, pluralist patterns of interest politics at the European level were expected to cause repercussions at the national level. Industry was seen to draw political strength from its organizational weakness at the European level, where it successfully rejected centralized negotiations with labour (Streeck and Schmitter 1991: 206ff.). This was expected to impact– at least in the long run – upon the balance of power in the member states. At the policy level, the absence of EC social policy harmonization might bring about regime competition and social dumping, thus weakening labour's bargaining power. Capital's threat of exit, by contrast, gained substantially in weight due to the market liberalization programme 'Europe 1992' (e.g. Falkner 1993a).[4] In a nutshell: much debated threats to national corporatism originate at the national, the European and the world market levels.

As regards the applicability of the corporatist approach at the *European level*, the mainstream assessment during the pre-Maastricht era was effectively summarized by Streeck and Schmitter's 1991 paper entitled 'From National Corporatism to Transnational Pluralism'. There, the authors state that:

> interest representation around and within the Community was always much more 'pluralist' than corporatist; more organizationally fragmented; less hierarchically integrated; more internally competitive; and with a lot less control vested in peak associations over their affiliates, or in associations over their members.
>
> (Streeck and Schmitter 1991: 200)

Concerning the procedural dimension, their major point was

> that in the uniting supra-national Europe, it was not only the case that labour was and continues to be *under-organized*, but there also was never a real possibility of a mutually organizing *interaction effect*, a *Wechselwirkung*, between labour and the two other major players in the political economy, capital and the state.
>
> (Ibid.: 204; emphasis in original)

The EC was thought to fall short of the indispensible contribution of public power, of an 'active, interventionist, non-liberal state which may . . . institutionalize labour as well as capital as principal participants in a centralized structure of political bargaining' (ibid.; see also Traxler and Schmitter 1995: 200). Streeck and Schmitter came to the conclusion that:

> The evolutionary alternative to neo-liberalism as a model for the European political economy is clearly not . . . neo-corporatism. More likely appears an American-style pattern of 'disjoint pluralism' . . . characterized by a profound absence of hierarchy and monopoly among a wide variety of players of different but uncertain status.
>
> (Ibid.: 227)

Many authors have since supported their conclusions.[5] However, while none of the above-mentioned arguments is wrong, others have tended to be neglected: mainly the usefulness of corporatist policy styles for the legitimation of both policies and polities – even at the EU level. My argument is that public–private co-operation in decision-taking, under conditions which privilege a few private interests, will persist as one among several modes of governance. There is indeed qualitative change rather than a general retreat of non-pluralist patterns.

The academic debate on (neo-)corporatism[6] has continued ever since the notion was rediscovered by Lehmbruch and Schmitter in 1974.[7] Over time, corporatism has developed into a 'highly complex phenomenon (or set of phenomena) of which different dimensions are covered by diverse conceptualizations' (Lehmbruch 1982: 2). Predominantly, there are two dimensions: the procedural and the structural ones. With regard to patterns of policy-making, Lehmbruch opposed 'corporatist' co-operation of organizations and public authorities to 'pluralist' pressure politics (e.g. Lehmbruch 1982: 8). A corporatist mode of policy formation was described as one 'in which formally designated interest associations are incorporated within the process of authoritative decision-making and implementation. As such they are officially recognized by the state not merely as interest intermediaries but as co-responsible 'partners' in governance and social guidance' (Schmitter 1981: 295). With regard to the institutional set-up of corporatist systems, Philippe Schmitter (1979: 13[8]) formulated the typical characteristics as a limited number of singular, compulsory, non-competitive, hierarchically ordered and functionally differentiated categories, recognized, or licensed (if not created) by the state, and granted a deliberate representational monopoly.[9] Already Schmitter stressed, however, that these ideal types would hardly ever be met in reality (ibid.: 14).

During the 1980s, corporatist patterns were already being traced outside the 'macro' level of trans-sectoral political systems. 'Meso-corporatism' or 'sectoral corporatism' were used to denominate corporatist 'arenas' at the level of industrial sectors, subnational units or single policy areas (Lehmbruch 1982: 27; Cawson (ed.) 1985; Streeck 1994: 17). Academic attention subsequently shifted to other fashionable labels such as, above all, 'policy networks' (Marsh and Rhodes 1992; Kenis and Schneider 1991). This theoretical shift paid tribute to the empirical finding that policy-making increasingly happens in sectoral or even issue specific sub-polities.[10]

Even long after the heyday of 'corporatism' in the late 1970s and early 1980s, the concept still belongs to the basic political science toolkit. To give just one example: when elaborating dimensions and types of policy networks, van Waarden used 'corporatism' as a distinctive feature, referring to it as 'the degree of integrated participation by economic interest groups in the public policy process' (1992: 29). Obviously, there is still a need for a label characterizing a form of public–private interaction which includes only a small number of privileged societal interests (typically: labour and employers) who are co-actors in public policy-making. That is notwithstanding the fact that due to economic and political developments, it is now less likely that, within otherwise fragmented polities, corporatist patterns should still cover *all* important areas of public policy as Lehmbruch's ideal type of macro-corporatism assumed.

Because of its connotations with regard to the systemic level, it seems advisable not to use the label 'corporatism' as such any longer, but rather to look for 'corporatist policy communities'[11] in specific policy areas or sectors. This concept allows us to capture corporatist patterns below the macro level. I hold that even in the absence of classic macro-corporatism across many or all policy areas, corporatist patterns may still today characterize policy processes in the European multi-level system. The functional scope of corporatist arrangements (cross-sectoral, sectoral/policy specific, or micro-level) and the specific economic policy orientation should both be seen as empirical questions.

My central argument is that even under the condition of a multiplicity of diverse sectoral systems (be it at the state or the EU levels), it is highly relevant to distinguish *specific* patterns of interest politics. The overall view might appear pluralist simply because of a variety of co-existing sub-systems (cf. also Cawson 1992: 117). But sectoral differences should not be overlooked and in specific areas, corporatist patterns may still prevail.

National politics: continuing diversity and supply-side corporatism

Against frequent expectation, recent studies have revealed that there is not convergence, but *continuing divergence* of the national structures of industrial interest intermediation in Europe (see Traxler 1995a and the contributions to Crouch and Traxler (eds) 1995). As far as corporatist patterns prevail, there are two particularly interesting factors to be mentioned: first, they may sometimes even be prompted (instead of harmed) by European integration; second, economic developments may bring about a new brand of 'supply-side corporatism' which is considered an asset in international market competition.

First, it seems that the effects of Europeanisation do not unilaterally prompt a decline in corporatist patterns, but may, depending, for example on the specific institutional set-up and the political situation in a member state, also favour the contrary. Thus, Andersen (1995) describes the implementation of the Single Market's banking policy in Denmark to have brought about increased centralization of collective bargaining, not a decentralization: 'cartels have developed into associations and industrial trade unions' (ibid.: 262). In this case, the institutional set-up of interest politics was changed in the direction of corporatist patterns[12]. In Norway, a procedural aspect developed similarly: Parliament approved a law on the extension of collective agreements in order to prevent social dumping when Norway became a member of the European Economic Area (Traxler 1995a: 12).

The brief history of Austrian EC membership shows that the well-known system of 'social partnership' managed to establish a system of co-ordinated tripartite policy-making with a view to adopting 'national' positions on EC draft law. Concerning the implementation of EC Directives, the major associations' de facto right to consultation in the legislative process was for the first time laid down by law. At least during the first years of EC membership, social partnership seems not to have suffered (Karlhofer and Tálos 1996).

A further important fact is that the Union increasingly builds on innovative regulatory patterns involving decision-making at lower levels and partly by the social partners. The recent European Works Councils Directive is a major example of this (see Falkner 1996). The Maastricht Social Agreement explicitly provides that the implementation of Directives at the member state level may be realized by management and labour (see below).

Already the Single Market Programme has made some governments try to revitalize incomes-policy concertation (e.g. the Portuguese, Spanish and Italian; Traxler and Schmitter 1995: 212). EMU could well induce a similar development with even wider functional scope: the Maastricht Treaty's convergence criteria have put considerable strain on the member states' budgets, but cuts in expenditure are hard to sell to the public without the consent of the major interest groups. Thus, we witness efforts to reach tripartite agreements between governments and societal interests with a view to imposing austerity in many member states (e.g. Italy, Portugal, Spain, Belgium, Ireland, Austria, France, etc.), even beyond those which used to be labelled corporatist (mainly Austria, Germany, the Netherlands and Sweden). The names for such pacts typically focus on the fight against unemployment, but they mostly aim at a whole bundle of measures which are often designed with a view to EMU membership (predominantly cuts in public spending, pay moderation and measures to enhance competitiveness).

To sum up: notwithstanding other effects of European integration, there are indicators that sometimes, corporatist patterns might also originate or be strenghtened as a sort of spillover from EC politics.

Second, when it comes to policy contents, many of the corporatist arrangements which are now prompted by European integration seem not really novel in kind. In fact, they fit into a broader trend: Traxler has observed that 'in contrast to the assumption of the disorganisation thesis . . . there seems to be a growing need for a new type of 'supply-side' corporatism aimed at backing a country's competitiveness' (1995a: 13). This refers to a change in the functions of corporatist systems rather than a general movement towards pluralist pressure politics. Compared to the Keynesian demand-side corporatism, the new version targets qualitative aspects of industrial relations rather than the regulation of aggregate demand or prices (see Traxler 1995c for the Austrian case). In fact, successful economic restructuring depends not in the least place on high-trust relations and collective goods, which the firms cannot provide themselves with satisfactorily (Traxler 1995b: 36f.). The prime areas for 'supply-side corporatism' are thus vocational training (Crouch 1995), environmentally friendly methods of production, and industrial policy. After all, productivity coalitions at the company level (Windolf 1989) might be 'a complement rather than an alternative to corporatist structures above this level' (Traxler 1995a: 14). While the tripartite pacts undertaken with a view to achieving EMU as outlined above usually stick with supply-side economics, they go beyond qualitative aspects of industrial relations only and target budgetary austerity and monetary stability.

Clearly, there are counter-examples (e.g. the failure of a tripartite employment pact in Germany under Chancellor Kohl) and countervailing trends to the ones outlined above (they are well known from the literature and were briefly outlined at the beginning). It is neither possible nor necessary here to give a full account of the development of interest inter-mediation patterns in all EC member states. A distinctive literature on the recent 'new social pacts' has emerged recently (see, for example, Schmitter and Grote 1997 who already referred to an earlier version of this article; Rhodes 1998; Hassel 1998).

The core of my argument is simply that there is no unidirectional decline of corporatist governance, even if the contemporary cases seem different in function and often more narrow in scope than before. But what about the prospects of corporatist patterns at the EU level?

Euro-politics: not only pluralism

Much of the literature focuses on the improbability of the emergence of a supranational form of macro-corporatism comparable to national patterns in the 1970s (e.g. Traxler and Schmitter 1995: 213; Kohler-Koch 1992: 103; Streeck and Schmitter 1991: 227). The very feature of the EU political system is, however, *fragmentation*. There are enormous cross-sectoral differences in policy style – a fact which has become increasingly topical during the 1990s (e.g. Greenwood *et al.* 1992a). Much more attention should thus be paid to co-operative public–private patterns at the meso level, where some authors have already detected structures alien to classic pluralism.[13] Furthermore, the possibility of co-evolution of political regimes and interest politics (Greenwood *et al.* 1992b: 243f.; Eichener and Voelzkow 1994a: 17; Kohler-Koch 1996: 215f.) has become of scientific interest. Implications for the development of more co-operative, maybe even 'corporatist' policy styles have yet to be revealed. If it is true that since the early days of European integration (against the expectations of neo-functionalists), private organizations have not taken the lead but rather followed political initiatives (see e.g. Kohler-Koch 1995: 16), then major constitutional innovations such as the Single European Act and the Maastricht Treaty should prompt specific developments of interest group organization and of their involvement in public policy-making alongside relevant new regimes at the sectoral level. This will be examined with regard to the Maastricht Social Agreement.

EC social policy: towards a corporatist policy community

A prime example of co-evolution of political/administrative structures (what might be called 'the state' at the national level) and interest politics is the recent development in the realm of EC social policy. Due to unanimity requirements, the 'social dimension' had traditionally lagged behind economic integration and was stuck in a classic 'decision-making trap' (Scharpf 1988). In 1991, however, the so-called Maastricht Social Agreement introduced a new social policy regime. Originally, it only applied to the member states, although not the UK.[14] Explicit Community competences were extended to many more social policy matters than before; majority voting is now possible for a much wider range of issues; and new patterns of 'corporatist decision-making' were introduced. The very establishment of the new regime is, in fact, attributable to the major European interest groups' *anticipation* of significant changes in the EC social policy provisions[15] which made UNICE (employers) conclude an agreement with ETUC (workers) and CEEP (public enterprises) in October 1991. Their joint proposals on the future involvement of the social partners were immediately submitted to the IGC. They promoted corporatist patterns of EC social policy along the lines which had earlier been developed by the Commission and the Belgian government (see e.g. Ross 1995: 183; Falkner 1998: 89–95).

The Social Agreement contains three layers of social partner participation in the policy process: first, the Commission now has a legal obligation to consult both management and labour before submitting social policy proposals. Second, a member state may entrust management and labour, at their joint request, with the implementation of Directives adopted pursuant to the Social Agreement. And third, but most importantly, management and labour may, on the occasion of such consultation, inform the Commission of their wish to initiate negotiations in order to reach agreements instead of traditional EC legislation. Such agreements may, at the joint request of the signatory parties, be implemented by a Council decision on a proposal from the Commission. In particular, the incorporation of the latter aspect in the Maastricht Treaty suggests that all major actors at the EU level (including not only the major interest groups and the Commission but also the governments in the Council) are ready to participate in 'a mode of policy formation in which formally designated interest associations are incorporated within the process of authoritative decision-making and implementation' (Schmitter 1981: 295) – the classic formula for procedural corporatism.

Under this new social policy regime, the procedures of decision-making (see next section) as well as the structure of interest representation (see p. 263) have undergone significant developments which brought them much closer than they were a few years ago to the above-mentioned procedural and structural definitions of corporatist patterns. In other words, a corporatist policy community has emerged.

Corporatist policy-making procedures

Although observers had initially doubted whether the far-reaching powers attributed to labour and management in the Maastricht Treaty would actually be put into practice, this happened in a number of cases has already.

The first application of the new procedures saw no formal negotiations but only 'talks on talks' (Gold and Hall 1994: 181) on a collective agreement between the two sides of industry. It eventually led to a traditional Council Directive on European Works Councils.[16] It was already a major innovation, however, that in autumn 1993, the UNICE had declared that it was 'ready to sit down with the Commission and/or the European unions to develop a . . . procedure for information and consultation that is acceptable to all parties . . .' (EIRR 238: 13). Until then, it had always strictly rejected any EC-level initiative on employee information and participation in the enterprise.[17]

The second decision-making process under the new social policy regime has indeed led to a Euro-collective agreement among the three major federations. On 14 December 1995, the ETUC, UNICE and CEEP adopted a Framework Agreement on Parental Leave,[18] providing an individual right for a minimum of three months' time off while employment rights are being retained. Via a Council Directive implementing the agreement, the standards agreed by the social partners were made binding for the member states (initially, for all except the UK, but since the Labour government has meanwhile adhered to the Social Agreement concluded at Amsterdam, all relevant Directives were extended to the UK). This procedure provided a solution to what had been perceived as a major obstacle to the development of corporatist patterns at the Euro-level (e.g. Keller 1995; Obradovich 1995; Traxler and Schmitter 1995), namely that CEEP, ETUC and UNICE (at least *de facto*) lack the powers to directly implement their agreements via their member organizations.

Like the issue of implementation, the fact that none of the three major Euro-federations has a general bargaining mandate has also worried scholarly writers on the Maastricht Social Agreement a great deal (e.g. Keller 1995; Obradovich 1995; Streeck 1995; Traxler and Schmitter 1995; Turner 1995). Indeed, negotiating mandates are being given on a case-to-case basis. After the parental leave case, this was repeated in the collective negotiations on atypical work which in summer 1997 led to the second Euro-level agreement, on part-time work; in the case of fixed-term work (see Europe, 16 January 1999, no. 13), on and most recently in the agreement on telework (*EIRR*, August 2002). Of the three issues which were not negotiated by the social partners since the Social Agreement came into force (the reversal of the burden of proof in sex discrimination cases, sexual harassment at work and information/consultation of workers in national enterprises), only the latter issue was controversial (a majority of UNICE members would have preferred to negotiate).[19] This led to pressures for further reform of the voting procedures in UNICE).

There is no space here to discuss details of the Agreements (but see Falkner 2003), whose standards have sometimes been harshly criticized (not least by unions from the socially more advanced member states, notably the German DGB). It is important to mention, however, that a realistic yardstick must be applied. This implies that, first, both the viewpoints of industry and of labour have to be taken into consideration (the former partly criticizes the agreements for going too far). Second, not only the highest national standards within the Community should be the reference point in the judgement of the results of a Euro-collective bargain, but also the lowest. Although three months of parental leave are below the existing amount in most member states, there are several whose labour law had so far not known a statutory right for parental leave at all (Ireland, Luxembourg and Belgium), and several details might bring improvements also elsewhere.[20] Third, one has to keep in mind the alternative of collective bargains, i.e. Council Directives on EU social standards. Like the recent collective agreements, recent social policy Directives decided by the Ministers themselves have also been criticized for being too minimalist in ambition. In fact, the huge differences in standards and the pressures of economic competition make it practically impossible for both governments and social partners to harmonize at a high speed, without paying attention to the costs involved. In any case, the Parental Leave Agreement was even somewhat more favourable for workers than various earlier compromise texts discussed in the Council. In the part-time case, too, the Council had already contemplated comparable low-ambition solutions before the social partners came into play. Just as at the national level, it seems that the results of corporatist deals thus depend on the politicians as much as on the interest representatives: there is not only dense contact but even interdependence within corporatist policy communities.

Replacing what is 'the State' at the national level, there are two EC institutions involved in corporatist patterns under the Social Agreement. The Commission has significant influence without directly participating in the negotiations because it supplies the social partners with a document that constitutes the basis of their talks. Furthermore, the Council may only implement a collective agreement on a proposal by the Commission. Thus, the Commission's power of initiative is extended to the corporatist procedures. In addition, the EC Council is involved in some 'corporatist exchange', too – not only at the stage of implementing an agreement but also during the decision-making process. Only if a necessary majority of Council members seems willing to adopt social law will the UNICE usually be interested in striking bargains (since it views them as a 'minor evil', see e.g. Tyskiewicz in Europe, 7 October 1996, no. 24). The Council, in turn, has an interest in successful collective bargains in order to legitimize both material EC social law, and (what was in the past at least as important) non-decisions, in front of a public which is increasingly critical about the lack of a 'social dimension' of European integration. Despite the fact that negotiations, in the narrow sense, are being conducted solely among the social partners, the co-operative policy-making style emerging under the Social Agreement therefore has features quite similar to 'tripartism' between the State, capital and labour at the national level.[21]

Since the ideal-typical description of procedural corporatism as developed by Lehmbruch and Schmitter fits well with the new decision-patterns which have developed under the Maastricht Social Agreement,[22] it is of interest if there are also developments regarding the relevant system of interest groups, i.e. in the structural dimension of the definition of corporatism as outlined above.

Corporatist structure follows strategy

Changes related to the structure of the system of interest representation concern intra-group reforms (towards more competences and decision capacity) as well as the development of a core group of decisive interest groups (towards monopolistic representation in the relevant social partner negotiations). These developments are even more significant if one considers that prior to the Maastricht Social Agreement, the participation of all relevant Euro-associations in binding negotiations with each other and the EC institutions was by no means undisputed in their member organisations (be it national unions or employer federations).

The ETUC was first to adapt its structure with a view to enhancing negotiating capacity at the European level. In 1991, the internal structure and the decision-making process (including voting by two-thirds majority) was reformed with a view to limiting dangers of blockade, and the European Industry Committees were allowed to vote too (except in financial and statutory matters; Ebbinghaus and Visser 1994: 239; for details see e.g. Dølvik 1997: 166ff.). This may be regarded as progress concerning the problem of co-ordinating territorial and functional interests – both now directly represented within the umbrella of the ETUC. Further amendments to the ETUC constitution were decided during its May 1995 Congress. The Executive Committee now has a responsibility to 'determine the composition and mandate of the delegation for negotiations with European employers' organisations', and to 'ensure the convergence at European level of the demands and contractual policies of affiliated organisations' (Article 11). A change in the UNICE's statute in June 1992 directly aimed at meeting the challenges of the Social Protocol. The organization was formally assigned the task of representing its members in the dialogue between the social partners provided for in the Social Agreement (Article 2.1 of the Statute). The Council of Presidents is in charge of defining the positions to be taken in the social dialogue. That collective agreements have still to be adopted unanimously has already been challenged recently (especially by the new President Georges Jacobs; see e.g. Europe, 11 July 1998: 14). That the federation of enterprises with public participation, CEEP, also adapted its Rules of Procedure in order to meet the challenges of the Social Agreement is less surprising since it had traditionally been more open to EU-level negotiations with labour than had UNICE.[23]

But what about the plethora of lobbies, expected to hinder any effective corporatist negotiations at the European level? Is there any help from European state institutions (e.g. Traxler and Schmitter 1994) which would prompt encompassing but monopolistic patterns of interest representation such as exist in some national systems? Empirical evidence shows that this is the case. Both the Council and the Commission actively supported the monopolization of collective negotiations under the Social Agreement by the three major cross-sectoral interest federations (ETUC, CEEP and UNICE). The EC institutions' involvement can be assimilated to the 'licensing' (Schmitter 1979) in corporatist national systems even though it partly relies only on giving incentives for self-organisation of the 'social partners'. In its 'Communication on the Application of the Social Agreement' (COM(93) 600 final, 14 December 1993; par. 22 ff.), the Commission defined a set of criteria for organizations to be included in consultations preceding legislative proposals pursuant to the Social Agreement. It is the same range of almost thirty associations which may, during the process of consultation, theoretically decide to negotiate on a collective agreement. However, the Commission considers that it is up to the organizations themselves to develop their own dialogue and negotiating structure (see ibid.: par. 26). Thus, responsibility lies with the representatives of labour and management. This was a successful tactical move since a formalized narrow definition of the 'social partners' under the Social Agreement might have been challenged in and finally reversed by the ECJ.

Support for the (not at all unexpected) constellation of *de facto* only three negotiating Euro-groups was nevertheless expressed when the Commission suspended several legislative processes on the joint request of the 'big three' (although it had received responses from many more organisations during the consultations; see e.g. *EIRR*, 260: 3). Subsequently, the Council indeed implemented the collective agreements signed by the same three peak federations. In the parental leave case, the European Council explicitly welcomed the fact that it was for the first time possible to reach agreement with 'the social partners' on a draft Directive (European Council 1995: point 6).

On both sides of industry, smaller interest groups[24] protested in vain against the three major federations' *de facto* monopoly (or rather: 'oligopoly') on negotiating as cross-sectoral social partners in the frame of the Social Agreement. The Euro-association of the small and medium-sized enterprises (UEAPME) even filed an unsuccessful law suit against the Council.[25] The Commission urged to seek ways of satisfying those groups in order not to endanger the legitimacy of the new corporatist decision patterns, e.g. via encouraging linking structures with the major groups (e.g. in COM(93) 600 final). Meanwhile, several Euro-groups on the employer side were included in the social partner negotiations on an observer basis. UEAPME concluded a co-operation agreement with UNICE. It must be consulted before UNICE represents employer positions in the social dialogue, but it does not have a veto right (see e.g. Europe, 17 December 1998: 16). Thus, the representativeness and public acceptance of the collective agreements seem improved, but the greater decision-taking capacity of the exclusive group with only three players was upheld.

To conclude: not all details of Schmitter's ideal-type description of a corporatist interest group system are met under the Social Agreement (but this is not the case for any extant national system, either).[26] However, the quintessence of structurally corporatist patterns is, maybe surprisingly to many observers, meanwhile present. Only a few groups, which are not under competition with each other for membership, negotiate. They proved capable of striking deals and were acknowledged by 'the state' (i.e. the Commission and the Council) as legitimate representatives of 'labour and industry' at the EU level.

In general, the patterns which evolved under the Maastricht Social Agreement (which replaced the EC-Treaty's old social provisions under the Amsterdam Treaty and are now binding for all member states) do not replicate exactly any of the various national patterns of corporatism. However, the crucial attributes of such a policy style can be found concerning the patterns of policy-making as well as the structure of interest representation. A corporatist policy style is thus no longer alien at the EU-level. The developments since the Maastricht IGC furthermore indicate that EU Treaty reforms should not be disregarded as potential agents for change in interest politics. Due to the fragmented system of EC politics, developments will certainly not lead in the same direction for all or even many policy areas.[27] At least in one other field, however, the post-Maastricht era has already brought developments in the direction of co-operative governance including labour and management, as well.

Employment policy concertation at the EU level

One of the most controversial aspects of the EMU, as provided for in the EU Treaty, is its effect on employment. While the convergence criteria were developed to fight nominal divergence (i.e. to reach convergence of the development of prices), no precautions were taken with regard to fighting divergence of the non-monetary aspects of the economies of the member states, particularly in terms of their unemployment rates.

> ... during the Maastricht negotiations, I proposed making employment part of the criteria. Not all the national delegations agreed to this. They committed an error, we see that today.
>
> (Jacques Delors quoted in Europe, 3 February 1996: 2b)

As austerity programmes with a view to reaching the convergence criteria are currently being implemented in the member states, a possible negative effect on employment is the subject of heated debate (Heylen and Van Poeck 1995; Busch 1994).[28] Even Jacques Santer admits that the fear of unemployment is 'undermining confidence in the single currency' (quoted in Europe, 1 February 1996: 4). These developments have brought about a trend towards co-ordination of national policies with a view to fighting unemployment. Although the decision process is not 'corporatist' is the narrow sense, involvement of the social partners is a distinctive feature. Subject of debate are measures to be carried out at the national level as well as possible greater effects on the employment of EU policies (structural funds; transeuropean networks).

The roots of this policy go back to the Delors White Paper on Growth, Competitiveness, and Employment (December 1993; cf. EC Bulletin Supplement 6/93). Together with a Commission report on the national employment policies, this programmatic discussion paper was presented to the European Council of Essen in December 1994. On this basis, the Heads of State and Government adopted a medium-term strategy for the fight against unemployment to be implemented via multi-annual employment programmes in the member states. Five major aims were defined: investment in vocational training, flexibility of the labour market, reduction in non-wage labour costs, improvements in active labour market policy and in measures to help groups particularly affected by unemployment. In order to analyse progress, the European Council of Essen introduced a surveillance procedure (so-called 'Essen follow-up'). In the context of this chapter, the most interesting aspect of this initiative is the collaboration of a wide range of actors at all levels of the EU system, including the social partner organisations both at the national and at the European level (see also European Council 1995: point 2). In the 1995 Joint Report, social partner participation was indeed given prime importance during all stages of the process (European Council 1995: Annex 2).

The 'Essen follow-up' has increased the social partner activities at the European level significantly, highlighting a growing belief in the need for 'concerted action' for employment by the EC institutions *and* the social partners at the Euro-level. During the 1996–7 Intergovernmental Conference, the possibility of giving more priority to employment within the EU's general objectives as well as an employment chapter in the EC Treaty were a major issue, and indeed, the 'Essen procedures' were formalized in the Amsterdam Treaty's new employment chapter.[29] On the basis of a report by the Council and the Commission, the European Council each year adopts conclusions on the employment situation in the Community. On this basis, the Council draws up guidelines which the member states must take into account in their employment policies. The Council annually examines the implementation of the employment policy guidelines and may, acting by a qualified majority on a recommendation from the Commission, make recommendations to member states (cf. Article 128 EC Treaty).[30]

The role allocated to the social partners under the new procedures does not repeat the corporatist patterns under the Maastricht Social Agreement. One may speculate that this might have been different if the Santer initiatives had been followed by any substantial social partner agreement. Contrary to the situation in 1991 when the pre-Maastricht social partner input to the Intergovernmental Conference was negotiated, there was, however, no realistic threat of legislation which might have made industry prefer corporatist deals instead. In fact, it was known already at an early stage of the pre-Amsterdam IGC that the majority of member states wanted no supranational employment policy in the narrow sense but only a co-ordination of national policies.

The decision patterns legally agreed in the Amsterdam Treaty's employment chapter are not explicitly corporatist (unlike those in the Social Chapter of that Treaty) since the social partners are only mentioned when the Employment Committee has to consult them. This new Committee consists of member state and Commission representatives and is to promote co-ordination between member states on employment and labour market policies (cf. Article 109s, i.e. now Article 130 EC Treaty, after renumbering). *De facto*, however, the three major federations of employers and workers (UNICE, CEEP and ETUC) have played a more significant role, particularly in the decision-shaping phase. Meetings before European Council summits which bring them together with the Heads of State and Governent (or the Troika representing them) were recently used to a large extent for the discussion of employment matters. Furthermore, a number of meetings were held between the Council of Social and Employment Ministers, the Commission, the President of the EP Committee of Social Affairs and ETUC/UNICE/CEEP, on employment matters. Twice a year, there are now meetings of the Troika and the social partners with a view to the major federations' participation in the implementation of the employment guidelines (on the first meeting see Europe, 8 November 1997: 5).

In December 1998, UNICE, CEEP and ETUC adopted two common positions which served as an input for the European Council, on the employment policy guidelines for 1999 and on the reform of the Standing Committee on Employment (Europe, 14 December 1998: 16). In the Presidency conclusions of the Vienna summit, the governments called for even more participation and responsibility of the social partners in employment matters (Europe, 13 December 1998: 11). In June 1999 the Cologne European Council finally established a so-called 'macro-economic dialogue' between various actors involved in wage negotiations and monetary, budget and fiscal policies, including most notably the Euro-level social partners and the European Central Bank.

The practice of employment policy co-ordination thus reveals how much the state(EU)–labour–employer relations at the European level have recently been in a state of flux. Even outside a corporatist Treaty basis, the three major cross-sectoral federations of employers and employees may be pragmatically included in EU decision processes in a variety of ways, according to area-specific circumstances and considerations. In the employment case, a few privileged interest groups (once again ETUC, UNICE and CEEP) have on occasion even been invited to the negotiation table of the Social Affairs and Employment Council. Since they are not formal co-decision-takers (as under social policy decision rules) this might best be termed a form of enhanced consultation. It nevertheless indicates that along the corporatist–pluralist continuum, manifold shades of inclusion/ exclusion of interest groups exist in the various fields of EU policy-making.

Conclusions

Contrary to certain scholarly expectations, a general fading out of cor-poratist policy styles has failed to occur in Europe. The future of public–private interaction in the European multi-level system does not purely consist in pluralistic pressure politics by an unlimited number of private interests acting in an uncoordinated way and without discrimination on the part of 'the state' (be it the national governments or the EC institutions). Definitely, the 1970s' Keynesian macro-corporatism has not come back and may never do so. However, a multiplicity of patterns continues to exist at the national level, and 'supply-side corporatism' (Traxler) coexists with more pluralist styles. In several cases, the establish-ment of the EMU has indeed prompted tripartite economic policy arrange-ments between governments, labour and industry. At the level of the fragmented EU political system, too, huge differences exist in the particip-ation of private interests in policy-making. Alongside with policy areas which fit the pluralist paradigm, there are corporatist patterns to be found elsewhere. The prime example is the post-Maastricht social policy regime which gives the 'social partners' the right to agree on standards which are subsequently made binding for the whole EC/EEA area, in a an outright corporatist policy community. Other policy fields, like employment pro-motion, are located somewhere along the pluralism–corporatism continuum of policy-making (but in this case at quite some distance from the extreme pluralist end, where lobbies individually try to influence governments in a competitive way).

In analysing social and employment policies, this contribution highlights one side of the coin only. However, this is the 'dark' side which was partly not even thought to exist (notably at the EU level). By contrast, arguments why corporatist patterns may increasingly be disadvantaged by recent economic and social trends as well as by European integration are well known from the literature (and they are not discarded here, although counter-tendencies are being studied).

If the argument is neither that classic national neo-corporatism will come back nor that there is a single EU system of interest intermediation (including all sectoral EC systems) developing along corporatist lines, what is the range and the weight of the argument presented here? With a view to the EU, my point is, first, that there is little use in searching for an overarching characteristic for the sum of all policy areas: too huge are the differences, and there is little indication for convergence. To label this deeply segmented system 'pluralist' simply because the bird's eye view on all sectors results in a non-corporatist picture seems an undue simplification. Second, due to the orientation towards both 'pluralism' and a 'systemic' viewpoint, the potentials of change in the European system of interest intermediation were often underrated. Evidence shows that there was indeed a co-evolution of the policy-making rules and the system of interest intermediation in the case of the Maastricht Social Policy Agreement. If Treaty changes had such a potential in one area, that might also hold true for others. This is of major interest for the political scientist and of impact for practitioners – even if potentials for change do not yet indicate a specific direction of that change (in other words: different Treaty changes might as well bring about more pluralist patterns instead of formerly more co-operative public–private interaction). With a view to the national systems, it seems that neither world-wide economic developments nor European integration simply put an end to all corporatist patterns. While Keynesian macro-corporatism might indeed be outdated, other but still non-pluralist forms such as area-specific corporatist policy communities might survive.

How can one explain the unexpected resilience of corporatist patterns? It seems that the dimension of the 'unburdening of the state' still matters. Governments need the legitimizing support of the major interest groups to a particularly great extent in times of tighter budgets. The need to push through welfare cuts, often against the will of large clusters of society, causes governments to attempt a dispersion of responsibility. The so-called 'social partners' often look like ideal co-actors: While they may gain some concessions for their clientele (normally at the expense of less organized interests), the involvement of the major interest groups supports both social legitimacy and compliance. The process of establishing EMU increased the need for co-operative governance in order to generate social acceptance for short-term austerity plans with a view to reaching the convergence criteria. At the European level, the Heads of State and Government seem to perceive a similar incentive. When the employment situation and discussions on the perceived absence of a 'social dimension of the EMU' endangered the permissive consensus for European integration, they tried to involve the 'social partners' in various activities with regard to employment policy and social policy.

Why do the major interest goups go along with this? With the progress of European integration, self-interest of national interest groups in the participation of Euro-level policy-making tends to increase. From the perspective of national 'social partners', strengthening the Euro-groups was, for a long time, considered as a loss in power. With tribute to the specific situation of multi-level governance, however, corporatist patterns at the EC-level might not be a zero-sum-game after all (see also Kohler-Koch 1992: 99f.). In areas where competences are meanwhile transferred to the EU and may be decided without unanimity, national interest groups have already lost their grip. They can only win if they are able to collectively, along with their counterparts from other member states within a Eurofederation, to act in the supranational arena. Indeed, to be one of several participants at the higher level is certainly more beneficial than not participating at all. In addition, innovative regulative patterns have recently allowed for mutually beneficial effects: if collective agreements at the Euro-level, such as on the issue of parental leave, are to be implemented in a 'cascading'-like pattern where politics filter down from the supranational to the national, sub-national and even enterprise-level, national and sub-national actors might in the end even be strengthened.[31] From the perspective of interest federations at the Euro-level, such decentralization will, in practice, cause a deflation of pressure on intra-group interest unification and thus facilitate agreement.[32]

Compared to Keynesian macro-corporatism in the 1970s and early 1980s, contemporary corporatist arrangements work under the condition of supply-side economics and open markets. Even tripartite deals in the member states now often differ from classic neo-corporatism in supposedly sovereign nation states in the sense that their objective is to implement EC level policies (or to facilitate adaptation to them), rather than independent policy-making.[33] Even if the patterns of interest representation and the participation of private interests in public policy-making show corporatist features, the action radius and the political weight of such arrangements tend to differ from those of the 1970s. All of the corporatist arrangements now work in the shadow of the internal market and of the EMU. Thus, they are not fully independent in their policy options. Notably measures which increase public spending or which put burdens on business are much harder to entertain because the convergence criteria and internationalized markets account for a hanging slope towards monetarist and neo-liberal policy options. In the words of Thomas Hüglin,[34] corporatist exchange now tends to take place *within* the neo-liberal agenda.

The smaller scope of policy influence is certainly a disadvantage mainly from the viewpoint of labour. Nevertheless, the participation in such schemes (in exchange for minor concessions by the employers) is frequently perceived as the only available option to secure jobs in times of open markets and restrictive public finances, while the employers and the governments, in turn, aim at increasing both the compliance with and the social legitimacy of the policies on the agenda. The balance of power between labour and management assumed for corporatist arrangements in earlier literature may always have been doubtful – but with completely open economic borders, the political resources of labour (mainly to strike) tend to be further devalued in comparison to capital's exit option. Only with an even stronger backing from 'the state' than before[35] and under great societal pressure can there nowadays be some sort of equal weight: e.g. if there is a realistic threat of legislation in the case of absence of industry's readiness to bargain with labour; or if a failure of collective negotiations could create social unrest. But in general, labour's leverage is significantly lessened under the conditions of austerity-oriented convergence criteria for

EMU, open economic borders and high unemployment. In fact, it seems no coincidence that social and employment policies are currently the prime areas of (non-pluralist) participation of the major societal interests in public policy-making, both at the national and the European level. These fields are of immediate interest to the citizens, so that *public opinion* may exert some counter-balance to the lessened bargaining power of the unions *vis-à-vis* capital. One might even speculate that it will be hard for both national governments and the emerging EU polity to afford *not* to employ, in these areas, a governance mode with a high potential for 'legitimizing' policy outputs, i.e. involving the major and privileged societal interests in corporatist policy communities.

This leads to the final conclusion that under specific circumstances, scenarios will persist that include a small and stable set of private actors with a high capability to act and implement in a way that is more 'para-state' (i.e. connected to public authority and binding in character) than 'social-political governance' (Kooiman 1993; the latter refers to an unstable and issue-oriented co-ordination of a wide range of societal actors). However, it appears that within the contemporary European multi-level system, such corporatist patterns represent only one mode of governance among many. Political scientists should neither at the national nor at the European level expect the convergence of different policy styles towards an overarching ideal-type, be that 'pluralist' or 'corporatist'. Finally, evidence suggests that, both at the national and the European levels, the cultivation of corporatist patches is quite instrumental, with a view to ensuring compliance with the politics of the EMU and liberalized world markets. In that sense, current corporatist patterns often seem to belong less to the realm of political structure than to political strategy.

Notes

1 The 'policy style' refers to both the patterns of policy-making and imple-mentation (Richardson *et al.* 1982).
2 In *Current Politics and Economics in Europe*, 8/4, 1999. An earlier version had appeared in the *European Integration online Papers* (EIoP) Vol. 1 (1997) no. 11 (*http://eiop.or.at/eiop/texte/1997–011a.htm*). Thanks for helpful comments to their anonymous referees, to Frans van Waarden, and to the participants of the conferences where the text was discussed.
3 By summer 2002, the emphasis in EU social policy (which makes up the main empirical part of this chapter) had shifted from minimum harmonization (where the quasi-corporatist mode of decision-making described below applies) to open co-ordination. There, the decision patterns are still remote from classic pluralism but nevertheless not outright corporatist. This does, however, not question the basic argument presented in this chapter. At least to date the corporatist design of decisions on EC social policy directives agreed in the EC Treaty has not been changed, and only very recently another collective Euro-agreement has been concluded (on telework). Although there are now fewer Commission proposals on social regulation than at earlier periods, there are a few relevant projects to which corporatist patterns could still be applied in the

near future. In any case, this is not the only example of a kind of corporatist policy community at EU level, and the fact that further ones could at least potentially develop (assuming there is backing from the Commission and the Council) is highlighted by the post-Maastricht developments in that field.

4 For an overview on the pessimist expectations concerning European integration's effects on national corporatism, see van Waarden (1994: 218ff.)

5 This was even the case with research carried out around the time of the Maastricht Treaty's signature or later (e.g. Keller 1993, 1997; Falkner 1993b; Traxler and Schmitter 1994, 1995; Sadowski and Timmesfeld 1994). For a nuanced view including 'possibly some signs of corporatism' see Mazey and Richardson (1994: 30) and most notably the authors mentioned in note 13. Andersen and Eliassen 1991 briefly mention that they expect Euro-corporatism if the European Parliament is significantly strengthened.

6 By calling the newly depicted features of democratic systems 'neocorporatism', 'liberal corporatism' or 'democratic corporatism', scholars wanted to distinguish them from their fascist counterparts predating the Second World War. After two decades of debate on contemporary corporatism, the evocation of the spectre of fascism and authoritarian rule seems less probable, hence the use of the term 'corporatism' without prefix here. On various concepts of corporatism within political science and industrial relations, see e.g. Williamson 1989; Streeck 1994.

7 In short, their concept opposed the pluralist way of analysing the role of organized interests in the political life of Western democracies, popular in post-war political science. Governments were no longer perceived as only passively influenced or 'captured' by a huge number of independenly acting pressure groups. The latter were seen as not only 'representing', but also actively governing their members' interests. The new perspective considered the state as a constituent actor in the organization of collective interests in society (Streeck 1994: 9).

8 First publication: 1974.

9 A pluralist system, by contrast, comprises an unspecified number of multiple, voluntary, competitive, non-hierarchically ordered and self-determined (as to type and scope of interest) categories not licensed, recognized, subsidized, created or otherwise controlled by the State, without monopoly of representational activity within their respective categories.

10 In fact, changes were over time noted even in the classic macro-corporatist system, i.e. the Austrian (e.g. Tálos 1994: 27; Tálos *et al.* 1993). Like during the early years of Austrian 'social partnership' immediately after the Second World War (Tálos 1985: 64), it is since the mid-1980s again a selection of issues rather than socio-economic policy in its full variety that is subject to such patterns of policy-making (Müller 1985: 220).

11 This typology was developed in a recent book on EU-level industrial relations and social policy (Falkner 1998).

12 Kohler-Koch (1992: 102f.) notes that the necessity of participating in the European policy process has indeed, at times, also increased the action potential of federations at the national level, e.g. the need to co-ordinate has favoured the merging of actors.

13 See Greenwood and Ronit (1992) for the pharmaceutical sector; Cawson (1992) for consumer electronics; Eichener and Voelzkow (1994b) for health and safety in the workplace; Eichener and Voelzkow (1994c) for technical harmonization and standardization.

14 For details see Falkner 1998.

15 This goes along well with established knowledge. With regard to the growth of European interest group federations, Kohler-Koch (1994: 171) observed that they did not develop parallel to an increase in the EC's policy-making powers,

but rather, 'the anticipation of a growing importance of the EC in a rather vague sense . . . stimulated the establishment of transnational organizations (and not) the actual transfer of powers'; see also Greenwood *et al.* 1992b: 244.

16 For details see e.g. Falkner 1998: 97–113.

17 That, in the end, the UNICE could not overcome the disapproval of the attempted compromise with regard to European Works Councils by its British member CBI in March 1994 (for details see below and Falkner 1996), however, prompted another significant intra-goup reform: according to an internal agreement of April 1994, the CBI participated later on but did not have a veto right in negotiations pursuant to the Social Agreement. Therefore, the CBI was not be bound by an agreement of which it did not approve.

18 For details see Falkner 1998: 114–28.

19 The others were broadly perceived not to represent 'appropriate' issues for collective bargaining since they are usually a matter of *legal* regulation even at the national level.

20 See e.g. Falkner 1998: 121–3.

21 It should furthermore be mentioned that the EC institutions were actively involved in the development of the Euro-level interest groups. Especially for labour, organizational and financial support is manifold.

22 It should be stressed that even in national corporatist systems, by no means each and every decision process is actually dominated by the social partners. If non-agreement of the major interest groups in one or the other case would already disqualify a political system or policy area from being ideal-typically corporatist, there would actually not be corporatism even in Austria which is usually traded as the hallmark of it (see e.g. Karlhofer and Tálos 1999). However, even where the most far-reaching possibility (i.e. a collective agreement instead of a Council decision specifying social standards) does not come into effect in current EU social policy, the social partners are not only repeatedly consulted but their quasi-compromises in pre-negotiations may even influence bargaining in the Council (they reportedly did so in the Works Councils case) and the interest groups may still come into play during the national implementation processes.

23 For details see e.g. Falkner 1998: 159f.

24 These are mainly the UEAPME (representing small and medium-sized enterprises) and the EuroCommerce (representing firms in retail, wholesale and international trade) on the employers' side, and the CESI (representing independent trade unions) and the CEC (representing professional and managerial staff) on the workers'.

25 The argument that the signatory parties of the parental leave collective agreement were not representative and that the Council should not have turned the agreement into a Directive was rejected by the ECJ (case T-135/96 decided 17 June 1998).

26 Absent is the criterion of compulsory group membership which is, however, also rare in typical corporatist systems at the national level. Even in Austria, not all decisive actors of the social partnership have compulsory membership (notably not the Trade Union Confederation). There is still a long way to go in the direction of a truly and formalized hierarchical internal structure of the Euro-groups. Most important is, however, the fact that the internal structures were already adapted and proved to be sufficiently potent to allow a number of deals to be adopted (which was not expected by most observers). It is, for example, a significant development which would have been unthinkable a few years ago that the ETUC now adopts binding agreements against the will of several influential members, including the DGB. While even more far-reaching reforms than those adopted so far were discussed (for the ETUC see e.g. Dølvik 1997) or are being

discussed at present (notably within UNICE), it is not surprising that internal group reform is a step-by-step process rather than a singular 'quantum leap'.

27 Due to extreme differences that tend to exist both in sectoral EC regimes and in patterns of interest representation in the single sectors, one should not expect the sum of diverse sectoral developments to add up to a coherent cross-sectoral system of interest politics (e.g. also Eising and Kohler-Koch 1994: 182f.).

28 A study by the rather pro-European Austrian Institute for Economic Research (WIFO) revealed that the austerity programmes might cost 2 per cent of the Union's purchasing power and actually increase unemployment by 1.5 per cent (*Der Standard*, 25 February 1996).

29 Cf. Articles 125–30 EC Treaty (formerly Articles 109n–s).

30 As opposed to the economic policy guidelines pursuant to Article 103 EC Treaty, there are no sanctions provided for in the new employment chapter (some governments, notably the Swedish and the Austrian, had promoted this in vain). Nor is there any mention the possibility of publishing such recommendations to a member state, which might have created public pressure.

31 See also the case of the European Works Councils Directive (e.g. Falkner 1996).

32 To some extent, there is also a normative pattern of response from interest groups to European integration: some peak representatives within the major national groups, in actual fact, rank the general goal of European unification quite high within their general political priorities (e.g. in Germany and Austria where securing peace in Europe via the EU is often opposed to the dark ages of fascism and the Second World War). When confronted with the post-Maastricht legitimacy crisis, some leaders fear a far-reaching backlash and thus feel urged to support the 'European enterprise'. One way for them to become active is to provide legitimation through co-operation with governments and EC institutions in the making and implementation of European policies.

33 For a study on the implementation of six labour law Directives in all fifteen EU member states, including the impact on national public–private relations, see http://www.mpi-fg-koeln.mpg.de/fo/multilevel_en.html#Proj5.

34 To whom I am very grateful for this suggestion!

35 Indeed, a significant role of the 'state' was always assumed for corporatist arrangements (cf. e.g. Schmitter's 1979 definition quoted above) but it seems to even gain in importance.

References

Andersen, S.S. and K.A. Eliassen (1991) 'European Community lobbying', *European Journal of Political Research*, 20/2: 173–89.

Andersen, T. (1995) 'Deregulation of the Danish Banking Industry: the Response of Employers' Associations and Trade Unions', in C. Crouch and F. Traxler (eds) *Organized Industrial Relations: What Future?*, Aldershot: Avebury.

Busch, K. (1994) *Europäische Integration und Tarifpolitik. Lohnpolitische Konsequenzen der Wirtschafts- und Währungsunion*, Köln: Hans-Böckler-Stiftung/Bund Verlag.

Cawson, A. (ed.) (1985) *Organized Interests and the State. Studies in Meso-Corporatism*, London: Sage.

Cawson, A. (1992) 'Interests, Groups and Public Policy-Making: the Case of the European Consumer Electronics Industry', in J. Greenwood, J.R. Grote and K. Ronit (eds) *Organized Interests and the European Community*, London: Sage.

Crouch, C. (1995) 'Organized Interests as Resources or as Constraint: Rival Logics of Vocational Training Policy', in C. Crouch and F. Traxler (eds) *Organized Industrial Relations: What Future?*, Aldershot: Avebury.

Crouch, C. and F. Traxler (eds) (1995) *Organized Industrial Relations: What Future?*, Aldershot: Avebury.

Dølvik, J. E. (1997) *Redrawing the Boundaries of Solidarity?* ARENA Report 5/97, Oslo.

Ebbinghaus, B. and J. Visser (1994) 'Barrieren und Wege "grenzenloser" Solidarität: Gewerkschaften und Europäische Integration', in W. Streeck (ed.) *Staat und Verbände*, Opladen: Westdeutscher Verlag.

Eichener, V, and H. Voelzkow (1994a) 'Europäische Integration und verbandliche Interessensvermittlung: Ko-Evolution von politisch-administrativem System und Verbändelandschaft', in V. Eichener and H. Voelzkow (eds) *Europäische Integration und verbandliche Interessenvermittlung*, Marburg: Metropolis-Verlag.

Eichener, V. and H. Voelzkow (1994b) 'Europäische Regulierung im Arbeitsschutz: Überraschungen aus Brüssel und ein erster Versuch ihrer Erklärung', in V. Eichener, and H. Voelzkow (eds) *Europäische Integration und verbandliche Interessenvermittlung*, Marburg: Metropolis-Verlag.

Eichener, V, and H. Voelzkow (1994c) 'Ko-Evolution politisch-administrativer und verbandlicher Strukturen: Am Beispiel der technischen Harmonisierung des europäischen Arbeits-, Verbraucher- und Umweltschutzes', in W. Streeck (ed.) *Staat und Verbände*, Opladen: Westdeutscher Verlag.

Eichener, V, and H. Voelzkow (eds) (1994) *Europäische Integration und verbandliche Interessenvermittlung*, Marburg: Metropolis-Verlag.

EIRR, *European Industrial Relations Review* (monthly), London: Andrew Brode.

Eising, R. and B. Kohler-Koch (1994) 'Inflation und Zerfaserung: Trends der Interessenvermittlung in der Europäischen Gemeinschaft', in W. Streeck (ed.) *Staat und Verbände*, Opladen: Westdeutscher Verlag.

Europe, *Agence internationale pour la presse*, daily news service on European affairs, Brussels and Luxembourg: Agence Europe S.A..

European Council (1995), Schlußfolgerungen des Vorsitzes, Europäischer Rat Madrid, 15–16 Dezember 1995, SN 400/95.

Falkner, G. (1993a) 'Sozialdumping' im EG-Binnenmarkt: Betrachtungen aus politikwissenschaftlicher Sicht', in *Österreichische Zeitschrift für Politikwissenschaft*, 3: 261–77.

Falkner, G. (1993b) 'Sozialpartnerschaftliche Politikmuster und Europäische Integration', in E. Tálos (ed.) *Sozialpartnerschaft zwischen Kontinuität und Wandel*: Wien.

Falkner, G. (1996) 'European Works Councils and the Maastricht Social Agreement: Towards a New Policy Style?', *Journal of European Public Policy*, 2.

Falkner, G. (1998) *Social Europe in the 1990s: Towards a Corporatist Policy Community?*, London: Routledge.

Falkner, G. (2003) 'The Interprofessional Social Dialogue at European Level: Past and Future', in B. Keller and H.-W. Platzer (eds) *Industrial Relations and European Integration. Developments and Prospects at EU-level*, Oxford: Blackwell.

Gold, M. and M. Hall (1994) 'Statutory European Works Councils: the final countdown?', *Industrial Relations*, 25/3: 177–86.

Goybet, C. (1994) 'Lutte pour l'emploi. Les douze adoptent un plan d'action', *Revue du Marché commun et de l'Union européenne*, 374: 5–8.

Greenwood, J., J.R. Grote and K. Ronit (1992a) 'Introduction: Organized Interests and the Transnational Dimension', in J. Greenwood, J.R. Grote and K. Ronit (eds) *Organized Interests and the European Community*, London: Sage.

Greenwood, J., J.R. Grote and K. Ronit, K. (1992b) 'Conclusions: Evolving Patterns of Organizing Interests in the European Community', in J. Greenwood, J.R.

Grote and K. Ronit (eds) *Organized Interests and the European Community*, London: Sage.

Greenwood, J., Grote, J. R., and Ronit, K. (eds) (1992) *Organized Interests and the European Community*, London: Sage.

Greenwood, J. and K. Ronit (1992) 'Established and Emergent Sectors: Organized Interests at the European Level in the Pharmaceutical Industry and the New Biotechnologies', in J. Greenwood, J.R. Grote and K. Ronit (eds) *Organized Interests and the European Community*, London: Sage.

Hassel, A. (1998) 'Soziale Pakte in Europa', *Gewerkschaftliche Monatshefte*, 10: 626–38.

Heylen, F. and A. v. Poeck (1995) 'National Labour Market Institutions and the European Economic and Monetary Integration Process', *Journal of Common Market Studies* 33/4: 573–95.

Karlhofer, F. and E. Tálos (1996) (eds) *Sozialpartnerschaft und EU. Integrationsdynamik und Handlungsrahmen der österreichischen Sozialpartnerschaft*, Wien: Signum.

Karlhofer, F. and E. Tálos (1999) (eds) *Sozialpartnerschaft: Wandel und Reformfähigkeit*, Wien: Signum.

Keller, B. (1993) 'Die soziale Sicht des Binnenmarktes. Zur Begründung einer europessimistischen Sicht', *Politische Vierteljahresschrift*, 4: 588–612.

Keller, B. (1995) 'Perspektiven europäischer Kollektivverhandlungen – vor und nach Maastricht', *Zeitschrift für Soziologie*, 4: 243–62.

Keller, B. (1997) *Europäische Arbeits- und Sozialpolitik*, München and Wien: Oldenbourg.

Kenis, P. and V. Schneider (1991) 'Policy Networks and Policy Analysis: Scrutinizing a New Analytical Toolbox', in B. Marin and R. Mayntz (eds) *Policy Networks. Empirical Evidence and Theoretical Considerations*, Frankfurt am Main: Campus Verlag/Westview Press.

Kohler-Koch, B. (1992) 'Interessen und Integration. Die Rolle organisierter Interessen im westeuropäischen Integrationsprozeß', *Politische Vierteljahresschrift*, Sonderheft 23: 81–120.

Kohler-Koch, B. (1994) 'Changing Patterns of Interest Intermediation in the European Union', *Government and Opposition* 29/2: 167–80.

Kohler-Koch, B. (1995) 'The Strength of Weakness. The Transformation of Governance in the EU', *Arbeitspapiere*, Mannheimer Zentrums für Europäische Sozialforschung (10).

Kohler-Koch, B. (1996) 'Die Gestaltungsmacht organisierter Interessen', in M. Jachtenfuchs and B. Kohler-Koch (eds) *Europäische Integration*, Opladen: Leske & Budrich.

Kooiman, J. (1993) 'Social-Political Governance: Introduction', in J. Kooiman (ed.) *Modern Governance. New Government – Society Interactions*, London: Sage.

Korinek, K. (1994) 'Interessenvertretungen im Wandel', in P. Gerlich and H. Neisser (eds) *Europa als Herausforderung. Wandlungsimpulse für das politische System Österreichs*, Wien: Signum.

Lash, S. and J. Urry (1987) *The End of Organized Capitalism*, Oxford: Polity Press.

Lehmbruch, G. (1982) 'Introduction: Neo-Corporatism in Comparative Perspective', in G. Lehmbruch and P.C. Schmitter (eds) *Patterns of Corporatist policy making*, London and Beverly Hills: Sage.

Marsh, D, and R.A.W. Rhodes (eds) (1992) *Policy Networks in British Government*, Oxford: Clarendon Press.

Mazey, S. and J. Richardson (1994) 'Promiscuous Policy-Making: The European Policy Style?', *European Public Policy Institute Occasional Papers*, 2.

Mazey, S. and J. Richardson (eds) (1993) *Lobbying in the European Community*, Oxford: Oxford University Press.

Müller, W. C. (1985) 'Die Rolle der Parteien bei Entstehung und Entwicklung der Sozialpartnerschaft', in P. Gerlich (ed.) *Sozialpartnerschaft in der Krise*, Wien: Böhlau.

Obradovich, D. (1995) 'Prospects for Corporatist Decision-Making in the European Union: The Social Policy Agreement', *Journal of European Public Policy* 2/2.

Rhodes, M. (1998) 'Globalisation, Labour Markets and Welfare States: A Future of 'Competitive Corporatism'?', in M. Rhodes, and Y. Mény (eds) *The Future of European Welfare: A New Social Contract?*, London: Macmillan.

Richardson, J.J., G. Gustavsson and G. Jordan, G. (1982) 'The Concept of Policy Style', in J.J. Richardson (ed.) *Policy Styles in Western Europe*, London: Allen and Unwin.

Richardson, J. J. and G. Jordan (1979) *Governing Under Pressure: The Policy Process in a Post-Parliamentary Democracy*, Oxford: Martin Robertson.

Ross, G. (1995) *Jacques Delors and European Integration*, Cambridge: Polity Press.

Sadowski, D. and A. Timmesfeld (1994) 'Sozialer Dialog: Die Chancen zur Selbstregulierung der europäischen Sozialparteien', in V. Eichener and H. Voelzkow (eds) *Europäische Integration und verbandliche Interessenvermittlung*, Marburg: Metropolis-Verlag.

Scharpf, F. (1988) 'The Joint Decision Trap: Lessons from German Federalism and European Integration, *Public Administration*, 88: 239–78.

Schmitter, P.C. (1979) 'Still the Century of Corporatism?', in P.C. Schmitter and G. Lehmbruch (eds) *Trends Towards Corporatist Intermediation*, Beverly Hills and London: Sage.

Schmitter, P.C. (1981) 'Interest Intermediation and Regime Governability in Contemporary Western Europe and North America', in S. Berger (ed.) *Organising Interests in Western Europe*, Cambridge: Cambridge University Press.

Schmitter, P. C., and Grote, J. R. (1997) 'Der korporatistische Sisyphus: Vergangenheit, Gegenwart und Zukunft, *Politische Vierteljahresschrift*, 3, 530–55. English version: J.R. Grote and P.C. Schmitter (1999) 'The Renaissance of National Corporatism: Unintended Side-effect of European Economic and Monetary Union or Calculated Response to the Absence of European Social Policy?' *Transfer*, 5/1–2: 34–63.

Seidel, H. (1989) 'Sozialpartnerschaft unter Anpassungsdruck', in H. Krejci (ed.) *Das reiche Land*, Wien: Signum.

Streeck, W. (1994) 'Staat und Verbände: Neue Fragen. Neue Antworten?', in W. Streeck (ed.) *Staat und Verbände*, Opladen: Westdeutscher Verlag.

Streeck, W. (1995) 'Politikverflechtung und Enscheidungslücke. Zum Verhältnis von zwischenstaatlichen Beziehungen und sozialen Interessen im europäischen Binnenmarkt', in K. Dentcle, B. Reissert and R. Schettkat (eds) *Die Reformfähigkeit von Industriegesellschaften. Fritz W. Scharpf – Festschrift zu seinem 60. Geburtstag*, Frankfurt and New York: Campus, pp. 101–30.

Streeck, W. (ed.) (1994) *Staat und Verbände*, Opladen: Westdeutscher Verlag.

Streeck, W. and P.C. Schmitter (1991) 'From National Corporatism to Transnational Pluralism: Organized Interests in the Single European Market', *Politics and Society*, 19/2: 133–65 (also published in W. Streeck (ed.) (1992) *Social Institutions and Economic Performance*, London: Sage (cited pages from this edition)).

Tálos, E. (1985) 'Sozialpartnerschaft: Zur Entwicklung und Entwicklungsdynamik kooperativ-konzertierter Politik in Österreich', in P. Gerlich, E. Grande and W. Müller (eds) *Sozialpartnerschaft in der Krise*: Wien: Böhlau.

Tálos, E. (1994) 'Interessenvermittlung und Interessenkonzertierung', in P. Gerlich and H. Neisser (eds) *Europa als Herausforderung. Wandlungsimpulse für das politische System Österreichs*, Wien: Signum.

Tálos, E., K. Leichsenring and E. Zeiner (1993) 'Verbände und politischer Entscheidungsprozeß – am Beispiel der Sozial- und Umweltpolitik', in E. Tálos (ed.) *Sozialpartnerschaft: Kontinuität und Wandel eines Modells*, Wien: Verlag für Gesellschaftskritik.

Traxler, F. (1995a) 'Farewell to Labour Market Associations? Organized versus Disorganized Decentralization as a Map for Industrial Relations', in C. Crouch and F. Traxler (eds) *Organized Industrial Relations: What Future?*, Aldershot: Avebury.

Traxler, F. (1995b) 'Two Logics of Collective Action in Industrial Relations', in C. Crouch and F. Traxler (eds) *Organized Industrial Relations: What Future?*, Aldershot: Avebury.

Traxler, F. (1995c) 'From Demand-side to Supply-side Corporatism? Austria's Labour Relations and Public Policy', in C. Crouch and F. Traxler (eds) *Organized Industrial Relations: What Future?*, Aldershot: Avebury.

Traxler, F. and P.C. Schmitter (1994) 'Perspektiven europäischer Integration, verbandlicher Interessenvermittlung und Politikformulierung', in V. Eichener and H. Voelzkow (eds) *Europäische Integration und verbandliche Interessenvermittlung*, Marburg: Metropolis-Verlag.

Traxler, F. and P.C. Schmitter (1995) 'The Emerging Euro-Polity and Organized Interests', *European Journal of International Relations*, 2: 191–218.

Turner, L. (1995) 'The Europeanization of Labor: Structure Before Action', paper prepared for presentation at the annual meeting of the European Community Studies Association, 11–14 May, Charleston, South Carolina).

van Waarden, F. (1992) 'Dimensions and Types of Policy Networks', *European Journal of Political Research*, 21: 29–52.

van Waarden, F. (1994) 'Is European Law a Threat to Associational Governance?', in V. Eichener and H. Voelzkow (eds) *Europäische Integration und verbandliche Interessenvermittlung*, Marburg: Metropolis-Verlag.

Williamson, P. J. (1989) *Corporatism in Perspective. An Introductory Guide to Corporatist Theory*, London: Sage.

Wimmer, N. and W. Mederer (1990) *EG-Recht in Österreich*, Wien: Böhlau.

Windolf, P. (1989) 'Productivity Coalitions and the Future of European Corporatism', *Industrial Relations*, 28: 1–20.

11 The renaissance of national corporatism

Unintended side-effect of European economic and monetary union, or calculated response to the absence of European social policy?

Jürgen Grote and Philippe Schmitter

Some years ago, we opened an earlier version of this chapter (Schmitter and Grote 1997) with the following remarks:

> The (re)discovery of corporatism in the mid-1970s was ironic. At the very moment that academics started using the concept to analyze trends in advanced capitalist societies, the practice had already peaked and it continued to decline during the 1980s. Then, just as many observers had announced its demise, corporatism has risen again and now seems to be carrying its twin burdens of interest associability and policy-making to new heights during the 1990s. Are students of European politics and society forever going to be condemned like Sisyphus to dragging this concept-*cum*-practice into their work, only to see it come crashing down later?

We concluded that corporatism would be heading back up the hill goaded as before by an architectonic national state. This would just be about on time. Corporatist practices had bottomed out after the mid-1980s and were likely to hitting their peak sometime after 1998–9 – more or less at the very moment that monetary unification was to occur!

Now, after monetary union, we see no reason to revise yesterday's assumption. Corporatism's (re)discovery in the 1970s may have been ironic, but no less so than in the premature death certificate issued to it by authors such as Scott Lash and John Urry (1987) in the 1980s. They proclaimed a new era of 'disorganized capitalism' at the very time when the 20–25 year political cycle that sustains corporatist practices had just begun to turn upwards. If anything, ensuing developments not foreseen (or even imaginable) three years ago seem to confirm our earlier hypothesis.

In Germany, a first attempt to reach a tripartite agreement had failed resoundingly in 1996. Two years (and one government) later, a comprehensive macro-level pact, the *Bündnis für Arbeit*, was signed by the peak associations of labour, capital and the government on 7 December 1998. In his New Year's address, the president of DGB, Dieter Schulte, seemed even to been affected by our Sisyphean metaphor when he observed that 'we are only at the beginning and still have a steep and upward way to go'.[1] Similarly, after the Agreement of 23 July 1993 had initiated a new system of binding rules in the area of industrial relations, Italy's social partners hammered out a comprehensive *Patto Sociale* on 22 December 1998.[2] Further east on the shores of the Mediterranean, the General Confederation of Greek Labour (GSEE) and the two national employer associations SEB (industry) and ESEE (trade) opened a dialogue with government on 'Competitiveness, Growth and Employment' on 14 May 1997. The social pact they signed on 11 November 1997 was the first in modern Greek history.

Of the fifteen EU member states, only France and the United Kingdom continue to abstain from 'concerted' policy-making among consenting peak associations. Even territorially and linguistically divided Belgium managed to solve the structural problems that had delayed the implementation of three comprehensive agreements reached in the 1990s. In France, the main obstacle has been the persistent ideological cleavage within the labour movement that had institutionalized such a process of *surenchère*, i.e. competitive overbidding between union federations, that state intervention became the default option. For example, the *Loi Robien* of 11 June 1996 was drafted by the Jospin government and passed by its parliamentary majority in an attempt to achieve economic and social goals that elsewhere in Europe have been the subject of voluntary social pacting. In Britain, the Labour Party still seems to be suffering from the trauma induced by the failed Social Contract of the mid-1970s. Together with the subsequent eighteen years of Thatcherism, the country seem to have passed the point of no return for the building of any kind of centralized policy concertation between capital and labour. Trade unions have been weakened more than elsewhere, and employer associations do not seem to be any better off (Crouch *et al.* 1999). Moreover, large parts of the British population seem to have given up any hope of combating unemployment by collective means, which has been one of the cornerstones of recent pacts in the rest of Europe.[3]

But let us first *reculer pour mieux sauter:* go back briefly to past experiences with national corporatism and to the reasons that were adduced for its demise in the latter half of the 1970s and 1980s and try to see if we can find any hints about why it was resuscitated in the 1990s.

The past

The 'corporatist approach' emerged as one subspecies of a much broader genus of theorizing in political economy that has been labeled 'institutionalist'. Its central claim was (and still is) that behaviour – economic, social or political – cannot be understood exclusively in terms of either the choices and preferences of private individuals or the habits and impositions of public agencies. Somewhere between markets and states existed a large number of 'self-organized' and 'semi-public' collectivities that individuals and firms relied upon more or less regularly to structure their expectations about each other's behaviour and to provide ready-made solutions for their recurrent conflicts. These corporatist practices might have seemed, from an abstract and external point of view, inflexible in their demands and sub-optimal in their performances, but they did save considerably on search and information costs, while supplying a psychologically reassuring famili-arity to those who worked within them. Normatively, they may have represented 'second best solutions' for all involved, but operationally, if one takes into consideration the uncertain 'shadow of the future', the particip-ants seemed prepared to bear the mutual burden of rigidities and inefficiencies – at least, until some manifestly better solution presented itself.[4]

Moreover – and this is especially important for the corporatist sub-species – their 'standard operating procedures' demanded specialized personnel. Those who came to occupy such positions developed a strong vested interest, not just in the maintenance of existing practices, but also in their future development. Some of the dues, rents and subsidies these associational leaders extracted from members and interlocutors could be 'invested' in further legitimation and task expansion. In other words, the trajectory of this non-market and non-state arrangement was not just a passive reflection of the demand for its services by individuals and authorities. It could (and did) acquire a dynamic of its own that served to carry its burdens further up the slope than might otherwise have been the case.

For corporatists – analysts as well as protagonists – differences in the nature of intermediary institutions at the national level were regarded as crucial in determining the policies adopted and their eventual outcomes. Only when specially organized intermediaries were involved and only when the process of negotiation empowered them as monopolies to represent the collective interests of some encompassing group and to take subsequent responsibility for any decisions made, could one speak of corporatism *strictu sensu*. It was not enough just to consult various interests. Effective participation was not open to any organization. The macro-process of interest conflict and compromise depended upon the 'active assent' of peak associations representing comprehensive class, sectoral or professional interests. In more specialized sectors and under very special auspices, this could even result in the creation of so-called 'private interest governments' that had a great deal of autonomy from and authority over both members and interlocutors in the way in which they allocated resources (Streeck and Schmitter 1985).[5]

The corporatist literature of the 1970s tended to stress two ideal-typical clusters of conditions: (1) associational properties; and (2) decision-making characteristics.[6] Under the former *rubrique*, they looked about for such things as monopoly of representation, hierarchic co-ordination across associations, functional differentiation into non-overlapping and comprehensive categories, official recognition by state agencies and semi-public status, involuntary or quasi-compulsory membership, and some degree of heteronomy with regard to the selection of leaders and the articulation of demands. In terms of decision-making the search was on for 'concertation,' i.e. for contexts in which there was regular interaction in functionally specialized domains, privileged and even exclusive access, consultation prior to legislative deliberation, parity in representation, active and concurrent consent and not just passive acquiescence or majority voting as the usual decision rule, and devolved responsibility for policy implementation.

Needless to say, in the real world these traits did not always cluster together: e.g. monopolies of representation were granted (often *de facto*) to associations without much public control over leadership or the nature of demands; functional councils were established within the administration or higher executive office, but legislatures refused to accept their status, much less to allow them to consider and amend proposals beforehand. Most disconcertingly, the associational properties and the decision-making characteristics did not co-vary in some instances. Supposedly, policy concertation could not persist without monopolistically structured, hierarchically ordered, officially recognized and functionally delimited associations. Even where the latter did not exist initially, once concertation was up and running it should have encouraged the development of these properties in collaborating interest associations. Sometimes, the incongruencies were temporary when, for example, negotiations for the annual or biannual 'social contract' broke down momentarily over a specific issue and yet the basic structure of intermediation remained unchanged, or when negotiations concerning macro-economic policies persisted between peak class associations, despite the fact that one or another of them had suffered a 'defection' by a faction that opted for exerting pressure through other channels. Occasionally, great efforts were made to bring about a concerted outcome despite the prevalence of class, sectoral and professional interests that were 'incorrectly' organized – if they were organized at all. Great Britain during the 1970s and Italy in the early 1980s were apposite cases – and they appropriately failed in short order.

In addition to the above-mentioned intrinsic causes (inappropriate associational formats and/or exclusionary decision-making arrangements), what have been the extrinsic factors that have been used to account for the demise of corporatism? The arguments advanced to explain this were, at the time, quite convincing. At first, the problem seemed to be just the persistently lower growth rates and slack labour markets that emerged in the aftermath of the two oil shocks – along with the consequent fiscal crisis of the state. The surplus was simply not there to make the sort of side-payments that had facilitated compromises in the past and organized intermediaries were noticeably reluctant to share responsibility for the management of declining resources.

Gradually, however, other difficulties emerged which suggested that merely reversing the decline in growth and the increase in unemployment might not result in a return to the *statu quo ante* at the level of macro-concertation. The displacement of employment from the traditional 'hard-core' of manufacturing to service and, in some cases, to public employment had a serious impact on the recruitment of union members. The very core interest categories upon which macro-corporatist compromises had been built were becoming increasingly disaggregated and dispersed. The whole process of centralized negotiations concerning wages, benefits and working conditions came under severe pressures.

Moreover, new production technologies based on micro-electronics cut across traditional job classification systems and professional categories, and created possibilities for flexible production in relatively small units. In one sense, these processes increased the need for 'active assent' on the part of workers – and, therefore, the need for capitalists to bargain with them over the quality as well as the quantity of their contribution, but in another sense this was occurring in highly differentiated settings not easy to reduce to a standard contract and, hence, difficult for either trade union or employer peak associations to capture and control. Both types of intermediaries found themselves increasingly shut out of the negotiation process – where it occurred at all.

Of course, the real culprit – everyone's favourite *deus ex machina* – was (and still is) globalization. Sharpened international competition (and greater international mobility of capital) lay behind many of these developments, but also played a more direct (and menacing) role. The overt threat to move to another site or to discontinue production altogether put great pressure on workers to make concessions at the level of the enterprise, thereby undermining what had previously been negotiated at the national or sectoral level. Similarly, the heightened competition between firms made unified responses and commitments from business associations more difficult. Governments and state agencies, sensitive to these trends in the international environment through the balance of payments as well as to the direct pressure from those involved, multiplied the subsidies and exemptions designed to benefit specific sectors – and sometimes even individual firms.

If low growth rates, labour force restructuring, technological innovation and global competitiveness were not material causes enough, the ideological attractions of neo-liberalism seemed to seal the fate of any serious attempt to negotiate one's way through the labyrinth of major economic restructuring. The upshot of these trends seemed quite clear to many analysts in the 1980s. At best, 'national corporatism' had to shift from the macro to the meso level of aggregation. And even then, the question remained whether the process would stop there or disintegrate even further until the only 'systematic dialogues' left would be taking place at the level of firms and the 'voluntary and active assent', so obviously necessary for improving competitiveness in a more globalized marketplace, would emerge from the interactions of individual workers and employers – stalked by the shadow of future dismissals and plant closures. Not a very encouraging prospect – but, so it seemed, a realistic one!

We now know that it was overdrawn. 'Systemic dialogues', even between representatives of *gesamtwirtschaftliche* interests, began re-emerging in the late 1980s and presently seem to be proliferating. A number of countries have been attempting in the 1990s to reap the benefits of policy concertation between consenting interest associations, not all of which have the 'appropriate' organizational structures. What is more, they have been trying to do this at the highly visible and comprehensive national level, even if they have occasionally tried to fulfil new purposes with these efforts. To what extent do these more recent arrangements involve a completely different bundle of substantive policies? And, does this mean that, this time, corporatist practices are likely to travel further, before they inevitably come tumbling down again?

The present

All those death certificates issued to corporatism in the 1980s carried the same generic signature.[7] Despite some difference in the symptoms of their agonizing, the autopsies uniformly declared that it had died of *disfunctionitis*, i.e. neo-corporatist arrangements could no longer perform the imperative tasks that had been assigned to it by neo-Keynesian policy makers operating within the confines of their respective nation-states. Lacking any legitimacy of its own, its demise passed virtually unnoticed by the mass public and was not even mourned by those academics who had made a career out of (re)discovering it.[8]

E pur si muove! The corpse of corporatism has risen – again – and is rolling its dual burdens back up the slope of interest politics during the 1990s. It seems that some sort of associative governance – intersectoral as well as intrasectoral – is still an imperative of the functioning of modern capitalism, *pace* the more extreme protestations of neo-liberals. For, if capitalism requires an effective mechanism for ensuring orderly competition among producers and a mutually acceptable distribution of income between capital and labour, then, where the firms and individuals involved are associated with each other and, hence, capable of articulating their interests collectively, active assent can only be obtained through a systematic dialogue between the organizations that represent these interests.

The diagnostic error of those who presided over the autopsy of corporatism in the 1980s seems to have been in assuming that the *same* functions would have to be performed by the *same* organizations at the *same* level for this particular mode of interest intermediation/policy-making to survive. They did not acknowledge the possibility that *different* functions might be performed at the *same* level of aggregation by the *same* (or analogous) organizations. In any case, studying national-level arrangements became an increasingly redundant exercise and many shifted their attention to the study of changes in levels and in the composition of sectoral and territorial pacts[9] – i.e. to dimensions where corporatism did survive the neo-liberal assault of the 1980s and, in part, quite successfully. All the more surprising must have been the resurgence of policy concertation at the macro-level – especially remarkable in countries which do not seem to possess, at least not *ex ante*, an appropriately configured set of interest associations. A rapid perusal of the descriptive literature would reveal that the negotiating and implementing of tripartite or bipartite *social pacts* is back on the agenda – but not always where one might have expected it on the basis of the experiences of the 1960s and 1970s.[10]

Ireland is a case in point. Having been previously described as hopelessly pluralist and non-macro-contractualist in the Anglo-Saxon tradition, the country quietly developed a tradition of centralized wage bargaining from 1987 to 1993. Four consecutive economic and social accords were signed between government, the FUEC (the Federated Union of Employers), and the ICTU (the Irish Congress of Trade Unions). The three year 'Programme for National Recovery' in 1987 aimed at creating a fiscal and monetary environment conducive to the promotion of higher rates of economic growth. It included a broad package of measures: greater equity in taxes, reduction of inequalities, employment-generating measures, a ceiling on pay increases, measures for the low-paid and working time reduction. The second agreement signed in 1990, the 'Programme for Economic and Social Progress', the third in 1993, the 'Programme for Competitiveness and Work', and the fourth, the 'Partnership 2000 for Inclusion, Employment and Competitiveness' (1997) contained essentially the same measures – despite their differences in nomenclature. As demonstrated by Anke Hassel (1998: 636), these accords were embedded and backed up by pre-existing bi- and tripartite institutions (National Economic and Social Council, Employer Labour Conference, Labour Court, Joint Labour Committees), but have themselves helped building up new formal structures for concertation (Labour Relations Commission, Central Review Committee, etc.).

Finland is a rather different case. Having been a relative late-comer to Scandinavian-style corporatism, it continued quietly, if fitfully, to practice corporatism throughout the 1980s. However, in the early 1990s when the collapse of the Soviet economy left them in exceptional economic distress, the Finns revived and expanded macro-level concertation. The initial tripartite deal between the government, the Confederation of Finnish Industry and Employers (TT) and the Confederation of Finnish Trade

Unions (SAK) covered the period from 1 January 1992 to 31 October 1993. It was successfully renegotiated after a massive currency devaluation when workers agreed to a freeze on wages in exchange for government promises to refrain from laying-off civil servants, to support housing programmes, to grant tax relief to the lower-paid and to impose new taxes on those still in full-time employment. This macro-concertation has subsequently continued in a bipartite fashion between the TT and the SAK, with the additional participation of the Confederation of Technical Workers (STTK) and the Confederation of Professional Workers (AKAVA). Leaving aside basic wage issues (still covered by the previous agreement), they focused on a comprehensive package of measures designed to alleviate unemployment: lower wages for apprentices and newly recruited workers, reform of unemployment insurance, greater scope for decentralized bargaining, restrictions of political or sympathy strikes, and modifications in working time and workplace consultation.

The situation that emerged in *Spain* was completely different, in both its initial timing and intent. Macro-level concertation began in the late 1970s — just as it was declining elsewhere in Europe. The famous Pacto de la Moncloa in 1977 did ostensibly deal with issues of economic and social recovery, but it was signed by the leaders of political parties and primarily aimed at improving the prospects for the consolidation of democracy. In the terminology of Terry Karl (1985), it constituted a 'foundational' pact among political elites, not a 'managerial' pact between economic and social groups. As such, it was quite successful and, as we shall see, closely observed and occasionally imitated by other countries involved in similarly uncertain regime transitions. The initial Moncloa Pact did give rise to a series of subsequent efforts as 'managerial tripartite concertation' between the government, the Spanish Confederation of Employers' Organizations (CEOE), and various combinations of the socialist-oriented General Workers Union (UGT) and/or the communist-oriented Workers' Commissions (CC.OO). After seven years of fitful success and five Acuerdos, these negotiations collapsed completely – ironically, during the protracted hegemony of the Socialist Party (PSOE) in government, a factor which elsewhere and earlier was of crucial importance for the success of macro-corporatism!

After a lengthy period of sporadic and inconclusive bipartite negotiations between government and business associations and government and trade unions, tripartite policy concertation raised its head again. A first attempt was made in 1993 to reach a comprehensive social pact by voluntary means. When this was abandoned by both employers´ and workers´ representatives, the Socialist government issued an ultimatum that if no agreement emerged before the end of the year, it would put its own proposal before parliament (where it then enjoyed a comfortable majority). Despite a general strike on 27 January 1994, the consequent law (containing less rigid recruitment hiring procedures, permission for private and part-time employment agencies, reformulated apprenticeship contracts, incentives for creating part-time work, greater flexibility in working hours and less rigidity in collective redundancies) was passed and the measures were successfully implemented. The reluctant social partners seemed to have learned from that experience at having been shut out. Although the Toledo Pact (1994) and the Agreement on the financing and structure of the state social security and pension system were only signed by government and the trade union confederations (CC.OO and UGT), the latter, together with the employers (CEOE and CEPYME), managed to agree to a proper bilateral pact on 8 April 1997. This occurred after years of difficult negotiations and, hardly astonishing, only after massive threats of government intervention. *El País* described this agreement as 'probably the most important social agreement signed in Spain over the past fifteen years'.

Adjacent Portugal also went through a major regime change in the mid-1970s, but it did so without the benefit of a Moncloa-style foundational *pacto*. Instead, after a much more tumultuous process of democratization, it gradually and more easily than Spain settled into a process of managerial pacting at the macro-level, beginning with the creation in 1984 of a Permanent Council for Social Concertation. From 1987 through 1992, peak associations of business (industry, commerce and sometimes even agriculture) reached regular agreements with the General Union of Workers (UGT) on incomes policy and other issues.[11] In a near-classic repetition of what had occurred in Northern Europe a decade or more earlier, the Portuguese 'social partners' exchanged moderation in wage demands and greater flexibility in management practices for more generous social measures and improvements in labour legislation, as well as for adjustments in the calculation of economic indicators to bring them more in line with the country's EU partners. As had been the case before, when conditions of growth and employment began to deteriorate after 1992, it became increasingly difficult to make the necessary concessions. No comprehensive agreement was signed for the next four years – just when the process was being revived next door in Spain (where, incidentally, economic conditions were even worse)! On 20 December 1996, however, government and Portuguese peak associations (UGT, CCP, CAP, CIP) hammered out a rather comprehensive tripartite deal (Acordo de Concertação Estratégica) including issues such as incomes policy, working time reduction, introduction of a minimum income on an experimental basis, and tax reductions for low income-earners. Interestingly, the Acordo also foresaw the reduction of social security contributions for those employers belonging to employers' associations – a measure clearly aimed at providing incentives for the strengthening of organizational cohesion (Rhodes 1997). While the UGT felt the agreement to be a 'historic event,' the larger of the two unions, the post-communist CGTP, claimed that 'it is providing corporatist arrangements by establishing a labour relations centre' and consequently abstained from signing it. In the words of Hassel

(1998: 643), the Portuguese case might have to be removed from the list of successful social pacts, if the CGTP were to persist in its hostile attitude toward concertation.

Belgium has had a long-standing tradition of centralized bargaining on social questions within the framework of its National Labour Council. Collective agreements, once reached voluntarily within it, subsequently acquire the coercive force of public law. Interrupted in the mid-1970s – as so often happened elsewhere – the practice of negotiating two-year bipartite agreements was revived in 1987 and has been in operation ever since. Nevertheless, the restricted scope of these accords led the government in 1991 and again in 1993 to attempt the sponsorship of a much broader (and tripartite) pact on national competitiveness, employment and welfare. The resistance of the General Labour Federation of Belgium (FGTB) ended these talks – before they could even begin. The government then responded by passing new legislation that aimed at accomplishing the same objectives: changing the basis of wage indexation, freezing real wages, reducing social security contributions, encouraging enterprise-level negotiations on job flexibility, instituting special employment contracts for young people and reducing social security expenditures. Despite strong labour resistance to these measures (including a 24-hour general strike), the bipartite concertation process in Belgium continued to function at least until 1997–8 when negotiations to conduct a central agreement totally broke down.[12] However, this did not mark the end of the era of centralized negotiations. Since the head of state and the government have signalled their willingness to grant more autonomy to bilateral negotiations, the relations between the partners have again improved. They claim that they are now willing to widen the scope of their negotiations and to accept a stronger commitment to reform.

Marino Regini has recently analysed the rather puzzling trajectory of macro-corporatism in Italy (Regini 1996). Not only does he demonstrate empirically that its practice is far from dead in a country that had always been regarded as unusually resistant to its appeal, but he argues theoretically that

> the recent attempts at concertation between [Italian] governments [NB the unusual plural] and interest associations are apparently more successful and acquiring greater stability in the countries whose political and organizational features do not meet the supposed 'preconditions' of neo-corporatism, and possibly because of such differences.

Italy has been (and remains) a country with a fragmented system of interest intermediation and patterns of interorganizational bargaining that have been characterized as a pathological mixture of pluralism and consociationalism (Pizzorno 1993). Its only prior tripartite agreement of any importance, the Anti-Inflation Accord of January 1983 , did not give rise to stable concertation in the subsequent decade, as did happen in Ireland and (as we shall see) the Netherlands. However, as Regini observes, it did give rise to a less visible, but quite encompassing, system of 'micro-concertation' at the level of enterprises or industrial districts, which were successful in satisfying the needs and expectations of both employers and workers. These, in turn, led to the development of a significant degree of trust and consensus so that when the issue of potential macro-level agreements emerged in the 1990s, the system could take advantage of the opportunity – which it had not been previously capable of doing.

Regini refers to three agreements which, he claims, marked 'the most radical reforms in the history of the Italian welfare state:' first, the Tripartite Agreement reached in July 1992 (under the Amato government); second, the 23 July 1993 Agreement on wage costs (signed by the Ciampi government); and, in particular, the May 1995 Pension Agreement (negoti-ated by the Dini government). In the later 1990s, these were followed by a tripartite agreement on employment (*Patto per il Lavoro*) and by the more recent Patto Sociale. The most challenging element of Regini's analysis, which only refers to the pre-1995 period, is the assertion that all this has been accomplished *without* any major changes in the organizational structure of either capital or labour.[13]

The 1993 agreement clearly remains the most important one achieved by Italian interest associations and the state throughout the 1990s (Telljohann 1998). It helped, first, to surmount the traditionally conflictual system of industrial relations by institutionalizing binding rules and, second, to re-legitimize the trade union movement. Since it was limited to this specific, 'institutional' type of political exchange (formal recognition of the role of unions in collective bargaining at central and enterprise levels against an agreement to dismantle the *scala mobile*, the automatic wage indexation system) and since it was not immediately followed by material concessions and an active labour market policy, the agreement remained rather precarious and, in any case, did not prevent rank and file unrest (ibid.).

All the above cases could be discounted for one reason or another. Some were bipartite; others were tripartite. Some have been conducted in exceptional circumstances; others have been convened more routinely. Most importantly, they have been either too recent to have produced any major effects or not yet sufficiently 'embedded' to survive major changes in government in power or shifts in the business cycle. Whatever their actual or potential contribution to 'the governance of contemporary capitalism,' they have yet to be picked up by anyone as a 'model' worthy of imitation.

This is definitely not true of the Netherlands. There is hardly a West European prime minister or central bank president who has not recently referred with admiration to the virtues of that country's macro-economic performance and, specifically, to its 'full part-time economy'.[14] Jelle Visser

(1996) has demonstrated that, since the late 1980s, the Dutch polity has achieved simultaneously several things that elsewhere have been impossible. It has reformed its welfare policies and social security system without severe cuts or protests. Moreover, unemployment has been reduced from a very high 13 per cent in the mid-1980s to only 6.7 per cent in 1996 – the lowest level in contemporary Europe.[15] This has been done despite following a policy of strict fiscal conservatism aimed at monetary stability and budgetary discipline. The Netherlands is currently one of the few countries that satisfy the convergence criteria imposed by European Monetary Union. And, contrary to other countries' experiences, privatization of public enterprises has played virtually no role in temporarily augmenting Dutch public receipts.

The key to this superior performance, Visser finds, is in a set of major changes in the Dutch system of industrial relations – both in the structures and the strategies of its component organizations. The turning point came in 1982, considerably before the other cases we have reviewed above. The Netherlands had been one of the first countries to drop out of the postwar 'high corporatist elite'. Growing worker mobilization had destroyed its well-established practice of macro-concertation; the domestic policy debate had come to equate it with institutional sclerosis (ibid.: 2); and economists were issuing stern warnings about the 'Dutch disease', i.e. about the way in which windfall revenues from the exploitation of natural gas discoveries had produced wage and price hikes, steady inflation, and a corresponding loss of international competitiveness and jobs. Visser quotes the Swedish political economist, Göran Therborn, who described the Dutch economy in 1986 as 'the most spectacular employment failure in the advanced capitalist world', and shows that it was precisely this sense of crisis, widely shared by the population, that resulted in the subsequent changes in structure and strategy. The trade unions, in particular, were vulnerable to loss of membership and the burden of soaring unemployment. They began to recognize that 'improving the profitability of Dutch industry was a *sine qua non* for any job strategy' (ibid.: 12).

Only in this context can one understand the novelty and comprehensiveness of what came to be known as the 1982 Agreement of Wassenaar – 'the mother of all accords' in Visser's words. Wassenaar, he argues, was for the Netherlands 'what Saltsjöbaden (1938) had been for post-war Swedish labor relations.' It contained in anticipation virtually all of the measures that began appearing a decade later in the other social pacts we have discussed above. It coupled rigid budgetary measures in a sort of Maastricht *avant la lettre* to wage restraint and major reforms in welfare institutions. The trade unions gave up their Holy Grail of automatic compensation for price inflation and the employers' associations withdrew their veto a reduction in the working week. Moreover, the Wassenaar Accord turned out not to be just a 'one-shot' exercise. It was followed by an array of no less than seventy-eight subsequent reports, guidelines, joint opinions, reports of advice, recommendations and agreements covering the most diverse labour market issues. They marked the beginning of a continuous process of bi- and tripartite bargaining most recent product of which was the New Direction Accord concluded in December 1993 in which worker and employer organizations 'renewed their pledge to continue a policy of wage moderation, in favour of investment, job creation, working-time reduction and extra measures for training'. Moreover, the more recent agreements have inserted provisions in favour of a more differentiated and flexible implementation through negotiations at lower levels, possibly with the involvement of works councils, personnel or union representatives. Visser calls this a policy of 'centralized decentralization.' Along with the central co-ordination between peak associations and their sectoral affiliates, strict monitoring procedures were introduced at the enterprise level. Employee consultation and participation rights spread throughout the country.

Corporatism, quite obviously, 'has again become the dominant figuration in Dutch industrial relations' (Visser 1996: 27). Its trade unions are broadly representative. Their membership has remained stable and even showed recent signs of increasing. Despite organizational pluralism, they do not compete sharply with each other. Employers are equally well organized – and have become less confessionally divided. Over the whole process, but discretely in the background, lurks the Dutch state with its coercive 'shadow of hierarchy' and there is always the 'shadow of the future' to remind the negotiators that they could both be worse off – if they fail to agree. Recurrent (but informal) interaction and mutual adjustment have discouraged short-term opportunism and contributed to the building of longer-term trust. That trust is decisive for this form of policy to work is demonstrated by Visser (1998) with a view to a couple of successive agreements. The one on 'Flexibility and Security' (April 1996) and the more comprehensive pact 'Agenda 2000' have both been prepared and discussed in the Foundation of Labour (*Stichting van de Arbeid*) and both contain quite innovative qualitative measures (more attention to the lower paid and to ethnic minorities and a further shift in industrial relations from a macro- towards a micro-economic perspective). All this leads the author to conclude by observing that the Dutch case proves that 'countries do have considerable autonomy in shaping institutions and policies, in spite of the common challenges and pressures of integration and internationalization' (Visser 1996: 29).

Austria with its extraordinary continuity in reaching class compromises between its 'chambered' peak associations proves the same point. Franz Traxler (1996) argues forcefully against assuming that either globalization or regional integration will undermine the prospects for national concert- ative arrangements, especially when – as in the Austrian case – the functional content of concertation has shifted from demand to supply issues (*Angebotskorporatismus*). Brigitte Unger (2002) shows that the pressures of internationalization have always be taken into account by the participants in Austria's *Sozialpartnerschaft* and that there is no reason to believe that the Single European Market or European Monetary Integration will lead to its demise. It has become more difficult to sustain specific mechanisms, such as the Paritätische Kommission. After its fifty years of existence, Unger finds that it has entered the organizational equivalent of a typical male 'mid-life crisis': the participants think that the best times are over; they look back with regret to the glorious past; they feel increasingly impotent in face of external pressures; and, finally, they attempt to overcome this with a *fuite en avant*, i.e. by leaving the (national) family and taking up with a (supra-national) lover in Brussels. Behind this imaginative metaphor (Is it just a metaphor?), Unger finds considerable evidence for a major shift in the substance of the more recent accords, for example, in the Joint Report on the Consolidation of the National Budget of September 1995 (see also: Grote 1999). Just as in other pacts reviewed in this chapter, the previous objectives of 'full-employment' – or 'a high level of employment' – have shifted to 'increases in employment'; and the former emphasis on 'solidarity' has changed to 'efficiency' and 'budget consolidation'. She concludes by dismissing the possibility of transposing the Austrian arrangements to the level of an EU Social Dialogue or set of collective agreements and stresses that the future of Austria's concerted political economy lies in Vienna, not in Brussels.[16]

Corporatism in Switzerland has not (yet) had to face the tensions generated by EU membership. Hence, it has essentially remained stable – not only with regard to its organizational structure – but, more peculiarly, with regard to the content of its agreements. As demonstrated by Klaus Armingeon (2002), Swiss social partnership has always differed in important aspects from that of Austria or Scandinavia. Its functional equivalent to the more formal structures of the other countries is the *Vernehmlassungsverfahren* procedure (Article 32.3 of the Swiss Constitution) according to which interest associations are granted the constitutional (and, hence, virtually irremovable) right to be consulted *before* drafts of legislation are debated and decided in parliament. Also, the actual negotiations under the terms of the Swiss Social Peace Treaty of 1937 take place at the sectoral level, which allows for more flexible accommodation to changing market conditions. Finally, Swiss practices are rooted in a very stable overlap between parliamentary and corporatist policy-making – itself rooted in a long-standing coalition between the Social Democratic Party and the trade union movement. Contrary to the general trend in Europe, the party affiliation of union members in Switzerland has increased, not decreased – and the famous 2+2+2+1 formula for establishing the national executive has guaranteed Social Democratic participation in government continuously since 1947.

Unchallenged by EU membership or the Maastricht convergence criteria (which, incidentally, Switzerland would have no difficulty in meeting) and unthreatened in the recent past by major economic crisis, the Swiss macro-concertation may, nevertheless, be facing an uncertain future. Real wages have stagnated and there has been little economic growth since 1992 (Armingeon 2002). The country never attempted to 'govern' the business cycle and, therefore, '[Swiss] corporatism could never profit from the rise of neo-Keynesian macro-economic steering and it never suffered from its failure' (ibid.: 2002). This also means that Switzerland may be singularly ill-equipped with policy instruments for dealing with its current economic stagnation. Any comprehensive wage-tax-welfare bargain between organized capital and labour would require the consent by the Federal government, all twenty-six cantonal governments and a large number of local authorities – not to mention a probable referendum. So, Switzerland has been working at its own, in terms of macro-level arrangements, much more steady and slow pace. The country is definitely 'out of synchrony' with its more Europeanized neighbours. In the 1990s, it hardly seemed likely that the system could be induced to take on new substantive burdens in response to an expanded policy agenda.

If this evidence from Western Europe were not enough to convince the reader that macro-corporatism was back on the agenda, consider what has been happening in Eastern Europe! There is virtually not a single country that has not, in the course of trying simultaneously to transform its economy and its polity, experimented formally with macro-level corporatism. Admittedly, there is an element of irony in these experiences: they look suspiciously like efforts at copying Western practices when these very same practices were no longer functioning as they used to. Which does not mean that macro-corporatism might not be of some utility in the Eastern cases; just that it is highly unlikely to produce the same effects.

Hungary was the first. Its National Interest Conciliation Council was set up in 1988 at the initiative of the government – even *before* the regime change had occurred. It was re-established and reformed in 1990 and seems to have played a significant role in drafting legislation on industrial relations and distributing the assets of the former trade union movement, despite the fact that it is very pluralist in its representative structure. No less than seven confederations of workers and seven confederations of employers participate, along with a shifting set of government representatives.

The Czech Council for Economic and Social Agreement was created in October 1990, hence, after democratization had begun. It has a more classic composition, with monopoly peak associations for capital and labour and designated seats for three ministries. Its relations with the neo-liberal government of Klaus have been tenuous, but it has produced annual agreements since 1991 that seem to have had some effect on wage and employment issues, as well as the content of new legislation. Interestingly, it was renamed in 1995: the Council for Dialogue of Social Partners in manifest tribute to its Austrian neighbour. Slovakia 'inherited' a similar arrangement when it became independent in 1993.

Bulgaria is another case in point. Its National Commission for the Co-ordination of Interests was established by national tripartite agreement – and not by government initiative as in the previous cases – and quickly acquired a monopolistic and hierarchic structure of representation. After producing three agreements on price liberalization, income indexation, pension levels, privatization and labour law reform, it was abruptly dissolved in November 1991 by the incoming neo-liberal government of Dimitrov, only to be recreated in May 1992 as the National Council for Social Partnership and then again in January 1993 as the National Council for Tripartite Partnership. These changes were brought about by strong pressures from the trade union movement, which in Bulgaria as in Czechoslovakia seem to have retained much of the monopolistic organiz-ational structure and high density of membership that it had under the *ancien régime communiste*.

Poland has been a bit of a deviant case – perhaps, precisely because of the enormous initial presence and subsequent fragmentation of the Solidarity Movement. It did not even get the semblance of a macro-corporatist arrangement until 1993 and then only for issues concerning privatization: the Tripartite Commission on Control over the Implementation of the Pact on State Enterprises. This subsequently converted itself in the Tripartite Commission on Socio-Economic Issues, but its effectiveness has been paralysed by conflicts between competing trade union confederations.

The list could be extended. Russia, the Ukraine, Belarus, Romania, even Kazakhstan have experimented with tripartism in one form or another. But let us not be misled by this explosion of activity. As Petra Stykow points out in the monograph, which we have used extensively in putting together the above survey of developments in Eastern Europe, 'the actual political importance of tripartite bodies paints a bleak picture for all (Eastern European) countries' (Stykow 1996: 3). They may be modelled on (largely defunct) Western experiences, but they are not performing the same functions. Their creation has been much more dependent upon govern-mental initiatives and their survival much more contingent upon eventual governmental defections; their internal structure much less organizationally concentrated and *paritätisch* (which is due in large part to the weakness of associations of capitalists); their policy impact much more symbolic. Which does not mean, she shrewdly argues, that these institutions are 'superfluous' or 'empty'. They have been, in fact, quite important – but not for their role in managing the economic transition. Just like the Spanish Pacto de Moncloa, their real purpose is to embody a 'foundational' agreement among members of an emerging national political elite. Eventually, macro-corporatist pacting may stimulate the development of 'appropriate' class, sectoral and professional associations (they did in Spain) and they might even facilitate the governance of an emerging capitalist economy, but their immediate functions have been to reduce uncertainty among competing elites and to broadcast an image of orderly cooperation to the citizenry at large.

The future

In a deservedly obscure article written at the height of despair with the neo-corporatist arrangements of the post-war period, one of us reminded his readers that corporatism has had a historical tendency to disappear and to reappear (Schmitter 1989). Its modern ideological revival can be conveniently traced to the papal encyclical, *Rerum Novarum* of 1891 – although the resuscitation and extension of the Chamber system for artisans, industry and commerce and even for agriculture in some parts of Central Europe had begun some twenty years earlier. The concept re-emerged after the First World War, this time in a more secular and statist guise, and found its most public expression in the *corporazioni* of Fascist Italy, followed by imitators in Portugal, Spain, Brazil, Vichy France, etc. Several of the smaller European democracies began practising something analogous after the Second World War — although they were carefully to avoid the previous label.

All this puts its ideology-*cum*-practice – roughly – on a *twenty to twenty-five year cycle*[17] – with, of course, lags for particular countries and exemptions for particular sectors. This was a very speculative conclusion when it was advanced in the mid-1980s. For it to have acquired the status of plausible theory, one would have to come up with variable and contingent conditions that 'drive' actors to shift their preference from one solution to another – and then back again in a period of twenty to twenty-five years. One obvious candidate could be found in Albert O. Hirschman's (1982) notion of 'shifting involvements.' Actors collectively prefer one set of goods over another – say, private goods – until diminishing marginal returns and crowding effects set in and they switch to a different set of preferences – say, for more public goods. Pluralist-pressure politics would correspond to the private 'phase;' corporatist-concertation politics to the public one – and involvement with each could be expected to shift back and forth *ad infinitum*. Another possible candidate would be the twists and turns of the business cycle. The fact that the ups and downs of the macro-economy do not quite seem to correspond exactly in time to those of corporatist arrangements could be dismissed on grounds that institutions tend to be 'viscous' and, therefore, to take more time to learn about the changing context, to reflect the new balance of forces and to overcome the resistance of their internally vested interests. Whatever the basic sentiment or calculus behind it, the cyclical theory of corporatism is appealing – at least, to those who advocate or study such arrangements. Presumably, once consumers were satiated with private goods or once workers were again fully employed, the appeal of neo-liberal diatribes against government planning, incomes policies, production of public goods and the regulation of sectors would decline and neo-corporatist concertation would become a more attractive policy option at whatever level (including the supra-national).

Unfortunately, neither of these elegant theoretical speculations about the mechanism underlying corporatism's twenty to twenty-five year cycle seems adequate to explain its present revival. There is no evidence that consuming individuals are fed up with private goods and shifting their preferences to public ones – although there is some indication that the appeal of manifest neo-liberalism has waned. As was shown above, problems such as unemployment, low growth rates, the decline of union membership and new production technologies have not only not diminished: they are dramatically persistent and even increasing in several of the polities that have recently been experimenting with macro-concertation.

European societies have long been affected by the challenges and opportunities noted above. More recently, they have had to face something novel: the European Union – or, more particularly, the completion of the Single European Market and monetary unification. Purely as a matter of temporal coincidence, there is reason to suspect that the resurgence of national corporatism has something to do with these supra-national developments. Albeit the institutions of the European Union may not have intended to produce such a change in interest politics within its member states, the indirect impact has been substantial. Market liberalization and enhanced competition has put enormous pressure on national welfare states without supplementing or substituting their policies with a Europe-wide set of labour standards or bargaining mechanisms.[18] Its expanded transnational economic citizenship (mainly for the benefit of capitalists and consumers) has not been accompanied by a corresponding development of supra-national social citizenship (that might benefit workers, the unemployed and the retired). Faced with this increase in the 'imbalance of class forces', trade unions in most member states seem to have recognized that policy concertation on wages and working conditions at the national level represented their best line of defence. Business associations have reluctantly gone along with this effort as a way of insuring social peace and gaining greater 'flexibility' in the workplace.

Of course, European imperatives are unlikely to have presided over the initial resurgence of macro-corporatism in such countries as the Netherlands, Belgium and Ireland. At the time, they were collectively more focused on improving competitiveness and diminishing unemployment, but once the provisions of the Treaty of Maastricht on EMU began to be taken seriously, making the requisite adjustments in budgetary and borrowing policies quickly moved to the top of the agenda for concertation.[19] National governments, faced with a manifest loss of sovereignty in an area – the fixing of exchange and interest rates – which had been essential to their macro-economic decision-making, were desperate to regain some degree of autonomy in their policy process. The European-national state, quite obviously, still possesses its capacity to act as 'the architect of a corporatist order' as Gerhard Lehmbruch has argued in the case of Germany (Lehmbruch 1996: 741) and that, internationalization notwithstanding, there is still quite some room for manœuvre has been demonstrated by Jelle Visser for the case of the Netherlands. We have found evidence in a broad range of countries that the nation-state is still capable of drawing up *and* implementing such plans.

The future of this new cycle of macro-corporatism will depend primarily on the future evolution of the European Union. And this, *not* because the EU is likely to be successful in constructing an edifice of Euro-corporatism around either its embryonic Social Dimension or its various sectoral policies. Schmitter and Streeck (1991) argued some time ago that the pattern of interest politics emerging around Brussels was much more pluralist than the patterns prevailing in most of its member states and that this trend was likely to continue for several reasons: size, complexity, multiple layers of access, differing national practices, and so forth. We see no reason to revise this assessment, *pace* those who have struggled to find traces of concertation in specific sectors (Greenwood 1997; Mazey and Richardson 1992) or those who predict a more promising future for collective negotiations on social and employment issues at the European level (Falkner 1998).[20] The EU has neither of the two qualities which were present at the founding of national corporatisms: (1) an autonomous redistributive capacity; or (2) a relative equilibrium of class forces. And it is highly unlikely to acquire such state-like properties in the foreseeable future (Schmitter 1996).

Where the impact will be felt is primarily *via* the 'Europeanization' of national interest politics, i.e. as member (and, even, non-member) governments strive to meet their increasing EU obligations. Especially in the event that monetary unification is accomplished, they will have to rely more and more on the negotiated consent of their respective social partners in order to obtain the 'voluntary and active assent' that is so important for competitive success. Most national interest associations are unlikely to 'supranationalize' themselves and shift their attention and allegiance exclusively to Brussels. The costs are too high and the uncertainty of depending on the cooperation of others is too great – especially when further enlargement means a growing number of less well-known and more diverse others. However, these associations will become deeply penetrated in their internal politics by issues defined at the level of 'Europe,' and they may find it increasingly expedient to ally with previous interest competitors in joint attempts to defend distinctive national policies. The primary 'growth potential' for macro-corporatist architects in the future lies in the feverish efforts of national governments to adapt to the single market directives, the product and professional standards, the judicial verdicts and the monetary convergence criteria that will increasingly be regulated by supra-national authorities. The boundaries, territorial and functional, of interest politics have shifted irrevocably, which paradoxically implies a greater not a lesser reliance on previous structures of national inter-mediation – provided they can be exploited to fulfil new tasks and still manage to reproduce the old loyalties.

Because the EU is incapable of replicating the experience of its member welfare states, i.e. of defining and defending a minimal degree of common social policies for its citizens by isolating them from the raw pressures of national and international competition (Streeck 1996a, 1996b), it must tolerate – even encourage – these national polities to adjust as best as they can on their own. Defending one's own institutions by investing in corporatist arrangements, even at the risk of alienating one's members, may be the best available option available to national labour movements. For the foreseeable future, the cyclical fate of such practices will depend less and less on the 'classic' variables of rising costs, diminishing returns, shifting involvements, perverse effects or declining legitimacy and more and more on the role that they play in promoting national competitiveness within a market increasingly regulated (but not redistributed) at the European level. Eventually, its Sisyphean burdens will get heavier and national corporatisms will decline in importance. The only hope of breaking the cycle may be to 'supranationalize' the practice of corporatism. Only by transposing its scale to cover all of Europe and by extending its scope to include a broad range of social citizenship rights may it finally and definitively deposit its twin burdens of associability and policy-making at the top of the hill where it will become a routine practice of an (enlarged) EU and an important component of its (eventual) democratization. Not a likely scenario, but one well worth simulating – and stimulating.

Notes

1 Dieter Schulte recommends that one should not overload the basket of demands while approaching the top of the hill. See: the DGB's web page (http://www. dgb.de/cgi/a/pms.cgi?id=564).
2 In contrast, however, to the German agreement that immediately preceded it, this one engaged no less than thirty-two signatories. Consultations conducted among the rank and file of the larger of the three unions (CGIL) immediately after the December 1998 Agreement demonstrated that about 85 per cent of its members approved of it (see CGIL 1999).
3 According to Lionel Fulton (1998: 647), TUC membership declined from 12.2 to 6.6 million between 1979 and 1997. At the same time, the figure of those believing unemployment to be 'the most important problem facing the country' dropped from 81 per cent in 1993 to 28 per cent in 1998.
4 This more appealing alternative appeared in the 1980s when the neo-liberal *mantra* of deregulation, privatization and internationalization became so 'hegemonic' among capitalists – in manifest conflict with the operative principles of neo-corporatism. It should be added that corporatist arrangements were potentially more vulnerable than their pluralist rivals because they never benefited from an elaborate, status-conferring, ideology. Their ideological origin in Catholic thought and their association with authoritarian practices in the interwar period made it difficult to justify them openly after 1945. Only in Austria under the label of 'Social Partnership' did they become an integral part of public ideology – which explains, in part, why its practice there has been less Sisyphean.
5 Needless to say, the conditions needed to produce stable private interest governments were much more demanding than for ordinary corporatist arrangements.

See Streeck (1992) and Grote (1992, 1995) for details on the German artisan and small firm sector – a prime example of this peculiar type of arrangement.

6 For early work contrasting these two enabling conditions, see Schmitter (1974) and Lehmbruch (1974).

7 Corporatism did survive in a few exceptional instances. Austria, of course, is everyone's extreme case and we shall return to it below. Norwegian corporatism in the 1980s exhibited clear signs of incipient morbidity, especially in tensions between sectors and between organizations representing white and blue collar workers, but it managed to survive. Of course, its survival can easily be dismissed due to the fortunate transfusion of petroleum revenues into the agonizing body politic. The peculiarities of the Swiss case, still in line with the *Sozialfriedensvertrag* of 1936, are commented upon later in the text.

8 For reflections on the various ways in which corporatism was evaluated in the 1970s and 1980s, see Offe (1995). Interestingly, the one cell of Offe's that might have keep corporatism alive despite its (allegedly) fatal case of *disfunctionitis* – the one that combines a favourable and a normatively based evaluation of it – has been 'almost empty' (p. 123). To fill it, Offe had either to go back to the 1920s (Otto Bauer) or forward to the 'real utopian' speculations of Joshua Cohen and Joel Rogers, Philippe C. Schmitter and Jane Mansbridge. These have been conveniently gathered in Erik Olin Wright (ed.), 1995 – along with the above-mentioned essay by Offe.

9 For example, the debates on the future of the European regions, on multi-level governance and on flexible specialization in industrial districts are replete with the most exotic references to the corporatist paradigm, usually with some qualifier attached: enterprise, techno-, staged, as well as corporatist policy networks of all kinds (see, among others, Heinze and Schmid 1994). So called 'territorial pacts' now belong to the most important instrument of structural policies in Italy. In other areas not directly related to labour market issues, but where capital and the state felt threatened by the emergence of new social movements, governments and interest associations have also been finding new ways to make use of arrangements for policy concertation. Lauber and Hofer (1997) have catalogued some 133 such voluntary agreements on environmental issues in the Netherlands, 25 to 30 in Denmark and 17 to 28 in Austria that deal with either product- or substance-related matters. According to the views of an Enquete Commission of the German Bundestag (Enquete Kommission 1998), corporatist concertation belongs to the essentials of 'Good Environmental Governance'.

10 Most of the following information has been taken from various issues of the *European Industrial Relations Review* (EIRR) and the *International Labour Review* (ILR), in particular, from a discussion of social pacts in ILR; No. 30 of September 1994. Further information comes from a Special Issue on 'Bündnisse für Arbeit in Europa' of the German DGB´s *Gewerkschaftliche Monatshefte* (10/1998) and the consultation of web sites of some of the major national trade unions and employer associations.

11 The communist-oriented General Confederation of Portuguese Workers (CGTP) participated in the negotiations, but steadfastly refused to sign the agreements.

12 Interestingly, the most important obstacle to the conclusion of the agreement was a refusal by the EU Commission to accept the system of reducing social security contributions to firms which were subject to international competition.

13 Organizational fragmentation remains a characteristic of Italy's system of interest intermediation. Note the thirty-two signatories to the most recent pact (22 December 1998) which we have mentioned in the introduction. The same argument could be extended – *mutatis mutandis* – to several other Mediterranean cases: Spain, Portugal and even Greece.

14 For example, the governor of the Banque de France, Jean-Claude Trichet, was

quoted in *Le Monde* (23 January 1997) as having said that 'la France devrait s'inspirer du modèle économique néerlandais; et notamment de sa réussite en matière de création d'emplois à temps partiel'. From one of the lowest levels in Europe in the 1970s, part-time work climbed to 35 per cent of total employment by 1995.

15 According to Visser, this is due in part to the substantial increase in part-time work which was not – at least, initially – an objective of the macro-concertation process. He cites an official who admits 'it just came our way' (Visser 1996: 4).

16 Unger cites a national survey carried out among the (obligatory) members of both the Wirtschaftskammer and the Arbeiterkammer in which 81.7 per cent of industrialists and 90.6 per cent of workers opted for the maintenance of the chamber system.

17 For example, an article in the *Financial Times* (4 July 1987) reminded readers that Britain's National Economic Development Council (Neddy), a corporatist experiment founded in 1962, was just being abolished – twenty-five years later – by the Thatcher government. The author (John Elliot) warned his readers in the title: 'Don't Dance on Neddy's Grave' and prophesied that '. . . the pendulum will swing back and someone in Downing Street will echo the sentiments of Edward Heath who [said] "We have to find a more sensible way of resolving our differences!"'

18 The exception to this generalization is agriculture, where a very comprehensive European-level welfare programme has been developed and where corporatist-type sectoral arrangements have largely replaced national negotiations and arrangements.

19 In fact the Netherlands, Belgium and Austria may have come to this revelation much earlier since their currencies became tied to the Deutschmark some time before Maastricht – hence, the relatively earlier revival of macro-corporatism in the first two cases and the new lease on life given to Austrian *Sozialpartnerschaft* in the late 1980s. The fact that Luxembourg has long ago given up its national currency may even help to explain why it has so persistently (if quietly) been practising corporatism since the 1950s!

20 Note that Grote (1992, 1995), in his contributions to the books which opened the debate on the fate of Euro-corporatism (Greenwood *et al*. 1992; Greenwood 1995), did not find incidents of the phenomenon – at least not in the sector/policy domain studied by him (small enterprise policy).

References

Armingeon, Klaus (2002) 'Renegotiating the Swiss Welfare State', in this volume.

CGIL (Confederazione Generale italiana del Lavoro) (1999) 'Patto per lo sviluppo'. http://www.cgil.it/ufficiostampa/Rinnovo%20accordo%2023%20luglio.htm

Crouch, Colin, David Finegold and Mari Sako (1999) *Are Skills the Answer? The Political Economy of Skill Creation in Advanced Industrial Countries*, Oxford: Oxford University Press.

Enquete Kommission 'Schutz des Menschen und der Umwelt' des 13. Deutschen Bundestages 1998 (ed.) *Institutionelle Reformen für eine Politik der Nachhaltigkeit*, Berlin and Heidelberg: Springer.

Falkner, Gerda (1998) *EU Social Policy in the 1990s: Towards a Corporatist Policy Community*, London: Routledge.

Fulton, Lionel 1998. 'Ein britisches Bündnis für Arbeit?', *Gewerkschaftliche Monatshefte* 10: 644–50.

Greenwood, Justin (1997) *Representing Interests in the European Union*, London: Macmillan.

Grote, Jürgen R. (1992) 'Small Firms and European Integration: Modes of Production, Governance, and Territorial Interest Representation in Italy and Germany', in Justin Greenwood, Jürgen R. Grote and Karsten Ronit (eds) *Organised Interests and the European Community*, London, Newbury Park and New Delhi: Sage Publications, pp. 119–73.

Grote, Jürgen R. (1995) 'The Relevance of Size and Territory for the Organisation of Business Interests in Europe', in Justin Greenwood (ed.) *European Business Alliances*, London: Prentice Hall, pp. 239–60.

Grote, Jürgen R. (1999) (forthcoming) 'Le camere di commercio in Europa', in Paolo Perulli and Maurizio Catino (eds) *Tra organizzazioni e istituzioni. La riforma delle camere di commercio e le nuove tendenze del sistema di rappresentanza degli interessi: i casi della Lombardia e dell'Emilia-Romagna*, Milano: Franco Angeli.

Hassel, Anke 1998. 'Soziale Pakte in Europa', *Gewerkschaftliche Monatshefte*, 10: 626–38.

Heinze, R.G. and J. Schmid (1994). 'Mesokorporatistische Strategien in Vergleich: Industrieller Strukturwandel und die Kontingenz politischer Steuerung in drei Bundesländern", in W. Streeck (ed.) *Staat und Verbände*, Opladen: Westdeutscher Verlag, pp. 65–99.

Hirschman, Albert O. (1982) *Shifting Involvements*, Princeton, Princeton University Press.

Karl, Terry (1985) 'Petroleum and Political Pacts: The Transition to Democracy in Venezuela', in Guillermo O'Donnell and Philippe C. Schmitter (eds) *Transitions from Authoritarian Rule: Latin America*, Baltimore and London: Johns Hopkins University Press, pp. 196–221.

Lash, Scott and John Urry (1987) *The End of Organised Capitalism*, Cambridge: Polity Press.

Lauber, Volkmar and Karin Hofer (1997) 'Business and Government Motives for Negotiating Voluntary Agreements. A Comparison of the Experiences in Austria, Denmark, and the Netherlands', paper presented at the 25th Joint Sessions of Workshops of the ECPR (European Consortium for Political Research), Bern, 27 February–4 March 1997.

Lehmbruch, Gerhard (1974) 'Consociational Democracy, Class Conflict, and the New Corporatism'. International Political Science Association, Round Table on 'Political Integration', Jerusalem.

Lehmbruch, Gerhard (1996) 'Der Beitrag der Korporatismusforschung zur Entwicklung der Steuerungstheorie', *Politische Vierteljahresschrift*, 37/4: 735–51.

Mazey, Sonia and Jeremy J. Richardson (1992) *Lobbying in the European Community*, Oxford: Oxford University Press.

Offe, Claus 1995. 'Some Skeptical Considerations on the Malleability of Representative Institutions', in Erik Olin Wright (ed.) *Associations and Democracy*, London and New York: Verso, pp. 114–33.

Pizzorno, Alessandro (1993) 'I problemi del consociativismo.' in *Le radici della politica assoluta ed altri saggi*, Milano: Feltrinelli.

Regini, Marino 1996. 'Still Engaging in Corporatism? Some Lessons from the Recent Italian Experience of Concertation', paper presented at the 8th International Conference on Socio-Economics; Session on 'Globalisation and the Future of Corporatism', Geneva, 12–14 July 1996.

Rhodes, Martin (1997) 'Globalisation, Labour Markets and Welfare State: A Future of "Competitive Corporatism"?', in Martin Rhodes and Yves Meny (eds) *The Future of European Welfare: A New Social Contract?*, London: Macmillan.

Schmitter, Philippe C. (1974) 'Still the Century of Corporatism?', *Review of Politics*, 36: 85–131.

Schmitter, Philippe C. (1989) 'Corporatism is Dead! Long Live Corporatism! Reflections on Andrew Shonfield's Modern Capitalism', *Government and Opposition*, 24: 54–73.

Schmitter, Philippe C. 1996. 'Imagining the Future of the Euro-Polity with the Help of New Concepts', in Gary Marks, Fritz W. Scharpf, Philippe C. Schmitter and Wolfgang Streeck (eds) *Governance in the Emerging Euro-Polity*, London: Sage Publications, pp. 121–51.

Schmitter, Philippe C. and Wolfgang Streeck (1991) 'From National Corporatism to Transnational Pluralism', *Politics and Society*, 19/2: 133–64.

Schmitter, Philippe C. and Jürgen R. Grote (1997) 'The Corporatist Sisyphus: Past, Present and Future', working paper of the European University Insitute SPS No. 97/4.

Streeck, Wolfgang (1992) 'The Territorial Organisation of Interests and the Logic of Associative Action: The Case of Handwerk Organization in West Germany', in Wolfgang Streeck (ed.) *Social Institutions and Economic Performance. Studies of Industrial Relations in Advanced Capitalist Economies*, London: Sage Publications, pp. 105–37.

Streeck, Wolfgang (1996a) 'Public Power Beyond the Nation-State. The Case of the European Community', in Robert Boyer and Daniel Drache (eds) *States Against Markets. The Limits of Globalization*, London and New York: Routledge, pp. 299–315.

Streeck, Wolfgang (1996b) 'Gewerkschaften zwischen Nationalstaat und Europäischer Union', MPIfG Working Paper 96/1 (http:www.mpi-fg-koeln.mpg.de/ publikation/ working_papers/wp96–1.html).

Streeck, Wolfgang and Philippe C. Schmitter (eds) (1985) 'Community, Market, State – and Associations? The Prospective Contribution of Interest Governance to Social Order', *European Sociological Review*, 1: 119–38.

Stykow, Petra (1996) 'Organized Interests in the Transformation Processes of Eastern Europe and Russia: Towards Corporatism?' Arbeitspapiere AG TRAP, No. 96/11, Max-Planck-Gesellschaft, Arbeitsgruppe Transformationsprozesse in den neuen Bundesländern an der Humboldt-Universität zu Berlin.

Telljohann, Volker (1998) 'Die Erfahrungen mit tripartistischen Abkommen in Italien', *Gewerkschaftliche Monatshefte*, 10: 650–61.

Traxler, Franz (1996) 'Sozialpartnerschaft am Scheideweg: Zwischen korporatistischer Kontinuität und neoliberalem Umbruch', *Wirtschaft und Gesellschaft*, 22/1: 13–33.

Unger, Brigitte (2002) 'Austrian social partnership: just a mid-life crisis?', in this volume.

Visser, Jelle (1996) 'Two Cheers for Corporatism, One for the Market. Industrial Relations, Unions, and Labour Markets in the Netherlands', typescript, Max Planck Institut für Gesellschaftsforschung, Köln and Department of Sociology, University of Amsterdam, December 1996; published version in *British Journal of Industrial Relations* (1997).

Visser, Jelle (1998) 'Fünfzehn Jahre Bündnis für Arbeit in den Niederlanden', *Gewerkschaftliche Monatshefte*, 10: 661–68.

Wright, Erik Olin (ed.) (1995) *Associations and Democracy. The Real Utopias Project*, Volume 1, London and New York: Verso.

Index